O'Nolan

The History of a People

Cor unum via una

By Rev. John Nolan and Art Kavanagh

**With extended notices of other great
Gaelic, Anglo Norman and English
Families of South East Leinster**
(see back cover for details)

O'Huidhrin, a poet who lived in the early 1400s wrote
O'Nuallain, hero without fault
Chief Prince, fine and bountiful, of Fothart.

O'Nolan

(A History of a People)

by
Fr. John O'Nolan
&
Art Kavanagh

1900 - 2000

Published by Irish Family Names
Bunclody, Co. Wexford. Ireland 2000

ISBN 0 9538485 0 7

Cover Picture by Tomas O'Baoill, Heraldic Artist, The Tower I.D.A. Centre -
Set in Times New Roman 11 pt.

This book is dedicated to the women of the Ua Nuallain,
the wives and mothers, the unsung heroines.

Acknowledgements

The Clan Nolan wish to acknowledge the support given by the following
sponsors and subscribers:-

Barrow Nore Suir
Rural Development Ltd.
ICC Bank
Bank of Ireland
AIB
Carton Brothers
Edward Nolan (Old Leighlin) Ltd.
Tullow Farm Machinery
Hi - Spec Engineering Ltd.
Nolan Transport
Lord Bagenal Inn
Eileen Dalton
John Nolan, Nurney.
Dolmen Hotel
Mannings
P. Nolan & P. Conlon
Nolan's Garage, Tralee
R.N. Murphy Associates Ltd.
John T. Nolan, Iowa
Dobbs Oil
Wexford Creamery
Sheehan's Cash & Carry

Author's Acknowledgements

Fr. John O'Nolan was the man who conceived the idea of this book and he was the person who did the ground work for the early chapters. Fr. Swayne, Matthew Nolan B.A. and his daughter Mary FitzSimons were the custodians of precious material for over half a century and we owe them a deep debt of gratitude for preserving the material. The author also wishes to thank the staffs of the National Library, Carlow County Library, the Land Registry and the National Archives for their assistance and anyone who has helped in any way to make this book a reality. Much gratitude is due also to Sean Nolan of Ardattin, acting Clan Chief, who was so generous with his time and most helpful in every way, Matt Nolan of Rosslee, Jim Nolan of Ballinrush, Michael Eustace of Tinnaclash, Edward Kennedy of Kilballyhue, Pat Nolan of Myshall, Mick Nolan of Coolasnaughta, Dick Nolan of Rathnageeragh and his nephew Dick of Fenagh, Noel Nolan of Kilconnor, Patrick Nolan (formerly of Shangarry) of Terenure, Fiachra Kavanagh of Bunclody for the photographs and Brother P.J. Kavanagh to whom this book owes its completion.

Preface

This history of the O'Nolans would not have happened but for a series of peculiar events. Prior to 1920 Fr. John O'Nolan, who was Parish Priest of Kirkcubbin,[1] in the north of Ireland, decided to write a history of the O'Nolan Clan. He, himself, had Co. Carlow roots and, in the course of correspondence, was called 'cousin' by the O'Nolans of Ballinrush, Myshall, Co. Carlow. During his quest for information about the O'Nolan sept he visited Co. Carlow quite frequently. However he died in the 1920s and the work was never completed.

His manuscripts and letters were passed on to Fr. Swayne of Clonegal, a noted scholar, for completion and possible publication, but he was unable to find the time to finish the work before he passed away. The manuscripts, in an old brown worn suitcase, were given to a professor in Newbridge College, Mr. Matthew Nolan, B.A., and upon his death in 1977 they came into the possession of his daughter, Mary FitzSimons (nee Nolan).

A cousin of Mary FitzSimons, Brother P.J. Kavanagh, read my book, *In the Shadow of Mount Leinster*, and felt that I might be in a position to bring the work to fruition, because of my knowledge of the period and because of my treatment of the Kavanagh material. He wrote to me in 1996/97 and urged me to get in touch with Mary FitzSimons. I did this and was given custody of the material, without promising anything other than to look at the documents.

My first job was to sort out the papers and I found out that Fr. O'Nolan had in fact written about 15 or 16 chapters dealing with the history of the sept beginning with the origins of the O'Nolans in prehistory and coming right up to the 17th. century.

Still undecided, I contacted Sean Nolan, the then Chieftain of the Clan O'Nolan, the late Tom Nolan of Slyguff, Mary FitzSimons and my friend Jim Nolan of Ballinrush. Through a contact called Dr. Eric Klingelhofer, an American professor of History, I got to know Dr. John Nolan, also an American professor of History, who was planning to honeymoon in Ireland and we all met in Bunclody in January of 1998. All present urged me to undertake the work and the members of Clan Nolan offered their full support.

I showed the material to Dr. John Nolan and he suggested that I keep Fr.O'Nolan's material intact, because it was so typical of the period in which he lived and he felt it would be a pity to restructure it. In doing this too, I feel the book is a special tribute to Fr. O'Nolan who must have spent such a huge amount of time in compiling and working with the data in those days when computers had not even been dreamt about.

---

[1] He must have retired by 1925 as his address then was Moneyglass, Toome, Co. Antrim.

In my treatment of the material I have decided to put in footnotes, where needed, to explain certain items and highlight differences between Fr. O'Nolans's ideas and mine. A certain amount of reconstruction was necessary also in the later chapters.

In writing about any Gaelic sept or clan it is impossible to write about them in isolation. The history of the O'Nolans or of the Kavanaghs is inextricably interwoven with the history of the general area and with the history of every other Gaelic clan of the area.

As one might expect the history presented here includes many important references to the history of the Kavanaghs, the O'Moores, the O'Byrnes, the O'Connors, the O'Tooles and others who were the important Gaelic families in the area. The entire book is a rich source of historical data dealing with the complex political and social structures that existed and evolved as the conquest proceeded.

There is also a wealth of information about the Norman and English families who were instrumental in the eventual downfall of the O'Nolan clan and of the other Gaelic clans as well. These include the Butlers of Ormonde, the Fitzgeralds of Kildare, Carews, Bagenals, Mastersons, Harpooles, Eustaces and very many others.

This work is not a simple, easily read book. It is a history of a people. I have given the book all the gravity such a work deserves. I have tried to avoid too many complexities but what had to be written was written. If at times this book seems to stray from the subject, remember again that the O'Nolans did not live in isolation. The little picture has to be seen to fit in the bigger picture. I sincerely hope Fr. John O'Nolan would approve.

Introduction

Fotharta Fea was a very ancient division within the kingdom of Ui Cheinnsealaigh and did in fact predate that kingdom which only came into existence in the 5th. or 6th. century. It is well documented that apart from the many very ancient sites that have been noted in Co. Carlow, burial sites that occurred prior to the time of Christ have also been unearthed. One such marvellous discovery was made at Ballon hill. A huge boulder which appears to have been the capstone of a dolmen is said by the archaeologists to mark the burial place of Cathair Mor, High King of Ireland in 177 A.D. and of many generations of Kings before him. According to the late William Nolan (the Ballon author), writing in Carloviana in 1968, historians and archaeologists have described the collection of urns, and artefacts discovered there as being representative of nearly a thousand years of pre history (1300 - 500 B.C.) Other ancient sites in Carlow are to be found at Browne's Hill and Tobinstown where there are examples of dolmens dating back to 2,500 B.C. and an ancient burial site was discovered at Baunogenasraid in 1969. There is also a dolmen at Kilgraney on the Kilgraney side of the stream across from Clonmoney.

According to Alfred P. Smyth the noted authority on ancient land divisions the Fothairt were an auxiliary tribe of, and lived adjacent to, the Ui Bairrche (their name is remembered in the parish of Barragh in the Barony of Forth in Carlow). It would seem that when the Ui Cheinnselaigh invaded south east Leinster they pushed some of the Fothairt and Ui Barraiche before them and these settled in what are now the baronies of Forth and Bargy in south Wexford, where the Fothairt later (11th. century) assumed the name Ua Lorcain or Larkin and the Ui Barraiche the name Cosgrave. In the north Wexford/Carlow area the Fothairt assumed the name Ua Nuallain or O'Nolan while the Ui Barraiche were called Ua Neill.[2]

---

[2] In some Elizabethan documents the area occupied by the O'Neills was called the Leverock. This is a corruption of Leath Bhearrice. The same area was later called Fearannoneale, a corruption of Fearann Ui Neill or the district of the O'Neills. This district was in the Kildavin, Clonegal, Kilbride and Ballinapark area and approximated to the area of Moyacomb Parish. Nelan, Donnell and Art, sons of Prior O'Neill were pardoned for their part in the Kavanagh/O'Nolan rebellion of 1550-52. In 1572 Neill O'Neill, alias McPrior O'Neill, of Kilcarry handed over to Gerald the Earl of Kildare, "the Great Woods and lands called Ayllagh Knock in Clonegal in Fearann O'Neill country. The Kavanagh overlord of this district in 1582 was Murrough Leigh McCahir. This man was executed in Wexford in 1584 and his lands were granted to Lord Esmonde and James Butler. In the Civil Survey of 1654 the lands were described as Kilcarry, Clongaule, Clonogan,

At a period shortly after this event occurred another branch of the Ui Cheinnselaigh appear to have taken over the area of Fotharta Fea bounded by the Rivers Barrow and Burren and they were known as the Ui Drona (from Dron a sobriquet of Eana Cheinnselach the 4th. century king of Leinster from whom they were descended). They also occupied lands on the west of the Barrow in Ossory territory and this area later became known as Idrone west. When surnames began to be adopted the Ui Drona took the name Ui Riain or O' Ryan.

It would seem that the Ua Nuallain sept and the Ua Neill had to adapt to the changing circumstances of the times they lived in and settled for the possession of what is today most of Co. Carlow (Idrone excepted), parts of South Kildare and South Wicklow and possibly portions of North Wexford. With the passage of time and succumbing to the external pressures of Viking and Norman invasions their territory shrunk even more until by the 12th. century it may have approximated to the size of the barony of Forth as we know it today.

In the following pages, Fr. O'Nolan has detailed the descent of the noble race of Ua Nuallain and he has attempted to chart their progress down the dim pathways of history up to the 17th. century. In the succeeding chapters I have attempted to trace the fortunes of this once renowned clan as their descendants emerged from the tomb of misfortune (that is the story of the conquest) into the present day where they now walk tall in the land of their fathers.

Monagharrin, Balliredmond, Collroe and Owlert. By the year 1641 the O'Neill ownership of lands in the area had shrunk to just over 1200 acres. - A.K.

Contents

Illustrations

Chapter 1

Fr. O'Nolan's Introduction

The race, whose history is outlined in the following pages, springs from a stock as noble, and as honourable as that from which any other family in Ireland can trace its origin.

In ancient Irish history they are known as the Fotharta from the seven Fotharts of Leinster, granted to Eochaidh Finn Fuathairt, progenitor of O'Nuallain, by Cu Corb, King of Leinster, as a reward for his services in expelling the Munstermen from his kingdom about the year 115A.D.

It is on record that a clever woman, Meadbh, Queen of Cu Corb, applotted these seven districts at a distance from each other, as knowing the prowess of Eochaidh, she feared that a homogenous territory under the sway of so celebrated a warrior and leader would be a standing menace to the safety of her husband's kingdoms.

As time went on these separate districts under the command of one or other of his descendants, owing allegiance to the "King of the Fotharta", but removed from his personal supervision, lost cohesion, and most of them became absorbed into the neighbouring territories.

Two, however, Fotharta Ui Nuallain and Fotharta an Chairn retained their separate identity and are today known, the one as the barony of Forth in the County of Carlow and the other as the barony of Forth in the County of Wexford.

The original patrimony of the O'Nolans was centred in the barony of Forth in the County of Carlow, which is so called in Grace's Annals and other Anglo - Irish records. There are townlands of Ballynolan in the barony of Idrone West, in the County of Carlow, in the barony of Cranagh in the County of Kilkenny and in the barony of Kenry in the County of Limerick. There is a townland of Ballynowlan near Stradbally, barony of Maryborough East in the Queen's County, and a considerable territory embracing, among others, the townlands of Clooaddyonoran, Kylbry, Tlyawer, Clonegowne, Clowlenemone, Clonenagh, Ballyfin, Cloughclone and Clonanne in the barony of Maryborough West in the Queen's County, which is defined in the Fiants of James 1 as "parcel of the Lordship of Farren O'Nolan". From these it is evident that the influence and ramifications of the O'Nolans extended far beyond the confines of the parent barony of Forth O'Nolan.

In the Annals of Ireland, page 5, we find "The age of the world 2527. Fea, son of Torton, son of Sru, died this year at Magh Fea and was interred at

Dolrai - Maigh - Fea[1]; so that it was from him that the plain was named". To which O'Donovan adds the following note - "Magh Fea: i.e. Fea's Plain. This was the name of a level plain in the present barony of Forth, county of Carlow. Keating states in his History of Ireland (reign of Olioll Molt) that the Church of Cill - Osnadha (now Kellistown), four (large Irish) miles to the east of Leighlin, was situated in this plain. The barony of Forth, or O'Nolan's country comprised all this plain, and was from it called Fotharta - Fea, to distinguish it from the barony of Forth in the County of Wexford which was called Fotharta - an - Chairn, from Carnsore Point."

After the introduction of surnames, the inhabitants of Fotharta - Fea or Fotharta Osnaidhe, for it was known by either name, adopted the name of O'Nuallain, anglicised, O'Nolan, or O'Nowlan, Nolan, Nowlan and Nowland, from Nuallain (which means "one who is famous"), lord of that territory a little before A.D. 1000, about which time surnames were first adopted by order of Brian Boroimhe, then Monarch of Ireland.

By right of their descent from Cobhtach, Caol mBreagh, eldest son of Ugaine Mor, 66th. Milesian Monarch of Ireland, A.M. 4567, the O'Nolans are the senior Sept of the Heremonian line in Leinster. The O'Neills and O'Donnells of the North and the O'Connors of the West trace their genealogical line to Cobhtach, but all Leinster Septs, O'Nolan excepted, derive their descent from Laeghaire Lorc, second son of Ugaine Mor.[2]

---

[1] Also called Fotharta Fea. The Onomasticon Goedelicum states that Ard Bresine (Ardristan), Cell Osnada (Kellistown) and Leighlin are in it, and that it is in the Barony of Forth, Co. Carlow. In the book of Invasions it is stated that "at the end of seven years after Partholon occupied Ireland, the first man of his people died, namely Fea, son of Tortu son of Sru, his father's brother. From him is called Magh Fea, for it was there he was buried in Oilre of Magh Fea; and of him is the first hurt, that is the first wounding in Leinster, for there was he slain in the top of the hill." According to Edward O'Toole in his publication entitled 'The Parish of Ballon' the name of Fea still persists in the townland of Drumphea in the parish of Myshall and the name of his father Tortu is perpetuated in the townland of Turtane in the same parish. - A.K.

[2] Alfred P.Smyth in his book Celtic Leinster says "It is interesting to observe that the Fothairt or Fotharta, an alien tribe in Leinster who have left their names on the baronies of Forth in Carlow and Forth in south Wexford bordered on Ui Bairrche lands in both areas; and remnants of Ui Bairrche and Fotharta survived side by side in Eastern Liffey (Airthir Life) in the north of the Province. The origin tales of the Fotharta show them to have been introduced into Leinster as auxiliaries of the Laigin. and the topographical evidence would point to the Ui Bairrche as their immediate overlords. When the Ui Bairrche were fragmented by the power of the Ui Cheinnselaig, their mercenaries, the Fotharta, seem to have suffered the same fate as their masters. From the eleventh century the Fotharta of Carlow took the family name Ua Nuallain (O'Nolan), while their Wexford cousins survived

Unfortunately most of the records dealing with the territory occupied by the O'Nolans, have perished through the ravages of time, and the still more destructive hand of the invading Danes and Normans, or of the raiding Irish septs, and only fragmentary references have survived, but such as they are they show that in the struggle to maintain the independence of their country and their own freedom, the O'Nolans played their part in a manner befitting their noble ancestry and were ever in the fore front of the battle.

When Dermot McMurrough, suffering from the consequences of his evil life and actions, bartered the independence of his native land for his own personal vengeance, he secured the assistance of his Norman allies, by the promise of rich rewards in lands and powers, which were not his to bestow.

On the arrival of his Norman allies, he carried out his evil intentions by granting the tribe lands of his people to the needy adventurers who flocked to his standard in the hope of their own aggrandisement. The very first portion of Irish soil alienated in this manner was "Wexford and two cantreds adjoining given to FitzStephen and FitzGirald, according to the former Agreement. And to oblige the Earl of Chepstow, Dermot bestowed two cantreds (situate between Wexford and Waterford) on Henry Mountmaurice; and to those three settled the first colony of British on those lands, which have continued through all the Change since to this Day." (Cox. pg.13 Vol.1).

These lands comprise the baronies of Forth and Bargy, County Wexford, portion of the original territory granted to Eochaidh Finn Fuathairt upwards of a thousand years previously. Immediately after these grants had been made, the lands of Forth O'Nolan were similarly made over to Raymond le Gros, another of Dermot's swashbucklers. This completed the alienation of the patrimonial lands of the O'Nolans who were thus the first to be up against the might of England; and the fact that the clan survived for upwards of five hundred years afterwards, as a separate element and as a serious factor in the wars raging during all those centuries, is a splendid tribute to their dogged perseverance, their unflagging powers of resistance and their love of country and freedom. Such a record tells its own tale of patient suffering, stern resolve, and undying patriotism. They were seated in the gap of danger, lying athwart the pass from Dublin to Waterford. Through their territory practically every raid on the southern and eastern clans, by the English and by those clans on the pale, had first to make its way. The barriers of the pale were for a time planted on the outermost confines of their lands, till their ceaseless assaults taught the governors of the English colony in Dublin the advisability of moving "the barriers from Carlow to Dublin' as the State papers tell us was done in the 16th. century.

---

alongside the Wexford Norsemen as Ua Lorcain (O'Larkin). The O'Nolan's of Carlow retreated into the Wicklow forests after Strongbow's arrival." - A.K.

Crushed between the upper and nether millstones, - between the English of the pale and the English of Lower Leinster and Munster - their situation was a most unenviable one; and that any of the race have survived to hand down their name, traditions and characteristics to future generations is a glorious evidence of their steadfastness of purpose, their strong vitality, and their grim determination to hold their own against all comers at all costs.

Down to the end of the 17th. Century they (the O'Nolans) were known and recognised as a separate entity, to be dealt with as a distinct nation, which required careful handling. The attrition of centuries had, by that time, reduced them to a low level in strength and numbers, so that from thence forward, they appear, in English records, to have become merged in the Clan Kavanagh or McMurroughs.

As senior princes of the province they were always the right hand of the Kings of Leinster in their wars with the English of the pale, and wherever a record is found dealing with the McMurroughs during all those centuries, one can read McMurrough and O'Nolan with unfailing truth in every instance.

That a history, so glorious, should perish in oblivion is repugnant to human nature, and hence we have, even at this late period, made an effort to collect into one volume, such records of their life and actions as we have been able to recover from the scattered fragments of Irish history which have escaped the general destruction.

To thoroughly comprehend their history it is necessary to know much of the times and people among whom their lot was cast, and we have accordingly dealt freely with such matters as we consider essential to that end.

That many records exist, with which we have not been able to get in touch is, alas! only self evident, but in compiling this volume, we have done so in the hope that future years may add to the results of our researches, and that other, more competent hands may yet amplify the skeleton history which we now lay before the public.

In the history of practically every other Irish sept, there have been one or more, to ingratiate themselves with the English governors, and to secure possession of the tribe lands to themselves and their immediate posterity, have been ready to sell their faith, and their country, for greed and gain, or an empty title. But so far as our researches have gone, we have not found a single instance in which an O'Nolan bartered his birthright for this "mess of pottage". Their loyalty to their faith has been unswerving. No persecutions, no repression, no bribes have been able to decoy them from their religious beliefs, and in like manner their undying love has been ever given to their native land. Had their disposition been like that of so many others, of a more accommodating nature, the position of some of their sons today would, in all probability, be on a higher social plane, but they would have been deprived of their proud boast of "incorruptibility".

"See too", writes Mac Firbis, "how ignoble of descent are now placed in high positions in Erin, in preference to the nobles, because they possess worldly wealth". Worldly wealth, at its best is evanescent, riches take wings and fly away, but a good name and a high reputation remain for all times, and are the proudest possessions one can transmit to posterity. These flourish in adversity, as in prosperity, and are a beacon light showing the way to high resolve and strenuous effort.

Friar Michael O' Clery in his dedication of the *Annals of the Four Masters* writes: "in every country enlightened by civilisation, and confirmed therein through a succession of ages, it has been customary to record the events produced by time. For sundry reasons, nothing was deemed more profitable or honourable, than to study and peruse the works of ancient writers, who gave a faithful account of the great men who figured on the stage of life in preceding ages, that posterity might be informed how their forefathers have employed their time, how long continued in power, and how they have finished their days".

In so writing he was merely expressing the opinion held by the people of Ireland from time immemorial. Literature, history and poetry were cultivated to high degree of excellence. Special privileges were allowed to, and special emoluments set apart for, the professors of each of these branches of education.

Even a limited acquaintance with our manuscript records will suffice to show us how the national poet, the historian and the musician, as well as the man of excellence in any other of the arts or sciences were cherished and honoured. We find them, indeed, from a very early period placed in a position, not merely of independence, but even of elevated rank; and their persons and property declared inviolate and protected specially by the law. Thus an Ollamh or Doctor of Filedecht (that system of education, which in ancient Erin preceded the University system, and which included the study of law, history, philosophy, languages, druidism, music and poetry) was, when ordained by the King or Chief, entitled to rank next in precedence to the Monarch himself at table. He was not permitted, when on his travels, to lodge with or take refection from, anyone below the rank of a Flaith (a noble or landlord chief).

He that was the Ollamh was allowed a standing income of "twenty one cows and their grass" in the chieftain's territory, besides ample refection for himself and for his attendants, to the number of twenty four; including his subordinate tutors, his advanced pupils, and his retinue of servants. He was entitled to have two hounds and six horses. He was, besides, entitled to a singular privilege within his territory; that of conferring a temporary sanctuary from injury or arrest, by carrying his wand, or having it carried around or over the person or place to be protected. His wife also enjoyed certain valuable privileges; and similar privileges were accorded to all the degrees of legal, historical, musical and poetic art below him, according to their rank."[3]

The early history of the Irish nation is unique in its amplitude and its accuracy. The different records, which have come down to us, when collated, have proved the care and truthfulness which were exercised in their compilation. The arrangements for keeping those records, for their comparison, and for the elimination of anything irregular or inconsistent with truth, were eminently calculated to further these ends. At the triennial Feis of Tara the records of the past period in each provincial territory were compared, and the natural jealousy of Sept and Poet would prevent too great elaboration on the one hand, or the glossing over of defects on the other.

Writing in the year 1650 Duald Mac Firbis says : " If there be any one who shall ask who preserved the history, let him know that there were very ancient and long lived old men, recording elders of great age, whom God permitted to preserve and hand down the history of Erin in books, in succession, one after another from the Deluge to the time of Saint Patrick, which was written on their knees in books, and which is now in the hands of sages and historians from that time for ever."

Sir James Macintosh, a learned and discriminating Scotsman, in his *History of England* Vol. 1, Chap.2, gives the following unprejudiced opinion as to the authenticity of our Irish Annals. "In one respect Irish History has been singularly fortunate. The Chronicles of Ireland, written in the Irish language from the second century to the landing of Henry Plantagenet have been recently published with fullest evidence of their genuineness. The Irish nation, though they are robbed of their legends by this authentic publication, are yet by it enabled to boast that they possess genuine history several centuries more ancient than any other European nation possesses in its present spoken language. They have exchanged their legendary antiquity for historical fame. Indeed, no other nation possesses any monument of literature in its present spoken language which goes back within several centuries of those chronicles. The ancient date of the M.S.S. coincides with the same internal proof as in the Saxon Chronicles to support the truth of the outline of the narrative."

Such evidence is a conclusive refutation to the assertions of those captious English critics, and their ignorant followers in Ireland, who sneer at the idea that any Irish family should be able to trace its genealogy for one, two, or three thousand years back. Yet each of these accepts without question the pedigree of the English Kings and Queens, who can show no antiquity of descent passing one thousand years or so, except that of which they boast through their Irish origin and support by Irish records.

---

[3] O'Curry M.S. Materials Lect.1

Those who cavil at the accuracy of Irish genealogy are oblivious to the fact that the Monarch of Erin had an officer of high rank and distinction attached to his court, whose duty it was to keep, from generation to generation, a written record or genealogical history of all the descending branches of the royal family, and the same officer was obliged to keep true records not only of these, but of the families of the provincial kings and of all the principal territorial chiefs in each province.

In addition, each provincial King and each great territorial prince had his own special seanchaidhe who was bound to preserve similar records in each territory. Every free born man of the tribe, was, according to the law of the country, entitled by blood, should it come to his turn, to succeed to the chieftaincy; and every principal family kept its own pedigree to check on the officer of the tribe or province and as an authority for its own claim, should the occasion arise.

In a country where the lands were the property of the sept and not of the individual, where every man of the tribe could prove his relationship and legal right to share in those lands, the genealogies became the titles to such lands, and were, as a matter of necessity most carefully kept for that purpose, and most jealously scanned by the other participants in the distribution.

Many hundreds of such records, once in existence, have been destroyed by age or by the ruthless hands of the foreign invader. Many others have been brought to distant lands by the enforced departure of their possessors and may still exist amid thousands of unexplored MSS in the continental libraries, but some few have been preserved from the general wreck in the *Book of Leinster* (about A.D.1130), the *Book of Ballymote* (A.D. 1391) and the *Book of Lecain* (A.D. 1416). But the fullest and most perfect of all is the *Book of Genealogies* compiled in 1650 - 1666 by Duald MacFirbis, descendant of a great family of hereditary historians, from a larger number of local records which have unfortunately since disappeared.

It is on record that the Pedigrees of the Gaelic nation were collected and written into a single book called the Cin - Droma - Snechta (or *Book of Drom Sneacht*) by the son of Duach Galach, King of Connacht and an Ollamh in history and genealogy, shortly before the arrival of Saint Patrick in Ireland which happened in the year 432. It follows necessarily that these pedigrees and genealogies must have already been in existence, doubtless in the various tribe books. It is more than probable that their leading portions had, before then, been entered in the *Book of Tara*.[4]

Among the pedigrees which have survived is that of O'Nuallain, which is found in the *Book of Leinster* and in MacFirbis's *Book of Genealogies* and we

---

[4] O'Curry MS Materials

have taken that as the basis of our work. It begins - like all the others- with Adam, and is continued down to the year 1409.

When the scripture period has been passed, it is founded on the records preserved as above, and while it is possible that lapses or slight variations might be discovered, if all the necessary material for comparison were available, it is, taken as a whole, entitled to rank as thoroughly authentic.

The profound knowledge of the world's early history possessed by the Irish annalists ,and their synchronisation's of the Kings and Rulers of Babylon, Judea, Egypt, Greece, Rome etc., which later historians have shown to be quite accurate, gives to their history of their own country a cachet for reliability which is unsurpassed in such documents elsewhere.

Chapter 2

Pedigree Of Milesius

The *Annals of Clonmacnoise* begin the genealogy of Milesius as follows :-

1. ADAM in the 130 yeare of his age begatt Seth and lived afterwards 800 yeares and in all he lived 930 yeares.

2. SETH in the 105th. yeare of his age begatt Enos and lived afterwards 137 yeares.

3. ENOS in the 90th. yeare of his age begatt Cainan and lived after his birth 815 yeares.

4. CAINAN in the 70th. yeare of his age begatt Malalle and lived himself after 840 yeares.

5. MALALLE in the 65th. yeare of his age begatt Jareth and lived after 830 yeares.

6. JARETH in the 62nd. yeare of his age begatt Enoche and lived after 800 yeares.

7. ENOCHE in the 65th. yeare of his age begatt Methusalem after whose birth he walked with God.

8. METHUSALEM in the age of 187 yeares begatt Lamech and lived himself after 782 yeares.

9. LAMECH in the yeare of his age 182 begatt Noeh and lived after 595 yeares.

10. NOEH A little before the flood the Arke was made and in the 600 yeares of Noeh's age came the flood, which is the first age of the world, from Adam to the flood and contayneth 1656 yeares and according to the 70 interpreters of the Hewbrews 2242.

Keating gives the pedigree of Milesius very extensively from which the following is condensed.

"Noah, was son of Lamech, son of Mathusalem, son of Enoche, son of Seth, son of Adam; for it is of the race of Seth are all those who live after the deluge, and all the race of Cain were drowned under the deluge. Those saved from the deluge were Noah and his wife, whose name was Coba, and his three sons Sem, Cham and Japheth and their three wives Olla, Oliva and Olivana.

11. JAPHET was son of Noah

12. MAGOG was son of Japhet. The Cin - Droma - Snechta, according to Keating stated that among the sons of Magog was Braath.

13. BRAATH was the son of Magog.

14. FENIUS FARSAIDH was the son of Braath. He was King of Scythia and chief at the building of the Tower of Babel. After the destruction of the Tower of Babel each of the seventy two nations engaged in the building spoke in a different tongue. Fenius Farsaidh at his own expense, sent seventy two disciples into the various countries of the three continents of the world that were inhabited, and charged them to remain abroad seven years, so that each might learn the language of the country in which he stayed during that time.

 On their return Fenius Farsaidh established a school of languages in the plain of Sinair. Two other sages, Caoi Caomhbreathach from Judea and Gaedheal, son of Eathor, from Greece, presided over the school with him. It is from this Gaedheal that the Gaelic language takes its name, and not from Gaedheal, son of Niul, son of Fenius Farsaidh. At his death he left his kingdom to his eldest son Neanui, and left to his other son, Niul, only what profit he derived from the sciences and the various languages which he used to teach in the public schools.

15. NIUL son of Fenius Farsaidh. He acquired such a reputation as a teacher that Pharaoh Cincris invited him to Egypt and gave him lands and his own daughter Scota in marriage. She was the mother of Gaedheal. While Niul sojourned in Egypt the children of Israel escaped from captivity and came to Capacyroub on the shores of the Red Sea where Niul dwelt. Learning that they were short of food Niul placed his store of provisions at their service, and was rewarded for so doing by Moses, who healed his son Gaedheal from the bite of a venomous serpent which had brought him to a dying condition. To the blessing then imparted by Moses and Aaron, Irish writers attribute the absence

of venomous reptiles from the countries possessed by the descendants of Gaedheal.

16. GAEDHEAL son of Niul. It is from him that all the Gaels are named,
Feine O Feinius Atbearta
Brig gan doctita
Gaedhil O Gaedheal Glas gharta
Scuit O Scota.

The Feni are named from Feinius
The meaning is not difficult
The Gaels from comely Gaedheal Glas
The Scots from Scota.
On the death of his father, Gaedheal took possession of the lands of Capacyroub and a son was born to him.

17. EASRU was son of Gaedheal, who dwelt on the same lands and had a son Sru born to him.

18. SRU was son of Easru. In his time, the Egyptians, having recovered from the losses inflicted by the destruction of Pharaoh Cincris and his army, "sixty thousand foot and fifty thousand horse", who were drowned in the Red Sea, fearing he would assume the sovereignty over them expelled him and his people from their country. They made their way to the island of Crete where Sru died.

19. EIBHEAR SCOT son of Sru, then became leader of his people, whom he brought into Scythia, where a contention as to leadership arose between he descendants of Niul and the descendants of his brother Neanui, which continued for a considerable period.

20. BEODHAMAN, son of Eibhear Scot.

21. AGHNAMAN, son of Beodhaman.

22. TAT OR TA - IT son of Aghnaman.

23. AGNON son of Tat. During the period which elapsed from the days of Eibhear Scot to the time of Agnon, the descendants of Neanni appear to have held the ruling power in Scythia. In contending with them for the sovereignty, Agnon slew his relative Reafloir, who was then King of Scythia. The two sons of Reafloir collected an army and marched against the descendants of

Gaedheal, who thereupon left the country and went to the shores of the Caspian Sea, and then made their way northwards to Gothia.

24. LAIMHFIONN, was son of Agnon. He was leader in the migration to Gothia. During their voyage Keating tells us, "Mermaids came on the sea before them, and these used to discourse music to the sailors as they passed them, so that they might lull them to sleep, and then fall upon them and slay them; and Caithear, the Druid, applied himself a remedy to this by melting wax in their ears so that they might not hear the music lest it might put them to sleep.

25. EIBHEAR GLUINFHIONN, was the son of Laimhfhionn. He was born in Gothia where his people dwelt for one hundred and fifty years during which time the following generations are recorded.
26. AGNOMAN son of Eibhear Gluinfhionn (Keating omits him)
27. EIBRIC, his son.
28. NEANUL, his son.
29. NUADHA, his son.
30. EALLOIT, his son.
31. EARCHAIDH, his son.
32. DEAGHAIDH, his son.
33. BRATHA, his son. Once more a party of the descendants of Gaedheal migrated, this time under the leadership of Bratha who brought a party in four ships, each ship having fourteen wedded couples and six servants. Giolla Caomhain writes:

> Bratha, son Deaghaidh the beloved,
> Came to Crete, to Sicily;
> The crews of four well rigged ships safely came,
> Having Europe on their right, to Spain.
> From him the Duchy of Braganza in Portugal is named
> In Spain after they had routed the natives , they settled here. A plague carried off all but ten of them, but afterwards they increased in number.

34. BREOGHAN, son of Bratha was born in Spain. A French writer called Lobhois says that the first King who obtained sovereignty over all Spain was "a person called Brigus", who built many castles and it is he who in the *Book of Invasions* is called Breoghan. He it was who built Bregansia near Corunna, and also the tower of Breoghan in Corunna. He had ten sons, of whom one was Bile.

35 BILE , son of Breoghan, was the eldest of ten brothers and the father of Milesius.

36. MILESIUS, of Spain, son of Bile, was originally known as Galamh, but earned the name of Milesius by his military prowess. Early in his life he returned to Scythia with a number of young men from Spain, where he was well received and became Commander of the forces of the Kingdom. He married Seang, the daughter of the King, by whom he had two sons, Donn and Aireach. He afterwards carried his own forces to Egypt and was there welcomed by the Pharaoh Nectombus who gave his a territory in which he and his followers might abide. A war broke out between the Egyptians and Aethiopians and Milesius joined the Egyptians. He became Commander of the army and conducted the campaign to a successful issue. Seang, having died before he left Scythia, Milesius espoused Scota, the daughter of Pharaoh, who bore him six sons, Eibhear, Fionn, Aimhirgean, Ir, Colpa, Arannan and Heremon. Eventually he returned to Spain, then being harassed by the Goths whom he defeated and expelled from the Kingdom. Ioth, uncle to Milesius, went on an expedition to Ireland, and after being well received by the Tuatha De Dannan, then in occupation of the island, was later attacked by them, just prior to his departure for Spain. They feared he would return with larger forces and take possession of their Kingdom. He departed for home, grievously wounded and died on the voyage. When the sons of Milesius and the descendants of Breoghan saw his mangled body they resolved to come to Ireland to avenge his death.

O' FLAHERTY'S PEDIGREE OF MILESIUS

10. NOEM
11. JAPHEL
12. MAGOG
13. BRATH
14. FENISIUS c.1758
15. NUIL
16. GAIDEL
17. ASRUTH
18. SRUTH
19. HEBER SCOTT
20. BEOGAMON
21. OGAMON
22. TA - IT

23. AGNOMON
24. LAMFINN c. 2245
25. HEBER GLUINFION
26. AGNOMAN
   27. FEBRICK GLAS
28. NENNUAL
29. NUAD
30. ALLAD
31. ARCAD
   32. DEAG
33. BRATHA c. 2767
34. BREOGEM
35. BILE
36. MILESIUS

Chapter 3

The Heremonians

37. HEREMON was the first Milesian Monarch of Ireland A.M. 3500. " The fleet of the sons of Milidh came to Ireland at the end of this year" (IV M) A.M. 3500. Nennius, a British writer who flourished about the year 850 gives the number of their ships as 150; Keating says "thirty ships in all with thirty warriors in each ship, besides their women and camp followers."

Of the eight sons, five viz. : Donn, Irr, Colpa, Aireach and Arannan lost their lives before a landing was effected, and only Heremon, Heber - Finn and Aimhergin succeeded in making good their footing against the Tuatha de Danann who then held and governed Ireland. At Tailteann, now Telltown between Trim and Navan, a decisive battle was fought and the De Dananns utterly routed. Their three kings, MacCuill, MacCeacht and MacGreine were slain by the three surviving sons of Milesius. Eire, Fodla and Banbha their three queens, lost their lives in the same battle.

The kingdom was divided between two brothers, Hermon and Heber Finn. The former ruled the territory north of the Boyne and the latter that to the south of the river. This division lasted one year only, as a dispute arose between the two brothers which led to the battle of BRU - BHRIODAIN, at a pass between two plains in the district of Geishill (Co. Offaly), in which Heber Finn was slain. Heremon became sole Monarch of an undivided Ireland , A.M.3502, and reigned for fourteen years. Aimhergin challenged his right to the sovereignty, but was defeated at the battle of Bile - Theineadh in Breagh (probably Billywood, parish of Moynalty, Co. Meath). Heremon died at his palace, Rathbeitheach, beside the Nore, in Arigeadros, and was there buried "with great and solme funerals" (Annals of Clonmacnoise).

One hundred and nine kings of his lineage succeeded him in the monarchy. During the reign of Heremon, the Cruithnigh or Picts came to Ireland and landed at the mouth of the river Slaney, from whence they eventually proceeded to Scotland. Criomthann Sciathbheal, who the sovereignty of Leinster from Heremon, made friends with them.

The leaders of that fleet were Gud and his son Cathluan; and the reason that Criomthann entered into friendship with them was because a tribe of Britons, who were called Tuatha Fiodhgha, were making conquests in the Fotharta on either side of the mouth of the Slaney. Such were these people that the weapons of every one of them were poisoned, so that, be the wound inflicted by them small or great, no remedy whatever availed the wounded man, but he must die.

Criomthann heard that there was a skilful druid, called Trostan, amongst the Cruithigh who could furnish himself and his people with an antidote against the poison with which the weapon of the Tuatha Fiodhgha were wont to be charged; and he asked Trostan what remedy he should use against the poison of the weapons of those people we have mentioned. "Get thrice fifty white hornless cows milked", he said, " and let the milk got from them be placed in a hollow in the middle of the plain in which you are wont to meet them in battle, and offer them battle on that same plain; and let each one of your followers who shall have been wounded by them, go to the hollow and bathe, and he will be healed from the venom of the poison."

Criomthann did as the druid had advised, and fought the Battle of Ard Leamhnachta against the Tuatha Fiodhgha. He defeated and executed great slaughter on them in that place. From this event, and from the battle which took place, the battle has been called the Battle of Ard Leamhnachta ever since.

Now as to the Cruithnigh, that is, Gud an his son Cathluan, they resolved to invade Leinster; and when Eireamhon heard this, he assembled a numerous army, and went on to meet them. When the Cruithnigh saw that they were not strong enough to fight Eireamhon, they entered into peace and friendship with him. Eireamhon told them that there was a country to the north - east of Ireland, and bade them go and occupy it. Then, according to Beda, in the first chapter of the first book of the History of the Sacsa, the Cruithigh asked Eireamhon to give some of his noble marriageable ladies he had with him, some of the wives of the leaders who had come with him from Spain, and whose husbands were slain; and they bound themselves by the sun and moon that the possession of the kingdom of Cruitheantuath, which is now called Alba, should be held by right of the female, rather than that by the male progeny to the end of the world. Upon these conditions Eireamhon gave them three women, namely the wife of Breas, the wife of Buas and the wife of Buaidhne; and Cathluan, who was their supreme leader, took one of those women to wife; and after that they proceeded to Cruitheantuath and Cathluan conquered that country, and was the first king of Alba of the race of Cruithnigh. There were seventy kings of the Cruithnigh or Picts on the throne of Alba after him, as we read in the Psalter of Cashel in the poem beginning "All ye learned of Alba". Thus it speaks on this matter:

> The Cruithnigh seized it after that,
> When they had come from the land of Erin;
> Ten and sixty very noble kings
> Of those that ruled the land of Cruithnigh.

> Cathluan, the first of these kings,

15

I will tell you briefly;
The last king of them was the stout champion Constantin.

But Trostan, the druid, and five other Cruithnigh mentioned in the above poem, remained in Ireland after Cathluan, and got lands from Eireamhon in the plain of Breagh in Co. Meath.[5]

The Fotharta in which the battle of Ard Leamhnachta (New Milk Hill) was fought, was portion of the territory granted in after years to Eochaid Fionn Fuathairt by the King of Leinster as a reward for his assistance in expelling the Munster men from his Kingdom.

38. IRIAL. FAIDH 10th. Monarch of Ireland. A.M. 3520

Irial, the prophet, youngest son of Heremon, wrested the Kingship from the sept of Heber, at the battle of Cuil - Martra. He slew the four sons of Heber, viz: Ere, Orba, Fearon and Feargna, thus avenging his brothers, Luighne and Laighne, who had been killed by them about six months previously in the battle of Ard - Ladhron (believed to be Ardamine, Co. Wexford).

He cleared sixteen plains of their timber so as to render them suitable for cultivation, among them being Magh - nAirbhrioch in Fotharta Airbhrioch (anciently called Bri - Eile near the hill of Croghan in King's Co.). In Leinster, he also built seven royal forts in various parts of Ireland. He was the first Irish born monarch of the Heremonian line. He died at Magh - Muaidhe (Knockmoy, near Tuam) after a reign of ten years, and was buried there.

39. EITHRIAL 11th. Monarch of Ireland. A.M. 3549

Eithrial, son of Irial Faidh, held the sovereignty for twenty years. He is recorded as having cleared seven plains. He was slain by Conmhaol, son of Heber, at the battle of Raeire (probably Magh - Reighne in Ossary) in Leinster.

40. FOLL AICH

Foll Aich, son Eithrial did not reach the throne.

41. TIGHERNMAS 13th. Monarch of Ireland. A.M. 3580

Tighernmas, son of Foll Aich, and grandson of Eithrial, recovered the throne from the line of Heber. Conmhaol, who occupied it fell by the hand of Eibhear,

---

[5] Keating Vol II pg. 115

son of Tighernmas, at the battle of Aonach - Macha (Emania or the Navan fort near Armagh). In one year, Tighernmas defeated the descendants of Heber in twenty seven battles and almost exterminated them. He made great improvements in the social life of his people. He introduced gold and silver goblets, pins and brooches, having caused them to be made by an artificer named Uchadan at Fotharta - Airthir - Liffe (Fotharta east of the Liffey). It is noteworthy that this is the precise territory where considerable quantities of gold have been mined or collected in later years. In his time also clothes were first dyed purple, green and violet, and distinctive colours allocated to the several ranks of society. During his reign many lakes burst out over Ireland, among them Lough Foyle, now an arm of the sea and Lough Key, in Moylurg on an island which the famous Annals of Loch Ce were compiled.

He has also the credit or discredit, of having originated the worship of idols in Ireland. He paid the penalty for this 'crime' at Magh - Sleacht, in Breifney, where he and a large number of his subjects were killed by lightning on the eve of Samhain (a festival held on the 31st. October), while offering sacrifice to their principal idol Crom - Cruach.

Crom - Cruach is described thus in the seventh life of St. Patrick (Colgan): " It was an idol embossed with gold and silver, and had ranged on either side of it, twelve brazen statues of less distinction.....but this is not usurping miscreant .... was subdued by the servant of the living God, and was publicly disrobed and divested of these honours which he had contaminated by usurpation, and at length tumbled to the earth with confusion, from his elevated station. For when Patrick saw at a distance, the idol standing near the river Gathard, and, as he was approaching, threatened to strike it with the staff of Jesus, which he had in his hand, the statue began to fall down to the right, towards the west, it had its face turned to Tara and had the impression of the staff on its left side, though the staff did not touch it, nor did it even leave the hand of the man of God. The other twelve smaller statues were swallowed up in the earth to their necks, and their heads are to be seen yet, as a lasting memorial of this prodigy, just over the ground."

Dr. Healy places the Plain of Adoration, where 'Crom Cruaich and his sub-gods twelve' were adored, in the baronies of Tullyhaw and Carrigallen at Edentinney, between Fenagh and Ballnamore-But O'Donovan holds that, Magh Sleacht was in the present barony of Mohill, county Leitrim. He say the place was afterwards known as Fiodhnach which may signify a wild or woody district. Cromeleacs and huge stones and other druidical remains are to be seen at Fenagh to this day. St.Patrick erected a church called Domnachmore in the immediate vicinity of the place where Crom Cruach stood. A considerable difference of opinion prevails among our Irish historians and annallists as to the length of time during which Tieghernmas reigned. The Four masters (A.M.3656) say "This was the seventeenth year before three score of

17

Tighearnmas as King of Ireland." Keating gives the number as fifty years or according to others sixty years." while O'Flaherty (ogygia) and the Annals of Clonmacnoise agree as to thirty years.

He was one of the most worthy and famous Kings of his time, but his record is marred by the introduction of idolatry into Ireland. (O'Donovan in note,a,pg.43. Annals of Ireland, says, Magh Sleacht "was the name of a plain in the barony of Tullyhaw and County of Cavan the village of Ballymagauran, and the island of Port, are mentioned as situated in this plain.")........

DINDSENCHAS says, "There was a King idol of Erin - namely Crom Cruaich, and around him twelve idols made of stones, but he was of gold. Until Patrick's advent he was the god of every folk that colonised Erin. To him they used to offer the firstlings of every issue and the chief scions of every clan. 'Tis to him that Erin's King Tighernmas, son of Follac, repaired on Hallow-tide together with the men and women of Erin in order to adore him, whence is Magh Sleacht, 'Plain of Prostration"

42. ENBOATH the son of Tighernmas comes next in the line of descent. It was in the lifetime of this prince that the Kingdom was divided in two parts by a line drawn from Drogheda to Limerick. Two brothers of the "line of Ir" usurped and held the Monarchy conjointly. They divided the Kingdom in two parts. One of these brothers, Cearmna, slain in a sanguinary battle at Dun Cearmna called the Old Head of Kinsale in County Cork.

43.
SMIRG0L.
   Smirgol, son of Eanboth, was slain by Eochaidh Feabharghlas at the battle of Dorymlehan (Drumlahan in County Cavan). During his lifetime, the Picts of Scotland who had revolted against the tribute imposed upon them by the Irish Monarch, were invaded and once more and reduced to subjection.

44. FEACHAIDH LABHRAINNE 18th. Monarch A.M.3728.

Feachaidh Labhrainne, son of Smirol having slain Eochaidh Feabharghlas, at the battle of Carman (Wexford) ascended the throne. He cleared seven plains, among them being Magh-Luirg (now the plain of Boyle, County of Roscommon) in Connaught. A list of nine battles fought by him is given by the Four Masters. During an attack by him on the Ernaans, a remnant of the Firbolgs in Fermanagn, the present Lough Erne burst forth and overwhelmed the Eraans from whom it is named. After a reign of twenty years, he was slain at the battle of Bealgadan, by Eochaidh Mumho, of the sept of Heber, whose name is preserved in that of the province of Munster (Bealgadon is near Kilmallock in County Limerick).

45. AENGUS OLMUCHADHA,20th Monarch A.M.3773.

Aengus Olmuchadha son of Feachaidh Labhrainne having killed Eochaidh Mumho at the battle of Cliach (Knockany, Co. Limerick) restored the line of Heremon once more to the Kingship. O'Flaherty derives his surname from ALL BHUADH HACH which signifies "grand conqueror" or "Victorious" and ridicules the derivation "OLL" that is "Great" and "MUCA" "hogs" since he had the largest hogs that were in Ireland in his time -which some Irish scholars give as the explanation of his surname. In view of the long list of battles in which he was victorious over the Heberians, Ernaans and Fomorians in Ireland, the Picts and the Belgae in Scotland and also over the Lombards it is much more probable his surname "Olmuch adha" originated from his victories rather than from his hogs. During his reign many plains were cleared, among them being "Maigh Mucruimhe" near Athenry in County Galway, where in later years (A.D.195) Art Aoinfhear, King of Ireland, was slain by Ligurn, grandson of Eochaidh Fionn Fuathairt, lineal ancestor of O'NUALLAIN.

After reigning eighteen years, Aengus was killed at the battle of Carman (Wexford) by Enna Airgthioch, of the line of Heber, who succeeded him in the monarchy.

46. MAEN son of Aengus Olmuchada, was deprived of his father's throne by Enna Airgthioch (Enna the Plunderer). It was during Enna's reign that silver shields were made at Airgead - Ros (Silver Wood in the parish of Rathbeagh, barony of Galmoy, County Kilkenny) "so that he gave them together with horses and chariots to the men of Ireland, as rewards for bravery."

47. RAITHEACHTAIGH, 22nd. Monarch , A.M. 3818

Raitheachtaigh, son of Maen, having slain Enna Airgtheach at the battle of Raighne (a plain in Ossary), became King of Ireland in his stead. Little is chronicled of him beyond his accession and his death, which occurred at Tara, from a wound received from Seadna, son of Airtri, at the battle of Rath Cruachain (now Rathcroghan, Co. Roscommon). Raitheachtaigh reigned eleven years.

48. DIAN or DEIGN is given by Keating as the son of Raitheachtaigh, while the Four Masters style him son of Deman. It is probable the latter is correct, as according to their chronology 177 years elapsed from the death of Raitheachtaigh to the accession of Siorna , the long lived. During this time it is recorded that noblemen first wore golden chains around their necks a sign of

their birth. The golden chains referred to are probably the "Torques" of which so many excellent specimens are to be seen in our present day Museums.

49. SIORNA SAEGHALACH, 34 th. Monarch, A.M.4020

Siorna Saeghalach, son of Dean, grandson of Denian and great grandson of Raitheachtaigh, was called Saeghalach (the long lived) because he was granted length of years beyond his contemporaries. The Annals of the Four Masters state that he reigned for "a century and a half". O'Flaherty (Ogygia Chp. XXXII) quotes from the book of Lecan, fol.291 b. "He was called long lived because he lived 150 years." Keating quotes a poem giving his reign as 21 years and the Annals of Clonmacnoise record his death at the hands of "Rohaghty Roha McRoayne when he had reigned 21 years." It is also reported of him that " he lived an outlawe one hundred years together, before he was King, and that only against the Ulstermen"

Siorna assisted King Oilioll to overthrow his cousin King Berngall, and sixteen years later rose up against Oilioll, slew him and secured the Monarchy for himself. Be his age what it may, he was a warrior of no mean capacity and waged successfully many battles. He conquered the Ultonians at Atas - Keltair (Downpatrick, memorable for the sepulchre of St. Patrick, which is mentioned in the will of St. Patrick, as "Dun a mbeam' eis erge a Raith Chealtair mhic Duach", that is, Down where my resurrection shall be in the fortifications of Keltair, the son of Duach). He also conquered the Martineans, the Ernai and the Fomorians in many engagements. In the fifteenth year of his reign Lughair, son of Lughaidh, of the race of Heber, brought in a force of Fomorians into Ireland with their King, Ceasarn; Siorna attacked them at the Bog of Trogaidhe (O'Donovan places this in the east of ancient Meath), "where a cruel battle was fought between them with such vehemensy that almost both sides perished therein, with overlabouring themselves and especially the Irish nation with their king also. Loway and Kiarme, King of the Formoraches were slaine, others write that King Siorna was slain by Rohaghty Roha McRoayme" [6]

The Four Masters write " As they were fighting the battle, a plague was sent upon them of which Lughair and Ceasarn perished, with their people, and a countless number of the men of Ireland along with them.

During the reign of Siorna the following rivers broke out, the Skirt in Leinster, the Doallt, a stream in the south of Monaghan, the Nith, an ancient name of the river of Ardee, the Laune, near Killarney and the Slaine, a small stream flowing into the Boyne, near Slane, Co. Meath. Keating quotes the following poem, beginning "Noble Eire, island of the Kings" which tells of the death of Siorna.

---

[6] Annals of Clonmacnoise

> "Siorna passed in government
> The length of thrice seven noble years
> The cutting off of Siorna with slaughter
> Was in Aillin by Raitheachtaigh."

Ailing is now known as Knockaulin, Co. Kildare.

50. OILIOLL OLCHAIN
Oilioll Olchain was the son of Siorna. During his life, chariots with four horses were first used in Ireland, by King Raitheachtaigh " Ericthonius the son of Vulcan, the fourth King of Athens, about the year of the world 2463 is said to be the first inventor of chariots to hide the deformity of his legs which were crooked." (Ogygia)

During one whole year, at this time, snow fell continuously in Ireland.

51. GIALLCHAIDH   37th. Monarch, A.M.4178
Giallchaidh, son of Oilioll Olchain, having defeated and slain Eilim son of Raitheachtaigh, in a battle, fought at the confluence of the Suir, the Nore and the Barrow, near New Ross, ascended the throne A.M. 4178 and signalised his coronation by demanding hostages from the Kings of the five provinces, which were duly delivered. He had a reputation of being rather a tyrannical king and lost his life at the hands of his successor Art Imleach, at the battle of Magh Muaidhe, after a reign of nine years. (Magh Muaidhe is either Knockmoy, Co. Galway or the plain of the river Moy in north Connaught.)

52. NUADHAT FINNFAIL 39th. Monarch, A.M.4199
Nuadhat Finnfail, son of Giallchaidh, avenged the death of his father by killing Art Imleach, and thus became possessed of his ancestral Crown, which he retained for forty years. He, in turn, fell by the hand of his successor, Breas, son of Art Imleach, of the sept of Heber.

53. AEDAN GLAS
Aedan Glas was the son of Nuadhat Finnfail. In his time the coast was infested with pirates. The Fomorians came again into Ireland, but were overthrown in many battles and were quite expelled out of the Kingdom. During one year a dreadful plague swept over the land and very many of the inhabitants were carried off by it. "There was a great faintness generally over all the Kingdom, once every month during that year, which synchronised with the reign of Eochaidh Apthach (A.M. 4248) of the race of Luaghaidh, son of Ith, who had usurped the Monarchy. He was slain at the end of the year by Finn son Bratha.

54. SIMON BREAC 44th. Monarch, A.M. 4291

Simon Breac, son of Aedan Glas, secured the throne by killing his predecessor, Seadna, whom he caused to be torn asunder. Simon held the sovereignty for six years. He was then taken prisoner by Duach Finn, son of Seadna, who remembering the cruel death inflicted on his father, paid back his torture in full by having Simon crucified.

55. MUIREADHACH BOLGRACH 46th. Monarch, A.M.4307,

son of Simon Breac, having slain his father's executioner, Duach Finn, at the battle of Magh, was raised to the Monarchy which he held but one year, falling a victim to Enda Dearg. Enda Dearg was the first to have money coined in Ireland at Airgeadros.

56. FIACHA TOLGRACH   55th. Monarch, A.M. 4395

Fiacha Tolgrach, son of Muireadach Bolgrach, with the assistance of his son Duach Ladhrgrach, and Argeadhmhar, of the Irian race, having killed Art, his predecessor, assumed the Monarchy and held it for ten years.

His elder brother, Duach Teamhrach, had two sons Eochaidh Fiadhmuine and Conaing Begeaglach who reigned conjointly for five years from A.M.4356, Eochaidh governing the south of Ireland and Conaing the north. In A.M. 4361 Eochaidh was slain by Lughaidh Laimhdhearg and Conaing was deposed. The latter, however, did not tamely submit to his deposition, as after seven years he equalized matters by slaying Lughaidh and a second time becoming Monarch of Ireland. Conaing was called Begeaglach "because he was never afraid on anyone during his life." After a reign of twenty years he suffered the fate of his brother at the hands of Art son of Lughaidh.

During the reign of Fiacha, his right to the crown was stubbornly contested by Oilioll Finn, who eventually fell by his hand, but the death of Oilioll brought him little relief, as Eochaidh, son of Oilioll, continued his father's efforts to recover his ancestral rights. He at length succeeded in attaining his objective by killing Fiacha at the battle of Breauie. There are two places of this name, one in Co. Mayo and the other in Co. Donegal.

57. DUACH LADHGRACH 59th. Monarch, A.M. 4453

Duach Ladhgrach, son of Fiachaidh Tolgrach, appears to have been a warrior of no mean capacity, and a diplomat of high order. He combined with Argeadhmhar to assist his father in securing the crown. After his father's death, while Eochaidh son of Oilioll Fionn occupied the throne, Duach took measures to remove Argeadhmhar, as a dangerous pretender and " drew Argeadhmhar to so narrow a plung (sic) that he was driven to go to sea for seven years". At length, Duach and Argeadhmhar made peace and combining their forces fell on Eochaidh Mac Oilioll Fionn at Knoc - aine (Knockaney,

Co. Limerick) where Eochaidh was attending the fair held in that place, and killed him. Argeadhmhar then became king and Duach, still aiming for the chief monarchy, combined with Lughaidh Laighdhe, son of Eochaidh, slew Argeadhmhar, and secured the coveted prize. He was called Ladhgrach from "Luaghagra" meaning "swift retribution" as he gave no respite to anyone who had committed injustice, but extracted retribution from such on the spot. After a reign of ten years he lost his life by his old ally Lughaidh Laighdhe.

58. EOCHAIDH BUADHACH
Eochaidh Buadhach, son of Duach Ladhgrach, is called in the Annals of Clonmacnoise, "King Eochie Bway". In the Rawlinson MS. 448 printed by Dr. O'Connor we find the passage : " In the 18th. year of Ptolemy, Cimbaoth, son of Fintan began to reign in Emania, who reigned eighteen years. Then Eochaidh the victorious, the father of Ugaine, reigned in Tara."

O'Curry MS. Materials writes in Appendix XXXV:- " But the most curious part of this entry is the assertion that Eochaidh Buadhach, the father of Ugaine Mor was King of all Erin and residing at Tara, contemporaneously with Cimbaoth, King of Emania; when in fact that Eochaidh Buadhach was never monarch in Erin at all; but by mistake of the original compiler, or some subsequent scribe, his name is substituted here for that of his father Duach Ladhrach who was the contemporary of Cimbaoth.

Badhbhchadh, son of Eochaidh Buadhach, having slain his brother Ugaine Mor A.M. 4606, held the sovereignty of Ireland for a day and a half, when he lost his life at the hands of Laeghaire Lorc.

59. UGAINE MOR 66th. Monarch, A.M.4567
Ugaine Mor, son of Eochaidh Buadhach, was fostered by Cimboath and his famous queen Macha, from whom Armagh (Ard Macha) is named, and who has the further distinction of being the only native born queen who ever held sovereignty in Ireland. Like almost all those who preceded him in the monarchy, he reached the throne over the dead body of its last occupant, Reachtaidh Righdearg, whom he killed to avenge the death of his foster mother Macha killed by Reachtaidh.

Some of our Antiquarists affirm in their old writings that this king conquered all the land to the Tirrhian (Mediterranean) sea. He married Cesarea, the daughter of the King of France with very great pomp and ceremony and had by her 25 children, that is to say, 22 sons and 3 daughters. He divided Ireland into 25 parts among them, a part to each of them, which division continued 300 years after. To his son Cobhtach Caol mBreagh was allotted " the country of Brey, where the lordship of Taragh" stood. To

Cobhthach - Minn Muirtheimhne, to Laeghaire Lorc the lands about the river Liffey. To Fuilne was allotted Moy Fea, now Forth O'Nolan in Carlow, etc, etc......Although the King had so many children, yet only two of them had male issue - Cobhthach Caol and Laeghaire Lorc.

King Uaigne reigned for 30 years. He was one of the noblest and most worthy of Kings that ever governed this land. He was of the sept of Heremon and was slain by his own half brother Badhbhchadh at Tealach an Chogair in Magh Muireada in Bregia. O'Flaherty states he was killed on the banks of the Boyne at a place called Kill Droicheat.

In his references to Ugaine Mor, Connellan writes : "in the early ages the Irish Kings made many military expeditions into foreign countries. Ugaine Mor called by O'Flaherty, in his Ogygia "Hugonious Magnus" was contemporary with Alexander the Great; and is stated to have sailed with a fleet into the Mediterranean, landed his forces in Africa, and also attacked Sicily; and having proceeded to Gaul was married to Caesair, daughter of the King of the Gauls. Hugonius was buried at Cruachan. The Irish sent during the Punic wars, auxiliary troops to their Celtic brethren, the Gauls; who in their alliance with the Carthagenians under Hannibal, fought against the Roman armies in Spain and Italy."

Ugaine Mor was he who exacted oaths by all the elements visible and invisible, from the men of Ireland in general that they would never contend for the sovereignty of Ireland with his children of his race.

60. COBHTHACH CAOL BHREAGH, son of Ugaine Mor was the 69th. Monarch, A.M. 4609, and the direct ancestor of O'Nuallain; anglicised O'Nowlan and O'Nolan. The O'Nolan is the only sept in Leinster that derives its descent from Cobhthach. All the other Leinster septs of the Heremonian race derive their descent from Laeghaire Lorc, the younger brother of Cobhthach. Hence The O'Nolan, as of the senior sept, has always been the hereditary Grand Marshal of Leinster, which office of King's Marshal, O'Nolan exercised even down to and during the reign of Queen Elizabeth. From Cobhthach also are descended some of the most illustrious septs in other parts of Ireland, including O'Neill of Tyrone and O'Donnell of Tyrconnell. From the days of Cobhthach down to King Feidhlemidh Reachtmhar, in the year of Our Lord 110, a period of seven hundred years, the stem of the old O'Nolan sept of Leinster is the stem of the O'Neills and O'Donnells. While from the same "Royal Stem of Ireland" as it is called, descended the Kings of Scotland, and we are told by Forman, who wrote in the eighteenth century that :- "The greatest antiquity which the august house of Hanover itself can boast is deduced from the Royal Stem of Ireland."

We are told that this famous King Cobhthach treacherously slew his brother Laeghaire Lorc and thus obtained the crown. Being at the Royal Palace of Dinree on the river Barrow, he feigned sickness, and was visited by Laeghaire, who received his death blow by Cobhthach plunging a dagger into his heart, as he leaned over the bed on which the pretended sick man lay. Cobhthach, moreover, it is said, put to death all the children of his brother Laeghaire, except one name Labhra Maen, who, being dumb, was considered incapable of reigning.

We shall presently come to the story of Labhra Maen, but first let us examine the motive, which, in those turbulent times, may have induced Cobhthach to commit such an unnatural act of cruelty. He must have felt deeply the injustice of his younger brother seizing the crown of Ireland. It belonged by right to Cobhthach. He was the oldest son of his father, the great Ugaine Mor, by Caesarea, the daughter of the King of France. To him was allotted by Ugaine Mor "the country of Brey, where the lordship of Taragh stood", while Laeghaire received the lands about the Liffey. The great plain between Dublin and Louth was called Magh Breagh and Tara also stood in the territory. This district was evidently given to Cobhthach by his father because Ugaine Mor regarded him as the Tanaist or lawful successor to the throne. Writhing under the injustice inflicted upon him by Laeghaire seizing the crown, he determined to secure his own legal inheritance by what was probably the only and certainly the most expeditious means available. O'Curry (MS. Materials p.452) states that Cobhthach adopted this method of securing the crown on the advice of a Druid.

Cobhthach, as we have seen, spared the life of one child of his brother Laeghaire, called Maen, and known in after life as Labrhraidh Loingseach. "Maen passed his childhood at Dinree," writes Lady Ferguson, "under the guardianship of Ferkertne, the poet, and Craftine, the harper of Cova (Cobhthach). As he grew into manhood he became distinguished for his personal beauty, and in a moment of excessive indignation at an insult offered to him by a companion, suddenly acquired the power of speech. The bards by a play on the words, "Labhra Maen" - (Maen speaks) - derive his subsequent name of Lavra Maen form this supposed exclamation of the bystanders who witnessed the scene. Cova (Cobhthach) having heard of the event, summoned the young prince and his attendants to Tara, and finding that he was dangerous from his popularity and munificence, sent him and his companions into banishment. He is claimed as the ancestor of all the Lagenian or Leinster families of the race of Heremon, with exception of the O'Nolans, who descend from Cobhthach.

O'Curry (MS. Materials, Lecture XII) deals extensively with the transactions leading up to the death of Cobhthach, in giving his summary of the Historic Tale "Argain Dinn Righ", from the Book of Leinster, from which the following extract is taken. " He made no delay in Britain, but passing over along to France, he entered the military service of the king of that country, in which he so distinguished himself that he soon became one of the chief commanders of the army there. After he had in course of time established himself in the full confidence and estimation of the king of France, Labhraidh Maen, who still kept up a correspondence with his friends in Erin, determined , if he could, to make one more effort to regain his rightful inheritance.

With this in view, he made himself known, and disclosed his whole history to the king of France, and concluded by asking of him such a body of troops as he should select, to accompany him to Erin, and assist him in conjunction with his friends there, to re-establish himself in his kingdom. The French king consented without difficulty and the expedition arrived safely in the mouth of the river Slaney, now the harbour of Wexford.

After resting a while there to recover from the fatigues of their voyage, and being joined by great numbers from Leinster and Munster, the expedition marched by night to Dinn Righ, where the monarch Cobhthach, entirely ignorant of their approach, happened to be at the time holding an assembly, accompanied by thirty five native princes and a bodyguard of seven hundred men. The palace was surprised and set on fire, and the monarch, the princes, the guards and the entire household were burned to death. This was the Argain Dinn Righ or Slaughter of Dinn Righ."

The Annals of Clonmacnoise tell a different story: "King Cobhthach was invited to a feast by his said nephew Lawrey, and there was treacherously burnt, together with thirty Irish princes, in his own house, after he had reigned 17 years. King Cobhthach had little care of the Irish proverb, (that one should never trust a reconciled adversary)"

DINN RIGH: This was a very ancient seat of the Kings of Leinster. It is named Dinn - Righ i.e. " the hill of the Kings" , and also Dumha -Slainge i.e. " Slainge's Mount". It is situated in the townland of Ballyknockan, about a quarter of a mile south of Leighlin Bridge, on the west bank of the Barrow. Nothing remains of the palace but a moat.

61. MELGHE MOLBHTHACH   71st. Monarch, A.M.4678
Melghe Molbhthach (the Praiseworthy) son of Cobhthach, avenged his father's death, nineteen years afterwards, by killing Labhraidh Loingseach. He, himself, held the sovereignty for seventeen years, and lost his life at the battle of Claire (a hill near Duntrileague in Co. Limerick) in which Modhcorb was the victor. When his grave was being dug, Lough Melghe burst forth over the land in Cuirbre, so that it is named from him. Lough Melghe, now Loch Melvin, a beautiful lake on the confines of Fermanagh, Leitrim and Donegal.

62. IREREO, 74th. Monarch A.M. 4720

Irereo, son of Melghe, having slain Aenghus Ollamh, succeeded to the crown, which he held for seven years. Keating calls him Irangleo Fathach - Iron- Fight the cautious. He was a king of great justice and wisdom, very learned and possessed of many accomplishments, and was slain by Fearcorb, son of Modhcorb.

63. CONLA CAOMH, 76th. Monarch, A.M.4738

Conla Caomh (Beautiful) son of Irereo avenged his father's death, by slaying Fearcorb. He then assumed the monarchy and appears to have broken the record of his predecessors as it is recorded of him that he died a natural death at Tara.

64. OILIOLL CAISFHIACHLACH, 77th. Monarch A.M. 4758

Oilioll Caisfhiachlach (twisted teeth), son of Conla, succeeded his father as chief King of Ireland and reigned twenty five years. Adhamair, son of Fear Corb deprived him of his life and his crown.

65. EOCHAIDH FOILTLEATHAN, 79th. Monarch, A.M. 4788

Eochaidh Foiltleathan, son of Oilioll recovered the throne by killing Adhamair and thus taking vengeance for the death of his father. He reigned seventeen years and fell by the hand of Fearghne Fortamhail , a descendant of Ugaine Mor.

66. AENGUS TUIRMHEACH, 81st. Monarch, A.M.4816

Aengus Tuirmheach (the Prolific) son of Eochaidh Foiltleathan was so called because he is common ancestor of the great families of Leath-Chuinn, Alba or Scotland, Dal-Riada and Dal-Feathach (Ogygia). His predecessor Fearghus, surnamed the powerful or brave, fell by his hand at Tara. Aengus had two sons. One, Fiacha Fermara (so called from having been exposed in a small boat on the sea) is ancestor of the Kings of Dal-Riada and Alba. The other, Enna Aighneach, was afterwards King of Ireland from whom most of the succeeding monarchs derive their descent. After a reign of sixty years Aengus died, "quietly at Tara, in his bed".

67. ENNA AIGHNEACH, 84th. Monarch, A.M. 4488

Enna Aighneach, son of Aengus Tuirmheach killed his predecessor Nia Seahamain and recovered the monarchy from which he had been ousted by its two previous occupants. He was called Aighneach by reason of his generosity or hospitality. He reigned twenty years and was slain in an engagement at Ard Crimthainn by Crimthann Cosgrach (the Victorious), so called because he was successful in every battle which he fought. O'Flaherty dubs him "The Champion of the Hermonians of Leinster".

68. ASSAMAN EAMHNA his son was excluded from the throne by his father's murderer, who held the crown for four years till he was "slain by Rowry McSitrick, ancestor of the Clanna Roweys (clan-na-Rory) as of Magennyes, O'Ferrall, O'More etc."

69. ROGHEN RUADH, his son, "in his time", the annals state, "there was such a murrain of cattle in this land that only one bull and one heifer survived in the whole kingdom and there lived in a place called Sawasge", that is the Heifer's Glen, in Co. Kerry. (See Ann. F.M. 1.86) -("a remarkable valley in the county of Kerry where this tradition is still vividly remembered" - O'Donovan).

70. FINNLOGH his son. "About this time Julius Cesar was murdered in the Senate with Bodkins " by Brutus and Cassius.

71. FIONN his son. This prince married Benia, the daughter of Criomthann by whom he had two sons.

72. EOCHAIDH FEIDHLIOCH, 93rd. Monarch, A.M.5058
Eochaidh, son of Fionn, having killed Fachtna Fathach, placed the line of Heremon once again in possession of the monarchy after a lapse of 150 years. He was father of Maedhbh, the celebrated Queen of Connaught, who is described by O'Flaherty (Ogygia), as a "powerful termagant, who lived to a very advanced age, a woman of very unruly and inordinate appetites."

In the first year of his reign (5058) Eochaidh rescinded the division of Ireland into 25 territories, instituted by Ugaine Mor, three hundred years previously, and divided it into five provinces, Leinster, two Munsters, Connaught and Ulster, each with a provincial king subordinate to the Ard Righ at Tara. In his time the great fortress of Rath Cruachain was erected at the residence of the King of Connaught, to whom he gave his daughter Meadhbh as wife. He was called Feedhleoch (a long sigh) "for his heart was never without a sigh until his death, since he slew his sons in the battle of Drom Criaidh."[7]

About the end of his reign is the period fixed by the Bards for the beautiful, but very sad, tale of Deirdre and the children of Uisneach. Eochaidh reigned twelve years and died a natural death at Tara.

Towards the end of his reign, or early in that of his brother Eochaidh Aireamh who succeeded him , occurred the cattle raid known as the "Tain Bo Cuailgne" one of the most interesting episodes preserved in the literature of this, or any country. The great war between Ulster and Connaught described in this work and the doings of the heroes engaged therein, are blazoned with

---

[7] Keating

28

poetical exaggerations. The fight between Cuchulainn and Ferdia as given by the bardic writer is a wonderful piece of word painting, while the information conveyed as to the habits, customs, arms and methods of warfare of those times render the tale invaluable to the student of early Irish history.

73. BREAS - NAR - LOTHAR

were sons of Eochaidh Feedhlioch, born at the same birth, their mother being Cloithfionn, daughter of Eochaidh Uichtleathan. They were known as the three Finneamhas and were slain at the battle of Drom Criaidh when in rebellion against their father.

74. LUGHAID RIABH nDEARG, 98th. Monarch, A.M.5166

Lughaid Riabh nDearg was son of one of the triplets named above. To cover their want of knowledge in this case the Bards and historians tell a highly coloured tale which is not only improbable but unnatural. Lughaid was called Riabh nDearg because of a number of red circles on his skin. He married Crifanga, daughter of the King of North Britain, and afterwards Dervogilla, daughter of the prince of Lochlainn (now Denmark).   During his reign it is recorded that Lough Neagh and Lough Ree burst forth. As a continuation of the improbable tale of the Bards it is said Lughaid killed himself by falling on his own sword, but the more natural ending as told by many writers is that he pined away after the death of his wife Dervogilla whom he loved passionately.

75. CRIOMTHANN NIADHNAIR, 100th. Monarch, A.M.5193

Criomthann Niadhnair was the son of Lughaidh Sreabhndearg. It was in the eighth year of his reign that our Lord and Saviour Jesus Christ was born. Criomthann made many expeditions to Britain and Gaul, and assisted the Picts and Britons in their wars against the Romans in Britain. It is fabled that he was accompanied on these expeditions by his Bainleannan or female sprite named Nair, from whom he was called Neadh Nair i.e. "Nair's Hero", which is a far more romantic explanation of his name than the disgusting one given by Keating, obviously from some Munster calumniator of the race of Heremon. The Annals of Clonmacnoise give this fable in a slightly different form. "It is reported that he was brought up by a fairy lady in her palace, where after great entertainment bestowed upon him, she bestowed a gilt coach with a sum of money on him as a love token". He brought back with him from his expeditions a splendid gilded war-chariot, and a golden chess board, inlaid with a hundred transparent gems, a beautiful cloak interwoven with threads of gold, a sword inlaid with many serpents in refined gold, a shield with bosses of bright silver, a spear, from the wound of which no one recovered, a sling from which no erring shot could be discharged and a pair of grey hounds coupled by a silver chain which was worth three hundred cumals (female slaves).

Shortly after returning with these spoils, in the sixteenth year of his reign, he was thrown from his horse and died at Dun Crimthainn, which was situated on the hill of Howth, and its site is now occupied by the Bailey lighthouse.

76. FEREDHACH FINNFEACHTHNACH, 102nd. Monarch:

A.D. 36 Feredhach Finnfeachtnach was son of Criomthann and held the sovereignty for twenty two years. During his reign the Chief Brehon was Morann Main, son to Cairbre Caitcheann, by his queen Maina, daughter to the king of Leinster. He was as celebrated for the strict tenor of justice and equity, which he invariably observed as for his learning and jurisprudence. He recognised that his father Cairbre had no legal right to the crown, which he had usurped , and spontaneously resigned the monarchy to Feredhach, the rightful heir to the dignity. As a supreme judge in deciding all litigation, he procured the epithet of the "the Just" for king Feredhach. He was so accurate and sagacious in investigating the truth and so careful that his delegates and subordinates would act with impartiality, that historians have attributed to him the possession of a collar which had the property of closing in and tightening on the neck of anyone wearing it who uttered an unjust judgement or gave false testimony, and so remained till truth and justice prevailed. Fearadhach died a natural death at Leath Druim (another name for Tara).

77. FIACHA FINNFOLAIDH, 104th. Monarch. A.D.56

Fiacha Finnfolaidh, son of Fearadhach Finnfeachtnach, stepped on to the throne over the dead body of his predecessor, Feathach Finn, who fell by his hand. His descriptive name, Finnfolaidh, signifies White Cows and was given to him because most of the cows in Ireland during his life were white.

During his reign there occurred "one of the most momentous troubles which interrupt the course of history" - the revolt of the Aitheach Tuatha (Rent payers or Rent paying tribes). The oppression of these people had become so great that they conceived a well planned scheme to put an end to it, and the domination of the Milesians, for ever.

These Aitheach Tuatha were the descendants of the original tribes who had been driven out of their possessions by Heremon and Heber, and comprised also a large number of debased Milesians who had fallen away from their caste, lost their civil independence, and had become reduced to a state akin to slavery - tillers of the soil and drudges engaged in the meanest occupations. They set aside one third of their crops for three years to provide a splendid banquet for the dominant faction, and so profoundly secret did they keep their aims, that not one of their intended victims received the faintest hint of the plot that ripened for their destruction. When their plans had fully matured they invited all the kings, princes and chief men of the nation to a sumptuous entertainment. The feast was prepared at Magh Cru (the plain of blood), believed to be situated near Lough Conn in County Mayo. Those invited came gladly and the feasting went on for nine days, and while the nobles were deep in their cups and enjoying the delicious (sic) music of the harpers, their treacherous hosts surrounded the banquet hall with armed men and murdered almost all of their unsuspecting victims. On this occasion the line of the Milesians was practically wiped out, and was only preserved from total extinction by the escape of three queens - Eithne (daughter of the King of Alba, wife of Fiachaidh Fionnoladh), Beartha (daughter of Gortnead, King of Britain, wife of Feig, King of Munster) and Aine (daughter of Cainnedle, King of Sacsa, who was wife to Breasa, King of Ulster). These three ladies escaped from the general slaughter, fled to Alba and there a son was born to each and thus, by little short of a miracle, the succession was preserved. Feachaidh Fionnoladh lost his life on that day also.[8]

78. TUATHAL TEACHTMHAR 106th. Monarch, A.D. 106

Tutathal Teachtmhar was a posthumous son of Fiacha Finnfolaidh. His mother, Eithne, daughter of the King of Scotland, having escaped from the massacre of Magh Cru, fled to her father's court and her son was born there and educated in the duties and accomplishments of a king until he was twenty years old. In the meantime, Elim, of the race of Ir, had been elevated to the monarchy and the Aitheach Tuatha found themselves still ground down and oppressed as before. Probably the recollection of their revolt and bloodthirsty massacre of the Irish Kings and prices led to still heavier exaction from them. Concluding that any change would be for the better, they invited Tuathal to return, and engaged to assist him in recovering his father's throne.

Tuathal readily consented and receiving considerable foreign levies from his grandfather, landed at Irrasdamanonia where "Feachra Cassan and others, evil contented with their estate, to the number of 800 chosen men, met him and presently saluted him as King". O'Flaherty states he fought eighty five battles for the crown. He met Elim and the forces under his command at the battle of Aichill (the ancient name for the hill of Skreen near Tara) where Elim was slain and his army utterly routed. It is worthy of remark that Tacitus, in his "Life of Agricola", states that one of the Irish Princes, who was in exile from his own country, waited on Agricola, who was then the Roman general in Britain, to solicit his support in the recovery of the kingdom of Ireland; for that, with one of the Roman legions and a few auxiliaries, Ireland could be subdued.

This Irish prince was probably Tuathal Teachtmhar, who was in Alba about that time. Tuathal afterwards became Monarch of Ireland, and, as the Four Masters place the first year of his reign at A.D. 76; and as Agricola with

---

[8] (A. MS. H.3. 18) in Trinity College gives details of the massacre

the Roman legions carried on the war against the Caledonians about A.D.75 to 78, the period coincides chronologically with the time Tuathal Teachtmhar was in exile in North Britain; and he might naturally be expected to apply to the Romans for aid to recover his sovereignty as heir to the Irish Monarchy.[9]

Having thus got possession of the crown, he called a convention of the provincial kings and prices at Tara, and administered to them an oath similar to that formerly exacted by Ugaine Mor, so that they and their posterity would observe an inviolable attachment, subjugation and homage to him and his posterity, and that no one should advance a claim to the monarchy against any of his progeny so long as Ireland should be surrounded by the sea. To this they swore by the Sun and the Moon and by all their heathen deities, celestial and terrestrial.

" It was then, too, he was given four portions of the provinces out of which he made the present Meath as the peculiar territory of the high kings of Ireland. For although Meath is the name of the territory which is beside Uisneach from the time of the children of Neimidh to the time of Tuathal, still, Meath was not the name of the portions that were taken from the provinces until the time of Tuathal, and he made it into a territory distinct from the provinces.

Now when Tuathal had put these four parts together and made them into one territory called Meath, he built therein four chief fortresses, that is, a fortress in each of the portions. Accordingly he built Tiachtgha in the portion of Munster which goes with Meath; and it was there that the Fire of Tiachtga was instituted, at which it was their custom to assemble and bring together the druids of Ireland on the eve of Samhain (31st. Oct.) to offer sacrifices to all the gods or commemoration was given to the first day of August (sic) on which is now held the feast of the Chains of Peter - although the mound and fair of Taillte existed from the time of Lughaidh Lamhfhada, still Taillte was not a royal fortress until the time of Tuathal Teachtmhar. Now since the place in which Taillte is, belongs to the part that was taken from the province of Ulster, the tax on the fair of Taillte went to the King of Ulster. This was the amount of that tax, namely, an ounce of silver for each couple that got married there.

The fourth royal fortress, Tara, is situated in the part of Leinster given to Meath, and there the Feis of Tara was held every third year after the sacrifice had been offered to all the gods at Tiachtgha (as we have said) as a prelude to that royal assembly called the Feis of Tara, at which they were wont to institute the laws and customs, and to confirm the annals and the records of Ireland, so that the ardollamhs might inscribe all that was approved of them in the Roll of the Kings, which was called the Psalter of Tara; and every custom

---

[9] Connellan

and record that was in Ireland that did not agree with that chief book were not regarded as genuine. We shall not give here in detail the laws or customs that were severally ordained at the Feis of Tara, for the books of the Breithemhuas Tuaiths are full of them.[10]

It was at that fire they used to burn their victims; and it was of obligation under penalty of fine to quench the fires of Ireland on that night, and the men of Ireland were forbidden to kindle fires except from that fire; and for each fire that was kindled from it in Ireland, the King of Munster received a tax of a screaball, or three pence, since the land on which Tiachtgha is belongs to the part of Munster given to Meath.

On the portion he had acquired from the province of Connaught he built the second fortress, namely Uisneach, where a general meeting of the men of Ireland used to be held, which was called the Convention of Uisneach, and it was at Bealtaine (1st. May) that this fair took place, at which it was their custom to exchange with one another their goods, their wares and their valuables. They also used to offer sacrifice to the chief god they adored, who was called Beil; and it was their wont to light two fires in honour of Beil in every district in Ireland, and to drive a weakling of each species of cattle that were in the district, between the two fires as a preservative to shield them from all diseases during the year; and it from that fire that was made in honour of Beil, that the name of Bealtaine is given to the noble festival on which falls the day of the two apostles, namely Philip and James; Bealtaine is derived from Beil Teine or the fire of Beil.

The horse and trappings of every chieftain who came to the great meeting of Uisneach were to be given as a tax to the king of Connaught, as the place in which Uisneach is, belongs to the part of the province of Connaught given to Meath.

The third fortress which Tuathal built, called Taillte, is in the portion of the province of Ulster joined to Meath; and it is here that the fair of Taillte was held (about the 1st. August), in which men of Ireland were wont to form alliances of marriage and friendship with one another. And a most becoming custom was observed in that assembly, namely, the men kept apart by themselves on the one side, and the women apart by themselves on the other side, while their fathers and mothers were making contract between them; and every couple who entered into treaty with one another were married, as the poet says,

> The men must not approach the women,
> Nor the women approach the fair bright men,
> But every one modestly biding apart

---

[10] Keating chpt. xxxix

In the dwelling of the great fair.

It was Lughaidh Lamhfhada that first instituted the fair of Taillte as a yearly commemoration of his own foster-mother Taillte, wife of Eochaidh son of Earc, the last king of the Fir Bolg and daughter of Maghmor, King of Spain. When Taillte had been buried in that mound, Lughaidh inaugurated the fair of Taillte as a nasadh or commemoration of her; It was for that reason that the name of Lughnasa (gracious nasadh) came into being.

Eochaidh Aincheann, King of Leinster, married Dairine, daughter of Tuathal, who according to the annals of Clonmacnoise, was deformed and by no means good-looking. The men of Leinster were dissatisfied that their king had married the plainer of the two daughters and Eochaidh, some time afterwards, returned to Tara, and representing to her father that Dairine had died, asked for, and obtained Fithir, her sister, as his second wife. When Fithir came as a bride to the palace at Naas she met Dairine, and both expired of grief and shame at the treachery practised on them.

King Tuathal, enraged at the fraud which had been perpetrated on him and because of the death of his two daughters, assembled a great army and marched into Leinster with intent to plunder and spoil the province. The Leinstermen, being unable to withstand him in the field, made terms with the monarch and agreed to pay the tribute called the "Boraimhe", as a fine or "Eruic" for the death of the daughters of Tuathal. In addition, Eochaidh was beheaded, and his brother Eric substituted in his place.

This tribute is variously given by different authorities, some placing it as high as 6000 cows, 6000 ounces of silver, 6000 hogs, 6000 sheep, 6000 brazen cauldrons and 6000 fine mantles. Such a mulet would be impossible to meet and the fact that it was exacted over 500 years, goes to prove such figures excessive. The annals of Clonmacnoise give the numbers as "150 cows, hogs, coverlets and cauldrons with 2 passing great cauldrons consisting in breadth and deepness five fists for King's own brewing, 150 couples of men and women in servitude to draw water on their backs for the said brewing, together with 150 maids with the King of Leinster's daughter in the like bondage and servitude." There is more semblance of probability about this enumeration.

The Boraimhe tribute led to endless wars and terrible slaughter, in enforcing its exaction, until it was abolished at the persuasion of St. Moling[11] of Tigh Moling (now called St. Mullins, in the Co. of Carlow) about the year 693 A.D. Brian, of Cinneidigh, monarch of Ireland, revived it again, about the beginning of the eleventh century, from which he obtained the surname of

---

[11] St. Moling died in A.D.695. According to Alfred P. Smyth St. Mullins had earlier claims to the patronage of the Ui Cheinnselaig than Ferns. - A.K.

"Boroimhe" (Brian Boru). The Book of Lecain and the Book of Leinster contain very valuable tracts dealing with the history of this tribute.[12]

After a reign of thirty years Tuathal was slain by Mal, son of Rocraidhe, King of Ulster, at Moin-an-chatha, in Dal-Araidhe, where, the two rivers, Ollar and Ollarbha spring - (now known as the Six Mile Water and the Larne River). The place where Tuathal fell, originally called Linn-an-ghobhann, is now known as Ballygowan.

A poem by Maelmura Othna (Maelmura, i.e. the servant of St. Mura, of Fahan, near Lough Swilly) whose death is recorded A.D. 884, preserved in the Leabhar-Gabhala by the O'Clerys. It contains 268 verses and it begins :

>   Lord over Lords, Tuathal the welcome
>   A flowing ocean:
>   A lion in strength, a wily serpent,
>   A wounding warrior. (Translation)

It gives an account of the great actions of Tuathal Teachtmhar; and recites the battles fought against Eochaidh, king of Leinster, and against Aitheach Tuatha, who had risen in arms against their legal sovereign, but who were completely subdued by Tuathal. In this poem the poet endeavours, by a recital of the glorious deeds of this King to stimulate Fiann Sionna, his own sovereign to emulate so illustrious an example.

79. FEIDHLIMIDH REACHTMHAR 108th. Monarch A.D. 111. Feidhlimidh Reachtmhar, was the son of Tuathal Teachtmhar, his mother being Baine,

---

[12] About this time the O'Nolans were in receipt of tribute also as the following reveals: The Book of Rights, ascribed to Saint Benignus, personal friend and earnest disciple of Saint Patrick, contains records of the tribute due to the King of Ireland and to the kings of the various provinces into which that Kingdom was sub-divided. Two copies of this are preserved, one in the Book of Leacan, compiled in the year 1418 A.D. by Giolla Ias Mor Mac Firbish of Leacan, the other, in the Book of Ballymote which was compiled by various persons, but chiefly by Solamh O'Droma from older MSS. about the year 1390 A.D. In addition to the tributes due to each King, it also enumerates the rights and stipends due from the king to his subordinate princes.

The following extracts are taken from the copy of this work issued in 1847 by the Celtic Society, Dublin, with notes by John O'Donovan Esq., M.R.I.A., which add enormously to its value as a work of reference.

>   "Eight swords, eight horns for drinking
>   From the King of defensive Carman,
>   Eight steeds of which not one has a bad mane,
>   To the King of Forthart Osnadhaigh"   A.K.

daughter of Scal, King of Finnland (sic.), which then embraced Sweden and Denmark as well as Finnland. Mal, his predecessor, who had killed Tuathal, fell in battle against Feidhlimidh, who thus avenged his father's death. His descriptive name "Reachtmhar" (the law giver) arose not more from his enacting good and salutary laws, than from his strict observance of existing laws. He changed the "Lex Talionis" which exacted " a life for a life, an eye for an eye and a tooth for a tooth" into the system of fine called Ernie (sic.) which apportioned the weight of the fine according to the enormity of the offence.

Chapter 4

Eochaidh Fionn Fuathairt ancestor of O'Nuallain

80 EOCHAIDH FIONN FUATHAIRT son of Feidlimidh Reachtmhar, was ancestor of the O'Nuallain, Anglicised O'Nowlan and O'Nolan. Fotharta the name by which the descendants of Eochaidh were called arises as a corruption of the genitive case of the word Fomhartach (meaning harvest). There are still two districts inhabited by them which still retain their name viz., the baronies of 'Forth O'Nolan' in Carlow and 'Forth' in Co. Wexford. Feidhlimidh Reachtmhar had three sons viz., Conn, Eochaidh and Fiacha. From these three brothers descend O'Neill and O'Donnell (Conn), O'Nolan and St. Brigid (Eochaidh) and from Fiacha came O'Dolan, O'Brick, O'Faelan (of Dun Faelan near Cashel) and Clan Campbell (known in the highlands of Scotland as Sliocht Diarmuid Ua Dhuibhne).

"Ffelym Reaghtwar", the Annals of Clonmacnoise relate, "succeeded in the government of the kingdom, in whose time there was a great war between Munster and Leinster, Dergaine being the King of Munster and Cowcorb McMoycorb King of Leinster. The Munstermen took from the Leinstermen from the borders of Leinster to a little ford near the hill of Mullamaisden, called Athantrosdan[13] (the ford of the crutch or pilgrim's staff). The Leinstermen were then very bare by reason of the yearly payment of the great tax of the Borowa before mentioned, and therefore they could not of themselves withstand the great power of the Munstermen, whereby their King was constrained to have recourse to the King of Ireland's court and there submissively to crave his aid, where he remained 3 months together, humbly beseeching the King (whose loyal subjects they did acknowledge themselves to be) not to remember the offences of their predecessors but presently to succour and aid them against the wrongful invasions and daily incursions of the Munstermen, being in his Royalty bound for their defence because he was their natural liege Lord and King, and they his dutiful subjects, wherefore they pittifully (sic) craved his assistance, that, in the meantime, under the shelter of his wings they might come to their own again.

---

[13] Ardristan in Carlow - A.K.

Whereupon, the King and Council deliberately considering how the cause stood and with the mature advice of all his Nobility, thought fit that the King of Leinster and the Leinstermen should be instantly aided, and the speedier to perform the same, decided to send King Felym's own second son, Eochye Finn McFeylym and Lowaye Lysie, son of Lisseagh Leanmore, King of Ulster, with all the King's forces to aid the King of Leinster against the Munstermen who were already possessed of the best part of Leinster. The King of Leinster covenanted with the King of Ireland's son and the King of Ulster's son that if they would recover all the lands that was in the Munstermen's hands, and drive them out by force of arms and withstand their forces still, he and his heirs would make good to them and their heirs all that was them possessed by the Munstermen, which was from the borders of Munster to the ford of Atharthrostan aforesaid, which with many other privileges were granted from the King of Leinster to them and their heirs, for ever, and for the performance thereof the King of Leinster, and all that were with him, did solemnly swear before the King of Ireland, at his palace at Taragh, in their own behalf as well as in the behalf of their posterity, to make the promises good forever to the said Eochy and Lowaye and their heirs in perpetual, which was presently enrolled in the Royal Charters of the King of Ireland who reigned at Taragh.

When the conditions were so strongly sworn to and confirmed, Eochy and Lowaye Lysie marched on with 7,000 Ulstermen in Loway's company, and 3,000 Meath and Connaught men in Eochy's company, who with all celerity came upon the Munstermen at Athrosta, where they assailed them unawares, and gave them a great overthrow. The Munstermen, thinking to recover their disgrace gathered all their forces together again, and met their enemies at Athy where they were likewise discomfited. The Munstermen were also overthrown at Leack Riada in Lease and at Athlayen (which is a ford on the river limiting Leinster from Munster) and after these great overthrows the Munstermen were quite driven out of Leinster. Eochy Finn and Loway then received the countries that were possessed by them (the Munstermen), which were there before called by the names of both the Fohertyes and the seven ould Leases. Which countries were ever since possessed by the said Eochy and Loway, their Issues and Posterities - O'Nolan, O'Ffaylan, O'Broyan etc. are issue of Eochy - O'More, O'Dowlen etc., are of the sept of Loway: when King Felym had reigned 10 years he died and was a very good King.

Feidhlimidh Reachtmhar had three sons, namely Conn Ceadchatach, Eochaidh Fionn and Fiachaidh Suighdhe, as we have said above. The descendants of Conn were at Tara, and held sovereignty ; the next brother Eochaidh Fionn went to Leinster and his descendants multiplied there and it was his descendants that possessed the seven Fotharta of Leinster. It was in his time that Cu Corb, son of Mogh Corb held the sovereignty of Leinster. It was, moreover, by this Eochaidh Fionn that Laoighseach Ceannmhor, son of Conall

Cearnach, was brought up and educated in politeness. It happened at that time that the Munstermen gained great sway in Leinster so that they were in possession of Osruighe and Laoighis as far as Mullach Maistean.

Now, when Cu Chorb saw the Munstermen gaining power in Leinster, he asked Eochaidh Fionn to help him in expelling them from Leinster. Eochaidh consented to this; he assembled his friends from all sides, and thus brought together a large army, and made his foster son Laoighseach Ceannmhor leader of the host; and he himself and Cu Corb, King of Leinster, with their hosts, marched against the Munstermen, having Laoighseach Ceannmhor as commander-in-chief of the forces; and they drove the Munstermen from Mullach Maistean to the Bearbha; and they followed up this rout until they defeated them a second time at Coirtheine in Magh Riada, which is called Laoighis Riada; and they continued the rout thence until they overthrew them a third time at Slighe Dhala - that is Bealach Mor Osruighe; and thus they delivered the province of Leinster from the bondage of the Munstermen; and in consideration of this Eochaidh obtained the seven Fotharta of Leinster for himself and his descendants; and similarly, his foster son got the seven Laoighises for himself and his descendants, as a handsel in consideration of his leadership in expelling the Munstermen from the places we have mentioned. Again the King of Laoighis was bound to make muster at general assemblies along with the King of Fotharta, because Eochaidh Fionn, son of Feidhlimidh Reachtmhar, ancestor of the King of the Fotharta, as foster father to Laoighseach Ceannmhor from whom sprung the King of Laoighis. And this custom was ever observed until the Norman invasion." (Keating, Vol. 11 pg. 307)

According to the ancient tract beginning " Mace Moga-Corbt celas Clu" in the Book of Leinster (folio 44) it was Cu Corb's queen, Meadhbh, that divided the Fotharta and Loigsi into seven divisions respectively as she did not desire those tribes to be united, so that their power against the King of Leinster might be weaker. Her strength and influence over the men of Erin was very great; "for it was she that would not permit any King in Tara without his having herself as his wife". Cu Corb was killed in battle by Feidhlimidh Reachtmhar, somewhere in Leinster. Meadhbh was present at his interment and pronounced an elegy over him in a poem of eight quatrains. Then she eloped with the man who slew him." (O'Curry MS Materials)

One thousand years afterwards, when the Normans came to Ireland, Dermot, King of Leinster broke this solemn and sacred agreement which had been sealed by the shedding of so much blood, and delivered up the overlordship of the fair valley of O'Nolan to the foreign invader. "Two cantreds of land lying between the towns of Wexford and Waterford were granted by Dermot to Harvey de Montmaurice (sic)". This land is comprised in the present baronies of Forth and Bargie (sic) in the County of Wexford, and was the first place in Ireland made over to the English.

A few years later, the Barony of Forth O'Nolan was granted to Raymond-le-Gros, thus completely transferring the ancestral territory of the sept to the English settlers.

In the Historic Tale of the Battle of Moylena, we find " He (Conn of the Hundred Battles) was aided by his fifty foster brothers", "strong unflinching Champions, who were never routed or subdued in battle, among whom were Eochaidh Fionn and Feachaidh Suighdhe, the sons of Feidhlimidh Reachtmhar, and brothers of Conn, attended by their high-spirited followers"

The following description of the arming of Conn for the battle is most interesting as giving in detail the costume and armour worn by the Princes of Ireland at that time, when about to engage in battle: " He arose and put upon his fair skin and beautiful body his battle and combat suit, namely, his dark grey flowing long wide sking (sic) shirt, with its three beautiful, varied, well-coloured wheels (brooches) of gold in it. He put on his well-fitting coat of distinction made of the wonderful cloth of the flock abounding in his beautiful mansioned Land of Promise, bound with girdles and buttons, and with embroidered borders of red gold, so that it fitted to every part which could be touched by the sharp point of a hard needle, from the top of his head to the calves of his legs. Outside this he put on his heavy, firm, strong-ringed coat of mail, with its firm head piece of the same kind. He put on his light, strong leg armour, made of the fine spun thread of Finndruinne (a kind of fine bronze used chiefly in ornamental works by the artists of ancient Erin) - giving a dignity to his noble carriage, and being a protection against cutting, and a support in its resistance. He put his two lacerating gloves upon his hands, having a colour of snow freely to be seen upon them, and possessing attributes of victory in the field of battle, and no erring cast should be thrown from them by day or by night; he put on his neck his easy, thick, noble, light collar, and upon his head his diadem of a chief-king, in which were fifty carbuncle gems of the beautiful rare stones of eastern India, artistically set with beautiful bright silver, and with well coloured gold and with other precious stones. He placed his blue, sharp-edged, rich-hilted sword at his convenience, and his strong, triumphant, wonderful, firm, embossed shield, of beautiful device, upon the convex slope of his back. He grasped his two thick-headed, wide-socketed battle spears with their rings of gold upon their necks".

During the ensuing battle - "then came the seven shooting sons of Doghar with their warriors...... and they made a fierce road, and a stout encircling and a general bone-cut carnage of champions; and there came to meet them the seven manly sons of Feidhlimidh Reachtmhar   viz:- Feachaidh Araidhe, Bries the blind, Curraoine, Eochaidh Fionn Fuath - Airt, and Feachaidh Suighdhe etc. It was not easy to withstand their onslaught, in the angry moments of the

Champions who, accompanied by a section of their paternal forces, unmercifully pressed their weapons into those nobles; and the seven shooting sons of Doghar were wounded, and reddened and killed and destroyed in those conflicts, and the seven sons of Feidhlimidh carried their heads in triumph to where Conn and Conall of Cruachain were".

Eochaidh Finn is recorded as having murdered his two nephews Conla and Crionan, sons of Conn of the hundred battles, and also as having assisted Tiobrade Tireach, son of Mal MacRochruidhe, King of Ulster, to gain access to Conn, who was staying at his palace of Tuthamors, near Tara, without his retinue. Tiobrade was accompanied by "fifty seven stout youths dressed in female attire" and having come into the Monarch's presence they at once assaulted him and killed him in the hundredth year of his reign.

"For Conn had two brothers, namely, Eochaidh Fionn and Feachaidh Suighdhe, and by them were slain Art's two brothers: and in testimony of this are these two quatrains from the seanchus:

> The two brothers of Conn without faults,
> Were Eochaidh Fionn and Feachaidh Suighdhe;
> They slew Conla and Crionna,
> Conn's two sons, two fair youths:
>
> Art hated Eochaidh Fionn
> After the two sons had been slain;
> And he took the name of Art Aoinfhear
> After his two brothers were slain. [14]

The statement that Conn was 100 years old when he was killed will not bear examination. According to the Four Masters, Tuathal Teachtmhar was a posthumous son of Feacha Finnfoladidh who was slain A.D.56. Conn was killed A.D. 157, so that to be 100 years old at that date he should have been born when his grandfather was not more than a year old!

From the determined efforts of Eochaidh Fionn to remove all obstacles that stood in his path to the crown it would seem that those historians who state that he was the elder brother of Conn have some justification for their opinion. His efforts in this direction proved fruitless as on the death of Conn the monarchy eventually devolved on his son Art, by whom Eochaidh and his brother Feacha Suidhe were forthwith banished from Tara. O'Flaherty[15] writes, " Art the melancholy the son of Conn, succeeds his brother-in-law, King Conary. King Art banished from the confines of Tara, his uncle, Eochaidh

---

[14] Keating Vol.11 pg.269
[15] Ogygia Part 111 Vol. LXIX

Fionn Fothart and his sons, because they assassinated their brothers Conla and Crinn, and betrayed his father, Conn, to the Ultonians. Uchdella, wife of Eochaidh, was the grand-daughter of Cather Mor, King of Ireland, by his son Currie. He marches into Leinster, and the King of that province divided the two districts called Fotharts from his surname, the one from the confines of Munster to the mouth of the Slane, the other from the opposite bank, the Slane running in the centre of both, to the harbour of Wexford. There his posterity enjoyed the sovereignty many ages to the death of O'Nuallain, the last proprietor who died not long ago. They also possessed other tracts called Fotharts; as Fothart Airbreach, which is also called Bri-eli, held by the posterity of Corc, Lugad and Crumath, the grandsons of Eochaidh (by his son Aengus). The posterity of Fergus Tarbry were in possession of Fothart to the east of the Liffey. The offspring of Sedny, the son of Artcorb, were masters of Fothart Imchlair, near Armagh, and the posterity of Adnad, the son of Artcorb inhabited Fothart Fea and Fothart Moyitha. There were besides Fothart File, Fothart Thurles and Fothart Bile. Bressal, the grandson of Conla, the son of Art Corb, by his son Deny, after whom Hy-breasail in Hyfalgia is denominated, was the great grandfather of St. Brigid, the patroness of Ireland.

81. Aengus Meann
82. Cormac
83. Carbru Niadh
84. Artcorb
85. Fergus Tarbry, Sedney, File, Adnad and Conla (236 A.D.)
86. Donogh
87. Bressal
88. Dremry
89. Dubthach
90. St. Brigid

It will be seen from the pedigree of St. Brigid that she is closely allied to the family of O'Nolan, and in like manner the celebrated St. Fintain of Clonenagh is a branch of the same stem. He was the son of Gaibrene, who was son of Breasal, great grandfather of St. Brigid.

Another very historic individual closely allied to the stem of O'Nolan is Diarmaid O'Duibhne, who pedigree is given by O'Flaherty as follows.[16]

79. Feidhlimidh Reachtmhar.
80. Feacha Suighdhe.
81. Feacha Raide.
82. Fothad.

---

[16] Ogygia Chapter LXIX

83. Dubney.

84. Donel.

85. Diermot O'Duibhne.

Diarmuid is the hero of the celebrated romantic tale "The pursuit of Diarmuid and Grainne" which O'Curry summarises as follows.[17]

"Of these, the only tale founded on fact, or, at least on ancient authority (though romantically told) is one in which Finn (MacCumhaill) himself was deeply involved. It is the pursuit of Diarmuid and Grainne. The facts on which it is founded are shortly these.

Finn, in his old age, solicited the monarch, Cormac Mac Art, for the hand of his celebrated daughter Grainne, in marriage. Cormac agreed to the hero's proposal, and invited Finn to go to Tara, to obtain from the princess herself, her consent (which was necessary in such matters in those days in Erin) to their union. Finn, on this invitation, proceeded to Tara, attended by a chosen body of his warriors, and among these were his son Oisin, his grandson, Oscar and Diarmuid O'Duibhne, one of his chief officers, a man of fine person and most fascinating manners. A magnificent feast was of course provided, at which the monarch presided, surrounded by all of the great men of his Court, among whom the Fianna were accorded a distinguished place.

It appears to have been a custom at great feasts in ancient Erin, for the mistress of the mansion, or some other distinguished lady, to fill her own rich, and favourite drinking cup or glass from a select vessel of choicest liquor, and to send it round by her favourite maid in waiting, to a certain number (which I believe to be four) in their immediate vicinity, so that every one of those invited should in turn enjoy the distinction of participating in this gracious favour. They in turn passed the cup on to four more etc. On the present occasion the lady Grainne did the honours in her royal father's court, and sent around her favourite cup, accordingly, until all had drunk from it, Oisin and Diarmuid O'Duibhne excepted. Scarcely had the company uttered their praise of the liquor, and their profound acknowledgements to the princess, when they all, almost simultaneously fell into a heavy sleep.

The liquor, was of course, drugged for this purpose, and no sooner had Grainne perceived the full success of her scheme, than she went and sat by the side of Oisin and Diarmuid, and addressing the former, complained to him of the folly of his father, Finn, in expecting that a maiden of her youth, beauty and celebrity, could ever consent to become the wife of so old and war-worn a man; that if Oisin, himself, were to seek her hand she would gladly accept him; but since that could not now be, that she had no chance of escaping the evil which her father's temerity had brought upon her, but by flight; and as Oisin could not dishonour his father by being her partner in such a proceeding, she

_____

[17] MS. Materials pg. 313

conjured Diarmuid my his manliness and by his vows of Chivalry, to take her away, to make her his wife and thus to save her from a fate to which he preferred even death itself.

After much persuasion (for the consequences of so grievous an offence to his leader must necessarily be serious) Diarmuid consented to the elopement; the parties took a hasty leave of Oisin; and as the royal palace was not very strictly guarded on such an occasion, Grainne found little difficulty in escaping the vigilance of the attendants and gaining the open country with her companion.

When the monarch and Finn awoke from their trance, their rage was boundless; both of them vowed vengeance against the unhappy delinquents, and Finn immediately set out from Tara in pursuit of them. He sent parties of his swiftest and best men to all parts of the country; but Diarmuid was such a favourite with his brethren in arms, and the peculiar circumstances of the elopement invested it with so much sympathy on the part of these young heroes, that they never could discover the retreat of the offenders, excepting when Finn, himself, happened to be of the party that immediately pursued them, and then they were sure to make their escape by some wonderful stratagem or feat of agility on the part of Diarmuid."

This then was the celebrated Pursuit of Diarmuid and Grainne. It extended all over Erin; and in the description of the progress of it, a great amount of curious information on topography, the natural productions of various localities, social manners and more ancient tales and superstitions is introduced.[18]

The Book of Rights, ascribed to Saint Benignus, personal friend and earnest disciple of Saint Patrick, contains records of the tribute due to the King of Ireland and to the kings of the various provinces into which that Kingdom was sub-divided. Two copies of this are preserved, one in the Book of Leacan, compiled in the year 1418 A.D. by Giolla Ias Mor Mac Firbish of Leacan, the other, in the Book of Ballymote which was compiled by various persons, but chiefly by Solamh O'Droma from older MSS. about the year 1390 A.D. In addition to the tributes due to each King, it also enumerates the rights and stipends due from the king to his subordinate princes.

The following extracts are taken from the copy of this work issued in 1847 by the Celtic Society, Dublin, with notes by John O'Donovan Esq., M.R.I.A., which add enormously to its value as a work of reference.

"Eight swords, eight horns for drinking
From the King of defensive Carman,
Eight steeds of which not one has a bad mane,
To the King of Fothart Osnadhaigh"

[18] The Tale is published by the Osseanic Society

44

Fothart Osnadhaigh is now the barony of Fotharta, Anglice "Forth" in the county Carlow. The people called Fotharta were, according to the Irish genealogists, the descendants of Eochaidh Finn Fuathart (the brother of the monarch Conn of the Hundred Battles), who, being banished from Midhe (Meath) by his nephew, Art, monarch of Ireland, settled in Laighin (Leinster), where his descendants acquired considerable territories, of which the barony of "Forth" in the county of Carlow and the better know barony of the same name in the county of Wexford, still preserve the name. The former is called Fotharta Osnadhaigh in the text, from Cill Osnadha, now currently Kellistown, one of its principal churches, but more frequently "Fotharta Fea", from the plain of Magh Fea, in which this church is situated.[19]

After the establishment of surnames the chief family of Fotharta Fea, or Fotharta Osnadhaigh, took the surname of O'Nuallain, Anglice, formerly, O'Nolan, now Nowlan, and from him this barony has been not unusually called "Forth O'Nolan". [20]

O'Flaherty states in his Ogygia, part iii c.54, that the posterity of (sic) "Two hundred cows and seven hundred wethers and seven hundred beeves and two hundred cloaks and two hundred oxen from the seven Fotharta." (Book of Rights, pages 211, 219)

> "From all the Fotharta
> Are due two hundred goodly cows
> And two hundred cloaks of tribute,
> Two hundred rough oxen of the yoke."

Besides the baronies of Forth, one in Carlow and the other in Wexford, there were two other territories of the name in Leinster, as Fothart Airbreach, around the hill of Cruachan Bri Eile (Croghan), in the north-east of the King's County; and Fothart Oirthir Life, in the now county of Wicklow; but these

---

[19] Book of Baile an Mhuta, fol.77.b. and Keating's History of Ireland, reign of Oilioll Molt, where it is stated that Cill Osnadha is situate in the plain of Magh Fea, four miles to the east of Leith-ghlinn (Leighlin), in the county of Carlow.

[20] Inquisitions, Lagenia, 14, 16 Car.1.Grace's Annals of Ireland ed. by Rev. Richard Butler, pg. 99 et passim.

sank under other tribes at the early period, and the probability is, that the Fotharta of Carlow and Wexford are the people referred to in the text.

Chapter 5

The Descent of O'Nuallain

Beyond the names preserved in the pedigree of O'Nuallain not much information is available as to the persons who constitute his line of descent from Eochaidh Fionn Fuathairt. There are, however, a few facts which are interspersed in the following incidents taken from O'Donovan's "Annals of Ireland" and some other sources. The incidents quoted refer mainly to battles in Leinster and battles of the Leinstermen against the King and princes of other territories. As senior sept of the Heremonian line, Chief Marshals of Leinster, and Nominator of the Kings of Leinster at their inauguration, it is a reasonable assumption that the Fotharta who had thus early earned a reputation as sturdy fighters and mighty men in battle, were engaged in most, if not all, of the battles chronicled. In many we find records of the "Fotharta" indicating the presence of the warriors of that line in the conflict, and in those which occurred in Carlow, Queen's County and Kilkenny, seeing that their territories stretched over considerable sections of these counties it is morally certain their arms were not idle while those districts were being assailed. The following line of descent is preserved in the Book of Leinster.

81. Aonghus, son of Eochaidh Fionn Fuathairt.
Keating (pg.313. Vol II) writes: " As to Conn's other brother, namely, Feachaidh Suighdhe, he got land near Tara, namely, the Deisi Teamhrach, and he did not become King of Ireland. Now he had three sons, namely, Rossa, Aonghus Gaoibuaibhtheach and Eoghan, the third son. But Aonghus Gaoibuaibhtheach surpassed his contemporaries in valour. And Corman at that time was at enmity with a powerful personage, and no one protected him from Cormac except Aonghus Gaoibuaibhtheach; and the King gave Aonghus to him as a security. Aonghus took this nobleman under his protection. But after this, Ceallach, son of Cormac took this nobleman prisoner in violation of the security of Aonghus,and took out his eyes without the king's permission. When Aonghus Gaoibuaibhtheach heard this he proceeded to Tara, accompanied by a numerous host, and slew Ceallach by a cast of his spear, he stood behind King Cormac in the court, and wounded the King himself in the eye, leaving him with only one eye. Cormac assembled a large host and banished Aonghus and his kinsmen.
These descendants of Eochaidh Suighdhe involved Cormac in much fighting . However, Cormac drove them into Leinster, and they remained there

a year; and thence they went to Osruighe, and thence they came to Oilioll Olom, whose wife Sadhbh, daughter of Conn was their kinswoman. Ollill Olom gave them the Deise in Munster, for their native territory was the Deise Teamhrach before they were banished by Cormac.

These three sons or Feachaidh Suighdhe divided that territory between them into three parts; and they are called the descendants of Oilill Earann and the Earna. However, they are not the Earna, but the descendants of Conaire, son of Mogh Lamha and it is these that were styled the Earna. It is Corc Duibhne son of Cairbre Nusc who was chief over the descendants of Feachaidh Suighdhe who came to Munster; and it was these descendants that were called the Deise; and Aonghus, son of Eochaidh Fionn, son of Feidhlimidh Reachtmhar was their leader when coming to Munster, and with him were the three sons of Feachaidh Suighdhe, namely, Rossa, Eoghan, and Aonghus.

82. CORMAC, son of Aonghus,
A.D.195. After Art, the son of Conn of the Hundred Battles had been thirty years in the sovereignty of Ireland he fell in the battle of Magh Mueruimhe by Maccon and his foreigners Lioghairne of the Long Cheeks (leacanfada) son of Aonghus Balbh, son of Eochaid Fionn Fuathairt was he who laid (violent) hands upon Art in this battle of Magh Mueruimhe after he had joined the forces of Maccon (IV.M.) This Lioghairne was brother of Cormac.

O'Flaherty calls him Lugurn and writes "Lugadh Lagha, the brother of Oilill, but related to Maccon, by his mother, and Ligurn of the Fotharta (80. Achy Fothart. 81. Aengus, the dumb. 82. Ligurn) whom Art had banished. Lughad's companion in his exile, pursuing Art after the battle, stood at a brook in Aidhnia, and attacking him there, tumbled him to the earth, and as he lay almost breathless, cut off his head, and brought it to the conqueror." Incensed at the expulsion of his family, Lioghairne joined the forces of Maccon, against his relative Art, and had the killing of him with his own hand, at Turloch Airt. The name is still preserved, between Moyseola and Kilconnan, near Athenry, and the spot where Art fell is still pointed out by local residents.
83. Cairbre, son of Cormac.
O'Flaherty calls him Carbry Neadh in his pedigree of St. Brigid.[21]
84. Art Corb, son of Cairbre.
85. Mughna, son of Art Corb.

O'Flaherty calls him Adnad. About this time occurred the battle of Gabhra Aichle referred to in the following: (It is probable Simeon son of Cerb was brother to Mughna - Cerb and Corb being interchanged.) " A.D. 284. After Cairbre Liffeachair had been seventeen years in the sovereignty of Ireland, he fell in the battle of Gabhra. Aichle (Gabhra of Aichill, so called from its

---

[21] Keating 317

contiguity to Aichill, now the hill of Skreen, near Tara, in Co. Meath, Gabhra, Anglice Gowra, is now the name of a stream which rises in a bog in the townland of Prantstown, parish of Skreen, receives a tributary from the well of Neamhnach on Tara Hill, joins the River Skene at Dowthstown and unites with the Boyne at Ardsallagh) by the hand of Simeon, son of Cearb, (one) of the Fotharta; (after the death of Finn Mac Cumhail Cairbre disbanded and outlawed the Clanna Baisgne, or Irish militia, of which Finn was the most distinguished chief.

The Clanna Baisgne then repaired to Munster, to their relative, Moghcorb who retained them in the service, contrary to the orders of Cairbre. This led to the bloody battle of Gabhra in which the Clanna Baoisgne, on the side of Moghcorb and the Clanna Morna, a Firbolg tribe of Connaught, almost exterminated each other. In this battle, Oscar, the son of Oisin, met the monarch in single combat, but he fell. Cairbre, retiring from the combat encountered his own relative, one of the Fotharta (who had been expelled from Leinster), and in the resulting fight, Cairbre was slain.

86. Cuibhe, son of Mughna.
87. Iar, son of Cuibhe.
88. Feach, son of Iar.

(Four Masters - Adan A.D. 457) The twenty ninth year of Laeghaire.[22] The battle of Ath-dara (The ford of the oak - in the Irish historical tract called

---

[22] It was around this time that the Ui Cheinnselaig arrived in southern Leinster. Alfred P. Smyth states "The Ui Cheinnselaig first appeared as an expanding and hostile political force in the heart of Leinster in the Carlow area, it is reasonable to assume that they invaded the Province, not earlier than the fifth century, through the pass of Gowran from Ossory. This would explain how St Mullins on the Barrow, and near the Ossory border, had early connections with the Ui Cheinnselaig. It would explain, too, how the Ui Cheinnselaig broke the power of Ui Bairrche by seizing the Slaney valley from Rathvilly (Rath Bilech) to Tullow (Tulach mic Fheilmeda), thereby separating the Ui Bairrche of northern Carlow from those of southern Wexford. The Fothairt, allies of Ui Bairrche, shared the same fate and were separated into two groups - one the Fothairt in Cairn in south-east Wexford, and the other Fothairt of Mag Fea in Carlow. The expansion of Ui Cheinnselaig from Carlow into Wexford took place by one of two possible routes. The first, and least probable, was by Scullogue Gap, a high mountain pass in the Blackstairs south of Mount Leinster which led into the forests of Bantry and Ross. The second, and more probable route, led from Rathvilly in Carlow down the Slaney valley into Wexford between the Blackstairs and the Wicklow mountains. This pass, which ran somewhere between Clonegal and Bunclody, was the gateway from Mag Ailbe in northern Carlow into Wexford. Here was the ancient Fid Dorcha (Dark Forest), later known as the fastness of

Borumha-Laighean, this ford is described as on the River Bearbha in the plain of Magh Ailbhe. There was a carn erected on the brink of the river in which the heads of the slaughtered forces of Leath- Chuinn were interred) between the Leinstermen and Laeghaire, son of Niall. Laeghaire was taken in that battle; and Laeghaire took oaths by the sun and the wind and (all) the elements, to the Leinstermen, that he would never come against them, after setting him at liberty- i.e. that he would forego the Boromean tribute during his life.

Two and a half years later, unmindful of his oaths, Laeghaire again marched into Leinster and seized a prey of cows at Siadh Neachlain, where the Boyne has its source. Continuing his march he came to Greallach - Daphill, near the Liffey and there met his death. The Annals of Clonmacnoise declare that, "he was stroken dead, by the Wynde and the Sun, for foreswearing himself to the Lynstermen". He was buried at Tara, with his weapons upon him and his face turned towards the Lagenians, as if in the attitude of fighting them.

(Four Masters A.D. 489) "Aenghus, son of Nadfraech, King of Munster, fell in the battle of Cell- Osnadha, (fought against him) by Muircheartach Mac Earca, by Illan, son of Dunlaing, by Aillil, son of Dunlaing and by Eochaidh Guineach."

The place called Cell- Osnadha is described by Keating as situated in the plain of Magh Fea four miles east of Leighlin, in the county of Carlow. This place is now called Kellistown, and is situated in the barony of Forth, in the county Carlow, and there exists among the old natives of the place a most curious and remarkably vivid tradition of this battle which explains the Irish name of the place as denoting the "Church of the groans" and which it received according to this tradition, from the lamentations of the Munster-women, after the loss of their husbands and brothers in the battle. This was once a place of considerable importance and contained up to about the year

---

Leverocke, (Leath Bhearraice) which guarded the gateway to southern Ui Cheinnselaig. It was through this pass that the high King Rory O'Conor forced his way with a Connaught army when he twice defeated Dermot MacMurrough, once in 1166 and again in 1167. On this second campaign the high king approached the pass from Kellistown (Cell Osnaid) in Carlow. A seventeenth-century map of the barony of Scarawalsh preserved in the Dublin Public Records Office shows this pass about the village of Bunclody to coincide with a break in the great forest that followed the line of the Blackstairs and Wicklow mountains. This cordon of forest and mountain completely sealed off Wexford from the rest of Leinster. So vast was the woodland here that as late as 1654 there was a rudimentary forestry department for Wicklow and Wexford. It was of these woods in Shillelagh that Chichester reported in 1608 as being sufficient to supply the King's navy for twenty years. - A.K

1800, considerable remains of an ancient Church, and round tower, which are now all effaced.

Aonghus, who fell in this battle, was baptised by St. Patrick at Cashel, who, by a singular accident, put his faith to the trial by piercing his foot with the end of his Crosier, which the King, thinking it part of the ceremony bore without flinching.

89. Ninneadh, son of Feach.

90. Baithin, son of Ninneadh.

91. Eochaidh, son of Baithin.

A.D. 593. Cumuscach, son of Aedh, son of Ainmire, was slain by Bran Dubh son of Eochaidh at Dun - Bucat (now Dunboyke, in the parish of Hollywood, barony of Lower Talbotstown in county Wicklow).

"According to the ancient historical tract called the Borumha Laighean, this Cumascach set out on his royal, free quarter, juvenile visitation of Ireland, on which he resolved to have the wife of every king and chieftain in Ireland for a night! He first set out for Leinster, with four battalions and crossed the river Righ (the Rye Water) which was the boundary between that province and Meath. He advanced to Bealach-Chonglais, now Baltinglass, where Bran Dubh, King of Leinster, resided (at Rathbran, near Baltinglass). He sent for the wife of Bran Dubh, who came to him, and requested that he would not detain her until she had exhibited her hospitality, in distributing food among his attendants. This request was granted; but the Queen of Leinster, instead of remaining to wait on his hosts, fled, like an honest woman, from her palace and betook herself to the fastness of the lonely forest of Dun Buichet.

After this the King of Leinster, attired in the garb of a menial, set fire to the house in which the young libertine Cumascach (who was dressing himself in the clothes of one of his satirical poets) climbed the ridge pole of the house, made his way out, escaped the flames and fled to Monaidh- Cumascaigh at the end of the Green of Cill-Ramnaireach (now Kilranelagh) where Lochine Lonn, Erenagh of that Church, and ancestor of the family of O'Lonain, discovered who he was, cut off his head and carried it to Rath Bran Dubh, where he presented it to the King of Leinster, who for this signal service, granted perpetual freedom (or exemption from Custom or tribute) to the Church of Cill Ramnairech."[23]

Four Masters A.D. 594. After Aedh, son of Ainmire, son of Sedna, had been twenty seven years in the sovereignty of Ireland, he was slain by Bran Dubh, son of Eochaidh, in the battle of Dun-Bolg, in Leinster, after Aedh had gone to exact the Borumha and to avenge his son Cumascach upon them.

"Dinn - Bolg i.e. Fort of the Sacks. This place is described in the historical tract (Borumha Laighean) as situated to the south of Dun Buchat (now

---

[23] note by John O'Donovan

51

Dunboyke, near Hollywood, Co. Wicklow) not far from a church called Cill Belat, now Kilbaylet, near Donard, in the same county. When the monarch Aedh heard that his son Cumascach had been killed at Dun - Buchat, he assembled his forces and marched into Leinster and proceeded to the place where his son had been killed and pitched camp at Baeth Eabha close to Dun Buchat.

When Bran Dubh, King of Leinster, heard of the monarch's arrival he moved northwards to his principal fort of Rath Brain Dubh, (Rathbran) near Bealach Conghlais or Baltinglass, and passed over Mointeach, Muinchin, Daimhne (the Deeps), Etar, Ard Choillidh and Ard mBresta, and crossing the river Slaney proceeded over the lands of Fe to Bealach Dubhthair, now Bealach Conghlais. Here he was met by Bishop Aidan, the monarch's half brother, who informed him the monarch of Ireland had pitched his camp near Dun Buaiche. Bran Dubh sent the bishop to request an armistice from the monarch until he could muster his forces when he would either make peace or give him battle. The monarch refused the request and used insulting language to his half brother who resented it and predicted his doom.

The monarch then marched to Bealach Dun- Bolg, which evidently extended along Hollywood glen, and over the great rocky surface called Lec Comaigh Crann (Flag of the broken bones) and onwards through Bearna an Sciath (Gap of the Shields) at Kilbelat, where he pitched a fortified camp in a strong position.

The Bishop, Aedan, returned to Bran Dubh and informed him that the monarch of Ireland was encamped at Kilbelat, and that he had treated him with indignity. As the King of Leinster had not time to muster his forces, the bishop advised him to have recourse to a stratagem which he planned for him and which ultimately proved successful. Bran Dubh and the bishop then set out to reconnoitre the royal camp, and they arrived, accompanied by 120 young heroes, on the side of Sleabh Neachtain, a mountain which then received its present name of Sliabh Cadaigh, and they perceived what appeared to them to be numerous flocks of birds of various colours, hovering over the camp. These they soon recognised to be the standards and ensigns of the Ui Neill, floating from poles and spears over their tents and pavilions; and the bishop, after encouraging the King of Leinster and his attendants by recounting the mighty deeds achieved by their ancestors, departed for his church.

After this, Bran Dubh saw a great multitude of people on the mountain of Sliabh Neachtain near him; and being reinforced by his household and some of the men of Leinster, who were now flocking to his assistance from every quarter, he surrounded this multitude and took them prisoners. These were the men of Ulidea, with their king, Diarmuid, son of Aedh Roin, who, being the hereditary enemies of the Race of Conn Ceadchathach, were glad to desert to the enemy; and they formed a solemn treaty of friendship with the

Leinstemen; in commemoration of which they erected a carn on the mountain and changed its name from Sliabh Neachtain i.e. Neachtain's Mountain to Sliabh Cadaigh i.e. The Mountain of the Covenant (which name it retains to this day though somewhat disguised under the anglicised form of Sliabh Gadoe). Then Bran Dubh told the Ulideans to separate from the monarch, and they retired to the insulated piece of land ever since called Inis - Uladh, i.e. the Island of the Ulideans. After this the King of Leinster asked who would go to spy on the camp of the monarch of Ireland for a rich reward and Ron Kerr, son of the chief of Imail undertook the difficult task in the garb of a leper. He rubbed his body and face all over with rye dough, moistened with the blood of a calf; fixed his knee in the socket of a wooden leg, which he borrowed from a cripple, and put on an ample cloak, under which he concealed his sword; and to complete the deception, he carried with him a begging wallet. In this plight he repaired to the royal camp and presented himself at the door of the monarch's pavilion. He was asked for tidings and he replied:

" I came from Kilbelat; this morning I went to the camp of the Leinstermen, and, in my absence some persons, certainly not Leinstermen, came and destroyed my cottage, and my church, and broke my quern and my spade."

The King made answer that should he himself survive that expedition, he would give him twenty milch cows as eric, or reparation for this injury, and inviting the leper into his pavilion asked him what the Leinstermen were doing. The leper, disguising his manly voice, and martial expression of eye and features as much as he could, said they were preparing victuals for the monarch and his army. The monarch, however, suspecting from the expression of the eye of Ron Kerr, that he was not a real leper, but a warrior in disguise, sent to spy the camp, despatched Dubhduin, Chief of the Orighialla with the forces of his territory, to Bun Aife (Buniff) and Cruidhabhall to prevent the Leinstermen from surprising his camp.

Now Bran Dubh had all things arranged for the stratagem which Bishop Aedan had planned. He had 3,600 oxen carrying hampers in which armed soldiers were concealed, though they seemed to be filled with provisions; he had also 150 untamed horses, for a purpose which will presently appear, and a huge candle; the light of which was concealed under the regal cauldron. With these he set out, in the depth of the night, for the monarch's camp. When the Orighialla, who were posted at Bun Aife, heard the din and tumult of this host - the snorting of the horses, and the lowing of the loaded oxen - they started to arms, and asked who were the party advancing. The others made answer that they were the calones of Leinster, who were conveying victuals for the entertainment of the people of the King of Ireland. The Orighialla, on examining the tops of the hampers, felt the dressed provisions, and their king, Dubhduin or Beg Mac Cuanach, said "they are telling the truth, let them pass".

And the Leinstermen advanced to the centre of the monarch's camp, and there, on a hill, called ever since Candle Hill, they removed the King's Cauldron off the Great Candle, and its light was seen far and wide. They were followed by the Orighialla, who wished to partake of the King of Leinster's hospitality.

"What a great light is this we see", said the monarch to the leper.

"The Leinstermen have arrived with their provisions", replied the leper, " and this is their light".

The stratagem was now effected. Small bags, filled with stones, were fastened to the tails of the wild horses, which were let loose among the tents of the men of Ireland; the oxen were disencumbered of their burdens, and the Leinster soldiers issued from the hampers, grasped their swords, raised their shields, and prepared for fighting. The leper also cast off his wooden leg and handled his sword. The Kinel-Connell and Kinel-Owen, perceiving that the camp was surprised, sprang up, and forming a rampart of spears and shields around the Monarch of Ireland, conveyed him on his steed to Bearna-na-Sciath. The leper, Ron Kerr, pursued the monarch with a select party of Leinstermen, and after much desperate fighting unhorsed him, and cut off his head on a flat rock, called Lec-Comaigh-cnamh. He emptied his wallet of the crumbs which he had got at the royal pavilion and put into it the head of the monarch. He then passed unobserved in the darkness of the night, from the confused fight, which ensued, into the wild recesses of the mountains, where he remained till morning. The Leinstermen routed the Ui-Neill and Orighialla with great courage, and slew among others, Beg, the son of Cuanach, chief of the Orighialla.

On the following day, Ron Kerr, son of Dubhanach, chief of Imaile, presented Bran Dubh with the head of the Monarch, Aedh, son Ainmire; and he obtained from the King the privilege of dining at the royal table, and his paternal inheritance free of tribute to him and his representatives for ever.

A.D. 601 the battle of Slaibhre (not identified) was gained by the Ui-Neill over Bran Dubh, son of Eochaidh, King of Leinster; and Bran Dubh i.e. son of Eochaidh was killed by the Ardchinneach[24] of Senboithe-Sine (now Templeshanbo at the foot of Mount Leinster) and his own tribe as it is said.

> Saran Soebhdhearc[25], a guide indeed, Ardchinneach
> Of Seanboith Sine
> Was he, it is no falsehood without bright judgement,

---

[24] Ardchinneach - the hereditary warden of the church, usually anglicised Erenagh or Herenagh.

[25] Saran Soebhdheard i.e. Saran of the crooked, foul or evil eye.

Who killed Bran Dubh, son of Eochaidh.

A certain Leinsterman said the following:-

> Were it in the time of the son of Eochaidh that
> The northern host had come
> From the battle which they gained,
> They would have been long panic driven
> If in a pillared house, were the son of Eochaidh
> Son of Muireadach
> I would not bring my full sack[26] to a church
> For the sake of Aedh Allan.

92. Ronan, son of Eochaidh.[27]
93. Fionnan son of Ronan.

A.D. 635 The first historical Ui Dunlainge king of Leinster was Faelan Mac Cholmain who ruled c.635. There are many uncertainties regarding the chronology of his reign, and on his death the Leinster kingship oscillated between the Ui Cheinnselaig and the Ui Mail until it was finally secured for Faelan's descendants on the death of the last Ui Mail king in 715 Already, however, in Faelan's reign over Leinster, the Ui Dunlainge were tightening their grip on the northern half of the province. Faelan's brother Aedh Dub, who died in 639, had become Bishop of Kildare, one of the wealthiest monasteries in Ireland, but situated within Ui Failge and under the immediate control of the Fothairt, to whose tribe, Bridget, the foundress had belonged. Faelan's nephew, Oengus, and a certain Brandubh, a distant cousin of the same generation as Oengus, were also abbots of Kildare.

Clearly, by the second quarter of the seventh century, the Ui Faelain were displacing both Ui Failge and the Fothairt at Kildare, and the rich estates round about it. The violent nature of this Dunlainge expansion is hinted at in a genealogical note attached to the name of Maelumai, a brother of Faelan, who ruled c. A.D. 635. This note states that Maelumai slew Deichtre Mac Findig of Ui Meic Cruaich of the Ui Ercain in his fortress or *dun* at Cell Rois and seized his wealth. The details of Deichtre's tribal origin hold the key to the meaning

---

[26] Full sack - this alludes to the tribute unwillingly paid by the Leinstermen to the monarch Aedh Allan; for the author regrets that Bran Dubh was not alive to resist the incursion of that northern potentate.

[27] During this time the church of Ferns was founded by Maedoc, a Welsh saint who had been trained by St. David in Wales and who died in 625 A.D. - Alfred P. Smyth in *Celtic Leinster* - A.K.

of this obscure record. The Ui Ercain were a branch of the Fothairt of Ui Failge and this branch was settled around Bile maicc Cruaich in Ui Ercain, the old name of Forrach Patraic, a low hill at Narraghmore in the Liffey Plain. Bile maicc Cruaich was an ancient inauguration site, as the name *bile* implies, and the fact that the Ui Dunlainge prince who seized this from the Fothairt was a brother of Faelan, the first Ui Dunlainge king of Leinster, is surely significant.

Further evidence of the violent suppression of older population-groups within the rich Central Region of Leinster by the Ui Dunlainge is provided in the case of Cellach Mac Cennfaelad. This Ui Dunlainge prince (*fl.* c.A.D. 720) was three generations later than Faelan, and descended from Faelan's brother, Ronan. The genealogists noted that he was defeated on an unidentified battleground at Ath Slabai. But the alliance of his enemies was a Munster and Ui Cheinnselaig coalition, which would suggest that he met an invading army somewhere in north Carlow. The genealogists also tell us that he destroyed the Ui Gabla Roirend and that he was cursed by a holy man called Mo-Chuille Dresna.

The Ui Gabla Roirend were a branch of the Dal Chormaic who took their name from Roiriu, now Mullaghreelion, five miles south-east of Athy in south Kildare. Dresan, the home of Mo-Chuille, who was offended by Cellach's suppression of older tribes, seems to have been in Mag Fea, not far to the south of Roiriu, and a plain in the Slaney valley near Tullow in Carlow. After the suppression of the Dal Chormaic the region was considered part of Ui Muiredaig (a branch of Ui Dunlainge) by later Irish writers.

The central stronghold of Ui Dunlainge from the seventh century until the Norman Invasion was at Naas, and the nearby mausoleum of the dynasty was at Cell Nais (Kill. Co. Kildare). In spite of genealogical statements alleging that two aunts of Faelan—Sodelb and Cumaine, the daughters of Coirpre Mor of Ui Dunlainge died as holy virgins in Cell Nais, it is believed that these associations of Ui Dunlainge saints with northern Kildare may be later inventions designed to give Ui Dunlainge ancestors a respectable place in the annals of early Leinster Christianity. There are other traditions claiming that two other holy women of the Ui Dunlainge- Eithne and Dar-carthaind, the daughters of Cormac the great-grandfather of Faelan - had lived as nuns at Tullow, Co. Carlow (Tulach Meic Fheilmeda). If these ladies ever existed, we might date their *floruit* to, c.A.D. 560 and at that time we should expect to find the Ui Dunlainge in the Carlow region if as the genealogists claimed, they originally derived along with the Ui Cheinnselaig from a common ancestor, Bressal Belach. It is significant that early genealogical traditions associated Ui Dunlainge ladies of the sixth century with Tullow - a place which was otherwise regarded as a palace of the Ui Cheinnselaig and of the Ui Felmeda Tuaid in particular. It may be, therefore, that we should view the north Carlow or

Gabair region as a dispersal area from which expanding political groups emerged. It was in this region, yet again, that the Osraige invaded Leinster in the eleventh and twelfth centuries in an effort to take over the entire Province, and we recall, too, that Leinster proto-history began at Dinn Righ on the banks of the Barrow near Leighlin when in the distant past Labraidh Loingsech stormed that fortress with his warriors from Gaul and Britain.[28]

A.D. 642 etc. The battle of Gabhra[29] was fought between the Leinstermen themselves.

A.D. 658 Faelan, son of Osraighe was slain by the Leinstermen.

A.D. 663 Cearnach Sotal, (Cearnach the arrogant), son of Aedh Slaine died of a mortality which arose in Ireland, on the Calends of the August of this year, in Magh Itha in Fotharta.[30]

A.D. 690 A battle was fought between the Osraighe (people of Ossary) and the Leinstermen, wherein Faelchar Ua Maelodhra was slain.[31] It rained a shower of blood in Leinster this year. Butter was there also turned into lumps of gore and blood, so that it was manifest to all in general. The wolf was heard speaking with a human voice which was horrific to all.

A.D. 705 A hosting made by Congal of Ceann Maghair, son of Fergus of Fanaid, against the Leinstermen, and he obtained his demand from them. On returning from his expedition Congal composed these lines:-

> Bid me farewell, O Liffe!
> Long enough have I been in your lap;
> Beautiful the fleece that is on thee;
> thou wert safe except thy roof, O fort of Nas!
> The plain of Liffe was so still now
> today it is a scorched plain
> I will come to rescorch it, that it may know a change.

---

[28] Alfred P. Smyth in *Celtic Leinster*

[29] Gabhra - Liffe, not Gabhra near the Boyne.

[30] Magh Itha was a plain in the barony of Forth in the south east of Co. Wexford.

[31] This was referred to in a tract known as the Testament of Cathair Mar in which the Ui Bairrche are praised for defending North Leinster from the tribes of Osraighe and for raiding around Gabran (Gowran) The Ui Bairrche adopted the name Mac Gormain or O'Gorman and were dispossessed by de Chalhull one of Strongbow's knights in the early days of the Norman invasion.

This would seem that he renewed the Borumean tribute. In the Leabhar Gabhala of the O'Clerys it is stated Congal made this expedition to wreak his vengeance on the Leinstermen for the death of his great grandfather Aedh Mac Ainmireach, whom the Leinstermen had slain in the Battle of Dunbolg; but that he obtained his oighreir or full demand from them without any opposition.

A.D. 710 A battle was fought by the south Leinstermen, and Bran Ua Maelduin and his son were slain.

A.D. 717 The battle of Finnabhair (Fennor, in the parish of Duneany, barony of Offaly, Co. Kildare) by the Leinstermen, in which Aedh, son of Ceallach was slain. Leinster was five times devastated in one year by the Ui Neill. Leinster was plundered and the Borumha again enjoined, and hostages taken by Fearghal.

A.D. 718 After Fearghal, son of Maelduin , son of Maelfishrigh, had been ten years in sovereignty over Ireland he was slain in the battle of Almhain (hill of Allen, Co. Kildare), by Donnchadh, son of Murchadh, and Aedh, son of Colgan, an heir presumptive to the sovereignty. The number which the race of Conn (of the hundred battles) brought to this battle was seventy one thousand and the number brought by the Leinstermen was nine thousand. A long list of the chieftains who fell on both sides is given but none of the Fotharta are specified. "Seven thousand was the number that fell on both sides between them" [32] The Leinstemen were nearly annihilated at this time, so that the remission of the Borumean tribute, through the intercession of St. Moling was but of little advantage to them.

The author of the Annals wrote a quaint note - "there were nine that flyed in the air as if they were winged fowle and so saved their lives".

---

[32] The Annals of Clonmacnoise

Chapter 6

Ireland during the time of the Vikings

94. Maonach, son of Fionnan
(Some of the descendants adopted the name of Maonagh, now Mooney, when the surnames were enforced about A.D. 1000

95. Fergus, son of Maonach. He is mentioned as Lord of Fotharta (Tighearna Fotharta) and he was killed at the battle of Ath Seanath in A.D. 733.

A.D. 737 The Fotharta of this period appear to have constituted into two lordships - namely Fotharta Fea afterwards known as Fothairt O'Nuallain in Co. Carlow and Fotharta an Chairn, now the barony of Forth in Co. Wexford. There were many other tribes of the Fotharta in earlier times.[33]

A.D. 761. Dondgal son of Laidcnen, a member of the main Ui Cheinnselaig line was killed in a battle at Gowran is described in the Book of Leinster as *'Dondgal a quo Cellach Bairne.i. taiseach Hua nDega'* (Dondgal from whom is descended Cellach Bairne head of the Ui Dega).[34]

A.D. 766 There arose a dissension between Ceallach, son of Donnchadh, King of Leinster and the monarch Donnchadh, son of Domhnall. Donnchadh made a full muster of the Ui Neill and marched into Leinster. The Leinstermen moved before the monarch and his forces until they arrived at Sciath Neachtain (near Castledermot in Co. Kildare). Donnchadh, with his forces remained at Aillinn (now Cnoc Aillinne - a hill on which are the remains of a very large fort, near old Kilcullen, in the Co. Kildare); his forces continued to fire, plunder and devastate the province for the space of a week until the Leinstermen submitted to his will.

A.D. 769 A battle was fought at Ferns between two rival Ui Cheinnselaig rulers. In that year Dubhcalgach, the reigning Ui Cheinnselaig king was slain by his successor, Cennselach of the

---

[33] By the middle of the eight century the Ui Cheinnselaig had expanded from Carlow into Wexford where they took over Ferns as their chief centre and turned its church into a royal monastery.

[34] Alfred P. Smyth in *Celtic Leinster*

southerly Sil Maeluidir (who gave the name Shelmalier to the present barony of that name).[35]

A.D. 790 The burning of Reachrainn (probably Lambay Island, near Dublin, took place. This was the first recorded attack on Ireland by the Danes. They plundered and broke its shrines.

96. Congall, son of Fergus
97. Dungus son of Congall.

A.D. 799 Aedh Oirdnidhe assembled a very great army to proceed into Leinster and devastated Leinster twice in one month. A full muster of the men of Ireland (except the Leinstermen) both laity and clergy was again made by him and he marched until he reached Dun Cuair (Rathcore - barony of Lower Moyferragh, Co. Meath) on the confines of Meath and Leinster. Thither came Connmhac, successor to Patrick, having the clergy of Leath -Chuinn along with him. It was not pleasing to the clergy to go upon any expedition; they complained of their grievance to the king and the king i.e. Aedh, said that he would abide by the award of Fothadh na Canoine; on which occasion Fothadh passed the decision by which he exempted the clergy of Ireland forever from expeditions and hostings, when he said:-

> The Church of the Living God, let her alone, waste her not
> Let her rights be apart as best it ever was.
> Every true monk, who is of a pure conscience,
> For the Church to which it is due, let him
> labour like every servant
> Every soldier from that out
> Who is without rule or obedience[36]
> Is permitted to aid the Aedh, son of Niall
> This is the true rule, neither more nor less,
> Let every one serve his vocation
> Without murmur or complaint.

Aedh Oirdnidhe, afterwards, went to the King of Leinster and obtained his full demand from the Leinstermen; and Finsneachta, King of Leinster gave hostages and pledges.

---

[35] Ibid.
[36] Religious rule or obedience

60

A.D. 804 A battle was fought between two septs of the Ui Cheinnselaigh , in which Ceallach, son of Dongal, was slain.

A.D. 817 Leinster as far as Gleann da locha and the territory of Cualann (now the Bray area) was devastated by Aedh Oirdnidhe.[37]

A.D. 818 An army led by Murchadh, son of Maelduin went to Drom-in-dech (probably Drimnagh in Dublin). He had with him the Ui Neill of the north. Conchubhair, King of Ireland, with the Ui Neill of the south, and the Leinstermen, came against him. And when they came to one place, it happened, through the miracles of God, that they separated from each other or that time without slaughter or one of them spilling a drop of the other's blood.

A.D. 825 This year there occurred the destruction of the fair of Colman, by Muiredhach, opposed by the South Leinstermen, where many were slain. Also this year the destruction of the Dun-Laighean at Druim, by the Pagans[38], where Conaing, son of Cuchongelt, Lord of the Fotharta was slain, with many others.[39]

A.D. 826 A battle was gained over the foreigners by Cairbre, son of Cathal, Lord of Ui Cheinnselaigh.

A.D. 829 Feidhlimidh, son of Crimthann, with the forces of Munster and Leinster, came to Finnabhair-Breagh (Fennor near Slane) to plunder the men of Breagh; and the Liffe was plundered by Conchubhair, son of Donnchadh, King of Ireland.

---

[37] "The monastic life at Ferns had become so degenerate by this time that in 817 the monastic communities of Ferns and Taghmon fought a pitched battle in which 400 were slain. Ferns grew even more powerful in the later Celtic period as its kings graduated to the throne of all Leinster." - Alfred P. Smyth in *Celtic Leinster* - A.K.

[38] The Vikings

[39] At this time the chief dynasties which controlled all of the Southern and Central Regions of Leinster were the Ui Cheinnselaigh and the related tribes of Ui Dega and Ui Drona. The sept name Ui Drona is preserved in the baronies of Idrone East and West in Carlow. The survival of this tribal name in a modern barony is misleading. Much of Idrone country once belonged to Ui Bairrche as far south as Lorum in Co. Carlow and across the Kilkenny border to Kilmacahill near Gowran. We know from the annals that from the tenth century at least, the territory was ruled by a branch of the Ui Cheinnselaig who later took the name Ua Riain (O'Ryan). - Alfred P. Smyth in *Celtic Leinster*. - A.K.

A.D. 831 Diarmuid, son of Ruadhrach, Lord of Airthear Life[40], died. Fotharta Airthir Life was held by the posterity of Fergus Tarbry, fifth in descent from Eochaidh Finn Fuathairt.[41]

A.D. 834 A hosting was made by Niall Coille, King of Ireland, into Leinster; and he appointed a king over them, namely Bran, son of Faelan, and obtained his demand.

A.D. 836 The first taking of Ath Cliath (i.e. Dublin) by the foreigners (Danes).

A.D. 841 The plundering of Cluain Eidhneach and the destruction of Cluain Iraird and Cill Achaidh - Droma Fota by the foreigners.

A.D. 845 Artuir, son of Muireadach, Lord of Airthear Life, died. Cathal, son of Cosgrach, Lord of Fotharta was slain by the Ui Neill.

A.D. 846 Another battle was gained by Olchobhar, King of Munster, and by Lorcan, son of Ceallach, King of Leinster, having the Munstermen and the Leinstermen with them, over the foreigners at Sciath Neachtain (near Castledermot in the south of Co. Kildare) wherein Tomhrair, Earl tanaist of the King of Lochlann and twelve hundred along with him, were slain.

A.D. 846 A defeat was given by Echthighern and the Leinstermen to the Osraighe (men of Ossary) at Uachtar Garadha (probably Oughteraghy in Co. Kilkenny).

A.D. 854 Dunlang, son of Dubhduin, Lord of Fotharta- tine died.[42]

A.D. 856 The plundering of Leinster by Cearbhall, son of Dunlang; and he took their hostages, together with Cairbre, son of Dunlang and Suithenen son of Arthur.

A.D. 857 A great meeting of the chieftains of Ireland was called by the King Maelseachlainn, to Rath Aedha Mic Bric (now Rathhugh, in the barony of Moycashel, Co. Westmeath), with Fethghna, successor of Patrick and Suairleach, successor of Finnia (i.e. abbot of Clonard), to establish peace and concord between the men of Ireland; and here Cearbhall, lord of Osraighe gave the award of the successors of Patrick and Finnia to the King of Ireland, after

---

[40] That part of Co. Kildare embraced by the Liffey in its horseshoe winding way called Airthir Life.
[41] O'Flaherty - Ogygia C. LXIV
[42] Fotharta- tine i.e. Barony of Forth O'Nolan

Cearbhall had been forty nights at Everoo (probably Oris in Co. Westmeath) and the son of the King of Lochlann at first along with him plundering Meath. And after they had awarded that the King of Osraighe should be in league with Leath Chuinn, Maelgualai, son of Donnghal, King of Munster, then tendered his allegiance (Maelgualai was stoned to death by the Danes, shortly afterwards).

98. Dunan, son of Dungus

99. Faelan, son of Dunan.

A.D. 858 A hosting of the men of Leinster, Munster and Connaught and of the southern Ui Neill into the north by Maelseachlainn, son of Maelruanaidh.; and he pitched a camp at Magh Dumha (Moy) in the vicinity of Armagh. Aedh Finnleach, son of Niall and Flann, son of Conang attacked the camp that night against the king and many persons were killed and destroyed by them in the middle of the camp; but Aedh was afterwards defeated and he lost many of his people.

A.D. 862 A prey was made by Cearbhall (Lord of Osraighe) from Leinster; and another prey in a fortnight afterwards from the Osraighe, by the Leinstermen.

A.D. 863 Colman, son of Dunlang, Lord of Fotharta - tire was slain by his own children.

A.D. 868 The plundering of Leinster by Aedh Finnliath (monarch of Ireland) from Ath Cliath to Gabhran (Gowran in Co. Kilkenny). Cearbhall, son of Dunghall plundered it on the other side as far as Dun Bolg (this was the ancient name of a fort near Donard in Co. Wicklow).
A.D. 872 An army was led by Aedh Finnliath into Leinster, so that he plundered the entire country.

A.D. 875 The plundering of Ui Cheinnselaigh by Cinneidigh, son of Gaethan, Lord of Leinster; and numbers were slain by him.

A.D. 876 A defeat was given to the Leinstermen at Uachtar-dara[43] when Bolgadhar, son of Maelceir was killed. A slaughter was made of the South Leinstermen at Fulachta (i.e. the Cooking Place - not identified) by the Osraighe, wherein Dunog, son of Anmchadh, and Dubhthoirthroigh, son of

---

[43] Probably Outrath, barony of Shillelophar, Co. Kilkenny.

Maelduin were slain, together with two hundred men (who were cut off) by slaying and drowning.

A.D. 881 Cairbre, son of Dunlang, lord of Airthear Life died.

A.D. 895 A prey was taken by the Leinstermen from the Osraighe on which occasion Buadhac, son of Ailell was slain.

A.D. 897 Fagarnach, son of Flann, Abbot of Laithreach- Briuin (now Laraghbrine, near Maynooth, Co. Kildare), and lord of Fotharta Airthear Life died. The expulsion of the foreigners from Ireland, from the fortress of Ath Cliath by Cearbhall, son of Muirigen and by the Leinstermen (was accomplished); by Maelfinnia with the men of Breagh about him; leaving great numbers of their ships behind them, they escaped half dead across the sea.

Chapter 7

Intertribal Wars

A.D. 908[44] This is the thirtieth year of the reign of Flann, son of Maelsechlainn. The great host of Munster was assembled by Flaithbhertach Mac Inmhainen, Abbot of Inis Cathaigh (now Scattery Island) and Cormac Mac Cuilemain, King of Munster and Bishop of Cashel. Their object was to demand hostages from the Leinstermen and the Osraighe. Flaithbhetach went through the camp on horseback and his horse fell under him into a steep trench and this was an evil omen to him. There were many of his own people and of the whole host who did not wish to go on the expedition after this, for they considered his fall as an ominous presage. Noble ambassadors, not knowing this, came from Leinster and they delivered a message of peace i.e. one peace in all Ireland, in return for which they would give hostages and pay fines.

Cormac appeared to be willing to accept the terms offered but Flaithbhertach refused and insisted that considerably more was needed. Cormac had an intuition that things would not go well for the Munstermen and he even forecast his own death.

According to the annals he made his will and ordered his body to be buried in Cloyne in Co. Cork or if not in the cemetery of Castledermot.[45] Some of the Munstermen were so annoyed that they went home. The remainder, unwillingly it seems, pressed on into Leinster via Old Leighlin, in Forth O'Nolan. They went as far as Sliabh Mairge, in Co. Laois, and then on to Co. Kildare, where they were opposed by the Leinstermen, aided by Flann, son of Maelsechlainn, with great forces of horse and foot.

The great battle was fought at Magh Ailbhe, a plain in the south of Co. Kildare, now called Ballymoon, near Carlow town.

Flaithbhertach, Cormac and another Cormac, the King of Kerry led the Munstermen. They were opposed by an army three times greater led by among

---

[44] There appears to be part of the Nolan manuscript missing but I found another document entitled " Annals of Ireland - Three Fragments copied from ancient sources by Dubhaltach Mac Firbisigh and edited by John O Donovan 1860." - I used these for this chapter - A.K. In addition I also used some material from my own book "In the Shadow of Mount Leinster".

[45] The Dermot who founded the church in what is now Castledermot, was the grandson of Aedh Roin, King of Uladh. He dedicated the church to St. Comhgall of Bangor about the year 800 A.D. - A.K.

others, Flann the son of the King of Ireland, Cearbhall the son of the King of Leinster, Tadhg, son of the king of Ui Cheinnselaigh, Inneirghe, son of the king of Idrone, and Follamhan, son of the king of Fotharta Fea (Barony of Forth in Carlow).

The battle itself was bloody and furious. Cormac the abbot, who had foretold his own death, was thrown from his horse and badly injured. He was seized and beheaded. After a short period the men of Munster gave way and began to retreat. The retreat turned to a rout and they fled back through Old Leighlin, pursued by the vengeful Leinstemen, who killed them in large numbers and took many more prisoners back to Leinster.

Flaithbhertach was captured and imprisoned for a time, but was later released. He went back to Munster and after a short period became king of Cashel and then King of Munster for thirty two years.

A.D. 909 Cearbhall, of Leinster died. He was killed accidentally
when his horse reared and he was flung against his own spear being carried by a servant. He was buried in Naas - as is stated in the following :-

> There are nine kings of famous career
> In Cill - Nais, of shining lustre;
> Muireagan, a hero without mistake,
> Ceallach and Cearbhall the sensible,
> Colman, Braen and Bran the lively,
> Finn, Faelan, Dunchadh the bold,
> In Corban's church, I have heard,
> Their warlike graves were made.

In this year also the men of Breffni went into revolt (it would appear that they were a rabble of peasants etc., as the King of Ireland, when told about their depredations said "the end of the world is nigh when plebeians like these dare to attack noblemen"). They were soundly defeated and many were taken into slavery.

A.D. 910 The men of Idrone led by their king Aedh, son of Dubhghioll and Diarmuid the King of Osraighe, destroyed the east of Magh Raighne and the church of Killinny (parish of Kells in Co. Kilkenny). Aedh the heir presumptive to the Ui Cheinnselaigh was afterwards slain by some 'plebeians' of the Osraighe as he returned to his house in Idrone. He was buried in Rath Aedhain (Ferns). The following was written about him at the time:

O Youths of pleasant Ailbhe[46]
Mourn ye the King of noble Slaine.
Slain is Aedh of hosts of the Bearbha,[47]
The just king of the land of peaceful Fearna.[48]
To great Fearna, of the thousand noble graces,
There came not, if I can remember,
A corpse of more illustrious fame
Since Bran Dubh of troops was slain.
My shelter, my protection has departed;
May the King of kings make smooth his way.
It is easily known by Rath Aedhain
That Aedh is dead, O youths!

A.D. 911   A wonderful sign was seen in the sky - two suns moving together during one day. [49]

A.D. 913 A very large fleet of Lochlanns settled at Port Lairge (Waterford) and plundered the north of Osraighe: they carried a great number of prisoners and many cows and small cattle to their ships.[50]

916 A.D. The Vikings plundered Leighlin.

951. A.D. The church of St. Mullins was plundered by the Vikings.

978 A.D. Leighlin[51] was plundered by the people of Osraighe

982 A.D. The people of Osraighe again devastated the town of Leighlin.

1002 A.D. Brian Boroimhe (Boru) became Monarch of Ireland.

---

[46] A plain on the east side of the Barrow.

[47] River Barrow

[48] Ferns in Co. Wexford.

[49] The annals of Clonmacnoise put this event as occurring in A.D.902.

[50] Annals of the four masters give the date as A.D.910.

[51] Old Leighlin not far from Dinn Righ, was a relatively late foundation of St. Mo -Laise who died in A.D. 639. His foundation became the centre of the diocese of Leighlin in the twelfth century. The Long Book of Leighlin, now lost, was an ancient manuscript which testified to this region of the Barrow Valley as being a centre for early scholarly activity. - Alfred P. Smyth in *Celtic Leinster*. - A.K.

1014. A.D. Brian Boru, then aged 80 years, was killed at the Battle of Clontarf after a fierce engagement between his forces and those of the Vikings. It was in his reign that surnames were extensively introduced. He was also said to be responsible for rebuilding roads, monasteries and towns.

1017 A.D. Donagan, King of Leinster, with many of his principal nobility was treacherously murdered at a feast in the home of Teige O'Riain of Idrone, by Donough MacGiolla Patrick, prince of Ossary. Malachy the monarch of Ireland, justly desirous of punishing so atrocious a crime, entered the territory of Mac Giolla Patrick, whom he slew with many of his followers and then retired to Tara bringing many prisoners.

1046 A.D. Diarmuid Mac Mael na mBo became King of Leinster. He was the first of the Ui Cheinnselaigh people to become King of Leinster. He was from the Sil nOnchon, a sept of the Ui Cheinnselaigh that lived in what is now the Bunclody/Kildavin area of north Wexford. In 1032 he was elected as King of Ui Cheinnselaigh (Wexford, Carlow, South Wicklow and East Kilkenny). The Fothairt owed allegiance to the Kings of Ui Cheinnselaigh, as indeed did the Ui Drona people and all the other sub septs that inhabited the region.

Diarmuid was an ambitious and ruthless man. He allied himself with the enemies of the Ui Dunlainge King (who was also the King of Leinster) and in 1037 he attacked the Ui Dunlainge (who lived largely in what is today called North Wicklow, Laois and Kildare)[52] and also plundered the Viking city of Waterford. His allies were the Osraighe (who lived mainly in what is now Co. Kilkenny and east Tipperary) and the Eoghanacht of Munster (the clans that lived in West Tipperary - centred around Cashel). He became such a threat that the two ancient enemies, the Kings of Leinster and Munster united and marched into Ui Cheinnselaigh. There they burned Ferns in 1046. Somewhere on their route back from Ferns those Kings were attacked by the Osraighe and the Eoghanacht, the allies of Diarmuid Mac Mael na mBo, and in the battle the King of Leinster was slain. This left the way open for Diarmuid to put himself forward as King of Leinster. The King of Munster was very unhappy about this turn of events and he mustered another army to invade Leinster. This he did and he took many hostages including some from Diarmuid.

Undeterred by this setback, Diarmuid turned his attentions to Dublin, the Viking city, which he attacked successfully and made himself King of Dublin. As the monarch of that city also claimed kingship over Wales, Diarmuid

---

[52] "The Ui Cheinnselaigh and the Ui Dunlainge invaded Leinster from Ossory in the fifth century and eventually took over the entire province from older groups such as the Ui Bairrche (and their allies the Fothairt), the Ui Failge, the Dal Messin Corb, the Dal Cormaic and the Ui Mail." - Alfred P. Smyth in *Celtic Leinster* - A.K.

declared himself King of Wales also. Many septs now flocked to his standards and thus empowered, Diarmuid invaded Munster. At a pitched battle at Sliabh Crot in Tipperary he inflicted a severe defeat on the Munstermen. The King of Munster now submitted to him and Diarmuid declared himself King of the Southern half of Ireland. In an attempt to become High King of all Ireland, Diarmuid, further strengthened by the Munstermen, now invaded Connaught, but this foray was unsuccessful.

1060 A.D. The Cathedral of Leighlin, a wooden structure, was burnt accidentally.

1070 A.D. Murchadh the great-grand father of Dermot McMurrogh and the son of Diarmuid Mac Mael na mBo was poisoned or killed by the Vikings of Dublin, where he had been installed as King.

1071 A.D. Diarmuid Mac Mael na mBo was killed in battle with the men of Meath. This unexpected event plunged the country into further turmoil. The new King of Munster, Turlough O'Brien, who had been placed on his throne by Diarmuid, moved to prevent the nephews of Diarmuid from becoming too powerful. He placed one of them, Donnchadh, on the throne of Ui Cheinnselaigh, and he made Diarmuid's grandson Donal (son of Murchadh) King of Dublin.

1077 A.D. Donnchadh the King of Ui Cheinnselaigh tried to assert himself and began to strive for the throne of Leinster. Turlough, the King of Munster, marched into Ui Cheinnselaigh to "place fetters on Donnchadh".

1089 A.D. Donnchadh died and was succeeded by his uncle Eanna Bacach, who had been excluded from the kingship previously. Eanna was the second son of Diarmuid Mac Mael na mBo.

1092 A.D. Eanna Bacach died and was succeeded by his sons in turn and later by Diarmuid a grandson of Murchadh who was killed in 1070.

1123 A.D. The King of Ui Cheinnselaigh, Eanna McMurrough, a grandson of Murchadh (above) allied himself with the McCarthys, Tighernan O Rourke of Breffni and the King of Meath to try to depose the High King, Turlough O'Connor of Connaught. This invasion of Connaught was a failure and Eanna McMurrough retired to Ui Cheinnselaigh.

1126 A.D. Eanna McMurrough, King of Ui Cheinnselaigh died and was succeeded by his son Diarmuid Mac Murrough. In this same year Turlough

O'Connor invaded Ui Cheinnselaigh and deposed Diarmuid. It is likely that Diarmuid was a young man of twenty years of age or less at that time.

1133 A.D. Eochaidh O'Nolan was slain.[53]

1154 A.D. The son of Eochaidh was slain.

---

[53] O'Hanlon in his book about the Queen's County - A.K.

Chapter 8

The Coming of the Normans

Dermot McMurrough, King of Leinster was a man of strong passions, arrogant, overbearing and aggressive. He aimed at attaining the position of Ard Ri, which many of his ancestors had filled and to this end engaged in numerous attacks on neighbouring princes. He overran and spoiled the city of Dublin, then practically (sic) a Danish settlement, and "bore a greater sway over them than any other had done for a long time"[54]

He forced O'Neill (of Leinster), O'Melaghlin and O'Carroll to give him hostages, and inflated by these successes, became so insolent and oppressive that at length the aggrieved princes rose up in rebellion against him. A short time previously he had carried off Dervorgilla, wife of Tiernan O'Rourke, prince of Breffni, who appealed to Roderick O'Connor, then High King, for vengeance on the disturber of his domestic happiness.

Roderick assembled a considerable army and with the forces of O'Rourke and O'Melaghlin, marched against Dermot, who (in the quaint words of Keating) "called together the nobles of Leinster from all sides, and when they came to one place, their answer to Diarmuid was that they would not go to defend the evil deed he had done, and thereupon many of them deserted him, and put themselves under the protection of the High King, and made known to him that Diarmuid, before that time, had committed many acts of injustice and tyranny against them.[55]

The people of his patrimonial lands in Wexford and Carlow, however, in great measure supported him, and fought for him against Roderick, but after sustaining several defeats Diarmuid dismissed the remnants of his followers and fled to England, where he besought the King, Henry 11, to aid him in regaining his kingdom.

Henry had long cast covetous eyes on the fair land so near his shores, and was even at the moment seeking a pretext for invading it. The coming of the exiled Diarmuid fitted in so smoothly with his own wishes, that Diarmuid was received with open arms, and had no difficulty in securing permission to enlist the sympathy and assistance of such English Knights, and others, as he could induce, by lavish promises of rewards, in land and treasure, to espouse his cause.

---

[54] Cox
[55] Irish Texts Ed. Vol. 111 pg. 321

The principal supported he secured was Richard de Clare, the Earl of Chepstow, Strigul and Pembroke, usually called "Strongbow", to whom he promised his daughter Eva[56] in marriage and the succession of the Kingdom of Leinster.

It is no part of this work to analyse the informality of such an action, or to dwell upon the fact that, though the crown was hereditary in a certain family, the actual recipient was selected by the people, and consequently such endowment was legally inoperative. The needy adventurers who flocked to Diarmuid's standards were in no mood to question any title which vested in them lands and power, and having got the grants, relied on their own strength to make good the title.

In October 1169 Diarmuid returned secretly to Ireland, and lived during the winter, quietly at his own house in Ferns, Co. Wexford. He spent the time working assiduously to procure assistance from the native clans for his forthcoming campaign.

In May 1170 the first detachments of his English adherents, consisting of 30 Knights, 60 men-at-arms and 300 choice archers, under the command of Robert FitzStephen, and ten Knights and a number of archers under Maurice de Prendergast, landed at Baginbun, in the south of Wexford. With them came Hervey de Montmorency (Mountmaurice in ms), as an emissary of Strongbow, his nephew. Hervey was to inform his nephew as to the state of the country, and the prospects of a successful invasion. FitzStephen had been for a considerable time detained in prison by Rhees ap Griffith, King of South Wales, for some infraction of the law, and it was only at the behest of Diarmuid and others, that he was released on the distinct understanding that he should proceed to Ireland.

Notice of the arrival of the Norman force reached Diarmuid, who hastened to his aid with such native levies as he could collect, and the united forces proceeded to lay siege to Wexford. The citizens of Wexford offered a sturdy resistance, and inflicted serious losses on the besiegers, but through the mediation of certain Bishops terms were arranged, and, after four days the town surrendered.

To reward their services Diarmuid granted to FitzStephen and Prendergast "the town of Wexford and two cantreds adjoining", and as a means of attaching Strongbow more securely to his cause, bestowed on his uncle Hervey de Montmorency "two cantreds on the sea coast, between Wexford and Waterford", which tract is comprised in the baronies of Forth and Bargy.

Thus, one of the first tracts of the fair lands of Ireland alienated to the invading Normans was part of the original territory possessed by the descendants of Eochaidh Fionn Fothart, ancestor of the O'Nolans.

---

[56] Aoife

The recovery of his Kingdom was not sufficient for Diarmuid, who thirsted for revenge on those who had opposed him in his hour of defeat. Strong in the military prowess of his English auxiliaries, he forthwith embarked on a series of filibustering raids into Ossory, Ofelan and O'Tooles country, which not only helped to slake his desire for revenge but also enabled his followers, both English and Irish, to enrich themselves with the spoils of the plundered territories.

Roderick, the High King, once more marched against Diarmuid, who knowing himself too weak to meet him in the open, withdrew into the fastnesses around Ferns, and while securely shielded in these dark woods, opened negotiations, and in due course made submission and gave his only legitimate son - Art - as hostage for his future loyalty. The impending fate of his son did not for a moment stay the prosecution of his designs.

The verdict of history is not favourable to Roderick, who appears to have been a weak ruler, wanting in genius, foresight and strength of will, which are necessary attributes to a great leader of men. Diarmuid, who appears to have been his superior in diplomacy, easily beguiled him into false security, and his duplicity, and timely submission, was enabled to stave off a decisive defeat, while awaiting the arrival of Strongbow and his much larger accession of strength. Had Roderick been of sterner mould he could have effectively stamped out the invasion in its inception and so have saved his country from the untold miseries which followed in its train.

Raymond le Gros landed in May 1171 at Dundowragh, eight miles east of Waterford, with the advance guard of Strongbow's army, consisting of ten Knights, 40 Esquires and 80 archers, who hastily entrenched themselves. An attack was made on them by a contingent from Waterford, Ofelan and Idrone, which was first successful, but Raymond, sallying out with his mail clad warriors, threw the attackers into confusion and beat them off with great loss, and captured seventy principal citizens who were forthwith put to death.

Strongbow landed in the haven of Waterford[57] in August 1171 with 200 Knights and upwards of 1000 men-at-arms. He was joined at once by Diarmuid, FitzStephen and Raymond le Gros, and the united forces immediately assaulted Waterford. After having been twice repulsed they succeeded in effecting an entrance to the city, put the inhabitants ruthlessly to the sword, and there, amid the red ruin of the desolated city, Strongbow and Eva were married.

The army of invasion, consisting of about 250 Knights and 1,500 men-at-arms, may seem small for the conquest of a people so warlike and so numerous as the Irish then were, but unfortunately the Irish Kings and Princes were torn asunder by internecine strife and personal jealousies, which left them an easy prey to the well-disciplined Normans. Again, the Irish fought without

---

[57] I assume Fr. Nolan meant that he landed at a haven near Waterford.

protective armour, and had as arms but spears and swords, whereas the English Knights were clad in armour of proof from head to foot, and were mounted on horses similarly caparisoned. Their archers were at the time, the most expert in the world, and the clouds of arrows discharged at the onrushing native levies kept them from engaging at close quarters; while the mail clad Knights rode through their ranks and cut them down almost with impunity.

" The Norman discipline, was, perhaps, the best suited for the purpose of aggression that had ever yet appeared in the world. Their feudal gradations of rank gave to their appearance the sharp edge and the wide base of a wedge. They were Danes in vigour, and more than Romans in art and armour. The despotic power of the leader, and the rigid requirements of their code of chivalry, perfected their capacity for overrunning a territory broken into several small states without a centre of union and power"[58]

Having reduced Waterford, Diarmuid and Strongbow marched through Wicklow to Dublin and laid siege to the city. The Archbishop, Lawrence O'Toole (Saint), entered negotiations for its surrender, and whilst terms were being discussed, and a truce existed, Raymond le Gros and Milo de Cogan, taking advantage of the cessation of hostilities, treacherously assaulted the city and sacked it with great slaughter.

Roderick, the High King, once more taking the field with a numerous but wretchedly organised army, besieged the Normans in Dublin, but his want of capacity as a leader was again evident. The siege was prolonged for a considerable time until the defenders were reduced to great straits. Finding starvation and submission were the certain effects of further inactivity, and no doubt being well informed of the lax discipline in the Irish army, Raymond and his fellow captains decided on making a dash for liberty, and sallying forth with every available man, fell with fury on Roderick's army, which was quite unprepared for such a desperate resolve, made dreadful havoc and slaughter and completely routed Roderick's men.

Diarmuid did not long enjoy the fruits of his victories, as he died in May 1172, but unfortunately the consequences of his evil deeds, and ill judged actions, did not die with him, but remain to this day.

Strongbow was recalled to England to account to the King for his actions and found considerable trouble in making peace with his irate sovereign, which he only succeeded in doing by an absolute surrender of all his rights in Ireland and an acknowledgement that the conquered territories were held in fee under the English Crown.

In October 1172 King Henry landed at Waterford with a considerable army, received a quasi homage from several of the Irish Kings, and took over possession of the invaded territories from his subordinates. He remained in

---

[58] T.D. McGee pg. xix

Dublin until Easter 1173 and before returning to England, parcelled out Ireland among his followers, making grants not only of the partially occupied territories but also portions of the country to which he could advance no shadow of a claim, and which remained independent of English control for some hundreds of years afterwards.

Hugo de Lacy got a grant of Meath and was appointed Chief Governor, but soon finding himself quite unequal to the responsibilities of such a position, asked to be relieved, and Strongbow being recalled from England, replaced him.

Soon afterwards, Raymond le Gros was married to Basilia, sister to Strongbow, and received as a marriage portion the lands of Idrone, Glascarrig and Fothart O'Nolan. Though Raymond was thus endowed with the patrimony of the O'Nolans, he, and his successors, derived small advantage from the gift, as the O'Nolans remained rooted in the soil, and lords of the territory for centuries thereafter. Many of their descendants still retain considerable portions of their ancient territory.

From the ready bestowal of these lands, which, from their mountainous character, were by no means among the most desirable with which Strongbow could with equal right dower his sister, it may fairly be assumed that O'Nolan was not a supporter of Diarmuid and Strongbow in their previous campaign. On his march from Waterford to Dublin, Strongbow was compelled to take the longer and more difficult route, by Glendalough, as the shorter road was held against him by the Irish. This shorter route passed through Forth O'Nolan, and the most difficult portion of the way, consequently the most easily defended, was in this territory. Though no record is extant which specifically states so, it is reasonable to assume that O'Nolan was hostile, and a factor in sending the army round by the longer route. On Diarmuid's flight into England, the only men of note who accompanied him were Auliffe and O'Kinede[59] and on his death the only Princes who threw in their lot with Strongbow were Donald Kavanagh (Diarmuid's natural son and successor in the Kingdom of Leinster), O'Reilly of Tirbruin (of Breffni) and Aulaff O'Garvie, a petty chieftain of the district round Rathvilly in Co. Carlow. [60]

O'Nolan, as senior Prince and Chief Marshall of Leinster, was a noteworthy figure, and his defection would account for the grant of his territory to Raymond le Gros. Another piece of circumstantial evidence which may be adduced in support of this view, is the fact that almost, if not quite the first, Norman Castle built in Ireland was in Forth O'Nolan, for " Hanmer informs us further that Lacey in 1179 built a castle in Fothart O'Nolan[61] for

---

[59] Cox pg. 11

[60] Regan B. and Orpen P.

[61] According to an anonymous writer in an article entitled "Visitation of Arms" the castle in question was Castle Grace. - A.K.

Raymond, and another for Griffen, his brother, the sons of William FitzGerald."[62]

---

[62] Ryan's Carlow pg. 54

Chapter 9

The 13th. Century

About the year 1175, Henry II bestowed the title of Lord of Ireland upon his son John, and with this title the English Kings were content for nearly 400 years, until the time of Henry VIII, when that autocrat, having constituted himself Head of the Church, also had himself nominated King of Ireland. Leland tells us that "to give weight and brilliancy to the English Government it was resolved to change the style of Lord of Ireland, with which the crown of England had hitherto been contented, to that of King .... It was resolved in the English cabinet that an Irish Parliament should confer the title of King of Ireland upon Henry and his heirs."[63]

In the year 1199 King John succeeded to the crown of England. He was a man of unscrupulous character and grossly licentious habits.[64] While yet a prince, some twenty five years before, he paid a visit to Ireland during which he gave serious offence to the ruling Irish Chieftains. Now, as King of England, he paid a second visit to Ireland, and in the month of June 1210 landed at Crook, near Waterford, with a fleet of over one hundred ships and a powerful army. In Juiy he proceeded to Meath, and thence he advanced to Downpatrick, Carrigfergus and other parts of Ulster, and in August returned by way of Carlingford, Drogheda, Duleek, Kells, Foure and Granard to Rathwire, where the De Lacys had a castle near Kinnegad. Here he received the submission and hostages of Cathal Crovedearg O'Connor, who refused to give his son as hostage, but gave four leading Chiefs in his place. These, King John brought with him on his return into England.[65]

Unfortunately for our country, when King John arrived on our shores with his powerful army, he met with no serious or combined opposition. Ireland was in a state of great distraction and unrest. Many of the native leaders, instead of uniting to defend their common country, were waging bitter and relentless war against each other. The English adventurers, who had already gained a foothold in Ireland, were ever ready to encourage these sanguinary feuds, playing off one party against the other, and even ready to take sides as occasion offered, in the hope that ultimately, by the destruction of both combatants, they themselves might obtain the mastery. Their policy then, as now, was "divide

---

[63] Leland III c. 7.

[64] Lingard

[65] O'Donovan - Four Masters

and conquer". Sometimes, indeed, these English barons quarrelled among themselves and enlisted the services of their Irish allies to prosecute their interests. But in all this it became apparent that plunder was their object in pursuit of which they hesitated not to perpetrate the most awful outrages and even to rifle the shrines of the saints and despoil their sanctuaries. They came to acquire wealth and so they plundered the natives and their churches without scruple and with impunity. So widespread, indeed, was the desolation brought about by their conduct that the Archbishop of Armagh went specially to England (1206) to complain to King John, of their sacrilegious action and insatiate greed.[66]

We do not, however, find any evidence of the O'Nolans bearing part in this internecine strife. On the contrary, the evidence at hand, meagre as it is, goes to show that the O'Nolans stood resolute "On the Frontier", facing the English invader.

The very first castle built by the usurpers was built within the borders of the fair lands of Forth O'Nolan[67] - "erectum est igitur apud Fotheret O'Nolan primo castrum Reimundo et aliud fratri ejusdem Griffino"[68]

Whether Hugh de Lacy was engaged in building these castles or not, when recalled to England in 1181, is a matter of conjecture. Certainly they were finished by his successors, during their three months stay in Ireland as Governors, for Dowling tells us that - " John Lacy, Constable of Cheshire, and Richard Peach (Bishop of Coventry) were sent as Governors into Ireland. They built castles on the Frontier, that is in Forth O'Nolan, Castledermot and Tullow and thence returned into England."

Within three months after his recall, Hugh de Lacy was sent back again to Ireland as Chief Governor. Since this leading English baron fills an important place in our history, we must take a hurried glance at his character and achievements.

Hugh de Lacy was a descendant of the De Lacys who came to England with William the Conqueror and were Earls of Lincoln, in England. He first came to Ireland in 1171 with Henry II and obtained from that monarch a grant of the whole Kingdom of Meath. He is thus described in Holingshead: " His eyes were dark and deep set, his neck short, his stature small, his body hairy, nor fleshy, but sinewy, strong and compact; a very good soldier but rather rash and hasty."

Hanmer says that he was an able and politic man in state affairs, but very ambitious and covetous of wealth and great possessions. He is said to have been a famous horseman. De Lacy's second wife was a daughter of King Roderick

---

[66] Four Masters
[67] Almost certainly Castle Grace near Ballon - A.K.
[68] Gir. Camb. Vol V. pg. 355

O'Connor and his descendants, the De Lacys, were Lords of Meath and Earls of Ulster.

In those days of primitive warfare the Irish warriors put their trust in the plashed woods and open moorland, while the Norman barons depended upon stout fortresses and strong Castles. These they erected at convenient places as soon as they had secured a footing, and, planting a garrison within, used them as safe retreats from attack, and secure bases from which to sally forth for aggression. Many of their strongholds are a wonder even at the present day.

"When Robert FitzStephen and the gallants of Britain entered the country," writes Hanmer, "they found neither dastards or cowards, but valiant men with horse and foot; they found the country fast with woods, bogges and paces trenched and plashed; yet the valour of the adventurers was such, presuming upon former fortunes, to have the like successes, with loose wings drove them out of the woods and bogges, into the plains and champion land, where the horsemen, with their spears, overthrew them, and the foote, finding them grovelling, runne them threw, and ended their days; the Gallowglasses followed and cut off their heads." [69]

Following out their policy of stout walls, the English Governors in Ireland had castles, as we have seen, erected at Forth O'Nolan, Castledermot and Tullow. A castle was also erected in Dublin and the work of erecting similar fortresses was prosecuted with great vigour wherever the English invader made the slightest headway. Hanmer tells us that Hugh de Lacy, "made bridges and builded townes, castles and forts throughout Leinster, as Sir John de Courcey did in Ulster in his time; the priest kept his church, the soldier his garrison and the ploughman his plough". He then goes on to describe the various castles erected by Hugh de Lacy, from which it appears that he planted many of these strongholds in the form of a rough semi-circle around the north and east boundaries of the principality of O'Nolan, but notwithstanding this systematic efforts to root them out, the hill country to the south, Croghaun, Slievebawn, Greenoge, Mount Leinster and the innumerable recesses of the Blackstairs Mountains were the eternal safeguard and sure retreat of the hard pressed Irish clansmen.

" The castle", says Hanmer, "which Lacie built for the good of the land, were these; first Laghlen, of old called the Blacke Castle, upon the Barrow, between Ossary and Idrone, of which Castle by Henry II's commandment Robert Poer had charge, until in cowardice sort he gave over the same and forsook it....this Black Castle now called New Leighlin, for difference of Old Leighlin, which is the Bishop's seate, standeth in the Barony of Ydrone, which was the antient inheritance of the Carews; who being Barons of Carew in Wales, so farre as I can learne. One of them married the daughter

---

[69] Hanmer pg. 228

and heiress of the Baron of Ydrone, and so the Carews became and were for the terms of many years Barons of Ydrone, until the troublesome time of Richard II when the Carews with all the English of Ireland in like manner, were driven to forsake the land.

He built in Leix for Meilerius Tachmeho, alias Cachmehe, and as for Kildare, with the country adjoining, the which, as Cambrensis writeth, as by the Earle Strongbow given him, the Governors, in Hugh de Lacy's absence, subtilly took it away from him, under colour of exchange, and gave him Leix, a wilde savage country, with woodes, paces, bogges and rebels farre from succour or rescue. In Meath he builded Clanarec, Dunach, Killar alias Killairie, the Castle of Adam de Ieypon, alias Sureport, and Gilbert de Nugents of Delvyn.

In Fothart of O'Nolan, alias Fethred Onolan, in Latin, Rotheric, he builded a Castle for Reimond, and another for Griffen his brother, the sonnes of William FitzGerald, for Walter of Ridensford, he builded in Omurchu, alias Morogh's country Trissledermot, otherwise called Trisdeldermot, about five miles from Catherlogh, and likewise Kilka, in the county of Kildare. For John de Gereford, he builded a Castle in Collach, otherwise called Tulacfelmeth; for John declawsa, alias Clavill, he builded a Castle upon the Barrow, not farre from Leighlin, now supposed to be Carlogh, though some attribute it to Eva, Earle Strongbow his wife; yet it is evident next after the Danes, that the English men builded all the Castles in Ireland. He builded also near Aboy, a Castle that he gave to Robert Bigaret, another not farre from thence, which he gave to Thomas Fleminge; another at Narach on the Barrow for Robert Fitz Richard; lastly he builded the Castle of Derwath, where he made a tragical end; for on a time when each man was busily occupied, some lading, some heaving, some plastering, some engraving, the General himself also digging with a Pickaxe, a desperate villaine among them, whose toole the Lord Lieutenant used, espying both his hands occupied, and his body bent downwards, with an axe cleft his head in sunder; his body, the two archbishops, John of Dublin and Mathew of Cashill, buried in the Monasterie of the Bectie, that is in Monasterio Beatitudinis (Bective Abbey), and his head in Saint Thomas Abbey at Dublin, whose death, (I read in Holinshed) the King was not sorry of, because he was always jealous of his greatnesse.

Upon the death of Lacy, Sir Roger le Poer, a most worthy knight, who served valiantly in Vister, in company with Sir John de Courcy, being made Governor of the country about Leighlin in Ossorie, was in most lamentable sort traitorously slaine; and upon that occasion, there was (saith Cambrensis) a privy conspiracy over all Ireland against English men."

Hanmer says that Idrone was "the ancient inheritance of the Carews". Raymond le Gros received this territory, " the ancient inheritance of the O'Ryans" from Strongbow. It is supposed that Maud, Countess of Norfolk, granted the barony of Idrone by certain services in fee to the family of

Carew.[70] But the O'Ryans and the McMurroughs held Idrone for many a day afterwards.

In these Castles were placed some of the stoutest and most daring of the invaders and the land beyond was to be their reward, provided they could crush or exterminate the ancient inhabitants. Every facility within the reach of the English Governors in Ireland was given them and from time to time large subsidies and drafts of recruits were sent over from England to assist them in pushing forward the conquest.

Against this strong and resolute combination, backed up by all the resources of the crown, O'Nolan and his confederates had to contend, and did so successfully for a space of over four hundred years. Nay, so well did the O'Nolans hold their ground during all the vicissitudes of the past seven hundred years since the Norman invasion, that it may be truly said there is no clan in Ireland even at the present day, better represented within the limits of its ancient territory by its sturdy and virile descendants, than the O'Nolans, so much so indeed, that some years ago, when Dr. Nolan was Bishop of Kildare and Leighlin, it was a trite saying among people that "every man from the Bishop to the Bellman in County Carlow was an O'Nolan," and today the bright laughing children of this ancient and noble race gather round the firesides at eventide to listen to some heroic tale of their glorious ancestors while the very name of Strongbow, Raymond le Gros and Hugh de Lacy are forgotten, and their strong stone Castles have long since crumbled to decay.

Raymond le Gros was married to Basilia, the sister of Earl Strongbow, at Wexford, in 1174. He was invested by Strongbow with the office of Constable and Standard Bearer of Leinster, and received with Basilia, as her dowry from Strongbow, the district known as Forth O'Nolan. Raymond's honeymoon was short, as, in the midst of the festivities, intelligence arrived that Roderick O'Connor had crossed the Shannon and invaded Meath.

"The very morning after the celebration of nuptials, the bridegroom was obliged to put on his armour."[71]

He led his troops to Dublin, but on his arrival there found that Roderick had retired after devastating the English settlement in Meath. It was at this time a castle was erected for Raymond in Forth O'Nolan and also for his brother Griffin. [72]

These castles have long since disappeared, but the position occupied by Raymond's castle has been identified.[73] It was situated at the motte of Castlemore, near Tullow. The proof rests upon certain contemporary Charters

---

[70] Harris

[71] Leland

[72] Giraldus Cambrensis Vol. 5 pg. 355

[73] Orpen, R.S.A., Journal Vol. xxxvi pg. 368

recorded in the Register of the Abbey of St. Thomas, Dublin, which were granted by Raymond and Basilia jointly and after Raymond's death by Basilia alone, and by her together with her second husband, Geoffrey FitzRobert, Seneschal of Leinster, concerning tithes, benefices and lands in Fodredunolan.

In the first of these charters in chronological order (CXXXI) Raymond and Basilia grant " to the Church of St. Mary and St. David of their castles of the theud (Ir. tuath) of Radeillan, the tithes of their lordship of Fothered and one carucate of land viz. by these boundaries marked : from the great rock which is on the east side of the cemetery along the road on the north as far as the pit which the said Raymond perambulated, and from that pit to a thorn hedge, and from the hedge along a ditch to the boundaries of the monks, and along the boundaries of the monks to the river Slaney, and from the boundaries of the monks in a southerly direction, so that the aforesaid carucate of land may be completed.......reserving, nevertheless, the site of a mill and of a fishery in the said carucate of land, in that part where it slopes down to the Slaney, if there should be a site for a mill or a fishery there." This deed is witnessed by Griffin Fitzwilliam, Raymond's brother, and by Robert, Jordan and William de Cat, which is evidently a contraction of de Cantitunne, sons of Raymond's sister Mabilla, who married a Nicholas de Cantitune.

"The cemetery along the road" can still be seen at the junction where the Carlow road divides for Ballon and Tullow, while the quarry hole from which the "great rock", has been in latter years blasted, lies to the east side of the cemetery and about 200 yards east of Castlemore.

In another Charter (CXXXV) the abbot of Baltinglass refers to " certain tithes of our land near our grange of Fothert". Now the grange of Forth is evidently the present parish of Grangeford to the north west of Fenagh, in which Castlemore is situated. Grangeford is at present in the barony of Carlow and Castlemore in the baorny of Rathvilly, from which it appears that in those times Forthart Ui Nuallain stretched much farther to the north and probably embraced the entire district now included in the baronies of Carlow and Rathvilly. This is evident from Charter CXXXII, in which Mabilla de Cantitune (who was sister of Raymond le Gros) made a grant of "Strupho in tenemento de Fothered", but this Straboe is a parish and townland in the barony of Rathvilly, altogether north of both Fenagh and Grangeford. It is called "Strabe in Fothard" in the Ecclesiastical Taxation 1302 - 6.

In Charter CXXX Raymond and Basilia grant to the church of St. Thomas, of Dublin, and to the canons there serving God, in the first place their bodies to be buried in the said church, and next, as regards the right of advowson, the church of Rasilan in Fodredunolan, together with one carucate of land which was assigned to the said church, and all the ecclesiastical benefices of their lordship, both of Englishmen and Irishmen in the land Fodred.

In Charter CXXIX, Geoffrey FitzRobert and Basilia his wife, grant the Church of St. Mary's and St. David the Confessor, of Fotharahonolan to the canons of St. Thomas of Dublin, with all its appurtenances and certain lands.

In Charter CXXXVIII William Mareschal jun. (1219- 1231) confirms the above grants after the death of Basilia.

Charter CXXXVIII is a grant of the Abbot of St. Thomas of seven lots, each containing a burgage and twelve acres of land to seven persons (named) " at Fothered, in the carucate of land which Thomas holds close to the vill of Fothered, between the river Slaney and the said vill, at a rent of five silver solidi."

Charter CCCLI described the boundaries of the parish of the parochial church of "Villa Castri in Foorthynolan."

We need not go into details regarding these boundaries but if we examine some of the names given in this Charter they tell their own tales. "Clochayn Acayth" is evidently meant to stand for Clochan a Chata - the stepping stones of the battle. "Roscaath" is the battle wood and "Glassecorp" means the stream of the corpses and is probably the more ancient name of the Aghalona river. O'Donovan has identified "Ceil Osnadaigh" with Kellistown, which is barely two miles away, and which has given its name to more than one historic battle, one in A.D. 487 which may be taken as marking the beginning of the supremacy of North Leinster over Ui Cheinnselaigh - a supremacy which lasted for six centuries, and another in 1167, between Tighearnan O'Rourke and Dermot McMurrough.

"The battle of Cill Osnaidh in Magh Fea, in which fell Aengus Mac Nathfraeich, King of Mumhan, and his wife Eithne, the hateful daughter of Criomthainn, son of Enna Cinnsealach.[74] Iollann, son of Dunlaing, and Oillill, his brother, and Eochaidh Guineach, and Muircertach Mac Erca, King of Aileach, were victors as was said :-

A branch of the great spreading tree died - Aengus the praiseworthy son of Nathfraeich. His head was left with Iollann in the battle of foul Cill Osnaigh"[75]

From the Four Masters we learn of particulars of the second battle. "A.D. 1167, Diarmuid Mac Murchadha returned from England with a force of Galls, and he took the Kingdom of Ui Cheinnselaigh. Another army was led by Ruaidhri Ua Conchubhair and Tighernan Ua Ruairc into Ui Cheinnselaigh, until they arrived at Cill Osnadh. A battle was fought between some of the recruits and the cavalry of Connaught, and the cavalry of Ui Cheinnselaigh, and six of the Connaughtmen, together with Domhnall, son of Tadgh, son of

---

[74] The progenitor of the Ui Cheinnselaig who was converted at Rathvilly in the fifth century. - A.K.

[75] Chronicum Scotorum

Maelruanaidhe, were slain in the first conflict; and there were slain in the second conflict by Tighernan Ua Ruairc twenty five of the Ui Cheinnselaigh, together with the son[76] of the King of Britain (i.e. the King of Wales) who was the battle-prop of the island of Britain, who had come across the sea in the army of McMurrough. Diarmuid McMurrough afterwards came to Ua Conchubhair and gave him seven hostages for ten cantreds of his own native territory, and one hundred ounces of gold to Tighernan Ua Ruairc for his eireach[77]"

From other Charters in the Register we can infer that Raymond made a grant of lands in Forth O'Nolan to his sister Mabilla, wife of Nicholas de Cantiton, and to his nephews, Raymond and Robert de Cantiton.

Charter CXXXII (as already mentioned above) is a grant by Mabilla to the Canons of St. Thomas of the ecclesiastical rights of "Strupho in tenemento de Fothered", now represented by Straboe, a parish in the barony of Rathvilly.

In Charters CXXI and CXXII Robert de Cantiton confirms a gift by Gilbert Longus of the Church of Barrach (now Barragh, a parish in the barony of Forth O'Nolan) and half a carucate of land.

By an important inquisition dated May 6, 1290, it was found that Raymond le Gros enfeoffed Griffin FitzWilliam, his brother, of Fynnore[78] and Kells in Fothered, for the service of two knights and suit of his court at the castle of Fothered. The inquisition goes on to tell how after Griffin's death, Gilbert his son and heir succeeded, and left a daughter Clarice, half a year old at her father's death; how Gilbert's brothers Matthew[79] and Raymond entered upon the lands and held them adversely to Clarice; and how Clarice eventually recovered them at the price of giving up two thirds to William de Dene and Richard de la Rochelle, the representatives of the judiciary, and John FitzGeoffrey. Clarice married John, the son of Dermot Mac Gillamocholmog and bore him a son, John FitzJohn, who gave up the remaining third of the

---

[76] He was probably the son of Rees ap Griffith, who had detained FitzStephen (O'Donovan).

[77] i.e. as an atonement for the wrong done him by Dermot (O'Donovan)

[78] Killenora a townland in Kellistown - A.K.

[79] Matthew was given lands in Carrick-on-Suir but usurped the lands of the infant Clarice. Matthew was a witness to the charter of Geoffrey FitzRobert of the Priory of Kells in Ossory, which priory he largely endowed with the churches and chapels of his land. By a deed of 1228 he granted it, for the souls of himself and Matilda, his wife, all the ecclesiastical benefices of all his land of Forth in Leinster, namely Kellistown, Killenora, Moyle, Busherstown and Ballyveal. He seems to have died about 1247 and he was succeeded in the Forth lands by his brother Raymond. - A.K.

lands to William de Dene, and was himself killed at the battle of Callan in 1261.[80]

Raymond le Gros died without issue, and on the death of his wife Basilia, there being no direct line of descent, the title which he had acquired reverted to the representatives of Strongbow - the Mareschals.

As the title of Raymond le Gros pertained to the principality of the O'Nolans, we must endeavour to follow that title through its various stages through the 13th. century.

In 1189, William, Lord Maxfield, Earl Marshal of England, married Isabel, the only daughter and heiress of Strongbow and Eva. He was fourth in descent from Walter Maxfield, who accompanied William the Conqueror to England as his marshal. In 1191 William was appointed Governor of Ireland, in which office he continued for about six years. In 1191, also, he was created Earl of Pembroke, thus attaining to the rank, as he had previously succeeded to the possessions of his father-in-law, Richard, Earl of Pembroke. He arrived in Ireland again as Chief Governor in 1207, having in the interval been employed as ambassador to France, and in other offices of trust.

Immediately upon his arrival, he began the erection of his castle of Kilkenny and in the following year, 1208, received a renewal of the grant from King John, of the principality of Leinster, which he claimed to enjoy in right of his wife Isabel. It must be remembered, however, that Isabel had no claim according to the laws of Ireland, and therefore the grant was fictitious. William was also appointed to the post of Marshal of Ireland in 1208.

---

[80] We know from Eric St. John Brooks 'Knights Fees in Cos. Wexford, Carlow and Kilkenny' published in 1950, that Matthew the son of Griffin held two knights fees in Kellistown in Forth. This supports Fr. Nolan's theory that Forth was at one time considerably larger than it is today. By 1307 this holding was in the possession of Reginald le Dene and one Robert Bremyll held a third of a knight's fee in Balyscandal (perhaps Ballycallon) in Forth. The lands of Robert de Cantiton were held in 1247 by William le Gras (who founded Castle Grace, which passed to the Butlers in 1305), a nephew of Robert de Cantiton. The lands consisted of one knight's fee in Barragh and seemed to include Ballon and part of Aghade. Robert de Cantiton gave the church of Barragh as a gift to St. Thomas Abbey in Dublin prior to his death.

It is interesting to note that the amount of land allocated as a knight's fee varied, sometimes being smaller in peaceful districts. (Colfer in Anglo Norman Settlement in Co. Wexford - an article in Wexford History and Society ed. by K. Whelan). The fact that Barragh, which is quite a large area was given as one knight's fee would suggest that the area was relatively peaceful in the early days of the conquest, while the Kellistown/Killenora fief which warranted two knight's fees may have been more troublesome. -A.K.

The Charter giving the grant of Leinster to William is still extant and may be seen among the records preserved in the Tower of London and is dated 9th. John March 18.

During the visit of King John to Ireland in 1210 he divided the territory over which he had established feigned jurisdiction into twelve counties - Dublin, Meath, Kildare, Argial, Katherlagh, Kilkenny, Wexford, Waterford, Cork, Kerry, Limerick and Tipperary. The term county signified the territory of a count or Earl, and thus we can form a rough conception of the districts allocated to the various English barons as overlords.

Some of the counties have since then changed their boundaries. Thus Carlow at that time embraced the northern part of Wexford.[81] Over these counties sheriffs and other officers were appointed.

King John died in 1216 and was succeeded by his son Henry III, then only nine years old, who was proclaimed King in the presence of William Earl Marshal and Earl Pembroke, the Pope's legate and others. William was appointed Protector and director of the affairs of England. He died March 16, 1219.

When William Marshal senior died his eldest son and heir, William junior was full grown. In 1215 this William appears as one of the twenty five " Magna Charta Barons". His first wife died young, and as Earl of Pembroke he married, secondly, Eleanor, a sister of Henry III. There was no issue, and he died it was believed from the effects of poison, in 1231, and was buried in the choir of the Franciscan Church in Kilkenny, murdered under the guise of medical treatment by his own friends. This happened after a battle at the Curragh of Kildare, against the O'Connors. Gilbert, the third brother, succeeded and he was twice married. His second wife was Margaret, daughter of William, King of Scotland. He died without issue, having been killed by a fall from his horse at Ware, Hertfordshire, June 27, 1241.

Walter, the fourth brother, next became heir and he married Margaret, daughter of Robert de Quency, Earl of Winchester. He died without issue at Goodrich Castle near Monmouth on Nov. 24, 1245 and was buried at Tintern in Wales. Anselm, the youngest of the five brothers became Earl of Pembroke. He married Maud, daughter of the Earl of Essex and died without issue, eleven days after his brother Walter at Steigue (Chepstow) castle and was buried at Tintern.

The five brothers having died without issue, their five sisters became co-heirs. Their names were Maud, Isabel, Joan, Sibyl and Eva. The Irish lands which the Earl of Pembroke held by authority of the English Crown and claimed through Eva, the daughter of Dermot McMurrough were divided as

---

[81] In fact in the Fiants of the Tudor monarchs Arklow is included in Co. Carlow - A.K.

follows before the King, May 1247: Maud being the eldest, received Carlow[82]; Isabel received Kilkenny; Joan Wexford; Sibyl Kildare and Eva Dunamase (Queen's Co.). Maud was married twice at least. Her husband was Hugh Bigod, third Earl of Norfolk and Lord of Carlow. Of this marriage there were three sons. They were Roger 4th. Earl of Norfolk and Marshal of England, who died without issue, Hugh, whose son Roger became the 5th. Earl of Norfolk and finally Ralph who died during the lifetime of his brothers and although married, died without issue.

Roger the 5th. Earl of Norfolk, did homage to the King for the lands claimed by his late uncle Roger, the 4th. Earl, on July 25th. 1270. He was twice married and dying without issue on Dec. 11th. 1306, his Earldom, marshalsy and estates, including County Carlow, with its castles mostly in ruinous despair, passed to the King, (Edward 1) by means of a surrender to that end which had been made in 1302.[83]

Maud de Marshal, who had received Carlow as her portion ("the Castle, Manor and Burgh of Katherlac and Futhoret, now the barony of Forth") was married to her second husband, William Plantagenet, Earl of Warren and Surrey, before October 13th. 1225. William died on the 27th. May 1240, when his heir by Maud, John, Earl of Surrey was five years old. Maud herself died eight years later. The representation of Maud and her second husband William, passed by the said John, Earl of Surrey, to the Fitz-Alans, and so through the Mowbrays to the Howards; and in the Mowbrays the descendants of Maud by her second marriage regained the marshalship which her grandson by the first husband had surrendered to the Crown.

"The county of Carlow and Marshalship of England were afterwards granted by King Edward 1 to Thomas de Brotherton, from whom the lordship and county of Carlow descended through the families of Howard, Dukes of Norfolk, and Lord of Carlow and Berkeley, who forfeited by reason of the statute of Absentees (time of Henry VIII)" [84]

At the partition of Leinster among the five sisters, in 1245, as mentioned above, the portion of Forth O'Nolan which Maud received was valued at £53. 5s. 2d. A cow in those days was valued at 3s. 4d.[85]

---

[82] Anthologia Hib. Vol. 1 pg.38

[83] C.D.I. V. 54 etc., 617 In fact, despite having a massive income from his lands (which included the liberty of Carlow) of 6,000 marks a year plus income from his various offices as marshal, he was in considerable debt. According to W.F. Nugent *Carlow in the Middle Ages* in RSAI Jrnl. lxxv (1955) pp 62-77, he owed the King £20,000 and had to take this course of action to have his debt cancelled. - A.K.

[84] O'Ryan's Carlow

[85] Chart. St. Mary's Dublin, Vol. 11 pg. 403   C.DI. Vol 11 No. 933

In 1249 the manor of Forth O'Nolan was assigned as part of the dower of Margaret, Countess of Lincoln, widow of Walter Marshall. From the accounts of Hugh Bigod, Earl of Norfolk, which are still extant, we learn that next to the town of Carlow, Fothered was the principal burg of the district. It contained "eighty burgesses, paying a rent of 1s. each and 29 cottages paying together 13s. 11d. and 14 geese. A smith's workshop paid 4 horse-shoes.

This English settlement planted within their territory was shortly afterwards completely swept away by the O'Nolans who recovered their rightful inheritance and held complete possession of it during the fourteenth and fifteenth centuries. As early as 1306 the English castles in Carlow were "mostly in ruinous disrepair", and we find O'Nolan, the hereditary grand marshal of Leinster, acting in his rightful capacity and as the senior Lord of the Kingdom on the death of Donnell Reagh (McMurrough), inaugurating his eldest son Art Bui Kavanagh, or Yellow Art, as he was called, King of Leinster on the summit of Knockanvocka in the year 1511. Hore gives us in a few words a succinct account of the tribes and territories which O'Nolan solemnly committed to his sway on the occasion of his inauguration.

"The greater portion of the dominion of Donnell Reagh extended over the counties of Wexford and Carlow, in which he governed many subordinate septs - namely: the Kinsellaghs under their immediate head Mac Edmond Duff; the Mac Vadocs - inhabitants of the country surrounding the present town of Gorey; the Doyles, inhabiting around Arklow; the MacDamores, in the district still known as "the Macamores"; the O'Morchoes, or Murroughes (Murphys), in the country lying to the south east of Enniscorthy, and still called "the Murroghs"; the McEoghs, hereditary bards of the clan and the O'Dorans the hereditary judges or brehons; the Breens or O'Breens in the woody district called the Duffry, north west of Enniscorthy and in the adjoining shire of Carlow, the strong and warlike septs of the O'Nolans, O'Riains etc."

"Walter de Riddlesford founded a Nunnery at Grany, in the present baronies of Kilkea and Moone, about the year 1200, under the invocation of the Blessed Virgin, for Cannonesses of the Order of St. Augustine" [86]

A Charter, dated Nov.12th. 1207, makes a grant and Confirmation to the Convent of St. Mary of Grane, and the nuns there, of certain lands (named) tithes, etc., and also of the Church of Tristledermot (Castledermot), with its tithes and benefices, and all his patrimony; and the tithes of the expenditure of his house in meat, drink, and everything belonging to his table; as is witnessed by Walter's Charters held by the nuns.[87]

Pope Innocent III by a Bull in the year 1207, takes this nunnery and all its possessions into his especial protection, and particularly the grants made to

---

[86] Ware

[87] Charter 9th. John, M.S. Sweetman's Calendar St. Papers, 1. 355

them by Walter de Riddlesford, ut supra, the right of patronage of the churches of Tristledermot, St. Nicholas of Balinsderic in Fothered onolan (Fortonolan), and Kenheigh; and all the churches throughout the whole barony of Bre..........

In 1209 there were 300 Dublin people killed on "Black Monday". [88]

In 1227 civil war raged between Hugh de Lacy and William Marshal so that Meath was laid waste.

In 1234 Richard Marshal, Earl of Pembroke, was wounded seriously by the Geraldines in the battle of the Great Heath near Kildare and died on April 4th. Some say he was taken captive by de Lacy.

In 1258 Stephen Longspear was Justiciary of Ireland. In the town of Down, on the Sunday within the octave of the Ascension he slew O'Neill, King of Ulster, together with 352 of his supporters.

In 1264 there was a war between the Geraldines and Walter de Burgh, Count of Ulster. A conference was held at Castledermot, attended by Richard de Rupella, Lord Chief Justice, to deliberate on the sanguinary feuds between the Geraldines and the de Burghs. During this conference Maurice FitzGerald and Maurice, his son, captured Richard de Rupella, Theobald Butler, Miles Cogan and John Cogan and detained them in the prison Ley and Dunamaise and thence Ireland was filled with civil war between the Geraldines and the Burkes.

In 1268 William le Gras (or Grace) and another William of the same name, acted as Governors of Carlow in the years 1268 and 1275 and as deputies of the Earl of Norfolk, Lord Palatine of the district.

In 1269 there was an earthquake in Ireland.

In 1270 the King of Connaught conquered Walter de Burgo at the Ford of Athkyppe. Many knights and Nobles on the side of Walter were slaughtered and drowned and he himself escaped with great difficulty. The site of this ford is somewhere near Carrig-on-Shannon. Its name was probably derived from Ath-an-Chip - the ford of the stock or trunk.[89]

In 1271 there was a great famine all over Ireland, accompanied by widespread disease, pestilence and death.

The castle of Roscommon, built in 1269 was captured by the Irish in 1272.

Dermot Mac Murrough (Kavanagh) was captured in 1280 and two years following, in 1282, Art McMurrough Kavanagh and Murtagh Kavanagh were slain by the Butlers in Athlone - others say they were beheaded in Arklow.[90]

---

[88] Four Masters

[89] Four Masters 1270

[90] It is generally accepted that Arklow was the place of execution of these two men. - A.K.

In the next year, 1283, Waterford and Dublin were accidentally destroyed by fire and in the same year many English were slain in Ophaley, where Sir Theobald Butler lost his horses and men.

The castle of Ley, near Portarlington, was captured by the Irish in 1284 and in the next year Sir Theobald Butler died at Arklow.

Gerald FitzMaurice, the captain of the Geraldines, was taken prisoner by the Irish in Ophaley, in 1286, and there was a great slaughter in Rathoth. Gerald died the next year and his estates passed to John FitzThomas who was the first created Earl of Kildare.

In 1290 O'Mulseaghlin, King of Meath, was slain by McCoughlan. There was great mortality in Ireland during this year and the two following years.

On the feast of St. Margaret the Virgin, in 1294, there was terrific thunder and lightning, burning up the green blade and thus causing a great famine in Ireland. Many died of hunger. Calough O'Connor captured Trim and burned all the records, rent books etc. in the castle. Richard Burke, Earl of Ulster and William Burke, were captured by John FitzThomas, Earl of Kildare, on the Saturday before the feast of St. Lucy.

In the year 1296 William de Ross, prior of Kilmainham, was appointed deputy in room of Sir John Wogan. The absence of the English adventurers, who had been summoned to attend Edward I in Scotland, afforded an opportunity to the Irish chieftains to assert their independence. They made a fresh and noble effort to rid themselves of the hated foreigners. From the slopes of Slievemargy the O'Moores and their allies swept down on Old Leighlin and burned it and other towns around. The O'Nolans drove back the invader from their fertile plains, and the native chiefs on every side regained much of their former power and possessions, so that at the beginning of the fourteenth century we are told:- " The O'Carrolls in Ely O'Carroll were able to defy Ormonde and all his power; the O'Mores were as firm in Leix as their own rock built castle of Dunamaise; the O'Nolans held their own in Carlow, and were able to inflict a serious defeat on Bermingham and his allies (1322); the O'Tooles and O'Byrnes[91], in their mountain fortresses at Wicklow, defied all attack, and a chief of the McMurrough Kavanagh family was acquiring such power that in the not distant future that family would overshadow all Leinster"[92]

---

[91] When the Fitzgeralds took possession of Ui Faelan in the northern half of Kildare they forced the O'Byrnes, who were kinsmen of the O'Tooles, to retreat into Wicklow. - A.K.
[92] Dalton, Vol II cxxl

Chapter 10

The 14th. Century

Sir John Wogan was Lord Justice of Ireland for thirteen years (1295 - 1305). When he arrived in Ireland a bitter feud raged between the Burkes and the Geraldines. Wogan reconciled both parties, after which he summoned a parliament which provided for a stricter guard over the Marches, so as " to keep out the Irish", and then proceeded "with a smart party" to aid the king of England in his Scots wars. Taking advantage of the opportunity thus offered, the Leinster Irish made a bold effort to assert their independence. They destroyed many of the English fortresses, burned Wicklow, Arklow and Rathdown and devastated the surrounding districts.[93]

The year 1305 "produced abundance of villainy" says Cox, " for Jordan Comin with his complices murdered Mortagh O'Connor, King of Ophaly and Calvagh his brother and some others, at the house of Pierce Bermingham (Piers Mac Fheorais) in Carbury, in County Kildare."

The O'Connors[94] of Offaly were for nearly two centuries amongst the most heroic and therefore the most dangerous of the "Irish enemies". Maurice and Calvagh were at this time the heads of their sept, Calvagh being called "the Great Rebel", from the fact that he had more than once defeated the English with great slaughter. The Chiefs of Offaly were invited to dinner on Trinity Sunday 1315 by Bermingham. They accepted the invitation in a spirit of unsuspecting hospitality, but as they rose up from table they were cruelly massacred in cold blood. There were in all thirty two murdered. Complaint of this treacherous outrage was made to Edward I, but no redress was ever obtained except what Irish swords secured.

Portion of this castle can still be seen at Carrick Feorais near Castle Carbury, Co. Kildare.

---

[93] Cox

[94] Co. Offaly was originally granted by Strongbow to de Bermingham. Before the reign of Edward II it had become divided between the Berminghams and the Fitzgeralds who became Barons of Offaly and the O'Connors who retained possession of the western wooded parts of the county. After the rebellion of Silken Thomas in 1536 the title of Baron of Offaly was granted to the O'Connor and Sir Wm. Birmingham was made 'lord over his country'.- A.K.

About this time also (1307) Murrough Ballagh Kavanagh was beheaded at Merton. " On the first of April, Murcard Ballagh is beheaded by that brave Knight, David Cantiton" [95]

Bermingham apparently was allowed to die in his bed, but for the last mentioned cowardly act of murder "that brave Knight" Cantiton was lodged in the castle of Dublin the following year.

"On the 13th. April 1308 died Peter Bermingham, the noble tamer of the Irish.....David Cantiton is hanged at Dublin."[96]

Two years before (1306) Peter Bermingham " the noble tamer of the Irish" was defeated in Meath, the castle of Ballymore Eustace was burned down and its Governor, Henry Celfe, there slain by O'Nolan and O'More and their confederates. A great war raged through Leinster. The castle of Geashill, built by Thomas FitzMaurice, in the territory of the O'Connor Faly was demolished by O'Connor and the castle of Lea laid siege to by the O'Dempseys.[97] But John FitzThomas and Edmund Butler appeared and raised the siege.[98]

On every side the castles of the settlers went down and their power was broken to such an extent that "the English were summoned out of the other provinces to the relief of Leinster. They had a notable battle at Clenfel where Sir Thomas Mandeville fought valiantly until his horse was killed under him. It is evident that Sir Thomas did not "fight valiantly"[99] after his horse was killed or it would have been recorded.

On February 3rd. 1308 the Knights Templars (who had built the castle of Ballymoon in Idrone in 1301) were suppressed and their effects confiscated to the Crown. In the same year William Burke became Deputy and Cox states that in his time the Irish burnt Athy. He was succeeded by Pierce de Gaveston, "an insolent Frenchman", detested by the English nobility, but favoured by their King. "He slew Dermot O'Dempsey, a great Irish Chieftain, at Tully; he marched into Munster and subdued O'Brien in Thomond; he rebuilt the new castle of Mackingham, in the Kevin's country and repaired the castle of Kevin and cut and cleaned the passes between that and Glendalough."[100]

In 1310 Edward II granted a charter to the burgesses of Old Leighlin in which it is recounted that the King "for the public good and to resist the wickedness of the Irish living in the neighbourhood of Leighlin, has granted the

---

[95] Grace

[96] Ibid

[97] The Chief of the O'Dempseys was created Viscount Clanmalier in the reign of Queen Elizabeth. - A.K.

[98] Lodge's Peerage

[99] Cox

[100] Ibid

said men a ' muragium' (i.e. a grant for building walls) for the purpose of enclosing the said town." [101]

A patent dated the previous year, appoints J. de Boneville, in His Majesty's castle at Carlow, Seneschal of Carlow and Kildare and refers to the robberies, depredations etc., committed in the County of Carlow. But Boneville did not long enjoy his preferment for on February 2nd. in the same year (1309) Sir John Boneville was slain by Sir Arnold Poer at Ardscoll. Afterwards at a Parliament, held in Kildare, Poer was acquitted of the death of Boneville as it was found to be in self defence.

In 1311 the O'Byrnes and O'Tooles invaded Saggard and Rathcoole and struck terror into the inhabitants of Dublin, by lurking up and down the woods of Glendelory (Glenmalure) and the state could not suppress them. But in the next year Sir Edmund Butler, Deputy of Lord Justice Wogan, besieged the O'Byrnes in Glenmalure and compelled them to submit and sue for peace.

Having defeated the O'Byrnes he reduced the country to such a state of tranquillity that, "from Arklow to Clonmore and thence to Carlow and even to Limerick, he was accustomed to travel with only three horsemen." [102]

But things were scarcely so rosy as all this for we find in 1313 that " Richard Lawless was Mayor of Dublin, and Hugh Lawless and others his adherents, were commissioned to parley with the Irishry of the south-eastern parts of the Pale - the O'Tooles, the O'Byrnes and the McMurrough Kavanaghs." [103]

"Commissioned to parley with the Irishry of the south-eastern parts of the Pale"! This is something new and we are forced to look for the reason. We find it in the following short paragraph from an English historian - " It was in full confidence of victory that Edward II had hastened to Bannockburn; he fled from it with a party of Scottish cavalry at his heels; nor did he dare to halt, till the Earl of March admitted him within the walls of Dunbar, whence he proceeded by sea to England. His privy seal and treasures, with the military engines and provisions for the army fell into the hands of the conquerors." [104]

Edward II was defeated by the Scots under Bruce at Bannockburn, and now the Scots were preparing to land and liberate Ireland - "but the Scots were not content with asserting their own independence; they undertook to free Ireland from the English yoke. That island was now divided between two races of men,

---

[101] Strangely in this year also all the sept of the O'Nolans were pardoned for good service fighting with the justiciar against the Cantitons. (B. Colfer - in an unpublished work relating to the Norman conquest). - A.K.

[102] Dowling

[103] State Papers

[104] Lingard 1315

of different language, habits and laws and animated with the most deadly hatred towards each other."[105]

From these extracts we learn what was at the root of the proposed parley with the Irish. But the overtures for peace were rejected by the Leinster Chiefs and soon their clansmen were mustering for the great struggle now so close at hand " to free Ireland from the English yoke."

In the midst of this mighty bustle of preparation Edward Bruce, brother of Robert Bruce, King of Scotland, landed at Cushendun in the north of Antrim with 6,000 men. He was immediately joined by Donal O'Neill, price of Tyrone and other Irish Chiefs. He encountered and defeated the Red Earl of Ulster at Coleraine and slew many of his followers. Proceeding onwards through Meath and Westmeath he ravaged all the towns of the English Pale and meeting Roger Mortimer, Earl of March at Kells, with an army of fifteen thousand men, Bruce defeated him with great slaughter. "Roger", says the annalist " takes flight towards Dublin, and Walter Cusake towards Trim."[106]

Bruce spent his Christmas at Lough Seudy, one of the castles belonging to his friends the Lacys of Westmeath.

During all this time the men of Leinster were busy. There was feverish preparation going on within the ranks of O'Nolan and his allies. All Leinster was ablaze and the anvils rang out night and day in Forth O'Nolan, Clopook and St. Mullins, in the Duffry, Glenmalure and the Glen of Imaal[107], whilst the brawny smith fashioned the white steel into broad -swords, battle-axes and spears. But the Norman barons were not less busily occupied. They were mustering mighty forces and when the fatal day arrived, the Lord Deputy, Edmund Butler, aided by Thomas, Earl of Kildare, Arnold le Poer and others commanded an army far superior in numbers and equipment to that of the Leinster Confederates.

The Lord Justice retired to Dublin and summoned a Council of the English to deliberate as to the best means of carrying on the war. It was decided to begin by attacking the O'Nolans, O'Moores and O'Tooles. The forces at their command were formed into three divisions. One proceeded to attack O'Toole, another O'Moore and the third was sent forward to deal with O'Nolan, in the vain hope that having reduced the Leinster Chieftains they might the more easily subdue Bruce and his northern allies. This plan eventually proved a failure, although the brave O'Moores of Leix suffered a severe defeat at the hands of Edmund Butler, the Lord Deputy himself, who "brought back 800

---

[105] Ibid

[106] Grace

[107] Got its name from a corruption of the Irish Ui Mail, i.e. the descendants of Mal. Mal was the brother of Cahir Mor, monarch of Ireland in the 2nd. century - (from A History of the Clan O'Toole) - A.K.

heads to Dublin."[108] As for the O'Byrnes they "burned the whole country south of Dublin, that is to say Arklow, Newcastle, Bray etc." [109]

The O'Tooles issued forth from the impenetrable fastnesses of Imaal and after a long and bitter struggle in which they lost 400 men, drove back the English forces at Baltinglass. " The Irish of Imaal attacked Tullow, and lost four hundred men, whose heads were brought to Dublin; marvellous things occurred - the dead rose again and fought with one another shouting their cry after their fashion - 'Fennock abu' -"[110]

It was the living and not the dead who raised the war cry of the O'Tooles, for the undaunted warriors who, at such heavy sacrifice, held the field at Baltinglass, thence swept westward through Wicklow and Kildare, carrying fire and sword into all the enemy's quarters till they reached Athy, "burning and spoiling Wicklow as far as Athy." [111]

The O'Nolans, McMurrough Kavanaghs and the O'Byrnes[112] of the Duffry, who had mustered at Myshall and Newtownbarry[113] marched north and encountered a strong force of the English at Castledermot, under the command of Sir Arnold Power (Le Poer), who must have had at his command between eight and ten thousand men.

O'Nolan and his confederates decided to give battle, and on the Feast of the Epiphany, January 7th. 1317, after a fierce and deadly combat in which the forces under O'Nolan were victorious, the English were forced with great slaughter to retreat to Narraghmore. It was on the very same day that the O'Mores were defeated in Ballylethan, that O'Nolan dealt this crushing blow to the English at Castledermot.

"The Lord Justice," says Cox, "was not less active in Leinster; for he defeated O'More at Ballylethan and made a great slaughter of the rebels at TristleDermot, and slew about four hundred of the Irish of Omayle." All the slaying was not, however, on the side of the Lord Justice for O'Nolan slew Sir Peter Rochford and Sir Oliver Grace two of the commanders of the army under Sir Arnold Power, and probably some six or eight hundred of his supporters.

"About the feast of the Epiphany, the O'Nolans slew Peter Rochford and Oliver the son of David le Grasse and about 80 others belong to the army of Arnold le Poer, who was their chief and leader"[114] When an English annalist sets down the number slain as 80 we may multiply by ten. But let the number

---

[108] Grace

[109] Ibid

[110] Ibid

[111] Clyn

[112] He means the Breens or Briens of the Duffry - the descendants of Sil Brain

[113] Then as now called Bunclody - A.K.

[114] Clyn

be small or great the fact remains that O'Nolan was victorious and the English did not try conclusions with him again until the arrival of the army of Edward Bruce. Early in the year 1317 Bruce "went to Totemoy, Rathangan and Kildare, the neighbourhood of Castledermot, Athy and Rheban, yet not without loss; afterwards he came to Skerries at Ardscoll in Leinster where Edmund Butler, Justiciary, John FitzThomas, Arnold Power and other nobles of Ireland opposed him and any one of them alone could easily have drove him back, but they quarrelled among themselves and all of them retreated. Hamond Grace was killed in action and William Prendergast; of the Scots fell Fergus Ardrossan and Walter de Moray with many others whose bodies are buried in the Convent of the Friars at Athy."[115]

Passing through Kildare, Bruce rapidly pushed forward his forces to Athy in the hope that he would there intercept Butler on his return from Leix, but the English forces had made a rapid retreat and reached the main army at Narraghmore safely, before the converging forces of Bruce and O'Nolan had time to cut them off at Athy. The English were, however, forced to give battle at the famous moat of Ardscoll, four miles east of Athy on January 26th. 1317.

The Lord Deputy, Edmund Butler, Earl of Carrick, commanded the English, and Bruce had by his side McMurrough (Kavanagh), O'Nolan, O'Toole and O'Byrne, together with the other Irish chieftains who had rallied to his standard. It was a fierce struggle. Long did the tide of battle ebb and flow. The recollection of the cruel wrongs they had suffered and the memory of their recent victory over Le Poer gave fresh vigour to O'Nolan and the men of Leinster. While the sturdy Northern clans dealt death around on every side, the heroes of Bannockburn were at Ardscoll. Numbers were more equal with the result that the English forces were overthrown and completely routed with enormous slaughter. Sir William Prendergast and Hamon le Grasse two of their generals died (as already alluded to above - A.K.), while the O'Nolans and O'Tooles found Sir John Lyvet among those that fell beneath their swords to rise no more.[116] These Knights fell on the same battle field and they sleep in death within the same sanctuary. They are all buried in the Dominican Abbey of Athy.

In the course of this year, Robert Bruce landed at Carrickfergus, with a large force to support his brother Edward. Their combined forces must have amounted to fully twenty thousand men. They ravaged the English Pale as far as Slane and thence marching towards Dublin, arrived at Castleknock, took Hugh Tyrell, baron of Castleknock prisoner and established their headquarters there. Fearing an assault on the city of Dublin the inhabitants burned the

---

[115] Grace
[116] Clyn

96

suburbs and Bruce seeing their determination turned south with his army and overran Leinster and Munster. "He swept the country coming south to Castleknock. He burned Naas, Castledermot, Carlow, Gowran alias Balla Gowran, Callan and Cashel and proceeded to Limerick for Easter where he proclaimed himself Monarch of Ireland."[117]

He laid siege to Kilkenny and demolished its castle, rooting out on his path every vestige of English power, while the Butlers, FitzGeralds, Le Poer and other English barons collected an army of over thirty thousand men to oppose him. The O'Nolans, O'Mores, McMurroughs and the rest rallied to his standard and gave him all the assistance in their power. Every native Chief with one exception stood by Bruce and that exception was O'Madden. " O'Madden of Hy Many alone of all the Irish chieftains remained faithful to the Earl of Ulster during the Scottish invasion. The Earl, to reward his fidelity, allowed one third of his province to be subject to O'Madden, that no English stewart should be over his Gaels, and that his stewards should be over the English of the entire territory, both towns and castles. O'Madden and his blood were also declared noble as the Earl and his blood, though the ordinary principle of the English lords was that the Gael, though a landholder, was ignoble, and that the Saxon was noble though without education or lands" [118]

It is said that Bruce defeated the English in no less than eighteen battles, but the Scots and Irish were at length compelled by a dreadful famine to retire to Ulster, with the remnant of their forces, now reduced to three thousand men. The English, having collected a great force the following year, met the army of Bruce at Faughart, near Dundalk, on May 28th. 1318. Bruce's force was defeated and he himself was slain. He was found amidst a heap of the dead, and his head was cut off, salted, brought in a box to England and presented to King Edward. For this act, Birmingham was created Earl of Louth. The body of Bruce was buried in the old church yard of Faughart, and a large pillarstone erected to mark his grave. Here sleeps this noble Knight, who struck for freedom at Bannockburn, and having gained the independence of his own country "undertook to free Ireland from the English yoke."

The death of Edward Bruce did not damp the ardour and determination of O'Nolan and his brave compatriots. He was ever vigilant, ever on the alert, watching and waiting another opportunity to strike home. It came in 1322. "The King," says Cox, " on the third of April in the 15th. year of his reign, wrote to the Lord Justice to meet him at Carlisle within the octave of the Trinity following, with three hundred men-at-arms, a thousand hoblers, and six thousand footmen armed with a Keton, a Sallet and Gloves of Mail, to serve against the Scots, besides three hundred men-at-arms which Richard de Burgo,

---

[117] Dowling
[118] Rites and Customs of Hy Many pg. 139

Earl of Ulster, had, for his own share, undertaken to conduct; and though the English suffered a defeat by O'Nolan, so that Andrew Birmingham, Nicholas de London, and many others were slain, and though the Lord Justice lost his son, Richard, Lord of Athenry, who died about this time; yet all this did not hinder him from attending the King; but he left in his place Ralph de Gorges, Lord Deputy or Governor."

This victory of O'Nolan is referred to by the Annalists as follows:- "About the vigil of St. Luke the Evangelist (Oct. 17th. 1322), the O'Nolans slew Andrew Birmingham and Sir Nicholas de la Launde with many of their followers." (Clyn) - "1322. Andrew Birmingham and Nicholas de la Launde with many others are killed by O'Nolan on the day of St. Michael (Sept. 29th.) - Anno 1322 died the Lord Richard Birmingham, Lord of Athenry, the Lord Edmund Butler, and the Lord Thomas Persival." (Marleburrough).

We meet with this Lord Andrew Birmingham in February 1317, where it is recorded that "Sir Hugh Canon, Chief Justice of the Court of Common Pleas, was murdered by Andrew Birmingham between Naas and Castlemartin." [119]

In 1318, immediately after the defeat of Bruce, "the Lord Justice caused John de Lacy to be pressed to death at Trim, because he would not plead to the indictment against him." [120] The de Lacys had supported Bruce.

Edward III was proclaimed King of England on January 25th. 1327. He was then but fifteen years old and the Queen Mother and Mortimer usurped and exercised all the powers of government. The Earl of Kildare was made Lord Justice of Ireland. His salary was £500 a year and Roger Outlaw, Prior of Kilmainham, was made Lord Chancellor. His salary was £40 a year. A bitter feud broke out between the Earl of Desmond, aided by the Butlers and Birminghams on one side and Lord Arnold Power aided by the Burkes on the other.

In the midst of this turmoil the undaunted Leinster Chiefs decided on making another effort to effect a complete liberation of Ireland. Donald Art McMurrough (Kavanagh) was solemnly inaugurated King of Leinster by O'Nolan on the hill of Knockavoca. "The men of Leinster made a King for themselves to wit Donald McMurrough, who had resolved to go through all Ireland and subdue it."[121] The Royal Standard of Leinster was unfurled and the valiant clansmen went forth to battle. They took possession of all the English castles in their march and advanced within a couple of miles of Dublin city. Here a bloody encounter was fought with the forces of the English Pale under the command of Sir Henry Trahern and Walter de Valle. The Leinster men

---

[119] Cox
[120] Ibid
[121] Grace

were defeated and suffered heavy losses. Donald Art McMurrough was taken prisoner and O'Nolan was killed together with twenty four of his Captains.[122]

McMurrough was brought to Leixlip by Sir Henry Trahern and there detained until a ransom was paid for him by the English Crown, when he was removed to Dublin Castle. "McMurrough was taken prisoner by Sir Henry Traharn, who first brought him to Leixlip, where he received a hundred pounds for his ransom, and then brought him to the Castle of Dublin, where he placed him until his case should be decided."[123]

In those days a prisoner was often released on payment of a ransom by his friends. Here, however, the Crown paid the ransom and thus bought McMurrough, lest his own friends might redeem him from captivity.

After the defeat at Dublin, the King of Leinster now being in the hands of the English, the confederate forces retired southward, by way of Rathcoole and Dunlavin, fighting a stubborn rearguard action every inch of the way.[124]

They were pursued by Lord John Wellesley who succeeded in capturing David O'Toole near Dunlavin. David was the grand old Chieftain who had been leader of the clan for over fifty years and had stood on the heights of Ardscoll with Bruce and O'Nolan when the English flag was humbled to the dust. "David O'Toole, a Strong Thief, who had been taken prisoner was executed at Dublin."[125] For this capture Wellesley received an order from the Government for the sum of £24.

The State Papers give further particulars:- 1328, Davie O'Toole was led from the Castle of Dublin to the Tholsol of the city, and there, before Nicholas Hastocke and Elias Ashbourne, who judged that he should be drawn through the city after a horse's tail to the gallows, and after being there hanged to be drawn and quartered, which was done. He was looked on as a Strong Thief, the King's great enemy and the destroyer of his people."

From this eulogy we learn what a fearless and undaunted hero David O'Toole must have been in the defence of the hearths and homes of Imayle. Aedh O'Toole succeeded his father as chief of the clan and very soon gave a good account of his prowess.

---

[122] Clyn

[123] Grace

[124] Fr. Nolan maintained that these forces were commanded by O'Nolan, as Grand Marshal of Leinster, but this was an error as O'Nolan had been killed in the battle. Therefore I omitted that sentence. (A.K.)

[125] Cox

O'Nolan immediately set about reorganising the Leinster army and was loyally supported by the McMurroughs, O'Tooles, O'Byrnes and other septs.[126]

The Butlers, in order to disconcert the plans of O'Nolan, made a raid upon his territory and endeavoured to burn or otherwise destroy what they were unable to carry off, but O'Nolan despatched a few companies of his men who came up with the marauders near Ballynakill and routed them with great slaughter, killing David Butler who was their Captain and in command of the party. "On the Saturday before the feast of St. Lawrence (Nov.14 1329) the O'Nolan slew David Butler and immediately afterwards on the vigil of St. Lawrence, Sir Thomas Butler and Sir J. Warrin and with more than one hundred others was slain."[127]

On November 21st. "Sir Henry Trahern and Lawrence, brother of Sir James Butler were captured by O'Nolan, on account of which Sir James Butler, having gathered a great army, on Thursday, the day after the feast of St. Lucy, Virgin, (Dec. 14th.) and Friday following laid waste his territory and almost left desolate his country with fire and sword."[128]

Another annalist says:- " Philip Staunton is slain. Henry Trahern is taken by stratagem in his own house at Kilbeg, by Richard, son of Philip O'Nolan. Sir James Butler burned Forth, the country of O'Nolan for the same cause." [129]

It is not quite certain where Kilbeg was situated. It may have been Kilbegs, in the barony of Clane, Co. Kildare, but more probably it was at Leixlip, where Trahern had evidently his stronghold and where he detained Donald McMurrough as a prisoner until the Crown paid his ransom. But it is evident that O'Nolan did not know of the removal of McMurrough to Dublin, which must have been done surreptitiously when he despatched his brave and loyal Captain, Richard O'Nolan, with a chosen band of stalwart men on the hazardous expedition above mentioned. The object was the liberation of the King of Leinster; but if in this they failed, they attained a great victory in securing two of their most virulent enemies - Sir Henry Trahern and Lawrence Butler. According to Grace they were taken by stratagem in Trahern's stronghold after which Richard O'Nolan immediately retreated south and placed his prisoners in a place of security.

When Ormonde learned the news he was very wrath and gathering together a great army he invaded Forth O'Nolan on December 13th. and 14th. and laid waste the country with fire and sword. He did not, however, do this

---

[126] This O'Nolan must have been the newly elected man who succeeded the O'Nolan who had been killed. (A.K.)

[127] Book of Ross

[128] Clyn

[129] Grace

100

without suffering severely nor did he succeed in liberating his friends, for Richard O'Nolan retired by Drumfea and Rathanna to Graigue- na- managh, where the O'Nolans had loyal friends.

Ormonde, having failed in his main object, led the battered remnant of his forces back to Gowran where he refitted them for an attack on Graigue-na-managh, in the great monastery of which Richard O'Nolan had lodged his prisoners. At the end of the month of December Butler appeared before the monastery and besieged it. Richard O'Nolan had but a few men and soon he was compelled to seek safety in the bell-tower, which was a place of great strength, the only approach to which was by a narrow crooked stone stairway. Here Richard and his valiant followers made a determined defence and dearly did Ormonde pay for any advantage that numbers gave him. The approach was narrow and the swords of the O'Nolans keen, and their arrows fled swift and sure. Richard might well have defied Ormonde's power for long enough had not hunger accomplished what numbers failed to do. He was compelled at length to capitulate, deliver up his prisoners and give his own son as a hostage. " Richard O'Nolan, on the vigil of the Feast of the Circumcision was besieged in the Campanile of the monastery of Dowsky and compelled to deliver up his own son as a hostage." [130]

This historic tower was octagonal in design and justly regarded as one of the most beautiful ecclesiastical structures in the Kingdom. The noble ruins of the abbey still remain to attest to its former greatness, but the tower has disappeared. On a spring day in 1744, some four hundred years later than the time when the events took place which we have just recorded, a number of children playing around suddenly heard a tremendous crash and beheld the tower fall to the ground, bringing with it three or four great arches which supported its weight. The traveller, however, who visits the ruins of this great abbey church of Graigue-na-managh today, may still see portion of the narrow stone stairway which Richard O'Nolan defended with such undaunted courage.

But Ormonde was determined to crush and if possible exterminate the royal race of O'Nolan and become possessor of their rich and fertile country. In this he was pampered and supported by all the strength and influence of England. Honours and riches and power were lavishly bestowed upon him and for centuries the O'Nolan was forced to contend not only with a grasping adventurer but with one hungering to death for his lands- and having at his command all the available resources of the English Crown.

It is difficult to clothe with life and animation the dead bones of the annalist - but we find Ormonde on January 14th. with a party of his murderers, without any apparent provocation, attacked Richard O'Nolan and killed him. "

---

[130] Clyn

On Monday, the feast of St. Hilary, Richard, the son of Philip O'Nolan was slain by Butler and his relations."[131]

Notwithstanding, however, all that Ormonde could do, the Lord Justice, Sir John D'Arcy, dreading the growing power of the Leinster army under O'Nolan, summoned his Council, and resolved to appeal to Maurice, afterwards, the Earl of Desmond, to support Ormonde in his efforts to conquer the Leinster forces. Maurice already had under his command a vast army with which he had been preparing to make war upon Lord Arnold Poer and the Burkes, and with this he marched immediately to the relief and aid of Ormonde who was sorely pressed. "But the Lord Justice, finding himself too weak to deal with such a vast number of rebels as were now in arms in all parts of the Kingdom, invited Maurice FitzGerald to take the field, and promised him the King's pay. Maurice came accordingly, with a considerable army and marched against the O'Nolans. He routed them and burned their country so that they were forced to submit and give hostages. He did the like to the Kavanaghs and took the castle of Ley from the O'Dempsies. But the Lord Justice was not able to pay so great an army (being near ten thousand men) and therefore he was fain to connive at their extorting coyne and livery which now was first practised by the English."[132]

Davis observes that " the revenue of the land was far too short and yet no supply of treasure was sent out of England." Consequently, in this war against O'Nolan the English for the first time adopted the brutal method of free quarters or 'coyn and livery' as it was called. The soldiers were quartered on the inhabitants and allowed to support themselves by the most arbitrary exactions. Riot, rapine, massacre and all the tremendous effects of anarchy were the natural consequences.[133] Every inconsiderable party, who under the pretence of loyalty, received the king's commission to repel the adversary in some particular district, became pestilent enemies to the inhabitants. Their properties, their lives, the chastity of their families, were all exposed to the barbarians who sought only to glut their brutal passions and by their horrible excesses, saith the annalist, "purchased the curse of God and man." [134]

In various parts of Ireland by arbitrary exactions and oppressions of this sort the more powerful English Palatine Lords banished the native inhabitants,[135] and erected themselves into independent sovereigns. To

---

[131] Clyn

[132] Cox

[133] The soldiers were quartered on the colonists not the Gaelic inhabitants as Fr. Nolan seems to think. (see D'Alton's History of Ireland pg. 371) - A.K.

[134] Leland Vol. 1 pg. 280

[135] The opposite was the case - the colonists were the ones who suffered - "their exactions while they ruined the English settlers, enriched Desmond and increased his power, for many

encourage and strengthen the power of Maurice Fitzgerald and James Butler, who were summoned by the Lord Justice to withstand the O'Nolans and their confederates, the one was created Earl of Desmond (Deas Mumhan- South Munster), the other Earl of Ormonde[136] (Ur- Mhumhain - east Munster) and their possessions were converted into counties palatinate. By this the number of palatinates was increased by nine; Carlow, Kilkenny, Wexford, Kildare and Leix, part of Meath, Desmond and Ormonde. The power of the palatine lord was unlimited. "Those absolute palatines made barons and Knights; exercised high justice in all areas within their territories; erected courts for criminal and civil cases and for their own revenue, in the same form in which the king's court was established at Dublin; made their own judges, seneschals, sheriffs, coroners and escheators: so that the King's writ did not run in those counties, which took up more that two parts of the English colonies, but only in church lands lying within the same which were called 'The Crosse', wherein the King made a sheriff."[137]

We can here learn the enormous power and influence wielded by the Earls of Kildare, Ormonde, Desmond etc. It was no wonder that O'Nolan and his allies rose up in their might and fought with such determination to shatter this intolerable yoke which it was sought to place upon their unwilling shoulders. The Earl of Desmond brought with him a vast army of over ten thousand men. He had also with him a renegade Irishman and his followers - "Bryan O'Bryan and one thousand soldiers." This O'Bryan had been chosen to command the English and Irish forces that opposed Bruce at Limerick.

The Earl of Desmond first marched on O'Nolan who met him with his forces near Nurney, and valiantly withstood the onslaught until the vast army arrayed against him threatened to envelope his lines; then retreating slowly through the rugged country towards Ballytarsna Castle, one of his outposts. O'Nolan hung on the outskirts of the invaders, and while they pillaged and burned his country, he, by sudden sallies and night attacks, exacted a heavy toll of life and limb from his adversaries. Eventually he safely conducted his army through Fenagh to the Burren river where fresh levies of his own men and others under the McMurrough chiefs joined him, and compelled the Earl of Desmond to open negotiations for a truce, when hostages were given by both O'Nolan and McMurrough that they would keep the peace.[138]

---

of the settlers gave up their lands which were immediately handed over to Irishmen, who held them under the Brehon system of tenure and willingly recognised Desmond as their chief." (D'Alton pg. 371) - A.K.

[136] According to D'Alton he quickly followed in the footsteps of Desmond and forced the ejectment of his English settlers. - A.K.

[137] Davis

[138] Pembridge

This happened in the month of January 1330 and here according to the annalists amidst the fair lands of Forth O'Nolan, coygn and livery were first practised by the English. The brutal soldiery were allotted quarters and allowed to rifle the churches, to pillage the country, to burn down the houses and haggards and to carry away enormous booty.[139]

The above account is further collaborated by Lewis as follows: "About this time the castle of Clonmore was taken by the English, yet, notwithstanding the advantage thus gained, Sir John D'Arcy, the Lord Justice, could devise no more effective means for repressing the spirit of insubordination than by calling in the assistance of Maurice FitzGerald, afterwards Earl of Desmond, whose services were purchased by a promise of remuneration from the treasury, and whose compliance changed the aspect of affairs. Advancing against the McMurrough Kavanaghs and the O'Nolans, he ravaged their district, compelled their subjection, and exacted hostages for its continuance. But the most disastrous effects were produced by this connection; the Lord Justice, unable to fulfil his pecuniary engagements was forced to connive at the extortion of coyne and livery now first practised by the English; a grievance the more intolerable as it was limited neither in place or time. Every lord of a castle, or warden of the marches, made war at his pleasure, until the desolation became universal and threatened to be perpetual. Still, however, the Irish, though worsted on most occasions, were in arms."

No wonder that the O'Nolans and Kavanaghs are soon on the march again to avenge, as they did, the cowardly and cruel wrongs inflicted by the spoilers of their country.

Within a week after the events just recorded "Donald Art McMurrough Kavanagh escaped from the Castle of Dublin. Adam Nangle had given him a rope for which he was afterwards hanged."[140]

Pembridge says:- "The said Adam, being discovered, was hanged and drawn."

No sooner had the McMurrough regained his freedom than the beacons flashed once more from the Leinster mountains and the English interests in his Kingdom shrunk almost to vanishing point. "The Lord Justice received the bad news that the Irish had taken and burned the castle of Ferns, whereupon he grew jealous."[141]

"The whole of the County Carlow and the best part of Wexford were once again under the control of their ancient dynasts."[142]

---

[139] See notes above re same - A.K.
[140] Grace
[141] Cox
[142] Sir C. Coote - Survey Queen's Co. pg.64

The country over which the McMurrough exercised immediate sway was known as Hy- Kinsellagh[143] and comprised the County of Wexford, the barony of Shillelagh in County Wicklow and Kavanagh's country in Co. Carlow. [144]

The English forces made a sudden onslaught probably towards Tullow or Clonegal, and committed serious depredations but they were soon driven back within the borders of the Pale and many of the castles still remaining in their hands were wrested from them. Marlborough informs me that :- "There was a great slaughter made of the Irish in O'Kenslie, and the castle of Arklow was taken by the Irish and great slaughter made of the English in the Cowlagh by Otothell, where Sir Philip Brint and many others were slain. The castle of Ferns was taken and burned by the Irish."

This Sir Philip Brint was Sheriff of Dublin in 1329. According to Grace " the Irish are slain in Hy Kinselagh by the English on 14th. of April: the castle of Arklow taken by stratagem by the Irish on the 21st. April: on the same day the O'Tooles carried off three hundred sheep belonging to the Archbishop of Dublin from Tallaght, and killed some of his men, the news being brought by word of mouth to Dublin: there are also killed by stratagem by the O'Tooles at Cullagh (Tullow?) Philip Bret, the brother of Maurice FitzGerald the Hospitaller and many others.......William Bermingham led an army against the robbers and killed some of them, but is deceived by their false promises." That is the O'Tooles led them into an ambuscade where many of them lost their lives. It will be noticed that every victory gained by the Irish, was, according to Grace, gained by stratagem.

About the end of the year 1331 the Leinster septs are again in arms. "The Leinster Irish rise against the English; they set fire to everything, even the churches, and burnt the Church of Freynstown with eighty persons in it; and even the priest in his sacred vestments, and carrying the host in his hands, tried to get out and they drove him back with their spears, and burned him; for this cause they were excommunicated by a Papal Bull sent to the Bishop of Dublin and the country put under interdict. They despised these things and again wasted the county of Wexford. But at Ballycarney (apud Carconnam) four hundred of them were killed by Richard Whitty, Richard FitzHenry and the townsmen of Wexford , and many others of them were drowned in the River Slaney." [145]

---

[143] Ui Cheinnselaigh (A.K.)

[144] St. Mullins Lower and Upper. (Actually the Kingdom of Ui Cheinnselaigh comprised all Carlow, Wexford, South Wicklow and east Kilkenny. - A.K.)

[145] Grace

The Church where the above incident took place was situated at Freynestown in the barony of Upper Talbotstown[146], Co. Wicklow, and lay to the east of Colbinstown and at the foot of Glen Imaal in the country of the O'Tooles. We cannot justify, but we may endeavour to palliate such conduct. There can be little doubt, however, that the outrage was grossly exaggerated by those who reported it to the Holy Father. Moreover, it was not necessary for the O'Tooles to have long memories to recall the acts of barbarity to which they had been subjected by the strangers who had seized their lands. Only a couple of years before their aged king David O'Toole, was dragged ignominiously to the scaffold, through the streets of Dublin, tied to the tail of a horse.

We also learn from Grace that:- " In 1316 the Irish of Imaal made an attack on Tullow (or Tallaght) and lost 400 men, whose heads were brought to Dublin Castle, and a marvellous thing occurred: the dead arose again and fought with one another, shouting their war-cry after this fashion- 'Farrah-aboo!"

Of course the dead did not rise and shout but the English annalist endeavoured to paint an imaginary picture for the amusement of his own patrons. But if the dead did not arise the living watched and waited for sixteen years until they had a chance of balancing the account, which evidently they did at Freynestown, when the murderers of their fathers were assembled within the Church.

In 1332 "the castle of Arklow is retaken by the Justiciary, who drove out the Irish and is repaired."[147] But at the same time the O'Tooles capture and burn the castle of Lyons or Newcastle, which had been built on the ruins of an old castle belonging to Teig O'Byrne.

In the year 1337 "James Butler, first Lord Ormonde died at Balligaveran. Lawrence Butler, brother of the Earl was slain by the O'Nolans on Friday the vigil of the Assumption."[148] This was the Lawrence Butler who was captured by Richard O'Nolan in the castle of Sir Henry Trahern.

Notwithstanding the life long efforts of the first Earl of Ormonde to exterminate and crush the O'Nolans, we find on his death that they were practically supreme in their own country, and the English Government had acknowledged the power, and recognised the position of the McMurrough as lawful King of Leinster, and agreed to pay him 80 marks a year on condition that he would not molest their possessions and also agreed to allow the English settlers on the borders to pay O'Nolan what afterwards became known as 'Black Rent' in recognition of his authority and as an acknowledgement of

---

[146] Talbotstown got its name from Piers Talbot, who after he had defeated and slain Tirlogh O'Toole got possession of a large portion of his lands. -A.K.

[147] Grace

[148] Clyn

their dependence upon him. "It appears further that a temporary protection from the predatory assaults of the borders could only be procured by the degrading payment of a tribute called the Black Rent."[149]

Theobald Walter was created Chief Butler of Ireland about 1177. In a charter to the burgesses of Ballygaveran he styles himself 'Theobaldus Walter, Pincerna Hiberniae', and grants to them certain lands at a rent of ten marks of silver a year (Carte's Ormonde - Introduction). Carte also says that by an entry in the Register of the diocese of Ossory, dated at Kilkenny November 2, 1312, William, Bishop of Ossory undertakes to support, in the church of the Blessed Virgin Mary at Ballygaveran, four priests to pray for the soul of Edmund Butler, his wife Joane, etc., etc. The church of the B.V.Mary still exists for the most part in ruins, except the chancel which is used for Protestant services.

These four priests lived collegiately as it appears from the Regal Visitation Book of 1615 at present in the Royal Academy.

The value of the vicarage of Gowran was reduced by more than one half by the devastations consequent on the invasion of Edward Bruce. Bruce, on raising the siege of Dublin in 1316, marched southwards and was at Gowran sometime before the 12th. March of that year, old style. [150]

James, grandson of the above named Edward and third Earl of Ormonde built the castle of Gowran in 1337. This castle was razed to the ground in the 19th. century by Viscount Clifden. The site is still shown.

In 1382 Richard II granted licence to Thomas Derkyn and Walter Cantwell "living in the marshes of Ballygaveran, in front of the Irish enemies, McMurrough and O'Nolan, to treat for themselves, their tenants and their followers."[151]

The castle of Walter Cantwell stood at Stroan and Cloghscregg on the verge of the barony of Gowran, in 1382 the "marshes" of the Pale. He died in 1409, as on the 18th. March in that year the custody of the lands of Robert, son and heir of Walter Cantwell in Rathcoull and Strowan, was committed rent free to Richard and Thomas Cantwell. These lands were on the following 16th. December granted by the King to Robert Cantwell (on his coming of age) - "all the land and tenements, rents and services which the said Robert held in Rathcoull and Strawan in the Co. of Kilkenny, then in the King's hands."[152]

In after years they were finally lost by the forfeiture of Thomas Cantwell of Cantwell's Court, who was appointed provost marshal by the Supreme Council of the Confederate Catholics sometime after 1641, and is called "that

---

[149] Lewis

[150] Annals in Camden and Grace's Annals pg. 81

[151] Rot.Pat.5 Rich.II prima pars. No. 192

[152] Rot. Pat. 10 Hen.IV 2a pars No. 18 and 87

cruel and bloody rebel" in one of the depositions given in Temple's Irish Rebellion.[153]

Hugh de Gundevilla supposed by some to be Hugh Cantwell, came to Ireland with Dermot McMurrough. One of these Cantwells - 'Hugh Cantoval' - was left afterwards in charge of Waterford by Henry II. The Kilkenny branch of the family had their principal castles at Cantwell's Court,[154] now Sandsford Court near Kilkenny, and at Stroan, Kilfane and Cloughscragg not far from Gowran. The massive keep of Cantwell's Court still exists, but the remains of Stroan and Cloughscragg are inconsiderable, while of Kilfane castle there is now no trace. The charter granted to Gowran by Theobald Walter, first Butler of Ireland is witnessed by D. Thomas de Kentewell, whence it is probable he had seized upon these lands before 1206, the year of Theobald Walter's death.

In 1338 Edmund (Burke) son of the Earl of Ulster, was taken prisoner by Edmund Burke (MacWilliam) who tied a stone about his neck and drowned him in Lough Mask (Co. Mayo).[155]

In the year 1339 there was a universal war throughout the whole of Ireland. Two hundred Irish were killed in Kerry by the Earl of Desmond and three hundred were slain at the river Barrow by the men of Kildare. "An enormous prey is taken and driven away from Idrone by the Bishop Justiciary."[156] "The greatest booty, that ever was taken in that country was brought by the Lord Justice and the English from Idrone in the county of Cather Lough about the latter end of February, and in the April following the Lord Justice being sent for to England, resigned."

This Episcopal cattle stealer was a brother of the preceding Lord Justice, Sir John Charleton. He was the Bishop of Hereford and succeeded his brother as Lord Justice in 1339, resigning in 1340. During his term of office, as representative of Edward III, King of England, he utilised the forces of the English Crown to rob the native Irish of their cattle. Aided by the Butlers and others he swept away the herds from whole stretches of country and was favoured by Edward III with a letter of commendation for his conduct and an order to the Treasurer at Dublin to pay the Viceroy's salary before that of any other official.

But the O'Nolans and the Kavanaghs knew how to bide their time and to await the proper moment to seek restitution of at least a portion of their

---

[153] 1812 Ed. Pg. 119

[154] One William Cantwell seems to have been an agent of the Government in the mid 1500s He was certainly a scribe as he was ordered to write to Shane O'Neill and he was threatened with having one of his ears cut off for "counterfeiting the hands of certain of the Privy Council" (CSP) - A.K.

[155] Annals of the Four Masters

[156] Grace

plundered property. Accordingly we find them in the following August advancing on Gowran, which they burned to the ground, slaying every follower of the Earl of Ormonde they could lay hands upon[157] and driving back to their own country the herds of cattle which had been surreptitiously carried away.

Such terror did they strike into the Butlers that steps were soon taken to wall around and fortify the town of Gowran. A grant of tolls, such as were levied in the town of Kilkenny, was made to Ballygaveran, for forty years, to enable the burgesses and community to pave and wall their town, which had been lately burned, and the lieges therein destroyed by the Irish enemy by whom it was surrounded "and who daily threatened to do so again"[158] Not many years later the Kavanaghs seized upon the lands and castles of Idrone and continued to hold them for centuries in spite of all the power of England.

"All Leinster was at war with the English during this year (1346), burning, spoiling and slaying all they could; not sparing ecclesiastics nor shrines, nor anything consecrated, even the very churches and cemeteries in various places they spoiled and burned."[159]

According to Grace the castles of Ley and Kilmehide were burned in April by the Irish. In June three hundred at least of the English of Uriel were slaughtered by the Ulster men. D'Arcy, the Lord Justice, invaded Leix and compelled O'Moore to submit, although he resisted obstinately. The following year Donald McMurrough son of Donald Art McMurrough Kavanagh, King of Leinster, was treacherously killed by his own people on the 5th. July 1347.

"A great pilgrimage took place to St. Mullins in September and October of the year 1348. Bishops, priests and princes together with the people of all sexes flocked to St. Mullins in multitudes, so that frequently there were many thousands present on one day. Some came out of devotion, others through fear of the great plague which spread over the country from Howth and Drogheda where it first appeared destroying and sweeping away vast numbers." So wrote Friar Clyn from the Franciscan monastery in Kilkenny, of which he was the first guardian. The great plague was carrying away hundreds under his very eyes every day. "The pestilence," he says, "was rife in Kilkenny in Lent, for, from Christmas day to the 6th. March eight friars, preachers, died of it. Scarcely one alone ever died in a house. Commonly husband, wife, children and servants went the one way, the way of death." He then goes on to say he had kept a record of the things he had seen and had learned from persons worthy of credit. While "waiting for death till it come", he leaves a parchment for continuing the work, "if haply any man survive, or any of the race of Adam

---

[157] Clyn
[158] Rot.Pat.2 Hen V. 153 - Calendar of Rolls
[159] Clyn

escape this pestilence." He draws a vivid picture of the manner in which the pestilence spread and of its symptoms and its effects.

"That pestilence deprived of human inhabitants villages and cities and castles and towns, so that there was scarcely found a man to dwell therein; the pestilence was so contagious that whatsoever touched the sick or the dead was immediately infected and died; and the penitent and the confessor were carried together to the grave; through fear and dread men scarcely dared to perform the offices of piety in visiting the sick and in burying the dead; many died of boils and abscesses, and pustules to their skins or under their armpits; others died frantic with the pain in their head, and others spitting blood; that year was beyond measure, wonderful, unusual and in many things prodigious, yet it was sufficiently abundant and fruitful however sickly and deadly."[160]

The pestilence referred to by Clyn was the 'Black Death.' It swept over Asia, Europe and Africa carrying away hundreds of thousands of victims. The number of deaths in Avignon, where the Pope at that time resided, from the Black Death was 500 a day with a total of 60,000 or more than double the entire modern population of the city. Between August and Christmas over 4,000 souls are said to have perished in Dublin alone. "Ireland," we learn from Dr. Hecker, "was much less heavily visited than England. The disease seems to have scarcely reached the mountainous districts of that kingdom."[161]

"In some religious houses," writes Walsingham who died in 1440, "of twenty members only two survived; the pestilence was followed by a mortality of animals and a fall of rents; the land was left untilled from the want of labourers; and such misery ensued that the world has never been able to recover its former state."

"A great plague raged in Ireland (1349) and particularly in Moylurg (Roscommon), by which an immense number of people were destroyed."[162]

A.D. 1354 The McMurrough was put to death by the English and a great war arose in consequence thereof, between the English and the Irish."[163]

We learn from Grace's Annals that Thomas Rokeby was made Justiciary for the second time in 1356[164] and died the same year. "He was a just and prudent man, who used to say that he had rather eat and drink out of wooden vessels so that he could spend gold and silver on food and clothing and hired

[160] Clyn

[161] The Epidemics of the Middle Ages - Hecker 1832 pg. 27

[162] Annals of the Four Masters

[163] Annals of the Four Masters

[164] In this year also the inhabitants of Tullow were given permission to levy a tax for the purpose of building a wall around the town - A.K.

soldiers." "I am served," said Rokeby, "without parade or splendour, but let my dishes be wooden rather than my creditors unpaid." [165]

It was probably at the suggestion of this "just and prudent man", who nevertheless was opposed to "the King's Irish enemies" that the King of England issued a writ to the Lord Justice and Chancellor on the subject of exactions known as coygn and livery. In this writ he denounces the purveyors of the Justiciary and other officers for being "in the habit of taking and carrying off without price or tally, as well in churches and church fees, as elsewhere, and chiefly from the poor, oxen, cows, sheep, pigs, capons, hens, chickens, fish, wheat, barley, oats, straw and litter against the will of the people, commonly without giving any price or tally, or at most scarcely a third part of the real value; and by this extortion, from which the rich who made presents to the officers were saved, oppressed the poor and people of the whole land were reduced to poverty."[166]

The nature and consequence of these exactions are set forth in the preamble of a Statute - (10 Hen. VII c.4 not printed) - which states, " that a long time there hath been used and exacted by the lords and gentlemen of this land, many and divers damnable customs and usages, which being called coin and livery and pay, that is, horse meat and man's meat for the finding of their horsemen and footmen, and over that 4d. or 6d. daily to every one of them, to be had and paid of the poor earth-tillers and tenants without anything doing or paying therefor. Besides many murders, robberies, rapes and other manifold oppressions by the said horsemen and footmen daily and nightly committed and done, which have been the principal causes of the desolation and destruction of the said land, so as the most part of the English freeholders and tenants be departed out of the land, some into the realm of England and other some to other strange lands, whereupon the foresaid lords and gentlemen of this land have intruded into the said freeholders and tenants' inheritances and the same keepeth as their own, and setteth under them in the same land the King's Irish enemies to the diminishing of Holy Church's rites, the desertion of the King and his obedient subjects, and the utter ruin and desolation of the land."[167]

In 1356 in consequence of the invasion threatened by the Leinster Irish under the McMurrough and O'Nolan aided by a great multitude of other Irish, a royal hosting of the English at Newcastle McKynegan was proclaimed through all Ireland, and the sheriffs of Dublin, Meath, Wexford, Connaught, Roscommon, Louth, Waterford, the Cross of Ulster, Kildare, Limerick, the

---

[165] Leland Vol.1 pg.312
[166] Rymer Vol.111 pg. 340
[167] Davis's Discovery pg. 143-44. See also Chpts. XVIII and XIX 10. Henry in printed Statute.

Cross of Kerry, Carlow, Cork, the Cross of Tipperary, Meath and Kilkenny were ordered to proclaim it in their several bailiwicks.[168]

During this war "the castle of Kibelle, the property of Sir John Cornwall was destroyed by the O'Nolans. Two fortalices at Galbarrstown and Rathlyn, near Leighlin, suffered the same fate at the hands of the Kavanaghs and Byrnes."[169]

On 22nd. August, William Vale, Sheriff of Carlow, who had lost all his goods and chattels and friends and relations in repulsing the O'Nolans, when the Confederated Irish were burning the towns and the corn fields, and carrying off everything without resistance, and who had killed Donald Tagsone O'Nolan,[170] and many others of their captains and had brought their heads to the Castle of Dublin by the King's order, when he could have had great ransom for delivering them elsewhere, had an order for £30.[171]

In the year 1358 an order was made that no English Lord or other person should leave Ireland without special licence, the reason probably being that their presence would be required in Ireland to meet the growing power of the Kavanaghs and O'Nolans and the confederate Irish.

On the 8th. May orders were given that no one should furnish horses, armour or victuals to Art Kavanagh, the McMurrough and Donal Reagh who with others had made insurrection in Leinster. To meet the expenses of this war and to pay the soldiers, the English districts were assessed in various amounts. Thus the subsidy for Kildare ordered to be levied in the barony of Kilcullen was a crannock of wheat, a crannock of oats and a fat cow for every carucate[172] of titled land. The Earl and county of Kildare also supplied the pay of twenty four men-at-arms with armed horses at 8d., two hundred hobelars at 4d. and four hundred foot at one and a half pence per diem for a fortnight , or as long as the war should last.[173]

This order was made on the 3rd. August but as the war terminated on 12th. August the levy was not imposed. The Earl of Kildare, however, was paid according to agreement with certain persons in Co. Carlow - 60s for preventing the O'Moores from burning the town of Killaban.

On the 9th. November Thomas Stafford had an order for £8 for a horse he had lost while in attendance upon the Justiciary in a raid upon the Kavanaghs and O'Moores of Slemargy and Thomas de Baa, Esquire of Almaric

---

[168] Rot.Cl. 29 et 30

[169] O'Ryan

[170] The son of the ruling king of the O'Nolans

[171] Rot. Pat. 32 Ed. III .57

[172] 120 acres

[173] Rot. Pat.32 Ed.III 92.

de St. Amand, Justiciary, had an order for £10 for a horse lost in like manner.[174]

Referring to this struggle the Four Masters under the year 1358 says:- "O'Moore gained a great victory over the English of Dublin and left two hundred and forty of them dead on the field of battle."

James Butler was appointed Justiciary on February 16th. 1359 and on the 20th. July following the king issued a writ ordering all proprietors of the marches to reside on their lands under penalty of forfeiture.

On the 18th. March a writ was issued summoning the Bishops, Lords, Knights and citizens of Leinster to a council to be held at Dublin on the Monday before the Feast of St. Ambrose (April 3rd.) and the Bishops, Lords, Knights and citizens of Waterford on the same day. The cause of the summoning of this council was the insurrection of Art McMurrough Kavanagh. The council granted a subsidy in Waterford, Cork, Limerick and some other places. Messengers were sent to England from a parliament held in Kilkenny. On June 6th. Fitzpatrick of Queen's County was allowed £10 for giving support to the Justiciary in his expedition to Slievemargy against the McMurrough and Maurice Boy O'Moore, Lord of Slievemargy, who were compelled to give hostages which hostages were placed in the custody of Adam de Grantham, constable of the castle of Carlow. Notwithstanding this partial success, the Justiciary was compelled on July 26th. to summon another council to be held in Dublin on the Monday following the feast of St. Peter ad Viacula (August 7th.) "on account of certain most urgent matters concerning the peace of Ireland and more especially of Leinster."[175] McMurrough and O'Nolan were about to break out in a resolute effort for freedom.[176]

"The most powerful princes of the Lagenian Heremonians were the Ui Cheinnselaigh, descendants of Fiacha Bacceda, the youngest son of Cahir the Great, the last monarch of the Lagenian Heremonians A.D. 177. They governed the province of Leinster for 993 years, to the death of that profligate prince Dermod Mac Murchadh."[177] The meaning of the word Ceinnselach in Irish is given as 'ceann' signifying head or chief and 'saeghlach' meaning an elder or judge or King (it also means a standard bearer, a president or a governor). Ceinnselach therefore means the Head King or Chief Governor, which would correctly represent the position of the McMurrough in Leinster among the other dynasts of that Kingdom.

---

[174] Rot. Cl. 32. Ed.III 1. pars. 9&10

[175] Grace's Annals ed. by Dr. Butler

[176] The concept of national freedom was unknown at the time in the Gaelic kingdoms. They fought just to secure their own patch. - A.K.

[177] O'Conor of Balengar

113

When Dermot McMurrough died at Ferns in 1172 he left no legitimate male issue, but he recognised as his own, two sons born to him out of wedlock, one of whom was named Donal "Kavanagh" from having been educated at Cill Caomhan or Caomhan's church, in the county of Wicklow."[178] " From this Dermot came the Kaevanaghs, a very worthy and powerful family more like to the ancestors of Dermot than to Dermot himself."[179] From the brother of Dermot whose name was David, descended the powerful family of MacDavid More, whose descendants are still numerous within the borders of the ancient royal patrimony in the county of Wexford. Donald, called the 'handsome' was loyal to his father, and fought by his side until the end. He was proclaimed the McMurrough in succession to Dermot. He was one of the Irish Kings who did homage to Henry II when that monarch came to Ireland, and possibly by so doing he brought upon himself the displeasure of O'Nolan who killed him in battle shortly afterwards.[180]

Donal was succeeded by his son Donal Oge, of whom nothing is heard and matters remain obscure till we find Murtogh McMurrough King of Leinster in 1283. "Murtogh McMurrough (Kavanagh) and his brother, Art, lost their heads at Arcloe, or, as some say at Wicklow."[181]

The next McMurrogh Kavanagh we meet with in history is Donald Art McMurrough (1316) who is thus referred to by an English historian: "The meanwhile Edward Bruce reigned in Ulster, held his courts, pronounced his enemies traytors, abandoned the English blood, exhorted the Irish of Leinster to doe the like, whereupon Donald the sonne of Arthur Mac Morrow, a slip of the royal family, displayed his banner within two miles of Dublin, but him Trahern tooke prisoner, sent him to the castle of Dublin, whence he escaped, slyding down from the Turret, by a cord that one Adam Nangle brought him. The said Nangle was drawne and hanged."[182]

To Donald succeeded Maurice, to whom the English Government agreed to pay the sum of 80 marks yearly (1335) on condition that he would not molest their possessions. To Maurice the rightful succession would have been Dermot, but as the English captured and kept this prince in prison till his death in 1369, Art, another son, became the McMurrough. In a parliament held by the English at Castledermot (1358), Art and Donald Reagh were proclaimed

---

[178] Keating

[179] O'Conor of Balengar

[180] This is at variance with the account of his death in my book "In the Shadow of Mount Leinster. He was killed in a battle near Dublin between the Irish (Donal had declared himself King of Leinster and joined forces with O'Connor) and the Normans, by a countryman of his own in the pay of the Normans

[181] Ware's Antiq.pg.58

[182] Campion pg. 123

rebels and great preparations were ordered to be made to crush them. In the midst of all the confusion of war, and preparation for war, a son called Art was born to Art McMurrough (1357). He was destined to even overshadow his own father as a just king, a fearless soldier and a persistent and successful avenger of the wrongs of his country. Trained and disciplined in arts of war and peace he grew up to manhood gifted and endowed with all the powers of mind and body of a great leader and a valiant champion. His youthful mind was only beginning to expand, when in 1367 he had an opportunity of grasping the full meaning of allowing to remain within our shores an unscrupulous and dominant foreign foe.

In the year 1360 the King of England's son came to Ireland. He was Lionel, Duke of Clarence, third son of Edward III, who, being appointed by his father, Lord Lieutenant of Ireland, landed at Dublin on the 15th. September with a force of fifteen hundred men, consisting of archers and men-at-arms, together with Ralph, Earl of Strafford, who was one of the commanders under the Black Prince, at the battle of Crecy; James Butler, Earl of Ormonde; Sir John Carew; Sir William Windsor and other knights. The Duke of Clarence was accompanied by his countess, Elizabeth, daughter of William de Burgo, Earl of Ulster, and in right of his wife he became Earl of Ulster and Lord of Connaught, titles still held by the royal family of England. The Duke of Clarence held the office of Lord Lieutenant till 1367 and it was during his administration that the celebrated Parliament of Kilkenny was held in which the Act called "The Statutes of Kilkenny" was passed.

Lionel was the first styled by patent Locumtenans or Lord Lieutenant. At his first coming he was about twenty years of age and had been married at the age of ten, in 1347 to Elizabeth, then sixteen years old, who was the only daughter of the murdered Earl of Ulster and Maud Plantagenet. The object of this early marriage was to secure to the English royal family the vast estates of William Burke, her father, known as the Red Earl.

"William Burke, Earl of Ulster, was on the 6th. June 1333, basely murdered by his own perfidious servants at Carrickfergus; whereupon his wife and only daughter sailed to England; the daughter was afterwards married to the Duke of Clarence and had only one daughter who was the wife of Roger (Edmund?) Mortimer, Earl of March and Lord of Trim and from her the Earldom of Ulster and the Lordship of Connaught came by descent to be annexed to the Crown."[183]

The only daughter of the Duke of Clarence was Phillippa and she was married in 1380 to Edmund Mortimer, Earl of March. He died at Cork, in the Dominican Abbey on December 26th. 1381. By this marriage there was an only son, named Roger heir to the Crown of England. The O'Nolans slew him

[183] Cox

in battle, and later we shall find Phillippa coming over to Ireland and imploring O'Nolan to grant her the dead body of her son, that she might carry it back to England. The roll of Lionel's army is still preserved in the office of the king's Remembrancer in England.

Lionel was allowed 13s. 4d. a day for himself, 2s. a day for eight knights, 6d. each for 360 archers on horseback, out of Lancashire, and 2d. each for 23 archers out of Wales. Under him came Ralph, Earl of Strafford with his man and Sir William Windsor and Sir John Carew, Banneret, who had 4s. a day and 2s. for each of two knights, 1s. each for 8 esquires and 6d. each for 10 archers on horseback. James, Earl of Ormonde had 4s. a day and 2s each for two knights and 1s. each for 27 esquires and 6d. each for 20 hoblers armed and 4d. each for 20 hoblers unarmed.

On March 15th. 1361 the King issued a writ to all the proprietors of lands or benefices in Ireland resident in England, declaring that because that the land of Ireland was almost totally lost to the Irish enemy on account of the weakness of the loyal subjects, arising from the absentee lords and others taking profit from their lands and doing nothing for their defence, and that he determined to send his son there with a great army, and summoning them to appear before him at Westminster to treat on the subject and in the meantime ordering them to make ready men and arms.[184] An aid was then granted by the absentees of two years profits of their lands and tithes to carry on the Irish wars.

We are told that in 1361, " Art, the McMurrough, King of Leinster, and Donald Rivach (Kavanagh), heir presumptive to the Crown of Leinster, were treacherously taken prisoners by the King of England's son, at his own residence and they died in prison." [185]

Lionel returned to England on April 2nd. 1364, leaving the Earl of Ormonde as Lord Deputy. This Lord obtained a licence from the King to purchase lands to the value of £60 per annum, non obstante the statute of ordinance, that no officer of the King should purchase within his jurisdiction. Lionel returned on December 8th. but made a very short stay. He returned again as Lord Deputy in 1367 and it was then he held the parliament at Kilkenny which passed the famous statute " the Bishops of Dublin, Cashel, Tuam, Lismore, Waterford, Killaloo, Ossory, Leighlin and Cloyne (who were present at this parliament) did fulminate an Excommunication against the transgressors of that Law."[186]

The importance attached by Lionel to the possession of the district of Forth O'Nolan is shown by his causing the King's Exchequer to be removed to

---

[184] Rymer Vol. III pg. 609
[185] Annals of the Four Masters
[186] Cox

Carlow, and by his spending the then very large sum of £500 in fortifying it with walls, of which at present there is no vestige.

Before long O'Nolan and his allies compelled the English to withdraw from Carlow and remove the boundaries of the Pale back again to the very gates of Dublin. There is extant in the Bermingham Tower a record of 37th. Edward III. "Pro Barrio Amovendo a Catterlogh usque ad Dublinium."

"Thus the works erected by Lionel, Duke of Clarence, at Carlow, proved totally useless, inasmuch as the retention of that place was no longer possible."[187]

In 1363, all the issues and profits of Ireland from whatever source were appropriated to the maintenance of the war in the country.[188]

We have already seen how the Red Earl of Ulster was treacherously slain by his own servants, and the McWilliam Burkes of Connaught had drowned the Earl's son in Lough Mask.[189] The marriage of Lionel to the Earl's only daughter gave him title in English law to the vast estates of the late Earl both in Ulster and in Connaught.

But the junior branches of the Burke family, fearing this transfer into strange hands of their family inheritance, seized and divided amongst themselves the Burke estates, renounced English laws and language, and adopted together with the titles and war cries, the language and customs of their Irish neighbours. They became more Irish than the Irish themselves. In fact most of the descendants of the first invaders were becoming rapidly assimilated and absorbed into the warm and generous soul of the Irish nation and it was greatly feared that England would soon lose all hold, even upon her own colonists. To meet this danger, as also to guard and defend the interests he himself had in the estates of the Earl of Ulster, Lionel summoned a parliament to meet in Kilkenny in 1367, over which he presided as the representative and Viceroy of the King of England. This parliament passed the famous "Statutes of Kilkenny," the main effect of which as set down by an English historian are as follows:-

"That the Brehon Law is an evil custom, and that it be Treason to use it; that marriage, nursing and gossiping with the Irish be Treason; that the use of Irish name, apparel or language be punished with the loss of Lands or imprisonment until the party give security to conform; that the English should not make war upon the Irish without Order of the State; that the English should not permit the Irish to Creaght or graze upon their lands nor present an Irishman to an Ecclesiastical Benefice, nor receive them into Monasteries or

---

[187] O'Ryan

[188] Rymer Vol. III pg. 714

[189] Fr. Nolan seems to have made a slight error here as there is no previous mention in his manuscript of the drowning of the Red Earl's son.

117

Religious Houses, nor entertain any of their Minstrels, Rhymers or News-tellers, nor cess Horse or Foot upon the English subject against his will on pain of Felony; that the Sheriffs might enter any Liberty or Franchise to apprehend Felons or Traytors; and that four Wardens of the Peace should be appointed in every county, equally to assess every man's proportion of the publick Charge for Men and Armour."

Notwithstanding these statutes, however, the Irish continued to use the Brehon Law until the third year of James I who was proclaimed King of England on March 24th. 1602.

By a study of the Statutes of Kilkenny we learn the relations then existing between the English Government and the Settlers, on the one hand and the Settlers and the native Irish on the other. From it we see at a glance the civil, social, commercial, military and religious state of Ireland in 1367. Friendly relationships were rapidly springing up between the descendants of the early English settlers and the native Irish. to prevent the growth of this kindly feeling a wall of separation wide and high was erected by the Statutes. It was a declaration of eternal antagonism to the native inhabitants, their race, name, customs, dress and language. To understand the position we must remember that certain parts of Ireland were subject to English dominion. These districts comprised what was called the "English Pale" and embraced portions at least of some twelve or thirteen counties.[190] Then there was the Irish territory subject to its own native chiefs. And between these two districts there was the borderland called the "marches". These marches were generally the base line of a mountain, the outskirts of a bog, a river, a deep wood or any other natural fortress which formed a secure defence for the persecuted natives. This border line fluctuated with the tide of war, but it is certain that at the period under consideration almost all Wicklow, the north of Wexford, practically the whole of County Carlow, together with the present Kings and Queens counties were occupied by the sturdy Irish clans, who maintained their independence and stoutly resisted all inroads on their rightful inheritance. These border septs were called in the statutes " the Irish enemy" and with them there was to be no alliance, no marriage, no fostering of children, no intercourse whatsoever. They were to be either trampled down or driven out. Even in times of peace neither horses nor armour were to be sold to them, and not even victuals, in time of war, under penalty of death. To attend fairs held amongst the Irish enemies, whether in peace or war, was afterwards made a felony in a parliament held in 1429. All barter and exchange were prohibited lest the Irish might be able to equip themselves more thoroughly with horses, armour etc.

---

[190] The barony of Forth in Wexford and part of the barony of Bargy constituted the Wexford Pale and in Carlow the area around Carlow and Leighlinbridge was the 'Carlow Pale'. (A.K.)

for use in time of war. The Irish knew well the disadvantage they suffered from deadly combat with the mail clad soldiers of the stranger as we learn from the lament of O'Neill's bard, MacNamee, at the death of O'Neill who was slain at the battle of Downpatrick in 1260, along with fifteen of the O'Kanes and many other Gaelic chieftains. " The Galls from London hither, the hosts from Waterford came, in a bright green body, in gold and iron armour; unequal they entered the battle, the Galls and the Irish of Tara. Fair satin shirts on the race of Con; the Galls in one mass of iron."

By these statutes we also find the wandering minstrel, the piper and the story teller were banned lest information might thereby be carried to the lines of the ever watchful border septs. The Irishman beyond the Pale was the 'the enemy'; within the Pale 'the outlawed slave'.

In spite of this enactment we find the Irish language almost universally spoken outside a few garrison towns as late as the year 1540.

Another part of the Kilkenny law stated that "no Irishman living on the March, or Frontier shall pasture or occupy the lands of the English or Irish (who are at peace)." Pasture in those days was the principal wealth of the border clans. The O'Nolans kept immense herds of cattle on the high lands of their lordly principality; in time of war these were driven across the borders and allowed to fatten on the well cultivated valleys of the Pale. The herd was called a creaght and the shepherd or guardian called a kreight was armed with a club or battle axe and a side sword to suit his character as a shepherd soldier. How often has not this lonely watchman sat on the slopes of Mount Leinster, Knockbrack or Kilbride and watched the glimmering waters of the river Slaney or traced at sunset the outlines of Slievemargy against the western skies, while his herds browsed peacefully in the valley below. The beautiful picture drawn by Gerald Griffin with little change must often have been that of the kreight of Forth O'Nolan.

> On Slaney's side the day is closing fair.
> The Kern sits musing by his shieling low,
> Or marks beyond the lonely hills afar
> Blue, rimmed with gold, the clouds of sunset glow;
> Along the sunny highland pacing slow
> The kreight lingers with his herd the while,
> And bells are tolling faint from fair Kildavin's Isle.

We learn, however, from the following extract from an act passed in 1440, that the statutes of Kilkenny did not frighten away the O'Nolans and their neighbours from grazing their herds upon the border lands and sometimes within the Pale itself.

"Whereas divers Irish .....living on the marches without the licence of our Lord the King, did, at the time of war lay waste and destroy the march lands and bring their creaghts, to wit, horses, heifers, oxen, sheep, calves, pigs great and small, goats and all their other goods and chattels within the land of peace called Maghers, and there dwell without leave of the lords of such lands and as well, cut and burn their woods and gardens as graze and destroy their meadows and pastures - it is enacted that neither in time of peace or war shall the creaghts pass from the march lands into the land of peace, under pain of imprisonment of the drivers and forfeiture of the whole creaght of which half to be given to the King and half to the injured party."

The 'land of peace' was the Pale and 'the land of war' was the marches which the O'Nolans and their confederates held so persistently and so well against all enactments, statutes and aggression.

"Some Anglo- Irish writers," says Hardiman, "have laboured to show that the statutes of Kilkenny mainly answered the purposes for which they were intended and it had been seen that those purposes were principally to keep the English and the Irish forever separate. But it was too short-lived to answer all the ends of the promoters. A paper, written in the time of Elizabeth and preserved in the British Museum, states, that after the death of Lionel. ' the laws died with him also; but the distrust and disunion which they created, survived and continued to disturb the country for more than two centuries after.' The result was such as might be expected. English power and influence declined, insomuch that, at the close of the century succeeding, they had almost ceased to be a force in Ireland. "At the beginning the native Irish, apprehending that the real object of the law was to root them out altogether naturally combined for safety and some of the more powerful chieftains resolved upon immediate hostilities..... the English of the Pale were seized with consternation and dismay while the natives continued to gain ground in every direction."[191]

As the O'Nolans marched against the Pale and stood their ground so nobly and so well through all these trying times, we give another extract which may be read with interest as exemplifying their position, customs and difficulties.

"The Statutes of Kilkenny were promulgated in several successive parliaments, but the settlers found the strict application of their provisions more prejudicial to themselves than to the natives. The King of England was thus fain to accede to petitions in which the commonalties of his towns declared their inability to pay taxes, and that they should be ruined or famished unless authorised to trade with and make purchases from the Irish.

Numerous applications were also made by the settlers for permission to send out their children to be fostered among the Irish; and we have on record

---

[191] Tracts relating to Ireland Vol.II

120

the official concession to a memorial from some liege English, praying that an Irish minstrel might be allowed to sojourn among them, notwithstanding the express prohibition under the Statutes. Governmental licences were also frequently issued for holding parleys with the Irish. These negotiations were usually held on the borders, the respective parties coming to the appointed place with a few attendants, while their troops were drawn up within call. The borders formed the resort of bodies of mercenary light foot soldiery styled 'kern' and battle axe men called Galloglaoigh or gallowglasses, who, living by war, were ever ready to accept service from either Irish or colonists, who secured payment and maintenance for them. Beyond the wasted and desolated marches or borders lay the Irish territories, almost inaccessible through woods and narrow defiles, rendered impassable with peculiar art in times of war. Within these and other defences were the habitations and the cultivated lands which supplied the septs with stores of corn and provender for their large herds of cattle. The rights of the chief, sub-chiefs and families of each sept were regulated under the Brehon code, which, with minute precision laid down the rules for adjudicating on almost every variety of dispute, encroachment, or breach of law. Although the main attribute of the head of a clan was that of unfailing vigour and prowess in arms, to defend his territory against both foreigners and encroaching Irish, there were other duties deemed scarcely secondary. Such were the improvement of the land, the observance of strict justice, the liberal support of religious establishments under the patronage of the saints of the tribe; implicit obedience to the decrees of hereditary Brehons or judges and the maintenance of the endowments made of old for the support of their learned men and chroniclers.

Their intimate relations with Scotland and frequent pilgrimages to France, Spain and Italy rendered the chiefs and their families conversant with the affairs of the Continent, with which constant communication was maintained by their clergy and ecclesiastical students. The internal condition of the settlement and the manifold injustices perpetrated by the officials of the colonial government on those under their control, tended to repel rather than to attract the independent Irish towards the English system as then administered. Many of the judges and chief legal officials of the colony were illiterate and ignorant of the law, obtained their appointments by purchase and leased them to deputies who promoted and encouraged litigation with the object of accumulating fees.

Commissioners of Oyer and Terminer were multiplied, before whom persons were constantly summoned, by irresponsible non-residents, to such an extent that no man could tell when he might be outlawed or indicted, or if a process had issued to eject him from his property. The king's officers often seized lands and appropriated their rents, so long as the legal subterfuges enabled them to baffle claims of the rightful proprietors; and thus agriculture and improvements were impeded.

Ecclesiastics, lords and gentlemen were not infrequently cast into prison by officers of the Crown, on unfounded charges, without indictment or process and detained in durance till compelled by rigorous treatment to purchase their liberation. The agricultural settlers and landholders were harassed by troops of armed 'kerns' and mounted 'idle-men', who levied distresses, maltreated and chained those who resisted and held forcible possession of the farmer's goods till redeemed with money. The troops engaged for the defence of the colonists became little less oppressive than enemies. Under the name of 'liverie' or livery the soldiery took, without payment, victuals for themselves and provender for their horses, and exacted weekly money payments, designated 'coygnes'. It was not unusual for a soldier having a billet for six or more horses to keep only three, but to exact provender for the entire number; and on a single billet the same trooper commonly demanded and took 'livery' in several parts of a county.

The constables of royal castles, and the purveyors of the households of the viceroys seldom paid for what they took; and for the purpose of obtaining bribes to release their seizures they made exactions much more frequently than needed. These grievances, wrote the Prelates, Lords and Commons, to the King of England, have reduced your loyal subjects in Ireland to a state of destruction and impoverishment and caused them even to hate their lives."

In 1367 a war raged between the Birminghams of Carberry and the men of Meath, because of the robberies of the Berminghams, "wherefore Robert Preston put a garrison in the Castle of Carberry."[192] In a parley held at Carberry the Berminghams seize upon the Chancellor and Sheriff of Meath "wherefore James Bermingham, who is held Trim Castle in handcuffs and fetters is immediately set at liberty in exchange for the Chancellor and the others set free on ransom."[193]

Referring to this incident Cox says:- "for the very English were now grown degenerate and they preyed and pillaged on one another, after the barbarous manner of the Irish."

In 1369 Sir William Windsor was Lord Lieutenant. A parliament called at Kilkenny granted £3,000 subsidy and soon after another held at Ballydoil gave £2,000 "towards the maintenance of the King's wars." Windsor vigorously prosecuted the war against the O'Tooles and the Rebels of Leinster.[194] But the English forces in Limerick being defeated by O'Connor, and the Earl of

---

[192] Grace

[193] Ibid

[194] Cox

122

Desmond slain, matters became so precarious there that Windsor was obliged to march with all haste to the relief of his party.

In 1374 Sir William Windsor, "a brave and active man,"[195] is again Lord Lieutenant arriving at Waterford on April 18th. 1374. "He undertook the Custody of Government of Ireland for eleven thousand two hundred and thirteen pounds six shillings and eight pence per annum. (£11,213. 6s. 8d. a year to govern Ireland) and obtained an order from the King and Council. That all those who had lands in Ireland should repair thither or send sufficient men in their room to defend the country on pain of forfeiting their estates. Nevertheless, the Lord Justice was so far from subduing the Irish that he confessed he could never get access to know their countries or habitations, and yet he had spent more time in the service of Ireland than any Englishman then living; so finding he could do not good he resigned to James, Earl of Ormonde."[196]

From this we can learn to estimate at its true value the statement of O'Ryan in his History of Carlow, that "in 1369 the rebels of Leinster were vigorously opposed by Sir William Windsor, Lord Deputy." - So vigorously indeed that he could never get access to their countries or habitations. In other words he never set foot in their territory!

In 1369 Art McMurrough and O'Nolan are again at war with the Lord Deputy Windsor who had succeeded Lionel. Windsor caused Dermot Lamhdearg Kavanagh, who had long been a prisoner among the English, to be cruelly put to death in Dublin, an outrage which only deepened the intense hatred of the Irish nobility against the English domination.[197]

In 1371 the English Parliament granted an annual sum of ten marks to the Prior of Old Leighlin for keeping the Bridge at that important pass against the Irishry.

In 1373, Carew, who claimed Idrone, the ancient inheritance of the O'Ryans, having died, Art McDermot, the McMurrough, seized the castles of Ballyloughan and Ballymoon and held them even against Sir William Windsor and his £11,213. 6s. 8d. for keeping Ireland in subjection.

Under date 1366 Dowling says:- "Thomas Carew was expelled from the territory of Idrone by McMurrough and fled into England. Idrone was held through Margaret alias Matilda, countess of Norfolk. Afterwards, when Henry Sydney was Deputy (during the reign of Queen Elizabeth), Sir Peter Carew

---

[195] Ibid

[196] Cox

[197] The Art McMurrough mentioned in this paragraph was in fact Art the son of Dermot - not to be confused with his very famous successor Art McMurrough Kavanagh son of Art More who had died c.1361 (A.K.)

finding evidence in the rolls came and claimed it - whence they were compelled to compound - Sydney went to hauke et cetera."

By an Inquisition taken in the eighteenth year of the reign of King Richard II it appears that Sir John Carew died seized of the barony of Idrone Anno 36 Edward III, and that Sir Leonard Carew at his decease 43rd. year of Edward (1369) had possession of it, but upon the death of Sir Leonard, the McMurrough, otherwise Kavanagh, chief of his name, possessed himself of the said barony and (as the inquisition declares) held it manu forti - (by a strong hand).[198]

"Thus it would seem that at this period, the English land owners were almost totally dispossessed in our County." [199]

According to Dowling Gilfrid le Wale slew Donatum McMurrough near Carlow in 1373.[200]

"And so we come to the twenty first day of June 1377, on which day this victorious King (Edward III) died at Shene in Surrey in the sixty fourth year of his age, and of his reign one and fiftieth. His revenue in Ireland did not exceed ten thousand pounds per annum, though the medium be taken from the best seven years of his reign."[201]

Richard II, son of the 'Black Prince' and grandson of Edward III became King of England in the eleventh year of his age in 1377. In the same year died the King of Leinster (Art McDermot Kavanagh - the McMurrough) and in the twentieth year of his age the young King of Leinster was inaugurated by O'Nolan.[202]

Here is a vivid picture drawn by D'Arcy Magee:- "In 1377 the victorious old monarch died. He had raised up his dynasty and standard to a great eminence. This he had done in the very midst of his enemies. He had reduced the annual revenues of the English settlement to ten thousand pounds. He had fixed his allies as well as his own family firmly in the land. The O'Moores felt secure in Leix as Dunamase itself - the O'Dempseys banked the Barrow for many a mile - the O'Tooles and O'Byrnes kept the glens and hills of Wicklow as firmly as the Spanish Arabs held their worshipped Grenada - the O'Nolans

---

[198] Harris

[199] Ryan

[200] It is not known who this man was but he must have been a member of the ruling family of the Kavanaghs of the time. - A.K.

[201] Cox

[202] In 1377 a grant of money was made by the Crown to Matthew FitzRaymond de Bermingham who lately went with the Justiciar's orders to Tullagh with 120 horsemen to oppose the Kavanaghs, the O'Nolans and the O'Byrnes. Another grant was made to John Wode for the loss of 2 horses and £20 worth of goods on the occasion the town of Tullow was burned by the O'Nolans. - A.K.

lorded it in Forth, the McGiolla Patricks in Ossory - the McDavid, McMurroghs and O'Dorans in Wexford and the standard of the king himself floated over, not only the halls of his old inheritance, but the towns of his conquest. No greater descendant of Donal the Handsome had yet been borne to an earthen bed in the churchyard of St. Mullins.[203]

Trained under such a father[204]the young Art now in his 20th. year sat in the chair of coronation at Cnoc-an-Bhogha and being nominated by O'Nolan and approved by the chiefs of the tribe assembled, he was invested by the Arch Brehon, O'Doran, with the title of 'the McMurrough', King of Leinster. A powerful frame and amazing activity were combined in the youthful prince, with an ardent love of poetry and music, and a sincere devotion. To his enemies he appeared 'very fierce and terrible' but to his friends as gentle as a hooded daughter of Saint Brigid. The year of his coronation he was recognised by the Pales-men who in parliament held in Castledermot voted him the annual tribute of eighty marks - 'as the late King had done to his ancestors'[205] he agreeing to open the highways of Kilkenny and Catherlogh".

In 1380 this tribute was again voted by Parliament and some smaller sums to Malachy McMurrough (his uncle), McDavid More and Manus McGerald and with similar conditions. Yet, in this year, even as the parliament of the Pale still sat, the King of England granted a title to Sir John Beaumont and his heirs forever of Art's entire patrimony; 'from the Slaney on the part of the south to the Blackwater at Arklow, on the part of the north and from the main sea on the east to the bounds of Catherlogh and Kildare on the west, saving only the lands of the Earl of Ormonde.' Truly, a liberal king and a rich grant, if Sir John's sword can make it good. We do not find, however, that Art or his kinsmen were further molested at this time."

In 1375 Donough Kavanagh McMurrogh, King of Leinster, was treacherously slain by the English, he having often before that spread destruction among them.[206] In the following year Hugh O'Tuathail of the Glen of Imaal was killed by the English.

---

[203] This cemetery had for generations been the burial place of the Leinster Kings. Saint Moling himself is believed to have been of the race of Cahir More. He was Bishop of Tuam and died about 697. He erected the church called after him. Tigh - Moling is situated on the Barrow in the south of County Carlow; and the church of the same name was also built by him in the village of that name Co. Kildare. - A.K.

[204] This is an error - Art was not the son of Art McDermot but a son of Art More. They were cousins.

[205] Pat. Rolls - Richd.II)

[206] If this Donough was the McMurrough in 1375 he must have succeeded Art McDermot, but according to Fr. Nolan, as noted earlier in this chapter, Art McDermot died in 1377 and was succeeded by the famous Art McMurrough Kavanagh. The other possibility is that

In the same year (1376) the English of Meath, Ulster and Leinster marched into Annally (Co. Longford) the dominion of the O'Ferralls, where they committed many depredations. O'Ferrall then collected all his forces and attacked by turns the English of Ulster, Leinster etc., and burned their farm houses and towns and plundered their territories, returning home with great booty. John Young, Bishop of Leighlin, who had expended a large sum on the repairs of the Episcopal houses in his manors, was plundered of all his goods by the rebels. He died eight years later.

An annual grant of twenty marks, out of the rents of Newcastle of Lyons was made to the friars of the Carmelite monastery of Leighlinbridge, in consideration of the great labour, burden and expense that these friars were put to in supporting their house, and the bridge contiguous thereto, against the King's enemies. The original grant was made in 1378 and confirmed by the King in 1394.[207]

An act was passed in 1379 in the English Parliament, "whereby it is ordained that all that have lands, rents or offices in Ireland, shall return thither; unless they have reasonable cause to absent, that then they shall send sufficient deputies to defend their castles and estates, or contribute two thirds of the yearly value towards the defence thereof, because the loss of Ireland would be a disinherison of the King and his Crown of England."[208]

In 1380 Edmond Mortimer, Earl of March, came to Ireland with sovereign power, as Lord Chief Justice. He was the son of Phillipa, daughter of Lionel, Duke of Clarence, the third son of Edward III. The Irish nobility, with heirs presumptive to the throne of Ireland, waited on him, namely, Niall O'Neill (Tyrone), O'Hanlon (Armagh), O'Ferrall (Longford), O'Reilly (Cavan), O'Mulloy (Offaly), MacGeoghan (Westmeath) with other chiefs. Edward Mortimer died in Cork the following year, 1381.

As the Mortimers play a prominent part in connection with the history of the O'Nolans it is well to devote a little attention to the new Viceroy. He was the grandson of Roger Mortimer, Viceroy under Edward II and was born in 1351.

In addition to his patrimonial estates in England and Ireland Roger acquired further lordships, in both countries, by his marriage to Duke Lionel's daughter Phillipa, through whom he claimed the Earldom of Ulster, and the lordships of Connaught and Trim. On his appointment he received 20,000 marks to provide archers and men-at-arms to enable him to withstand the Irish enemies. But he also practised deceit as it is recorded that in his own house he

---

Donough was the Tanaist in Dermot's time and was captured and held prisoner. He would not have been able to fulfil his duties which then devolved on Art McDermot. - A.K.

[207] Monast. Hib.

[208] Cox

outraged hospitality by treacherously seizing upon Magennis, Lord of Iveagh, in Down. Being unable to procure timber from the vast woods of Western Ulster, owing to the opposition of the O'Neills he brought over, from his own estate in Wales, oaks of great length, with which he constructed a bridge across the river Bann, near Coleraine, to maintain which, against the natives, he was compelled to erect a fortress at each end, and a castle in the centre.

In return for certain privileges granted to them, the monks of Coleraine covenanted to pray for the Earl, his countess Phillipa and their ancestors and successors. Mortimer seized much spoil and cattle from the Irish clergy and laity, which he transmitted to the monks of his Augustinian Priory of Wygemore, in Herefordshire, on the border or marches of Wales, whence his grandfather, Viceroy of Edward II, received the title of Earl of March, or de la Marche. The priory of Wygemore had been founded by his ancestor Raoul de Mortimer, who wrested lands from the Saxon Edric. It is said that Raoul was the bravest of the knights who came over to England with his kinsman William the Conqueror.

Edmond who came to Ireland in 1380 was unable to penetrate further than Athlone, towards the west of Ireland, but this fortress he succeeded in capturing from O'Connor by a great force of horse and foot soldiers. He gave the Constable, he appointed there, power to arrest all artificers of all classes and compel them to complete its repair at reasonable rates. Mortimer proceeded southwards, took cold from crossing a river and expired unexpectedly at mid-night on 26th. December 1381 in the Dominican Abbey at Cork.

After his death a council of the English was convened, at which the Earls of Ormonde and Desmond were requested to accept the Viceroyalty, but they declined, alleging that the war on the borders would prevent them from executing the office, unless they left their own territories unprotected. Even Sir Thomas Mortimer, the Treasurer, refused declaring that the revenues could not defray the wages of the archers and men-at-arms whom he would require. [209]

Art, son of Thomas Fionn, of the family of the McMurroughs, Tanaist to Art Kavanagh, the McMurrough, was killed by the English of Wexford in 1383.

Roger Mortimer, Edmond's eleven year old son was appointed Viceroy in 1382 and the King ordained that Sir Thomas Mortimer should act as his deputy. Roger was proclaimed Heir Apparent to the Crown of England in a parliament held at Westminster in 1385.

Roger was succeeded as Viceroy in 1383 by Philip Courtenay, a cousin of King Richard, who had served under the Duke of Lancaster in Spain. In 1385

---

[209] Gilbert

Philip sent messengers to the King to inform him that " they despaired of being able to preserve the land from being soon wholly conquered by his enemies."[210]

In 1388 the Provost of Dublin was required to swear he would "ride the franchises, and not suffer the liberties to be intruded on by the rebels or foreigners." [211]

At this time the Pale or liberties did not extend beyond Bray on the one side and Drogheda on the other and towards the south west they did not extend beyond Saggard.

John Roe O'Tuathail, Lord of Hy Murray (in Wicklow), the most distinguished of his tribe for hospitality and feats of arms, was slain by a peasant of his own clan, within the precincts of his own fortress, and the bodach (clown) who slew him was immediately put to death.[212]

In 1389 Sir John Stanley acted as Deputy. He wrote to the King about the sorry state of affairs:- " In Kildare, the centre of the Leinster colony, many towns were sacked, despite the exertions of the armed settlers and their sheriff, Sir William Wellesley, who lost many of his kinsmen in resisting the attempts of the Irish to re-enter upon their lands. The settlers in Carlow were reduced so low by the McMurrough and his confederate septs (including the O'Nolans) that John Griffin, the bishop of Leighlin could neither approach or dwell in any portion of his diocese in consequence of the destruction and pressure of the Irish enemies."[213]

Richard II issued a writ in 1389 to the effect that the diocese of Leighlin being so much devastated by the Irish enemies as to render it impossible for Bishop John Griffin to reside within it, he therefore granted him the village of Galroestown, in the county of Dublin, near the marches of the O'Tooles, with all its appurtenances (being then part of the temporalities of the see of Killaloe, and then in the King's hands during the vacancy by the death of the late bishop, predecessor to the present, who is a mere Irishman, abiding among the Irish enemies, and not amenable to law or government) to hold by the said Bishop of Leighlin, as long as from that cause the villages should continue in

---

[210] Gilbert pg. 252
[211] Walsh & Whitelaw's Dublin Vol.1 pg.174
[212] Annals of the F.M.
[213] Gilbert pg.261

the King's hands. The bishop of Leighlin held Galroestown until September 1391, when Matthew MacCragh was restored to the temporalities of Killaloe, having been deprived of them for upwards of two years from the date of his advancement.[214]

---

[214] Harris's Ware

Chapter 11

Richard II in Ireland

The Viceroyalty was transferred to James le Botiller, third Earl of Ormonde, in 1391. He was granted 3000 marks a year to maintain the army. He was styled 'Earl of Gowran' because he erected a castle at Gowran after the native chiefs had expelled him from Nenagh.

About this time Ormonde fixed his chief residence at Kilkenny which he had lately purchased from the heirs of Sir Hugh Spencer, Earl of Gloucester, and Isabel, his wife, daughter and co-heir of Gilbert de Clare, who claimed through Eva McMurrough. To aid the settlers within the walls of Carlow, the English government engaged Richard Sonner, an armourer, who with his attendants, agreed, for the payment of one shilling per day, to dwell there, in the King's service for three months, for the purpose of making guns, harness and other articles of defence against the "malice of the Irish, then proposing to destroy and devastate the town."

Most of the parliaments in England, during Richard's reign, dwelt upon the heavy cost of maintaining the war in Ireland, in which country the King's revenues continued to diminish steadily, and the settlers, flying from the pressure of the O'Nolans and other border Irish, flocked to England in large numbers, much to the dissatisfaction of the English, on whose trades and avocations they encroached. Things looked so bad for England that in 1393 a parliament held at Wynton, voted a subsidy to enable Richard II to go in person and wage war in Ireland. All Anglo-Irish were required to return to Ireland before September 8th. and wait there for the King's arrival. "The King's squires and archers were summoned to arm and proceed with the royal troops to repress the increasing malice and opposition of the Irish enemy."[215]

The "Irish enemy" were the Irish people, the native Kings and Chieftains who with their own clans possessed the country, of which Richard and his supporters determined to rob them. Thus when Dermot McMurrough died the kingship of Leinster devolved on his next kinsman suitably endowed with capacity and valour. This was the Brehon law - the law of Ireland. As hereditary Grand Marshal of Leinster it was O'Nolan's high office to select[216] and nominate the new King. This duty O'Nolan faithfully discharged and as a consequence the line of the lawful successors was regularly maintained from Brandubh to Dermot and from Dermot to Art McMurrough Kavanagh, who

---

[215] Gilbert

[216] It is doubtful if selection was part of the Grand Marshal's function. - A.K.

130

was the lawful King of Leinster when Richard invaded his kingdom. He was acknowledged as King of Leinster by all the other dynasts of the province and they knew no king but Art the McMurrough, and looked upon Richard of Bordeaux as a fraud and impostor. Art held in "his fair hand the sovereignty and the charters of the province" and was regarded as "replete with hospitality, knowledge and chivalry; the prosperous and Kingly enricher of churches and monasteries with his alms and his offerings."

He had married a beautiful woman, Eliza de Veele, Baroness of Norragh, who, even in English law, held large estates in Kildare. These the English crown seized and granted to others on the ground that she had married one of the principle enemies of the King of England.

It was to support this aggressive action, to wrest, if possible, the kingship of Leinster from the McMurrough, and to trample on the ancient rights of O'Nolan and the other dynasts of that province, that Richard Bordeaux came to Ireland with all the panoply and power he could command. And it was to defend the lands of their own nation and people that the McMurrough, O'Nolan and their brave allies - O'Tooles, O'Byrnes, O'Connors and O'Moores determined to make Richard rue the day that he set out to rob them of their patrimony.

Richard landed in Waterford on October 2nd. 1394, accompanied by the Duke of Gloucester, Roger, the young Earl of March, four thousand squires and thirty thousand archers. He was then in his twenty-eight year, middle size, yellow hair, round ruddy face and effeminate mien. He had more troops with him than were present under Edward III at the battle of Crecy, and yet these were augmented still more by the forces of the Anglo Irish Earls of Kildare, Desmond and Ormonde.

In Leinster, which had been the chief seat of Anglo-Norman power, and the portion of Ireland most readily assailable from England, the O'Nolans and the other native chiefs refused to yield one single inch of ground. They had sustained a perpetual war for a period of over two hundred years, and even, in the face of Richard's mighty hosts, nobly defended their ancient inheritance. "The representatives of the original Irish proprietors never abandoned their claims, although in this struggle such numbers of them fell that one writer styled Leinster as *the cemetery of the glorious Gaels*."[217]

After landing in Waterford, Richard set out on his march, with the intention of making New Ross, then a walled town, his next resting place, and the base from which he might ravage the country about. But in the meantime, the McMurrough and O'Nolan descended upon New Ross and having plundered

---

[217] Gilbert - There seems to be an error here as other writers notably Hore quotes this saying as 'The cemetery of the valorous Gauls' referring to the great numbers of Anglo-Normans who lost their lives in Leinster at the period. - A.K.

it of all its supplies set it on fire and left behind them for Richard and his army nothing but a mass of calcified ruins. They burned it "with its houses and castles and carried away gold, silver and hostages."[218]

The McMurrough, O'Nolan, O'Connor Faly and their allies had decided that it would be imprudent to risk a pitched battle with such a formidable force and that their best policy was to adopt guerrilla warfare, in the tactics of which the Irish in those days had no equals. The result was the total defeat of Richard's mighty force and his return to England without accomplishing anything worthy of note.[219]

"Although guided by the Earl of Ormonde, who was inured to Irish warfare, Richard's troops were discomfited in an attempt upon Offaly, the territory of O'Connor, who repelled them and captured several of their steeds. The Earl of March encountered a similar repulse from O'Carroll, into whose district of Ely he essayed to make a predatory incursion. .....With his large army, skilled in all the military arts of the age, the king and his experienced English Commanders were, however, unable, from the character of the country and the mode of warfare of the natives, to make any progress in subjecting the Irish beyond the frontier of the settlement. The English troops were constantly assailed and surprised by the border Irish, who astonished them by their hardihood and determination, of which many alarming tales were circulated among the soldiery, unused to warfare amidst mountain passes, woods and perilous morasses."[220]

In the 'Chronicles of England, France and Spain' written by Sir John Froissart, a French priest and historian who died about 1400, there is contained an account of Richard's campaign in Ireland in 1394. When on a visit to England shortly after Richard's return, Froissart was a guest at Richard's court and while there he met Henry Castede, one of Richard's creatures, who had served with the Duke of Ormonde in Ireland and had been made a prisoner by the Irish, and from him Froissart learned the story which we append in full, as Froissart's works are not easily procurable.[221]

Froissart's account varies considerably from the version given in the Four Masters which states:- " The McMurrough, that is, Arthur Kavanagh, son of Art More, waged war against the King of England and his people, and many of them were slain by him. He finally came to the King's residence (Dublin Castle), at the request of the English and Irish of Leinster, where he was made prisoner, on a charge made against him by the Earl of Ormonde, the Lord

---

[218] Four Masters

[219] These comments relate to the ignominious defeat suffered by Richard when he invaded Ireland for the second time in 1399. - A.K.

[220] Gilbert

[221] See Appendix I for the full text as supplied by Fr. Nolan.

Justice; he was soon after set at liberty, but O'Byrne, O'Moore and John O'Nolan were kept in prison after him."

John O'Nolan was the dynast of Forth O'Nolan in 1394, and it is evident from the Four Masters there was treachery at work and that Richard, having invited the Leinster Chieftains to a conference in Dublin Castle basely seized upon them and cast them into prison. John O'Nolan must either have been beheaded or kept in close confinement for his son Donal takes the place of O'Nolan at the conference held on February 16th. 1395. As we learn from another English version of the history of this expedition.

"Richard II, King of England," says Cox, "landed at Waterford, on the second day of October 1394, with a mighty army, whereof he made but small use; for the Irish betook themselves to their old stratagems of feigned and crafty submissions, wherewith they deluded and abused King Henry II and King John in former times; However, Mowbray (Earl of Nottingham and Marshal of England) had a special commission to receive the homage and Oaths of Fidelity of all the Irish of Leinster; by virtue whereof, Gerald O'Byrne, Donald O'Nolan, Malachias O'Morough, Rory Oge O'Moore, Arthur McMurrough, Murrough O'Connor and others made their humble submission by an Interpreter, in the open field at Baligory (Baunogephlure), near Carlow, on the 16th. February 1395.[222] They did Homage in solemn manner, and made their oaths of fidelity to the Earl Marshal, laying aside their Girdles, Skeins and Caps, and falling down at his feet upon their knees; which being performed, the Marshal gave each of them the Osculum Pacis (the kiss of peace). Moreover, they were bound by several indentures upon great penalties, to be paid to the Apostolic Chamber (viz. O'Byrne twenty thousand marks, O'Nolan ten thousand pounds, etc.) not only to continue Loyal Subjects, but that by a certain day prefixed, they and all their Sword men should clearly relinquish and give up unto the King and his successors, all the Land and possessions which they held in Leinster, and, taking with them only their moveable goods, should serve him in his Wars against other Rebels; in consideration whereof, the King was to give them pay and pensions during their lives, and to bestow the inheritance of all such lands upon them as they should recover from the Rebels in any other part of the Realm: and whereupon a pension of eighty marks per annum was granted to Art McMurrough, chief of the Kavanaghs, which was continued to his posterity till the time of Henry VIII, although they did nothing for it.

But the King having received letters from O'Neal (wherein he styles himself Prince of the Irishry of Ulster, and yet acknowledges the King to be his Sovereign Lord and Dominus perpetuus Hiberniae) removed to Drogheda,

---

[222] The 'Treaty Stone' was pointed out to Mr. Edward O'Toole of Rathvilly in the early 19th. century according to Fr. Miller in 'The Barrow Valley and its History'. - A.K.

to take the Submissions of the Irish of Ulster. Thither came to him O'Neal, O'Hanlon, O'Donnell, MacMahon and others, who with the like humility and ceremony as aforesaid, performed their Homage and Fealty to the King's own person, in these or the like words:- Ego Nelanus O'Neal Senior, tam pro meipso, quam pro filiis meis, devinio Ligeus Homo vester etc. - and in the indenture between O'Neal and the King, he is bound not only to remain faithful to the Crown of England, but also to restore the Bonnaught of Ulster to the Earl of Ulster, as of right belonging to that Earldom, and (amongst other things) usurped by the O'Neals.

These indentures and submissions, with many more of the same (for there was not a Chieftain or Head of an Irish Sept, but submitted himself in one form or the other) the King himself caused to be enrolled and testified by a Notary Public, and with his own hands, delivered the Enrolments to the Bishop of Salisbury, who on the 25th. June delivered to the Court of Exchequer two Hanapers; one containing thirty nine, and the other thirty six instruments which were all there recorded or enrolled, so that they have been carefully preserved, and are now to be found in the Remembrance's Office; and the copies of them all are to be seen at Lambeth, Libro.D."

On the 1st. February 1395, Richard wrote from Dublin to his uncle the Duke of York, saying, "in our land of Ireland there are three kinds of people - wild Irish, our enemies; Irish rebels and obedient English. To us and our Council here, it appears that the Irish rebels have rebelled in consequence of the injustice and grievances practised towards them, for which they have been afforded no redress; and that, if not wisely treated, and given hope of grace, they will, most likely, ally themselves with our enemies." In response to his appeal the English Parliament voted a subsidy, the clergy a tenth and the Lords and Commons a fifteenth of their income to enable the King to conquer the rebels and enemies within his land of Ireland."[223]

The English versions of the history of this period as given above, bear the brand of falsehood on every line. If the four Irish kings submitted to Richard and all the chieftains and heads of clans who were enrolled submitted why did the English Parliament vote a subsidy as noted in the previous paragraph. Again if all the Irish kings and chieftains submitted who was left to be conquered?

Richard's campaign of 1394 was one of the greatest failures on record. A short experience of McMurrough and O'Nolan taught him that "Ireland is one of the worst countries to make war in or conquer." The young English squires soon discovered that they had to deal with brave and valiant men who taught them a much more severe lesson than even their historian admit. For Richard and his "four thousand men-at-arms and thirty thousand archers" cowered

---

[223] Gilbert's Viceroys

behind the ramparts of the Pale, and spent nine months there in terror of their lives, after which they were heartily glad to scurry back to England.

When Richard was leaving Ireland he appointed Roger Mortimer, his cousin, then twenty one years of age, as his Viceroy. Roger had married Alianore, daughter of Thomas Holland, Duke of Surrey, the King's half brother. As Richard had no children Roger was next in succession to the Crown of England, his right to which had been formally declared by the English Parliament in 1385, on the ground of his being eldest son of Phillipa, only child of Lionel, Duke of Clarence, third son of Edward III. In addition to his royal rights, Roger inherited the Earldom of March, the Lordship of Wygmore, in Herefordshire, and of Clare in Suffolk. He was also entitled to principalities in Ireland with almost regal jurisdiction. Through the various alliances of his family he had become the chief male representative of Marechal, de Lacy, De Burgh, De Braose and De Joinville, in right of whom he assumed the titles of Earl of Ulster, Lord of Connaught, Trim, Leix and Ossory. When he came of age his guardians delivered to him all his English mansions in good repair and 80,000 marks in money. But the position of his nominal estates in Ireland was different.

The Crown of England which undertook to guard Roger's Irish Estates had been unable to hold them against the native proprietors who repudiated his claims. Roger, in 1393, obtained from the Privy Council of England, a grant of one thousand pounds in consideration of the devastation and entire destruction of his estates by Irish enemies. He was legally authorised by the same Council to enter by force upon possessions of his lordships and manors in Ireland.[224]

A monastic chronicler of the Mortimer family records that Roger was distinguished for the qualities held in estimation in his time - a stout champion at tournaments, a famous speaker, a bounteous giver, in conversation affable and jocose, in beauty and form surpassing his fellows but dissolute and remiss in matters of religion.[225] In addition he was related to some of the most powerful nobles of the period. His brother married a daughter of Owen Glendower and his sister, Elizabeth, became the wife of Henry Percy, surnamed 'Hotspur', son of the Earl of Northumberland.

Roger had joined King Richard's army in Ireland with his own retinue of one hundred men-at-arms, of which two were bannerets and five knights; two hundred mounted and four hundred archers on foot. He subsequently attended the Parliament at Shrewsbury in great pomp, with a troop of retainers attired in white and crimson, the colours of the house of Mortimer.

When he became Viceroy he renewed war upon the borders and captured one of the chief houses of the O'Byrnes. But he was defeated by the O'Tooles,

---

[224] Gilbert
[225] Ibid

who on Ascension Day drove back his army with great slaughter carrying back to Imaal six score of their heads. "Amongst which were those of forty principal Englishmen." [226]

In 1397 the castle of Carlow was captured by Donal the eldest son of Art McMurrough. In the following year Roger Mortimer went into the dominions of the McMurrough where he had an encounter with the O'Nolans, O'Byrnes, McDavid More, Mortagh McLoaghlen and other allies at Kellistown. In the course of the battle Roger Mortimer was killed. [227] This battle occurred on St. Margaret's Day (June 10th.).

His mother gave to them two chalices, one to Myshall and the other to Garghill (Garryhill) so that she might have the body of her son, alive or dead to carry back with her to England. [228]

When the Viceroy marched against the O'Nolans who occupied the lands which he claimed in Forth O'Nolan, he was "attired in the dress and accoutrements" of an Irish cavalier. "He encountered them at Callestown, in Carlow, and fell at the head of his soldiery, which were routed with slaughter. By a gift of chalices to two of the churches of the district, Roger's mother, Phillipa, Duchess of Clarence, obtained his corpse, which was interred in the De Mortimer Priory at Wigmore."[229]

The effects of this famous battle were felt in England for many a day. It was the turning point in the history of that country for in it "were involved the destinies of the British Empire; for it was to revenge the death of his cousin and presumptive heir that Richard II came a second time into Ireland, and so left the field open to Bolingbroke, to whose towering ambition the superior claims of Mortimer's orphan children offered only a feeble obstacle; and hence the disputed succession, the thinning of the old nobles of England, the rise of the landed gentry, and all the thousand ever spreading consequences of the wars of York and Lancaster." [230]

On the death of the Earl of March, Reginald Grey was nominated Governor. He held nominal title of Lord of Wexford, and had long experience in border warfare in Wales. Soon afterwards Richard appointed as Viceroy, Thomas Holland, Duke of Surrey, his own half brother, who was also Marshal of England, and whose daughter Alianore was Roger's wife. Forgetting all compacts with the Irish he granted Surrey the barony of Norragh, which was the property of Art McMurrough's wife, together with the Castle and Lordship of Carlow, which was the property of the O'Nolans. He also allocated to

---

[226] Cox

[227] Dowling

[228] Ibid

[229] Gilbert's Viceroys pg. 278

[230] Dean Butler Intro. Dowling

Surrey 11,500 marks a year to support himself and his men against O'Nolan and Art the McMurrough and furthermore covenanted that he should have out of every parish in England, at the royal cost, a man and wife to dwell on the border lands of the settlement in Ireland. Surrey, aided by Janico d'Artois, a Gascon military leader, bravely endeavoured to enforce his claims against the Gaels. His efforts proving unsuccessful, Richard, already bitterly incensed against the O'Nolans and their allies, determined that he would make another expedition into Ireland to wreak his vengeance.

Conveyances of every kind were requisitioned to transport stores, and ships from all English ports were ordered to be in readiness at Milford for the embarkation of the royal army. Horses, cows, calves, salted meats, fresh water, bread and all the necessaries were taken on board. Knights, squires, men-at-arms and archers to the number of thirty thousand were mustered at Milford. Richard having set sail with his hosts arrived at Waterford on the first of June. He was attended by the Bishops of London, Lincoln, Carlisle, the Abbot of Westminster, the Duke of Exeter and the Earl of Salisbury. After six days rest at Waterford, Richard rode with his army in close array to Kilkenny. Early on a summer's morning, the 23rd. June, Richard marched against the McMurrough and the O'Nolan. These chieftains rejected the overtures of Richard, who regardless of his former compact had given the barony of Norragh to the Duke of Surrey; granted the territory of O'Nolan to John de Beaumont, and now proposed to expel the clansmen of McMurrough and O'Nolan and people their lands with compulsory emigration from England. The answer of the McMurrough was that he "would neither submit nor obey Richard in any way", and he affirmed that he was the rightful King of Ireland and that he would never cease from war and the defence of his country until death, declaring that the wish to deprive him of his land by conquest was unlawful.

Richard then advanced with all his forces into the territory of the McMurrough who with O'Nolan and some 3,000 men took up a strong position in a wood. Richard caused a space to be cleared and hoisted the pennons and standards of England, after which he ordered the surrounding villages and houses to be set on fire, and while they burned he knighted Henry, afterwards Henry V, son of the Duke of Lancaster.[231] Nero fiddled while Rome was burning. Richard burned the homes of the Kavanaghs and O'Nolans while Bolingbroke (whose son he knighted in their ruddy glare) was plotting to deprive him of his throne and kingdom.

Then Richard despatched messengers to the McMurrough promising him on submission both pardon and grants of territories and castles elsewhere. But having some years previously narrowly escaped by his own strength, from an attempt made to capture him by surprise in Dublin, the Chieftain rejected this

---

[231] Gilbert

proposal and declared, "that for all the gold in the world he would not submit, but would continue to war upon and harass the King."

Seeing that all hope of compromise was vain, Richard had two thousand five hundred of the English settlers employed to hew down the wood in which the Irish lay concealed, but this availed very little, for they were assailed with deadly effect by the Irish, who raising deafening war cries drove their darts through armour and cuirass. Foraging parties were also cut off by the native cavalry, who scoured the hills and valleys with a fleetness which astonished the English.[232]

It was while leading his men in one of these rapid attacks, probably on the outskirts of Killoughrum Forest, O'Nolan, the bravest of the brave, fell pierced through the heart by an arrow fired by one of Richard's famous Cheshire archers. On the death of Donald, the Tanaist, Sean, his son, became the O'Nolan.[233]

Eleven days were spent in unsuccessful attempts against the Irish allies - McMurrough, O'Nolan, Breens of the Duffry and McDavid More, who now cut off all supplies, so that the English army could obtain little more than green oats for their horses, of which many perished from exposure to rain and wind. The soldiery and their commanders also suffered from want of provisions. On some days five or six had but a single loaf between them, while the squires and knights were without regular supplies for five days together. They were compelled to march through mud and rain and storm, their horses up to their girth and their men up to their waist at times in bogs and quagmires. The journey was made, probably by the same route as the march of 1394 viz. by Pollmonty, Clonroche, Ferns, Gorey and Arklow.

At length the army arrived at Arklow, where they met three ships that had just arrived with stores from Dublin. Before the ships were moored, the soldiers, plunging into the water, contended for the supplies, and becoming intoxicated with the wine began to quarrel among themselves. All this time McMurrough and O'Nolan hung upon the line of march with their brave and nimble kerns and gallowglasses, seizing every opportunity of inflicting injury on the royal army. Depressed and disappointed Richard decided to decamp for Dublin, amidst loud war-cries and shouts of defiance from the Irish, who, says a French eye witness were "as bold as lions and gave many a hard blow to the King."

The McMurrough now decided to send a messenger to the King expressing his desire for peace, and requesting that some one might be deputised to meet him and discuss terms. Richard held a council of war as a result of which

---

[232] Gilbert
[233] Ogygia chpt. 64 pg. 325

138

Thomas de Spencer, Earl of Gloucester, who had married the King's cousin was selected for the mission.

Attended by the rearguard, consisting of two hundred lancers and a thousand archers, Gloucester proceeded to the appointed place of meeting, between two woods at some distance from the sea. He found the adjacent mountain covered with Irish, under the leading of the McMurrough, who is described by Creton, as a "fine, large, able man, wondrously active; of stern indomitable mien, wielding in his right hand a long dart, which he cast with much skill. His steed which was so good that he was said to have purchased it, by barter, for four hundred cows, was, although without housing or saddle, managed by him with the greatest dexterity."

In descending from the mountain he galloped so swiftly, says the French writer, "that I never, in all my life, saw hare, deer or other animal, go with such speed as his horse."

Gloucester and the McMurrough, meeting at a little brook, exchanged much discourse. The McMurrough declared he would have no terms, but peace without reservation, free from molestation of any kind, and asserted that otherwise he would never come to a compact so long as he lived. Failing to agree, they parted hastily; and on learning the result of the conference, Richard's usually ruddy face grew pale with anger, and he swore in great wrath, by St. Edward, that he would never depart from Ireland until he had taken the McMurrough dead or alive. He then resumed his march to Dublin, where, in the midst of plenty, the army for a time forgot the hardships they had endured. From Dublin, the King despatched three bodies of well appointed soldiery against the McMurrough and exhorted them to behave bravely, promising a hundred marks of pure gold to any who might kill or capture him. He declared that should they fail, he would himself pursue Art and burn all the woods after the fall of the leaves in autumn.

Tempests and adverse winds setting in prevented communication with England during six weeks. The first ship which arrived brought messengers, who informed the King that the Duke of Lancaster, landing in Yorkshire early in July had essayed to assume the sovereignty of England; seized the castles and fortresses; executed those who opposed him; and was received by the citizens of London. The King, on hearing the news turned pale with anger and exclaimed, "Good Lord! this man designs to deprive me of my realm."

(Richard subsequently sailed to England where he lost his kingdom and his life)

A remarkable fatality attended the English nobles connected with the colony in Ireland and its government under Richard II. The Duke of Ireland,[234] died from a wound, in exile. The Duke of Gloucester perished

---

[234] I'm sure this must be an error -probably the Duke of Exeter. - A.K.

mysteriously in the castle of Calais. The Duke of Surrey and Sir William le Scrop were beheaded by Henry IV. Mowbray, Duke of Norfolk and Lord of Carlow ended his days in banishment at Venice. Edmund de Mortimer was cut off by disease. Sir Thomas de Mortimer became an outlaw among the native Irish; while the death of his nephew, Roger, opened the path for the intrusion of Henry IV, leading to the bloody English wars of York and Lancaster.[235]

---

[235] Gilbert

Chapter 12

The 15th. Century

King Henry IV was crowned on October 13th. 1399. At this time the native Irish chieftains had regained so much lost ground that only part of four counties of Dublin, Meath, Kildare and Louth were subject to English jurisdiction.[236]

A daring Scottish Chieftain, Donald of the Isles, made many descents upon the Irish coast. His fleet was encountered in Strangford Lough by the Constable of Dublin, but Donald proved himself victorious and gave the English a total defeat. Many Englishmen were slain and many more were drowned.

A great number of the Anglo-Norman families began to repudiate the authority of England and ally themselves with the Irish, so that a Viceregal despatch says:- "These English rebels style themselves noble blood and Idlemen, whereas in truth, they are strong marauders."

McMurrough had declared "open war" against the English and with O'Nolan was at this time helping to crush the Earl of Ormonde. "He (McMurrough) is now", wrote the Council, "gone to the aid of the Earl of Desmond, to suppress the Earl of Ormonde, after which he will return with all the powers he can lead from Munster to destroy the country...the Irish have become strong and haughty, the border English are unable to make successful attacks upon them: thus the loyal subjects are destroyed and harassed, and the settlement in peril of final destruction."

Henry IV claimed the crown of England as the eldest son of the famous John of Gaunt, fourth son of Edward III, but the right of succession was in Ann, daughter of Roger Mortimer, slain by O'Nolan, son of Phillipa, daughter of Lionel, third son of Edward III, and accordingly Ann's grandson afterwards became Edward IV.

Henry IV in 1402 sent over his second son, Thomas, Duke of Lancaster, then in his twelfth year, as Viceroy. On the fifth of July following " John Drake, Mayor of Dublin, with a band of citizens, encountered and defeated four thousand Irish outlaws, near Bray, in the borders of Wicklow, and slew four hundred and ninety of their best men."[237] The scene of this bloody encounter

---

[236] Fr. Nolan is somewhat in error here as the Wexford pale was still in place though subject to serious attack by the Kavanaghs - see *In the Shadow of Mount Leinster* by Art Kavanagh.
[237] Cox

141

was long known as "bloody bank", but now it is called "sunny bank". Three months afterwards, in October "Daniel O'Byrn, for him and his Sept or Nation, submitted to the Lord Lieutenant, and promised allegiance and good behaviour; and to manifest his sincerity he granted to the king the castle of Mackenigan."[238]

Soon after the arrival of Prince Thomas, the Council wrote to King Henry a letter which is still extant and which gives a deplorable picture of the condition of the English garrison at the time. Our friend Janico D'Artois, a Gascon knight, who had made a brutal incursion into Forth O'Nolan some years before was a member of this lachrymose council. "With heavy hearts," they say, "we testify anew to your Highness that our lord, your son, is now so destitute of money, that he has not a penny in the world, nor can borrow a single penny, because all his jewels, and his plate that he can spare of those which he must of necessity keep, are pledged and lie in pawn. Also his soldiers have departed from him, and the people of his household are on the point of leaving; and however much they might wish to remain, it is not in our lord's power to keep together, with a view to his aid, twenty or a dozen persons with me, your humble suppliant, (Archbishop) of Dublin, and your humble liege, Janico, who has paid for your use his very all, but we will render our entire duty to him so long as we shall live, as we are bound by our sovereign obligation to you. And the country is so weakened and impoverished by the long non-payment, as well in the time of our lord, your son, as in the time of the other Lieutenants before him, that the same land can no longer bear such charge, as they affirm, and on this account have they importuned me. In good faith, our most sovereign lord, it is marvellous that they have borne such a charge so long. Wherefore, we entreat, with all our humility and fullness that we may, that you will please to ordain speedy remedy of these said dangers and inconveniences, and to hold as excused, also, if any peril or disaster (which God may avert!) befall our lord, your son, by the said causes. For the more full declaring of these matters to your Highness, three or two of us should have come to your high presence; but such is the great danger on this side, that not one of us dares to depart from the person of our lord."[239]

The submission of O'Byrne did not make any difference, however, to the attitude of O'Nolan. Like the brave King of Leinster, by whose side he fought and bled for freedom, O'Nolan scorned all overtures for submission. With Art the McMurrough, "he lay like a canker," as Leland says, " in the very heart of the Leinster territory. He exulted in the honour of having foiled a royal army; he despised the impotent attempt of Henry's deputies and had discernment to

---

[238] Ibid.
[239] Gilbert

consider that the title and dignity of his son, unsupported by a competent military force, was not sufficient to subdue him."

Sir Stephen Scroop was appointed Deputy to Prince Thomas. He was a soldier of experience in France and Flanders and was consequently commissioned to conduct the wars in Ireland under the youthful Viceroy. He was empowered to march against, destroy or pardon, as he should deem fit, the Irish enemies and English Rebels, who "continually devise war, and, to their utmost power, contend to destroy the land."

In 1402 Prince Thomas wrote to his father: - "I, by the advice of my council, rode against the Irish, your enemies, did my utmost to harass them, and, God be thanked, have returned with my people in safety."[240]

"To save their towns from the fate of Leighlin, the burgesses of which were reduced to the number of eighty six, the commonalty of New Ross obtained royal permission to pay an annual sum to Art the McMurrough, for protecting them."[241]

James, Earl of Ormonde, became Lord Justice of Ireland and held a Parliament in Dublin, which confirmed the Statutes of Kilkenny. "The Charter of Irish Liberty and the Statutes of Kilkenny were confirmed by parliament in the presence of the Earl of Ormonde, and the King's army slew 100 Irish enemies at Kilkea, the clergy, in the meantime, praying, holding a procession for their success at Castledermot."[242]

Elsewhere, the Dublin forces " on Corpus Christi, vanquished the Irish enemies and took three Ensigns, and brought to Dublin the heads of those they had slain. And the Prior of Conal had a good success in the plains of Kildare for with twenty Englishmen he defeated 200 Irish and killed many of them."[243]

While these things were going on in Kildare, O'Nolan and McMurrough were pressing the English settlers out in Wexford. Long had these Leinster chiefs and their allies beheld the stranger occupy their ancestral lands, and now, they resolved to have their own back again. Wherever the English gained a foothold they immediately erected strong castles. From the hill tops of Wexford the ruins of these impenetrable fortresses can even yet be seen studded thickly throughout the land. Breaking in upon these intruders they seized upon the castles of Camolin and Ferns and proceeding south they took the castle of Enniscorthy and captured the city of Wexford. On every side the castles of the Norman lords fell before their fury and those they did not garrison they destroyed. Turning north they marched on Castledermot which they sacked, and from which they carried away great spoil, bending their course

---

[240] Ibid. pg. 297
[241] Gilbert
[242] Dowling
[243] Cox

thence towards Conall, they taught the militant Prior thereof a severe lesson. "McMurrough raged war against the English, in the course of which he plundered and burned Contae Riabhach (Wexford[244]), Carlow and Disert Diarmada (Castledermot in Kildare).[245]

"As Deputy to Prince Thomas, Scrope returned to Ireland in 1407, and with the Earls of Ormonde and Desmond, the Prior of Kilmainham and other chief colonists he waged war upon the McMurrough, O'Nolan and O'Carroll. The settlers, deeming their cause specially favoured by heaven, believed, according to their chronicles, that on this occasion, the sun did not set at the natural hour, but continued to shine till the English Knights had ridden six miles in their raid upon the Irish."[246]

"About May, the Lord Deputy (accompanied by the Earls of Ormonde and Desmond, the Prior of Kilmainham and other chief colonists) set out from Dublin and invaded the territory of the McMurrough; at first the Irish had the better, but at length the constancy and resolution of the English prevailed, and O'Nolan and his son and others were taken prisoners; and after this was done, they marched speedily to Callan, in the County of Kilkenny, upon some intelligence they had of the rebels being thereabouts, and they so surprised them, that the whole party was routed and O'Carroll and eight hundred men slain upon the place."[247]

Another annalist gives us the following account:- "The Earl of Ormonde, the Earl of Desmond and the Prior of Kilmainham, with other nobles and captains, invaded the McMurrough country. First the Irish enemies set themselves to resist fiercely and fought with great determination, but at length, these being conquered, the Earl of Ormonde, by pursuing vigorously, in the end captured O'Nolan with his two sons and many others whom he led captive to the Castle of Dublin, but these O'Nolans were afterwards quite extirpated."

O'Carroll and 800 of his allies were slain by the Earl of Ormonde and other English under his command at Callan, and the Sun is said to have stood still and protracted its natural time of setting until the English had ridden six miles in pursuit of their enemies.[248]

During the winter of 1407-08 the Leinster clans were under rigid training for the work that lay ahead and in the following spring they had brought together a powerful army under the leadership of the McMurrough and the O'Nolan. They also entered into an alliance with O'Carroll of Ely and several of the chieftains of Desmond. O'Moore of Leix and O'Connor Faly prepared

---

[244] Probably South Wexford or the Wexford Pale - A.K.

[245] The Four Masters

[246] Gilbert pg. 300

[247] Cox

[248] Dowling

144

with vigour for the campaign. On the other side nothing was left undone to combat this strong alliance. Scroop made careful preparations for the expedition and on September the 14th. he marched out of the gates of Dublin and proceeded by Kildare to Carlow.

When the McMurrough and the O'Nolan learned of this they determined to carry the war into the enemy's country, for two reasons, first that they might strike a blow at the Butlers and secondly that they might the more quickly effect a junction with their southern allies. Soon the information was carried to Scroop that they had reached and sacked Gowran, and were on their march to the castle of Dunfert, which had only been erected in 1405 by the Earl of Ormonde. It was evident that they meant to direct their course towards Kilkenny. Instead of invading Forth O'Nolan and Idrone, as was his first intention, Scroop pushed forward by forced marches and eventually came up with the Leinster forces at Danesfort, six miles from Callan. The old people living around the district still call the place Dhoon -fartha, that is, the Fort of the Graves. The name has been anglicised, first into Dunfert and later into Danesfort. But the fort of the Graves tells its own story.

Here the Irish and English forces met in deadly combat. The Irish, under the command of the McMurrough and the O'Nolan; and the English under the command of Scroop, Ormonde and Desmond. It was one of the fiercest battles ever fought in defence of liberty. Art McMurrough, and O'Nolan led their men with such martial prowess as to have almost carried the day. The English forces were driven back, leaving their dead and dying to be trampled beneath the hoofs of the Irish cavalry. They wavered, they broke and were about to fly when a strong body of fresh forces arrived under the command of some 'Captains and gentlemen of Meath.'[249]

Again the English began to form up and O'Nolan, seeing the danger and desirous to deal with it without loss of time, called on his faithful clansmen to follow him and pressed forward his cavalry behind him making the welkin ring as they rapidly advanced with their dread war cry 'O'Nuallain Aboo'.

> "For he must have come from a conquering race,
> The heir of their valour, their glory, their grace;
> His frame must be stately, his step must be fleet,
> His hand must be trained to each warrior feat,
> His face, as the harvest moon, steadfast and clear,
> A head to enlighten, a spirit to cheer,
> While the foremost to rush where the battle brands ring,
> And the last to retreat, is a true Irish King."
> (Thomas Davis)

---

[249] Cox

"Terrible is the destruction O'Nolan deals around on every side, while the enemy encouraged by the fresh levies gradually begun to somewhat recover themselves. They close around O'Nolan and eventually the Earl of Ormonde and his men capture this brave warrior and his dauntless son Donald. While Art, the Tanaist of O'Nolan lies dead on the field of glory."[250]

Learning that O'Carroll of Ely and O'Moore of Leix were coming up, and now only six miles away, the English retire, hastily bearing O'Nolan and his son captive away with them, and riding to Callan, where, owing to their superior numbers and to the rapid and unexpected movement they met and defeated with great slaughter, the advancing Irish army. And the sun, we are told by the English chroniclers, stood still while these Joshuas of the Pale emerge from the Ajalon of their disasters.

Dowling tells us that it was the Earl of Ormonde "captured O'Nolan with his two sons and many others, whom he led captives to the Castle of Dublin." An addition to the chronicles by some unknown hand adds "but these O'Nolans were afterwards quite extirpated." This would seem to convey that O'Nolan and his brave son, Donald, met the usual fate of our Irish chiefs, and had their heads cut off to adorn the embattled walls of the citadels of the enemy. But the O'Nolans were not quite extirpated as we shall see.

Referring to this battle Leland tells us that:- "The Deputy was enabled, with the zealous concurrence of Ormonde, Desmond and some other lords, of the English race, and the assistance of the subjects of Meath, to march against them. After a desperate and well disputed battle they were defeated but not reduced. The victors were suddenly called off to other insurgents; and all their vigour and bravery could but acquire some temporary advantages with little damage to the enemy and no permanent security to the subjects."[251]

The Lion of Leinster, who knew not defeat, in other words, according to Leland, held the field but did not deem it judicious to pursue the retreating foe. Slowly did he turn the steps of his gallant steed up the steep side of the ancient rath, and in the light of the sun that is said to have 'stood still', watched the pennons of the English as they became less and less distinct across the undulating plain carrying with them into captivity O'Nolan, his noble marshal, his prudent councillor, his gallant ally and his faithful friend. The Chieftains gathered around him to offer their congratulations on his victory and their condolence on his loss, while the faithful kern and gallowglasses hollowed out the graves that were soon filled with the mangled remains of their fallen clansmen. When we hear people calling this historic spot Danesfort in future, let us remember that its true name is not Danesfort but Dun - fartha meaning the Fort of the Graves, the spot where so many of our brave countrymen are

---

[250] Ware
[251] Leland Vol.2 pg.5

interred, who died that we might enjoy freedom in the land of our forefathers.[252]

And if, perchance, we should ever travel through Forth O'Nolan by the road leading from Myshall to Carlow, let us breathe a prayer for the soul of Art O'Nolan as we pass the ancient ivy clad church of Temple Peter where his mortal remains rest, side by side with the Kings and heroes of his noble race.

In 1406 Leyseach O'Nollan, Tanaist of ffohertye & Hugh O'Twhaile, tanaist of Imaile, & also Bran O'Broyne, Tanaist of ffoylan, Thomas McThomas McMurrough, died all of the plague this yeare.[253]

"The English of Ireland with Scroope, the king's Deputy, gave an overthrow to the Irish of Munster, by whom Teige O'Keruell, prince of the territory of Elye was slaine. This Teige was deservedly a man of great accompt and fame with the professors of poetry and musick of Ireland and Scotland, for his Liberality extended towards them and every of them in generall."[254]

Scroope died at Castledermot in 1407 and was succeeded by Prince Thomas who returned as Viceroy in 1408. "Immediately on his arrival "he confined the Earl of Kildare, the Deputy Governor, in prison in the Castle of Dublin, till he paid a fine of three hundred marks, for having with Adam Nolan, interfered with the right claimed by the Crown of appointing a Prebendary to Maynooth. The Prince held a parliament at Kilkenny, the burger of which town, on the occasion of his visit, presented him with a butt of wine. Although he mustered in hostile array all the Crown tenants in Ireland, the border Irish pressed so closely upon Dublin, that in an engagement near Kilmainham, where he for a time resided, he was severely wounded and narrowly escaped being slain."[255]

When Lord Thomas of Lancaster resolved to attack the Leinster Chiefs, whose standards now flew within sight of Dublin Castle, he summoned a council of the chief men of the Pale and it was decided that preparations should be made to crush the growing power of the King of Leinster.

McMurrough, and O'Nolan, aided by O'Byrne, O'Toole and probably O'Connor Faly, marched north and descending the Dublin hills crossed the lowlands, while the tenants of the Marches fled precipitately within the walls of Dublin. The Irish encamped at Kilmainham. On the right hand they were protected by the Oaks of Inchicore and on the left by the Liffey, beyond which rose the undulating sward of the area later called the Phoenix Park. Before them lay the Priory of St. John, and farther southward the spires of St.

---

[252] Of course this was not the case. The idea of national freedom was a concept that only came into being at a much later date. - A.K.

[253] Ann. Clonm.

[254] Ibid.

[255] Gilbert pg. 300

Patrick's and St. Bride's churches, the towers of Christ's Cathedral and the Castle a grim background to the gated wall which stretched in front.

The Lord Thomas resolving to give battle, divided his forces into four parts. The first he commanded in person, Sir Jenico d'Artois (the Lawless) the second, Sir Edward Perrers the third and Sir Thomas Butler, the lame prior of Kilmainham, the fourth. The English then marched out in two divisions, one by the north side of the Liffey to the ford of Kilmainham and the other by St. John's Priory. On either side there were between twelve and fifteen thousand men. The battle was long and violently contested. The thickest of the fight was on the river side at the ford, which from the slaughter of that day is known as Athcroe or the Ford of the Blood. Lord Thomas was dangerously wounded and carried into Dublin and eventually the English were totally routed and fled pell mell casting away their swords and armour.

So great was the slaughter that McMurrough and O'Nolan could not carry back all the spoils of war, so taking the swords of the slain and those abandoned by the retreating English they bent them across their knees and buried them in the graves in which they interred their dead. Unfortunately the equipment of the Leinster forces did not warrant their attacking the strongly fortified city of Dublin, one of the best fortified cities in Europe in those days, so with victorious banners floating in the breeze they recrossed the mountains in triumph. Of all the slain that day the only name handed down is that of Hitsin (Hudson) Tuite, a Meath captain who fell on the side of the English.

In the excavations carried on at Kilmainham in 1846, for the laying of the South Western Railway, a great number of swords, bent in two, were dug up. Mr. Petrie explained this circumstance, as stated in the text, in a paper read before the Royal Irish Academy, in whose museum these swords are now preserved. The style of their workmanship shows them to be Medieval and I have no doubt they are the very same taken by McMurrough and his allies from the English at this battle. More recently many other relics of the battle have been discovered in the neighbourhood of Island Bridge and are now in the Royal Irish Academy.

The condition of Lord Thomas after this debacle is set forth in a letter sent to the King, giving an account of his dangers and difficulties. "His soldier have deserted him; the people of his household are on the point of leaving him; and though they were willing to remain, our Lord is not able to keep them together; our said lord, your son, is so destitute of money he hath not a penny in the world, nor a penny can he get credit for."[256]

He came over with 7,000 marks a short time ago and received the spoils and ransom money of Lord Kildare. He soon returned to England pleading his

---

[256] Biblm Cotton M.S. Titus. B. XI folio 22

148

wounds as an excuse. Prior Butler became his Deputy. He was surnamed Baccagh - lame.

In 1410 the Prior of Kilmainham, Lord Justice, led an army of 1500 and devastated the territory of the O'Byrnes.[257] Another Annalist says that the 1500 men were "Kerns or Irish soldiers" and that half of them went over to the enemy "so that it had gone hard with the Lord Justice if the power of Dublin had not been there and yet he escaped not without loss".[258]   Two years later the O'Nolans with O'Connor Faly and the Moores inflicted heavy losses on the English and took 140 prisoners at Kil Echain - Killucan - Co. Westmeath. Sir Thomas Mereward, Baron of Screen was slain and Christopher Fleming, son of the Baron of Slane was taken prisoner and 1400 marks paid for him.

Henry IV died in 1412 and was succeeded by his son Henry V, who had been knighted by King Richard in Ireland during his last campaign.

In 1414 the Irish of Leinster fought another battle with the English, led by the Archbishop of Dublin, at Kilkea, near Castledermot in Co. Kildare and according to Dowling 3,000 were slain but this is probably an exaggeration.[259]

Lord John Talbot was appointed Viceroy in 1413 and he determined to take on the Irish enemies. He didn't bother with the Carlow/Wexford clans but he carried fire and sword into Laois and then proceeded onwards to Meath and Louth where he firmly established English rule. During his time in office he continually made a circuit of the Pale, occasionally making forays against the Irish enemy but he was "in no wise able to reduce them to a state of obedience or enlarge the limits of the Pale."[260]

The English of the Wexford Pale (i.e the baronies of Forth & Bargy), heartened by the news of the victory of the English king at Agincourt in the previous year, rose in revolt against Art the McMurrough, to whom they had been paying an annual Black Rent. It would appear that they killed over 300 Irish in some raids but when Art appeared in the area they quickly made peace with him. He retired to New Ross to spend Christmas of 1416. His son, Donough and his chief Brehon, O'Doran, feasted with him.

Merry was the Christmas at Ros mhic Treoin and New Year's Day dawned happily but on the following morning, January 2nd. 1417 there was sorrow and dismay for the McMurrough and his chief Brehon lay dead - done to death, it was supposed, by drinking a poisonous draught which a woman gave them.

---

[257] Dowling

[258] Cox

[259] It is interesting to note that at that time one Thomas O'Nuallain was abbot of St. Fiacc's church in Clonegal (*A Christian Calling - Whelan and Murphy*)- A.K.

[260] Gilbert

Donough, son of Art, was proclaimed King of Leinster by O'Nolan. Two years later in 1419, Donough and his father's friend Calvach O'Connor Faly were entrapped by Sir John Talbot. O'Connor managed to escape, but Donough was brought a prisoner to London. He was held captive for nine years and then he was ransomed by his clansmen. During his imprisonment his brother Gerald was acting King of Leinster, but upon Donough's return Gerald relinquished the title.

During the ten year period from 1420 to 1430 there was intermittent war between the new Deputy Ormonde and the Irish of Leinster. The tide of victories ebbed and flowed. Because of the very disturbed state of the country many of the colonists became impoverished. A statement of grievances was made to the King in which it was said that "your land has descended to so great a decline that it will never be relieved ...without your most gracious presence ... but the same your land and your lieges there, in a short time, will be utterly lost and forever destroyed, which God forbid."[261] Henry V died in 1422 and he was succeeded by his son, an infant of nine months, as Henry VI.

Edmund Mortimer was appointed Viceroy in Ireland in 1423. He was entitled fifth Earl of March and Ulster, Lord of Connaught and Trim. He arrived in Ireland in 1424 but he died of the plague in 1425. His titles and estates devolved upon his nephew, Richard Plantagenet, Duke of York.

Ormonde was appointed Viceroy in 1426 but he only lasted one year and a new Viceroy arrived in Ireland in 1427. He was Sir John de Grey. This man was forced "to make large disbursements from his own proper gold to provide soldiery to defend the settlement from the attentions of the O'Nolans, McMurroughs and other hostile forces."[262]

Sir Thomas Stanley became Viceroy in 1431 and in the same year Donough the McMurrough, lately ransomed from his prison in London, aided by the O'Nolans, the O'Connors, the O'Tooles and the O'Byrnes made two attacks on Dublin. He was successful in the first but he was defeated in the second and the chief of the O'Tooles was captured. Every vestige of English power was swept out of Carlow and marching to Wexford the people of that city were compelled to pay an eric (fine) of 800 marks for the slaying of Murtogh McMurrough, one of the King's sons and compelled also to restore hostages they had taken.

The state of the country can be seen from the following passages taken from a submission sent to the King of England (or his acting advisers) by the hard pressed colonists. Stanley was the bearer of the letter which stated:-

"The county of Catherlogh, in the south west part of the city of Dublin, within this thirty years, was one of the keys of the land, midway between the

---

[261] Gilbert pg.313
[262] Ibid. pg. 323

said city and the outparts, that is to say, the counties of Kilkenny and Tipperary; and the province of Cashel also is inhabited by enemies and rebels, save the castles of Ceatharlogh and Tillagh. Within these nine years, there were, in the said county of Ceatharlogh one hundred and forty eight castles and piles defensible, well vaulted, embattled and inhabited, that are now destroyed and under the subjection of the said enemies."[263]

English ecclesiastics were forced to abandon their establishments on the frontiers, having vainly attempted to maintain and fortify them against the Gaelic clans. The settlers in Southern Leinster were compelled to pay heavy tributes and the sheriffs had recourse to forced labour to repair the fortifications and defences of Carlow and other border towns. Gerald Kavanagh, Donough's brother, died in 1431. Later on in 1444 his sons rose in rebellion against Donough and were supported by the O'Byrnes and the O'Tooles. Donough was sustained by the O'Nolans and O'Connor Faly and the other dynasts of Leinster. Matters seem to have been amicably adjusted for we find these Kavanaghs fighting with the O'Nolans[264] and the McMurrough against the common enemy in 1445. But in the following year King Donough[265] was slain in battle by the Kavanaghs.

One of the daughters of Donough was married to O'Neill and another to James, Earl of Ormonde. O'Neill repudiated his wife who was called Gormley, to take another but he was induced by the Earl of Ormonde in 1452 to separate himself from the second and to restore the first. Gormley died in 1465.[266]

---

[263] Gilbert pg. 330

[264] It must have been at this time that a branch of the O'Nolans went to Galway. According to Hamilton in his History of Galway the O'Nolans first went to Galway during the reign of King Henry VI. - A.K.

[265] Another man Donal seems to have been the man killed and his seal is to be seen in the British Museum. He was titled King of Leinster and he was a nephew of Gerald, Lord of Ferns. - A.K.

[266] Fr. Nolan seems to be somewhat in error here. Donough became blind in 1450 and he relinquished the title of King of Leinster to his nephew Donal Reagh or Riabhach, but retained the title of McMurrough until his death in 1478. Donal Reagh himself died in 1476 having been badly injured in a fall from a horse the previous year. Fr. Nolan is also mistaken about the family relationships. Donough's brother Gerald had three sons and no daughters. Gerald married his second cousin, Sadbh O'Byrne, by whom he already had his three sons - Donal Reagh, Dermot and Art More. One of Donal Reagh's daughters married one of the O'Nolans and after his death she married James FitzEdmond Butler. It was her son Piers Roe who became the 8th. Earl of Ormonde. If Fr. Nolan's sources are correct her sister married Henry O'Neill of Tyrone. Henry put away his McMurrough wife and married the widow of O'Donnell (she was formerly a De Burgo), but he was compelled by the Duke of Ormonde to reverse his actions. - A.K.

In 1446 John Talbot, Earl of Shrewsbury, was again appointed Viceroy. He held a parliament at Trim which enacted amongst other things that "every man must keep his upper lip shaved, or else may be used as an Irish enemy. If any Irishman that is denizen kill or rob, he may be used as an Irish enemy and slain".[267]

This parliament also passed an act which decreed that the sons of labourers and travailers of the ground should, under penalty of fine and imprisonment follow the avocation of their parents. It further ordered that "no man shall be so hardy henceforth as to use any gilt bridles, peytrells or any other gilt harness, in no place or the said land, except knights and prelates of the Holy Church; and if any be found with such bridles, peytrells or other gilt harness from the 1st of May next, it shall be lawful to every man that will, to take the said man, his horse and harness and possess the same as his own goods."[268]

According to the Irish authorities on the subject, O'Reilly, chief of the Breifney of Cavan was treacherously seized by the Viceroy on whose invitation he had come to Trim, where he was carried off by disease while "in durance". He had earned such a terrible reputation in France that the womenfolk of the common people, in order to instil fear into their children would call out to them "the Talbot will get you". The Irish chroniclers denounced him as " a son of curses for his venom, and a devil for his evils" and they added, "the learned say of him, that there came not, from the time of Herod, by whom Christ was crucified, any one so wicked in evil deeds."[269]

Talbot was succeeded by Richard, Duke of York, who was the head of the "White Rose" party in England. He was descended paternally from Edmund of Langley, youngest son of Edward III and by his mother, Anne, daughter of Roger Mortimer who was slain by the O'Nolans. He was legally entitled to the Crown of England, as representative of Lionel, third son of Edward III. His wife was Cecilia, one of twenty two children of Ralph Neville, Earl of Westmoreland. Most of these children married with the greatest nobles of England. Cecilia was remarkable for her beauty, her mental capacity and for the fact that she was the mother of two kings - Edward IV and Richard III.

" Instead of attempting to advance northwards under the banner of the 'black dragon', the English ensign of his Earldom of Ulster, the Duke adopted propitiatory measures with such effect that, before he had been a month in Ireland, he succeeded in enlisting the services of Magennis of Iveagh with six hundred horse and foot; Mac Mahon of Farney with eight hundred; MacArtan with a similar number and the two chiefs of the O'Reilly clans with seven

---

[267] Cox
[268] Gilbert pg. 349
[269] Ibid. pg. 350

152

hundred men. At the head of his combined forces the Duke advanced into the country of the O'Byrnes, ravaged their territory until O'Byrne came to terms and agreed to swear allegiance; to pay a tribute of two pence per acre of his land; to provide six hundred men, at his own cost, to do service where ordered; to permit the law of England to be put in execution in his district; and promised that he, his wife, children, and chief adherents should wear English attire and learn the language of England. On this expedition, the Duke, at Symond's Wood, in O'Byrne's country, conferred knighthood on Robert Preston, Lord of Gormanstown and others. Many score beeves were sent to the Duke by the Leinster Irish and those of Eastern Ulster. O'Neill, Magennis, MacMahon, O'Farrell, O'Moore, O'Dempsey, the McMurrough, O'Nolan, MacGeoghegan and Brian O'Byrne, in addition to four hundred kine presented two hobbies for the Duchess of York."[270]

Mac Geoghegan, native Lord of Kinelea or Cineal Fhiacha, in Westmeath, had, on the arrival of the Viceroy in 1449, presented him with nineteen score kine; but in consequence of subsequent transactions, he invaded the neighbouring ducal demesnes in Meath. He burned the Duke's "large town of Rathmore" with some adjacent villages and remained "assembling in woods and forts, waiting to do hurt and grievance to the king's subjects". Thither the Viceroy marched with his soldiery, under the banner of England; but MacGeoghegan advanced against them, at Mullingar, with so large a force of well appointed cavalry, that it was considered expedient to enter into terms, and to forego all claims for the injuries which he had inflicted both upon the Viceroy's lands and liege subjects. Smarting under this insult the Duke wrote to England for money to prosecute the war finishing his letter with this gloomy paragraph :- " If payment be not had in all haste, for to have men of war in defence and safeguard of this land, my power cannot stretch to keep it in the King's obeisance. And very necessity will compel me to come into England, to live there upon my poor livelihood, for I had lever be dead than any inconvenience should fall thereto in my default; for it shall never be chronicled, nor remain in scripture, by the grace of God, that Ireland was lost by my negligence."[271]

The Duke returned to England, unexpectedly, in September 1450 and left as his Deputy in Ireland, Sir James Le Botiller, eldest son of the Earl of Ormonde.

---

[270] Gilbert pg. 353 - This paragraph is followed in Nolan's MSS with a lengthy description of the general state of the country. It would appear from his sources that law and order was almost non existent. The main sufferers appear to have been the English tenants and 'husbandmen' who had to provide coyne and livery for their English overlords and their Irish 'friends'.

[271] Ibid. pg. 360

James, 4th. Earl of Ormonde, usually styled "the white" died in 1452, and was succeeded by his eldest son James. The kinsmen of the 'white Earl' intermarried with some of the principal septs in their vicinity, among whom were the Kavanaghs, O'Carrolls and O'Reillys. This Earl, who had frequently ruled the colony, was described by the Irish as "the best captain of the English nation that was in Ireland and England in those ages."[272]

His son, James, became the new Viceroy and appears to have spent the next two years warring against the FitzGeralds of Kildare. That country was wasted and despoiled and many people taken captive and held for ransom. Several appeals were made to the Duke of York to have the situation rectified. He was appointed Viceroy again in 1454 and nominated the Earl of Kildare as his Deputy. Later, when he Duke sought safety in Ireland, it would seem he received the sympathy of the O'Nolans and other Leinster septs. Any party that opposed the interests of the Ormonde faction was sure to receive the support of the O'Nolans. All through the latter part of the century the O'Nolans and FitzGeralds seem to have been closely allied against the Butler party.[273]

"The Deputy, Desmond, made two expeditions against the O'Byrnes in 1466; but at this period the English of Leinster suffered continuous reverses from the O'Nolans and other border septs, who defeated them in several encounters and carried off as prisoners some of their chief ecclesiastic and lay personages. Much of Meath having been regained from the settlers part of the natives projected to establish as King, at Tara, Tadgh, son of Turlogh O'Brien, Lord of Thomond. This chief crossed the Shannon with an army greater than any that had been mustered in Ireland since the time of Brian Borumha, and coerced the city of Limerick to agree to pay him an annual tribute, but was soon after cut off by a fever."[274]

An act was passed about this time halving the value of the currency and determining the actual cost of many items; a peck of wheat to be sold for sixteen pence; of oats for four pence; of barley eight pence; a barrel of herrings, six and eight pence; a cow, of the better sort, six and eight pence; an

---

[272] Gilbert pg. 364

[273] There follows in the Nolan MSS a lengthy description of the turmoil that occurred in Ireland as a result of the Wars of the Roses in England. Most of the battles were fought between the supporters of either faction - e.g. the Ormondes supported the Lancastrians and the FitzGeralds the Yorkists. During the period from 1450 to 1460 the native chiefs were left pretty much to their own devices. South east Leinster seems to have been relatively calm as Donal Reagh was able to found a Franciscan Abbey in Enniscorthy in the early 1460s.- where he was subsequently buried. The present Bank of Ireland now stands on the site. - A.K.

[274] Gilbert pg. 394

ox, ten shillings; a sheep, eight pence; a good hog, three and four pence; a gallon of the best ale, three half-pence; wine of Rochelle, six pence; of Gascoigne, eight pence and of Spain, ten pence per gallon."[275]

Sometime about the year 1480, Gerald the Earl of Kildare was appointed Lord Deputy and he enacted laws prohibiting trading with the Irish. He made an exception of ecclesiastical establishments. The principals of those foundations were given licences to trade with the Irish, to maintain communications with them in war and peace and to become godfathers to their children.[276]

During the closing years of the reign of Edward IV, the Earl of Kildare became a very powerful man. As Deputy he was empowered to seize the lands of absentee owners and he had powers to levy huge sums on all the baronies under his jurisdiction in Leinster. A most astute man, he made peace with most of the great Irish families of Leinster and practised fostering and gave the chiefs valuable presents in return for their recognition of his power.

So it was that the Earl was authorised to take possession of the county of Carlow, from the town of Calveston to Carlow Castle, unless the absentee claimants came, within twelve months and undertook the recovery of those lands from the Irish. The Deputy built a castle at Tristle Dermot or Castle Dermot in Co. Kildare, which it was expected would be "the true means of causing the waste lands of the County Carlow to be inhabited by the English subjects." To aid in this erection the Council authorised the Deputy to impress wagons, horses etc., from baronies in Dublin and Meath and to oblige every person holding one ploughland in the barony of Newcastle, to provide an able man to labour gratuitously at the work for four days. At the same time, the Earl was granted as Deputy, a subsidy of thirteen shillings and four pence to be levied from every ploughland under English jurisdiction in the four Leinster shires.

The nominal English Lordship of Carlow, descended through the female line to Sir William de Berkeley, created Earl of Nottingham by Richard III. De Berkeley, as Lord of Carlow, in 1484, transferred the advowson and patronage of the parish church of the Blessed Virgin there to St. Mary's Abbey, Dublin.[277]

The intelligence of the result of the battle of Bosworth was received with dissatisfaction by the heads of the Anglo-Irish, who were chagrined that Richard III, a son of their favourite Duke of York, should have been overthrown by Henry Tudor, whom they "regarded as an obscure Welsh adventurer, sprung from a doubly illegitimate stock."[278]

---

[275] Gilbert pg. 398
[276] Ibid. pg. 402
[277] Gilbert pg. 603
[278] Ibid. pg. 422

John the sixth Duke of Ormonde, died on a pilgrimage in Palestine in 1478 and he was succeeded by his brother, Thomas, who, inheriting great wealth, resided on his English estates and became a member of Henry's privy council. This absenteeism led to a reduction in the influence of the Ormondes in Ireland and the O'Nolans were left in comparative peace. Even FitzGerald, who had built the castle at Castledermot was not anxious to disturb the status quo to any great extent and he left the O'Nolans undisturbed to any great degree.

A junior line of the Ormonde family acquired much influence in Kilkenny and Tipperary during this period. This branch descended from the third Earl's son Richard, so named from his godfather, Richard II. Richard Botiller received knighthood and married Catherine, daughter of Gildas O'Reilly, lord of Cavan; their son, Edmund, surnamed Mac Richard Botiller, became further allied with the native Irish by marrying Catherine the daughter of Melrunad O'Carroll. Mac Richard's son, Sir James Botiller adhered to the Lancastrian cause, was pardoned by Edward IV and appointed Deputy in Ireland to his kinsman John, the absentee Earl of Ormonde. He reformed the government of the town of Carrick and built the castle of Nehom, near Gowran. He obtained influence with the Irish by his marriage with Sabina or Sadbh, daughter of Donal Reagh Kavanagh, the McMurrough. She was the widow of O'Nolan. An act of Parliament granted Sadbh rights under English law.[279] They were married in the Church of Listerlin in Ossory. Sir Piers Roe Botiller was the third child of this union. He later became the 8th. Earl of Ormonde. Sir James, himself, died in 1468 and was succeeded by his son Piers who was designated in James's will as 'chief captain of his nation' and given custody and defence of the lands of the Earl of Ormonde as they had been entrusted to himself. He also bequeathed to Piers his horse, cuirass and all his holy relics, beads, rings and hereditary jewels. Another important alliance was forged when Piers Roe married Margaret, a sister of Gerald, Earl of Kildare. However his right to administer the Ormonde estates was soon disputed when Sir James (the Black Knight) a nephew of Thomas the 7th. Earl was entrusted with this commission by his uncle. Kildare, on behalf of his brother-in-law appealed to Thomas without success.

Kildare was now removed from office as was Fitz Eustace the King's Chancellor and Treasurer. The office of Treasurer was granted to the Black Knight who was educated at the court of England. He was also appointed as Captain of the royal troops for Kilkenny and Tipperary and was given a grant of lands in those counties which had belonged to the Earl of March.[280]

The Black Knight was joined in commission with Thomas Gaith as Captain and Governor of the King's army. Some of their soldiers killed

---

[279] She was given a grant of 'English Liberty' - A.K.
[280] Gilbert pg. 444

Calvagh, son of O'Connor of Offaly, the ally and kinsman of the Earl of Kildare. In retaliation the Earl seized the Royal commissioner, Gaith, placed him in prison and hanged his son.

Prince Henry (later Henry VIII), then an infant was appointed Lord Lieutenant of Ireland. His Deputy was Sir Edward Poynings, the author of the famous Poyning's law.

Poynings was commissioned to "punish the King's delinquent subjects in Ireland; to receive rebels into peace; to accept fines or compositions from them and to issue pardons under the great seal. He was also empowered, with the King's forces, and those summoned to the 'royal service' and by all other means to invade, suppress, punish or bring to peace, contumelious English or Irish, warring upon or despoiling the territories of the Crown or the lands of its subjects.[281]

Poynings joined forces with Sir James Botiller and ordered the Earl of Kildare to bring his forces also for a punitive expedition against Magennis and O'Hanlon. While they devastated the lands of those chiefs Sir James assured Poynings that the Earl of Kildare in concert with O'Hanlon and the Scots had devised a plot against his life. Intelligence also arrived that the Earl's brother had seized the King's castle of Carlow. Peace was hastily arranged with Magennis and O'Hanlon and the Deputy hastened to Carlow.

There he was defied by James FitzGerald, the brother of the Earl of Kildare who refused to hand over the castle. A siege ensued which lasted for ten days. At the famous Parliament in Drogheda in December of 1494[282] the Earl of Kildare was attainted. He was shortly afterwards arrested and sent a prisoner to London. While he languished in the Tower, his kinsman in Munster, the Earl of Desmond, supported the claims of the pretender Perkin Warbeck and attacked Waterford city. Poynings marched on Waterford and after eleven days of fighting he repelled Desmond.

Fearing that the native chiefs might become embroiled in the attempt by Desmond, the Council in Dublin sent agents to O'Byrne soliciting his aid for the safe keeping of the borders and to influence him they sent a bolt of velvet to his wife! They also offered regular payments to O'Neill, the McMurrough, Mac Mahon, O'Connor, De Bermingham and others. They also entrusted the castle of Carlow to Gerald Kavanagh.[283]

---

[281] Ibid. pg. 449

[282] An event of some significance to the O'Nolans occurred in this year. The Crown took possession of the estates of absentee landlords and in this way the manors of Tullowphelim, Rathvilly, Clonmore, Kellistown, Powerston and Leighlin were granted to the Earl of Ormonde.

[283] He was the 2nd. son of Donal Reagh and he became the McMurrough in 1517 after the death of his brother Art Bui.

Wars were renewed upon the English by James, surnamed Earleson, brother to the Earl of Kildare. These movements became so formidable that in 1496 the Deputy ordered that fires be kindled on various parts of the hills of Tara, Lyons, Athboy and Slane, as beacons to warn the King's people when James Earleson with the Irish enemies should be seen advancing on the English territories.

Chapter 13

The 16th. Century

Historical incidents of vast importance come crowding in upon us so rapidly during the sixteenth century that it becomes quite impossible to deal fully with them, within the limits at our disposal.

The rebellion of Silken Thomas may broadly be taken as the beginning of the end of the power of O'Nolan and other Irish chieftains. Indeed, in the case of O'Nolan the fall of the Geraldines opened the way to the usurpation of the Butlers who had long sought for possession of the fair lands of Forth O'Nolan. The Butlers and FitzGeralds were hereditary enemies and so also were the Butlers and the O'Nolans. This opposition to the Butlers led to an understanding between O'Nolans and FitzGeralds the consequence of which was that while power remained in the hands of the Earls of Kildare the O'Nolans lived in comparative peace, and even when misfortune overtook the Geraldines, Lord Leonard Grey, who was sent over as Deputy, being brother-in-law to the Earl, exercised considerable clemency towards the O'Nolans and other supporters of the Kildare family, so much so, indeed that the Butlers charged Lord Grey before the King with manifesting too much sympathy with the King's enemies.

The position of Deputy was held almost continuously by the FitzGeralds between 1478 and 1534. Piers Roe Butler, the Earl of Ossory and later the 8th. Earl of Ormonde (1537) only held the office twice in 1521 and in 1528.

There is extant a wonderfully interesting document which bears testimony to the alliance between the FitzGeralds and the O'Nolans. This is the rental of Gerald, 9th. Earl of Kildare, commenced in 1518. In this we find a record of tributes granted by Morogh O'Nolan, captain of his nation, and certain other Irish chieftains, in consideration of which those chieftains and their clansmen were entitled to the protection and guardianship of this powerful nobleman. The payments took many and varied shaped. Eels from one, hawks from another, fat beasts, sheep, hogs, honey, butter etc., and of course a modicum of cash. Sir Henry Wallop states that down to 1584 there was hardly a native lord in the kingdom who was not dependant on either the Earl of Kildare or the Earl of Ormonde for his defence. The following entries in the rental show the tribute paid by the O'Nolan.

Folio XIII

O'Nolan's country called Fohirt

159

Upon the said O'Nolan yerely at Mich
For his defence, graunted by Morg
Nydfre Captain of his Nation   XII Kyne or
                              VI Mares

In Rathto yevin by Gerald Duffe
O'Nolan, upon every cow at Mech yerely   iii j d
and upon every Croe or Shepe   1 shepe
Item in Ballycalden in likewise.

The Morg Nydfre mentioned herein is that Morogh Niy Doiory O'Nolan whose lands, then owned by his direct descendant, were granted in 1605 to Sir Oliver Lambert,[284] after he had been 'attainted of felony' and Gerald Duffe O'Nolan's lands were granted partly to Lambert and the remainder to the Earl of Ormonde.

Gerald the 8th. Earl of Kildare was known to the Irish as 'Gearoid More' or the Great Earl. He succeeded his father in 1477 and died in 1513. In the year 1488[285] for a great rarity, six hand guns or muskets were sent to the Earl out of Germany. With these and other weapons he marched through the Pale destroying the property of the Butlers and their supporters, while in revenge for this Sir James Botiller plundered and burned the whole county and town of Kildare.

In 1513 he marched against Lemyvannan or O'Carroll's castle, now Leap Castle in the King's county; but as he was watering his horse in the river

---

[284] Sir Oliver Lambert was an English solider who came to Ireland in 1600 with Lord Mountjoy. He was stationed at Enniscorthy where he was in charge of the garrison there. In August of that year he was responsible for a huge prey of cattle and horses taken from the O'Byrne/O'Nolan/Kavanagh country. The area in question was the Forth/Shillelagh/Clonegal area. He set out to bring the cattle to the fort of Laois (Dunamace) to provision the garrison there. He was pursued by the Leinstermen and fought a running battle with them that lasted all day. Later he was made commander of the English garrison in Cavan town after Mountjoy captured it in 1601. In the Plantation of Ulster he was granted 1500 acres in the barony of Clonmahon, mostly in the parish of Mountnugent and Ballymachugh. His widow and son were granted more land in Mullahoran.

The Lamberts became the "Earls of Cavan" but their lofty title did not stop them losing their lands in Cavan (and Carlow) due to bad financial management. The family still own land in Co. Westmeath and retain the title Earls of Cavan. - A.K.

[285] In this year also Edmund O'Toole was killed by the O'Byrnes in a row about boundaries - The Book of the O'Tooles

160

Greese, at Kilkea, he was shot by one of the O'Moores of Leix. He died in Kildare a few days later.

When Henry VIII ascended the throne of England in 1509 the lawful and legitimate King of Leinster was Murrough McMurrough or "Mauritius Woodkern" as Dowling calls him. He died in 1512. He was also known as Murrough Ballach. He was the son of Donogh, son of Art.

About the same time Nicholas MacGuire, Bishop of Leighlin died. He was born in Idrone, but brought up in the University of Oxford. Thomas Halsay, an Englishman and Doctor of Laws was his successor. This Halsay was afterwards present at the Latern Council in the years 1515 and 1516. In his absence he constituted Charles or Cahir Kavanagh, Abbot of the Abbey of Duiske as his Vicar General.

About this time also, Patrick Finglas, one of the Barons of the Exchequer in Ireland, wrote a treatise on the 'Decay of Ireland'. This extract is of interest to us: "Earl Strongbow obtained Leinster not only by conquest but by the gift of McMurrough, then King thereof, who gave him his daughter. This Earl enjoyed all Leinster in rest and peace during his life, which was 14 years after the said conquest, so that at the time of his death all the inhabitants of the same obeyed the King's laws, except certain kinsmen of McMurrough, whom by reason of the alliance of his wife the Earl had permitted to inhabit the midst of the said country under tribute, in a little country (as it were a barony) called Ydron."

Finglas went on to give a brief description of how the lands of Carlow and Wexford were lost to the Irish during the succeeding centuries. He then goes on to say:- "If the King purpose to make a thorough reformation of this land, he should begin with Leinster, which was not these 500 years so likely to be conquered, for the Kavanaghs and Nolans, the Byrnes and Tooles are but feeble in regard of the strength they have been of in former times."

He then goes on to suggest how by suppressing the abbeys and taking over the church lands and castles the native Irish would be much weakened. He mentions the abbeys of Dunbrody and Tintern in Wexford, Duiske in Carlow and Baltinglass in Wicklow, the castles of Leighlin, Carlow, Rathvilly and Clonmore, and the other castles and abbeys in Wexford and Wicklow e.g. Ferns, Wicklow, Powerscourt, Arklow and CastleKevin.

His suggestion on placing English captains included the placing of such men in many of the castles and piles in McMurrough's country, O'Nolan's country and Byrne's country.

"The least of these captains would expend yearly 200 or 300 marks; besides giving lands to the freeholders under him. It were requisite that all of them should have no great possessions in England. As they cannot without the King's aid recover the lands that the Kavanaghs, O'Nolans, Byrnes and Tooles now have in possession , or banish them out of the country, the King should find an army, so as every of the said captains might have a retinue of men of war for their defence for 2 or 3 years, until they be settled and the land tilled and inhabited.

Touching inhabitants, as it might be dangerous to depeople the realm of England the lands might be inhabited by some sorts of the Irishry as at the first conquest, for there be no better labourers than the poor commons of Ireland, nor sooner will be brought to good frame, if they be kept under the law."

Another planner writing later in the century tried to delineate the extent of the territories of the Gaelic clans and the names of their chiefs.

"Hereafter issueth the names of the chief Irish regions and countries of Leinster and the chief captains of the same.

McMurrough, called also Kavanagh, of Idrone, in the west part of Carlow.

O'Byrne's country was in that part of the county of Wicklow between Wicklow head and Arklow, while the O'Tooles had four strong septs left - at Carnew, Castleruddery[286], Talbotstown (Glen of Imaal) and Powerscourt.

O'Morogh (O'Morchoe - Murphy)held the east part of the county of Wexford between Enniscorthy and the coast formerly called the barony of Deeps.

O'Toole's country was formerly called the barony of CastleKevin and comprised that part of Wicklow which lies between Talbotstown, Newcastle and Ballinacor.

O'Nolan inhabited the south west point of Wexford.[287]

McGilpatrick, afterwards called FitzPatrick of Upper Ossory in the Queen's county.

O'Moore of Leix, which was by the Irish statute 3&4 Philip and Mary constituted part of the new counties thereby erected, called Queen's county.

O'Dempsey of Glinmality near Portnehinch in the north part of the Queen's county.

O'Boyle of Oregan, in the barony of Tinnehinch, in Queen's county. All these were the chief Captains of their nation."

Gerald, ninth Earl of Kildare was born in 1487. He is called by the annalists Gearoid Oge. He appears to have followed the example of his father in considering it his duty, as representing the King, to govern and defend the Pale alone, and to have ruled the rest of his possessions as an Irish chief. Several of his Irish neighbours, having, at the end of 1513, ravaged parts of the Pale, the Earl, in the beginning of 1514 marched into Leix, where he defeated O'Moore and his followers and pursued them until they took refuge in their woods.

---

[286] Site of an Anglo Norman settlement near Imaal. - A.K.

[287] There is obviously confusion here. The chronicler thought that the O'Nolans lived in Forth in South Wexford, but he must not have known about Forth in Carlow. - A.K.

162

Again in 1516 he invaded Imaal, in the county of Wicklow and sent the head of Shane O'Toole, who had been slain[288], as a present to the Mayor of Dublin. He then marched into Ely O'Carroll, where he besieged the castle of Lemyvannan, against which his father had been marching before his death in 1513. The garrison, having defended it for a week, abandoned the castle under cover of darkness and the Earl when it fell to him had it razed. After this he marched so rapidly upon Clonmel that it at once surrendered on conditions. In December he returned to Dublin, "laden with booty, hostages and honour."[289]

But the enemies of Gearoid Oge had in the meantime "done what they could underhand to disgrace him in England,"[290] and eventually succeeded in having him called to answer for his conduct. He appointed Maurice, son of Sir Thomas Fitzgerald of Lackagh, a Knight of his own family, as Lord Justice. The chief charges against the Earl were that he enriched himself and his followers by the King's revenues and land; and that he had contracted an alliance with and had 'won' many of the Irish Natives to him and his heirs.[291]

Sometime shortly after this, Maurice, the Lord Justice, was killed by the O'Moores of Leix near Lackagh where a cross was erected in his memory. The place was called Maurice's Cross.[292]

During this year, 1519, McMurrough i.e. Art Bui Kavanagh, [293]Lord of Leinster died and also in the same year Donough Kavanagh, a prosperous and affluent man, of the chief nobles of Leinster died.[294] Art Bui was succeeded by his brother, Gerald, Lord of Ferns.

The Earl of Kildare was deposed and Thomas Howard, Earl of Surrey later created Duke of Norfolk, came as Deputy. He marched against and reduced Desmond and other Irish to subjection.

In 1521 Norfolk marched against the O'Connors of Offaly where he burnt towns and villages and great quantities of corn. In writing to the King, later, he stated his opinion that "the people will be forced to either to forsake their country or die of hunger next winter." However he did not get by unscathed. The Irish divided their forces into several parties and having intelligence that

---

[288] He was killed in his bed according to the Book of the O'Tooles

[289] Ware's Annals

[290] Cox

[291] Ware

[292] According to Fr. Nolan the base of that cross was still there in the 1920s while broken portions of the cross were built into the walls of an adjacent cottage.

[293] He may have died in 1517. He was buried in the Abbey in Enniscorthy. That site is now occupied by the Bank of Ireland. - A.K.

[294] Four Masters - He was the second son of Murrough Ballagh, King of Leinster who died in 1511 - A.K.

the baggage wagons of the army were slenderly guarded they attacked that part and did it so briskly that several of the Lord Deputy's soldiers fled.

While on the march, Norfolk was shot at by a rebel in ambush. The shot struck his vizor but he was unhurt. "Much ado they had to find the stubborn Tory, but at last they got him and FitzWilliam and Bedlow were forced to hew him to pieces for he would not yield."[295]

Bishop Halsay, of Leighlin, died and was succeeded by Maurice Doran of the Order of Friars Minor or of the Friars Preachers, a man highly esteemed for his excellent qualities and eloquent preaching.

At this time also Pope Leo the tenth decreed that King Henry VIII should be styled Defender of the Faith for the book he wrote against Luther.

Surrey was recalled to England in 1522 and Piers Roe Butler, the Earl of Ossory and claimant to the title of Earl of Ormonde, was appointed in his place. There was tremendous rivalry between the Ormonde - Ossory faction and the Fitzgeralds.[296] Judging by the correspondence of the period between the Fitzgeralds and the Crown, Piers Roe was gaining the upper hand and had taken castles, lands and livestock belonging to the Kildares. In one of the documents he complains that :- " (1)the servants of Ormonde burned, robbed and spoiled a town of the Deputy's called Levitstown, in the county of Kildare where they cruelly murdered and burned 17 men and women, divers of them being with child, and one of them fled out of the fire to the church was slain on the high altar; and burned and took with them goods to the value of £200.
(2) The Earl of Ormonde keeps a ward of evil disposed persons in a pyle adjoining the sea called Arclow, who rob and spoil the King's subjects passing thereby and ravish women, maidens and widows."

The Earl of Kildare was allowed to return to Ireland in 1523 and one of his first acts was to march against the O'Moores and O'Connors who had been colluding with the Earl of Ormonde.[297] Kildare was accompanied by the English of Meath and the O'Neills. A peace was brokered and the Irish chiefs agreed to give hostages. In this same year Gerald [298]Kavanagh, the McMurrough, died and was succeeded by Maurice, his brother.[299]

---

[295] Cox

[296] This is all the more surprising since Piers Roe was married to Gearoid Oge's sister - Margaret Fitzgerald.

[297] This is somewhat mystifying as O'Connor was married to Gearoid Oge's daughter. - A.K.

[298] Gerald was buried in Leighlin - A.K.

[299] It was about this time that the Kavanaghs transferred certain clan lands into the ownership of Piers Roe the Earl of Ossory (later the 8th. Earl of Ormonde) The lands in question were the Rower in Kilkenny, some townlands near Leighlin and lands in and

The Earl of Kildare was reappointed as Lord Deputy in 1524 and remained in that post until 1528.

In 1525 Maurice Doran the Bishop of Leighlin was murdered by Maurice Kavanagh, the son of Charles Kavanagh[300], the Abbot of Duiske, a kinsmen.[301] Maurice Kavanagh was the Archdeacon of the Diocese. The Bishop had threatened to correct him for "insolent stubbornness and other crimes". Maurice Kavanagh had some accomplices and they were all captured and hanged on the spot where the murder took place, by the order of Gearoid Oge Fitzgerald.

Cahir McArt of Polmonty the ancestor of the Borris Kavanaghs was married to a daughter of Gearoid Oge. In 1526 Cahir McArt attacked and burned Drumphea castle the home of Cahir McMoriertagh Og Kavanagh and his mother Maeve, both of whom perished in the flames along with many retainers.[302]

In 1527 the title of Earl of Ormonde was taken away from Piers Roe and granted to Sir Thomas Boleyn the grandson of the 7th. Earl of Ormonde who had died in 1517. Sir Thomas was the father of the unfortunate Ann Boleyn wife of Henry VIII who along with her brother George was executed in May of 1536. The title was restored to Piers Roe upon the death of Sir Thomas Boleyn in 1537.[303]

At this time the Earl of Kildare was shot while attacking O'Carroll and the Castle of Birr. A soldier who had also been wounded is said to have spoken to the Earl; "why are you so downcast when you see how well I am, although I

---

around Arklow. The sons of Brian Kavanagh of the Rower were relocated to Killcollatrim in Co. Carlow.

[300] Charles was the 3rd. son of Murrough Ballach, the king of Leinster who died in 1511. Daniel, the grandson of Charles was the Protestant Bishop of Leighlin later in the century.

[301] In those days abbots were laymen.

[302] It is not known why this attack took place but it is significant that three years earlier Moriertagh Og of Garryhill and Drumphea had been in contention for the title of McMurrough and King of Leinster. The Garryhill Kavanaghs were descended from Blind Donough the 2nd. son of the famous Art McMurrough while the Polmonty Kavanaghs were descended from Gerald Lord of Ferns who died in 1523. This attack probably took place in order to dispose of a future rival for the chieftaincy. - A.K.

[303] In the same year, 1537, a list of the lands (and the annual value of same) granted to Piers Roe and his son James was drawn up. The lands lay in counties Kilkenny, Tipperary, Catherlagh, Wexford, Waterford, Kildare, Meath and Dublin. James, Lord Butler, (Piers's eldest son) was also appointed Constable of the castles of Catherlagh and Kilkea. It was also noted by the Commission that the King's lands in Carlow, Kilkenny, Tipperary, Waterford, Dublin and Kildare were much depopulated and wasted. - Calendar of State Papers - A.K.

have no less than 3 bullets in me." The Earl quietly replied in his agony "I wish that you also had this bullet in you along with the others."[304]

He seems to have recovered well because in 1529 he was called upon to answer charges made against him by Piers Roe, the Earl of Ossory, his brother-in-law. Ossory accused him of contracting alliances with several of the King's enemies, with having executed many of the dependants of Ormonde and with conspiring to invade the territories of the Ormondes with the help of Irish enemies. He was also charged with conspiring with his two sons-in-law, O'Connor and O'Neill to have the Pale invaded. He was committed to the Tower of London and deprived of his office of Lord Deputy. He was further charged with exacting coyne and livery[305] in the counties of Kildare and Carlow as far as the bridge of Leighlin. It was asserted that he had great influence over the native chiefs many of whom, including O'Nolan, were paying tribute to him

Piers Roe was now appointed Lord Deputy but his tenure of that office was short-lived, because Gearoid Oge was allowed to return to Ireland in 1530 with the new Deputy, Sir William Skeffington. The reason for this was that the English officials, in particular, Wolsley the Chancellor, feared that the entire Pale would be overrun by the Irish and English 'rebels' unless their patron, the Earl, was allowed to return.

1530 "In the absence of the Earl of Kildare the Irish rose up in fierce rebellion and seized upon the country whence the King sent over the Earl of Kildare and Wm. Skeffington who quickly reformed the ferocity of the rebels. Cahir McInnycross Kavanagh[306] was made McMurrough who succeeded

---

[304] Ware

[305] Coyne and livery was widely practised by the Irish. According to Hore and Graves in 'The Social State of the Southern & Eastern Counties' coyne and livery were essential in an uncommercial society where money was scarce. Payment by cash was impossible and if the chief was to abide by the law of "spend me and defend me" he had to have himself and his bands fed and looked after by the general populace. - During the reign of Queen Elizabeth and also during the reign of James I the practice was outlawed and there were serious penalties attaching to anyone caught demanding them. The abolition of coyne and livery gave rise to a need for inns and hostelries and during the reign of James I many licences were issued for that purpose. - A.K.

[306] Cahir Mac na hInione Crosda - the son of the 'cross' daughter. This Cahir was either the bastard son of Gearoid Mor the 8th. Earl by a daughter of Donal Reagh, the King of Leinster who died in 1475 or else he was the illegitimate son of Gerald (the McMurrough who died in 1523) by a sister of Gearoid Oge the 9th. Earl. He was raised in the Fitzgerald household. In Hore's History of Wexford he is called Cahir Mac Gearailt.. There appears to have been some kind of unrest in the Wexford - Carlow area due to the office being contested. Cahir's opponent was Dulaing the 4th. son of Dermot Lamhdearg Kavanagh

166

Maurice Nemoroso Lagenie. An edict was issued from Parliament that no one in England or Ireland should receive a rescript from Rome."[307]

Piers Roe now sought to win friends at court and began a correspondence with Thomas Cromwell,[308] one of the most influential men in London. In the course of one letter he accused the Earl of Kildare of trying to take over "such garrisons and fortalices as I have. And whereas Thomas, late Earl of Ormonde, by deed gave to me and my heirs male the manors of Tullagh and Arcloe, I with force, danger of my life and great charge recovered the possession of the said manors out of the Irishmen's hands who had held them for 200 years;[309] and I made thereupon great buildings and reparations; but now the Earl of Kildare says he has obtained of Lord Wiltshire[310] a lease of the said manors, which are the very keys of the country, whereby Kildare with his Irish allies might destroy me, and win all the country from the King. The King should be wareful how he suffer him to have all the strength of the land, considering the seditious practices of his ancestors and himself."[311]

During 1533 John Alen, Master of the Rolls, was sent to England and instructed by the Council to declare to King Henry the state of the country and to charge the Earl of Kildare with appropriating the King's revenue. (1) " You shall instruct the King of the great decay of this land; that neither the English order, tongue nor habit has been used, nor the king's laws obeyed above twenty

---

who seems to have been domiciled in Tincurry near Ferns, Co. Wexford. Dulaing was the uncle of Cahir McArt of St. Mullins who was married to the daughter of Gearoid Og the 9th. Earl of Kildare. In the contest for the title the Earl gave his support to Cahir McInnycross. Dulaing sought and got support from Skeffington the Deputy. Two sons of Maurice, who had been the McMurrough prior to his death in 1531, were killed in a skirmish which occurred between the two parties. Cahir McInnycross was the last Kavanagh to be recognised as King of Leinster by the English.- A.K.

[307] Dowling

[308] Not to be confused with Oliver Cromwell who came to Ireland in 1649. This man was Thomas Cromwell later the Earl of Essex, who was at various times Lord Chancellor of England, Chief Secretary and Master of the Rolls. He was beheaded in the Tower of London in 1540 having fallen foul of Henry VIII. - A.K.

[309] Piers Roe was, as we have seen, the son of Sadhbh Kavanagh, daughter of Donal Reagh and widow of the O'Nolan. In 1525 Maurice the McMurrough surrendered Arklow to his nephew Piers Roe and in 1530 his cousins the sons of Cahir Kavanagh (3rd. son of Donal Reagh) conveyed the Rower in Co. Kilkenny to Piers Roe. It may well be the case that the O'Nolans likewise ceded Tullow to Piers Roe at this time.- A.K.

[310] Lord Wiltshire was Thomas Boleyn the grandson of Thomas Butler the 7th. Earl of Ormonde and he was made Earl of Ormonde by Henry VIII in 1527. Thomas Boleyn was the father of Ann Boleyn as mentioned above. - A.K.

[311] Vol. 616 p.46. St. P. 11. 153

miles in compass....(3) also by default of English inhabitants which in times past were archers and had feats of war, and good servants in their houses for defence of the country in time of necessity... but now the inheritors of the land of the Englishry have admitted to be their tenants those of the Irishry which can live hardily without bread or other good victuals; and some for lucre to have of them more rent, and some for other impositions than English husbands be able to give, together with the oppression of coyne and livery have expelled them; and so is all the country in effect made Irish.."

(6) "The black rents and tributes which Irishmen by violence have obtained of the King's subjects are a great mischief; and yet when the Deputies go upon Irishmen by the aid of the King's subjects for redress of their nightly and daily robberies, they keep all they get to their own use and restore nothing to the poor people."[312]

We now come to a stirring period, fatal alike to the Geraldines and the native Irish clans including the O'Nolans. "A Parliament was convoked by Gerald, Earl of Kildare, which ended, he was accused before the Council in England, thrown into the Tower of London and there ended his life."[313]

When Gerald Oge was summoned into England he appointed his son Thomas Fitzgerald, Lord Offaly, as Deputy. This Thomas was known as "Silken Thomas" because his followers had silk fringes about their head pieces.[314] Born in England in 1513, he was only twenty years old when appointed Vice Deputy.

The enemies of the Fitzgeralds who were jealous of their power and hungered for their estates spread a report in 1534 that Henry VIII had executed the Earl. When Thomas heard this he at once revolted and induced many nobles and chiefs to swear fidelity to him, sending such as refused prisoners to Maynooth Castle. Toward the end of August of this year, Piers Roe, the Earl of Ossory, having assembled all the forces he could in opposition invaded Forth O'Nolan and Kildare, carrying off a great number of cattle.

In revenge for this Silken Thomas, Cahir Mac Innycross the McMurrough, O'Nolan, O'Neill, O'Connor Offaly and O'Moore and their adherents laid siege to the castle of Tullow, then held by the Butlers, which they took after five days.[315] They then invaded Kilkenny, with banners displayed, and plundered the lands of the Butlers.

---

[312] Carew MSS No. 39

[313] Dowling

[314] Ibid.

[315] "The traitor Thomas prepared a great host with 4 weeks victuals and first besieged an old manor of the Earl of Ormonde called Tullow and there the ward for 5 days made defence where gathered from all quarters great numbers of men to whom he exbursed no small

The following castles were at this time in the hands of Thomas and his allies:- Maynooth, Portlester, Rathdangan, Lea, Athy, Kilkea, Castledermot, Carlow and Tullow, all strongly fortified and garrisoned.

Piers Roe again appeared with a large force. He once more invaded and ravaged Forth O'Nolan and Kildare.[316] Having taken the castle of Kilkea he purposed carrying the war into the heart of the enemies country, but the Deputy being ill, was unable to support him. Piers Roe, however, took the castle of Athy and soon afterwards succeeded in detaching the McMurrough from the forces of Silken Thomas.

In January 1535, the English forces under Brereton, Salisbury, Dacres, Musgrave and Alymer, marched into Kildare. Silken Thomas with O'Moore and O'Connor feigned an attack on them but did not abide the battle. The English forces then marched to Maynooth and burnt the town together with some five or six surrounding villages. The winter being stormy and wet matters so rested until the Spring.

Silken Thomas had by this time succeeded in raising 7,000 men in Offaly and Connaught and was on his way to relieve the Castle of Maynooth when he heard of its fall. At the news of the "Pardon of Maynooth" as it is called in the State Papers, the greater part of his forces dispersed and returned to their homes. With such, however, as remained, he advanced to Clane, where he was met by the Deputy and the royal forces. The cavalry could act on neither side, as a bog lay between them. The Deputy, however, brought two or three field pieces to bear on the enemy, whom he thus dispersed, and took prisoners 140 Gallowglasses, all of whom, he, on being threatened with an attack, put to death, except one who made his escape.[317]

Seeing that all hope of success was past the Irish chiefs now gradually submitted to the Deputy. In May the Earl of Ossory brought the McMurrough and O'Moore to Maynooth and induced them to join the royal cause. All the Earl of Kildare's castles were taken in succession except those of Crom and Adare in County Limerick.[318]

In July, aided by O'Connor of Offaly, Silken Thomas assaulted and took the Castle of Rathdangan. Sir William Brabazon, ancestor to the Earl of Meath, then laid siege to it hoping to capture Thomas but he managed to escape during the night. From the State Papers we learn that Naas would have

---

treasure and at last that castle was won and the Earl of Ormonde's men, the ward, slain." - A.K.

[316] It is not quite clear what this means. As the barony of Forth was being claimed by the Butlers it is unlikely that he did more than attack and burn dwellings and fortifications belonging to the English adherents of the Fitzgeralds. - A.K.

[317] Holinshed

[318] State Papers Vol.II pg. 254

fallen had it not been well fortified and the 'rest of Kildare and the county of Dublin would have been destroyed to the Gates of Dublin.'

Silken Thomas retired to Allen and fortified himself on the outskirts of the bog. He had in a wood near the bog a 'strong house, made all of earth, and so ditched and watered and of such force as men of experience said, that being manned, ordnanced and vitteled it would not have been pregnable.' This the English burned and destroyed.[319]

Brought at length to bay, Silken Thomas sent the following letter to Lord Leonard Grey, which is now in the State Paper Office and is wholly in his own handwriting:-

"After all due recommendations, I heartily recommend me unto your Lordship certifying you, that whereas I have done anything contrary against my Sovereign Lord the King's Grace's mind, came nothing of my own mere musing, but only by your council, the which being in your Lordhship's company now, as being Thomas Eustace, Gerald Gerrot, Shane, his son with divers others, by the which I was governed at that time, and did nothing but after their mind; the which I report me to all the Lords of the English Pale. Wherefore I heartily desire your Lordship to be intercessor betwixt my said His Grace and me, that I may have my pardon for me and my life and lands, the which shall not be undeserved to the uttermost of my power; and if I cannot obtain my foresaid pardon, I have no other to do but shift for myself the best I can; trusting in God, who preserves your lordship.

Your Loving Friend
T. FitzGeralde."

Thomas was accordingly admitted to a conference on the 18th. August. Lord Leonard Grey (his uncle) rode from Maynooth into Offaly where on the border of the bog of Allen, Thomas met him and surrendered himself to him and Lord Butler,[320] to be disposed of according to the royal pleasure. But the royal pleasure was soon made manifest for the Fitzgeralds had enemies enough to poison the brutal King's mind. Brabazon recommended that Thomas's five uncles should also be sent prisoners to England. This was done and all six were executed in 1537.

John Alen, the chancellor, now advised Cromwell the King's secretary about the conquest of Irish Ireland. "If the Tooles, the Byrnes, the Nolans and Kavanaghs, which is McMurrough and his sect, were banished and destroyed

---

[319] State Papers Vol II pg 266

[320] It should be remembered that Thomas was related to both men. Two of his aunts were married to them. Interestingly Grey himself was executed for treason in 1541, having been accused of extreme leniency towards the Fitzgeralds in the late rebellion. - A.K.

and it inhabited with Englishmen, then the King would have there a goodly country and no Irishmen who could make wars against him."[321]

We now come to a very important document which is dated May 12th. 1536. The original, in Latin, is still preserved. Namely the "Treaty of Peace and final concord between Lord Leonard Grey, Deputy, and Charles McInnycross Kavanagh, otherwise called McMurrough, principal captain of his nation.

(1) McMurrough promised to be a faithful liege subject to the King.

(2) He will pay to the King all the tribute, refections and sustentations of Scots and other men of war, annually accustomed to be paid.

(3) He will not adhere to any rebels of the King, nor permit them to be assisted by his people.

(4) He shall always be content solely with the peace and war of the King, and will rise up with the Deputy and issue forth with his entire band in every journey for three days at his own expense, and in every voyage called hostings with 12 horsemen and banners and 30 kerne.

(5) He will inform all damages by him or his adherents heretofore committed against the King and his subjects.

(6) He will allow the King's subjects to pass through his dominions without molestation; and the Lord Deputy will make proclamation that all persons coming from his dominions to the English parts shall not be molested for any fault committed heretofore; and neither the said Lord McMurrough now being, nor any others for the time being, shall have in his peace or war those whom the Lord Deputy now being, has taken into his peace, namely Lord O'Murgho,[322] Edmund Duff McDonagh, Arthur, his son, and all the country of the said Edmund of Kinselagh[323] to whom or to any of whom he will do no damage.

(7) In these and all controversies between McMurrough and Arthur, son of Edmund Duff McDonagh, they shall stand to the decision of the Lord Deputy and Council.

(8) The Lord Deputy shall give to McMurrough such annual stipend as other Deputies have been accustomed to give him and his ancestors, if he shall show that he has any just title to such stipend within half a year hence before the Lord Deputy and Council.

---

[321] Carew MSS No. 70

[322] This was the O'Morchoe (head of the Murphy clan) whose territory was the Murrowes a district in and around Oulart in Co. Wexford.- A.K.

[323] The Kinselaghs was a district in and around Gorey.

(9) He had delivered Edmund, son of John Juvenis O'Bryn,[324] and the son of John Baulagh, commonly called Shane Ballagh's son,[325] as hostages, into the custody of the Lord Deputy.

(10) As often as McMurrough shall infringe any of these articles the Lord Deputy is to receive 200 cows from him.

(11) Provided that, although the arbitration concerning controversies[326] between McMurrough and Edmund Duffe should rest with the Lord Deputy, nevertheless, if by senior and indifferent persons of that country they can otherwise agree, that agreement shall be ratified by the Lord Deputy.[327]

Lord Brabazon wrote to Cromwell (Henry VIII's secretary) recommending among other items that "300 horsemen to be resident in the castle of Ferns. From there they could survey the said county, now the King's and win the castles, holds and cattle of the O'Nolans, Kavanaghs and Briens between Dublin, the English Pale and Earl of Ossory, the Butlers and the said county, so that by next March it would be desolate of the Irishry and made habitable. Thus all the Englishry in Leinster and Munster, which contains three parts of the five parts of Ireland would be linked together."[328]

Another important document is the Indenture made 14th. July 1536 between Lord Leonard Grey, the Deputy, and Charles McInnycross, the McMurrough, principal captain of his nation.[329]

---

[324] This man was probably the son of the chieftain of the O'Briens or Breens of the Duffry. This sept originally lived in the region of Fethard, in south Wexford, and were descended from Bran Dubh the 6th. century King of Leinster. They were called the Sil Brain. They moved to the Duffry (a huge region sprawling across the south western slopes of the Blackstairs embracing most of the barony of Bantry and some of the barony of Scarawalsh) during the period of the Viking invasions. In 1548 they were noted by the Sovereign and Council of the town of Wexford who stated "As for all laths used in our town, we have them of the dwellers of the Duffir and the carters thereabouts under the jurisdiction of Cahir McArt, McMurrough. (CSP) - A.K.

[325] This branch of the Kavanaghs descended from Blind Donough who died in 1476 and whose grandson Murrough Ballagh was King of Leinster in the latter years of the 15th. century. - A.K.

[326] The tone of this condition would imply that the controversy was about land ownership or distribution. - A.K.

[327] Carew MSS No. 77

[328] Carew MSS No. 81

[329] This followed the invasion of Ui Cheinnselaigh by the Deputy who easily captured Ferns castle. He had a sniper shoot the castle gunner and the other few defenders surrendered. Cahir McInnycross seems to have disassociated himself from the defenders as the Deputy stated he captured the castle from 'certain rebels'. - A.K.

(1) McMurrough shall be keeper and constable of the castle and dominion of Ferns, lately recovered by the Lord Deputy out of the possession of certain rebels, during the King's pleasure, paying for the first year eighty marks and afterwards as by the Lord Deputy and Council and the Lord McMurrough shall be agreed.

(2) Gerald Kavanagh, commonly called Gerald Sutton,[330] shall be sub-constable and governor of the said castle.

(3) McMurrough and Gerald shall safely guard and defend the said castle and dominions and surrender them to the Deputy when required.

(4) Maurice, son of McMurrough, now in the castle of Dublin, and Arthur, son of the said Gerald, now in the custody of the Earl of Ossory, and of James his son, shall remain with the Lord Deputy as hostages; and the same Charles and Gerald promise that if they fail in the promises they shall forfeit their possessions forever. Moreover, the Earl of Ossory and his son James Butler, Lord O'Moore and Mortagh McArt Boy and his son Charles Kavanagh[331] are their sureties for the performance of the promises.

"The said castle is one of the ancientest and strongest castles within this land, and of the Earl of Shrewbury's or the Duke of Norfolk's old inheritance, being worth some time 500 marks by the year, situated nobly within 10 miles of Wexford and 12 miles of Arcloe, so as there dwelling a good captain may quiet, order and rule all those parts. From thence the Deputy departed ' by seaside' to Dublin, taking order in the country as he went, camping in the fields nightly; which way no English Deputy came this 100 years." [332]

In August 1537 the Deputy reported:- "Since our other letters concerning our proceedings against O'Connor and upon the wilful proceedings of the Kavanaghs (of whom we have made so oft mention to be exiled and that place

---

[330] This Gerald Sutton was the 5th. son of Murrough Ballagh, King of Leinster (d. 1511). In 1548 Gerald and his son had claimed ownership to a castle within 3 miles of Carlow town. It formerly belonged to Donal McCahir (may have been a grandson of Moriertagh Og of Garryhill and therefore a near relative of Gerald Sutton) who slew Kedagh O'More and was attainted, thereby forfeiting to the King, according to Brian Jones. CSP - A.K.

[331] Moragh or Murtagh McArt Boy was the son of Art Bui the King of Leinster who died in 1518. Murtagh was the tanaiste to Cahir McInnycross. He was the ancestor of the Clonmullen Kavanaghs. Murtagh became the McMurrough when Cahir McInnycross died and continued so until his own death in 1548. His son Charles or Cahir known as Cahir Carrgh or Carragh Duff was killed in 1538 by the English, probably in the skirmishing that followed a hosting by the Lord Deputy against the Kavanaghs in that year, (CSP) or because he was one of the hostages given by the McMurrough in 1537. Cahir built the castle of Carragh Duff, now called Carrigduff near Bunclody, which is in the Barony of Forth. - A.K.

[332] Carew MSS No. 83

to be inhabited by your Grace) I, your Deputy, marched towards them with 14 days victuals and took two of the piles of the O'Nolans their adherents, which we prostrated. Thus the Kavanaghs were constrained to put in their pledges[333]. So much has never been done with 14 days victuals, but if your army had been furnished with money at all seasons in due time since their coming hither, it had proceeded after a far higher sort. We begin to come to such knowledge of Irishmen and their countries that we consider no such difficulty to subdue or exile them as had been thought...."

The letter was signed by Leonard Grey; John, Lord of Trimleston, Chancellor; William Brabazon; Gerald Alymer, Justice; John Allen; Thomas Nothe, Justice.

During all this time the Butlers were pressing their cause, to get possession of the dominions of O'Nolan. Here is a statement in favour of Piers Roe, Earl of Ossory. " Thomas Boleyn, Earl of Ormonde, made a gift unto Piers Butler (afterwards the Earl of Ormonde) of Tully Phelim and Arklow[334] to him and his heirs, yielding unto the said Earl Thomas and his heirs the fourth part of all the profits growing out of them, the charges in keeping the same being defrayed; the said manors had been intruded upon by the Irish (the O'Nolans and the O'Byrnes[335]) for the space of two hundred years which the said Piers Butler recovered from them,[336] as appeareth in letters written by the said Piers (and now remaining in Sir Robert Cotton's custody) to Mr. Cromwell the King's secretary, and to the above mentioned Thomas Boleyn, Earl of Ormonde and Wiltshire. The rents of the said manors were paid to the Earl by the said Piers Butler and also he wrote to the said Earl to be his tenant on his manor of Carrick McGriffen."[337]

"Letters patent for Peter Butler, Earl of Ossory & Ormonde, and James Butler, Lord Butler, Treasurer of Ireland, (who had shed his blood in the wars against the Geraldines, O'Nolans and other rebels) granting them the manors, castles and towns of ...Rathvilly, Clonmore, Tullagh, Offellym, Kallasue, Powerston and Leighlin in Co. Ceatherlagh; Dunbrordyesland alias Great Island in Co. Wexford; the little Island in Co. Waterford; Oughterard, Castell Warninge, Donadea and Clyntonskourte in Co. Kildare." [338]

---

[333] This means that the hostages promised the previous year were taken into custody, including Cahir Duff or Charles Kavanagh.

[334] This grant was made in 1505 - A.K.

[335] Fr. Nolan is in error here. It was the Kavanaghs who were in possession of Arklow. - A.K.

[336] See footnotes on pages 267 & 271.

[337] Carew MSS No. 106

[338] Carew MSS No. 107

County of Carlow 1537. "Devices for the ordering of the O'Nolans, Kavanaghs, Byrnes, Tooles and O'Mayles for such lands as they shall have within the county of Carlow and the marches of the same county, and also of the marches of the county of Dublin.

(1) He that is now called McMurrough and every one of the gentlemen of the O'Nolans and Kavanaghs have certain lands appointed to them and the heirs of their bodies, to hold of the King by knight service, some by a whole knight's fee, some by half a knight's fee, some by a fourth part, and some by a sixth part after the rate of the land appointed to them.

(2) It shall be lawful to each of them to make freeholders under them.

(3) None of them to be "Obeisant to any other of them," but to the King's Majesty only, or to such as shall have the rule there under his Highness.

(4) Every gentleman's freeholder to be obedient to his Lord, unless he do not keep his duty of allegiance to the King.

(5) Every gentleman to pay a small yearly rent 'for a knowledge to his Majesty'.

(6) Considering how miserably the gentlemen and men of war do handle the poor husbandmen with coyne and livery in those parts, and also forasmuch as the said gentlemen's countries are not marching upon any Irishmen, but that the counties of Dublin, Kildare and Kilkenny do lie between them and the said Irishmen, it is thought they should no more need to charge the poor tenants with coyne and livery than the county of Dublin, and therefore the King will not allow the said gentlemen to take coyne and livery of any of his tenants, or to keep or wage any gallowglass or kerne; and the countries shall be charged with such impositions only by the Deputy in time of great need and when he shall put the like upon the county of Dublin.

(7) All the said gentlemen to answer the King's Lieutenant or Deputy at all times of war, as gentlemen of the county of Dublin do.

(8) As no part of the county of Carlow is above 45 o 46 miles distant from Dublin, where the King's courts are kept, it is thought convenient that his writs should run there like they do in counties Dublin, Meath, Uryell and Kildare.

(9) All the King's holds and fortresses within the said countries, that is to say the castles of Carlow, Leighlin, Duiske Abbey, Baltinglass, Ferns, Tyntern, Arklow and Wicklow to be occupied and kept by such as his Highness or his Lieutenant and Council shall appoint; and no man of inheritance dwelling beyond the water of the Barrow to keep or meddle with any of them.

(10) All the gentlemen and inhabitants of those countries do clearly relinquish and leave all their Irish apparel, save only their harness and habiliments of war in time of need and go arrayed of such sort as those of the county Dublin do.

175

(11) That all the Byrnes be order of like sort as the O'Nolans and Kavanaghs and that the Tooles and O'Mayles[339] be in like manner ordered.

(12) As the county of Waterford has no Irishman dwelling within it and is environed by the main sea, by the river that cometh to the city of Rosse, which is not passable but only by boat by the county of Kilkenny which is wholly under the Earl of Ormonde and by the lordship of Dungarvan which the said Earl now has of the King's gift, it is thought that all its inhabitants should not only answer the King's writs, but also wear English apparel, and that coyne and livery should not be levied upon the King's subjects without licence of the Deputy and Council.

(13) Finally it is thought that those parts being reduced to this good order the rest...will call themselves good Englishmen and the King's kinsmen will ensure the said order, and consequently the rest of all Irishmen of that land will follow the same for their own commodity; and nothing shall sooner bring them thereunto than the good handling of the said O'Nolans, Kavanaghs, Byrnes, Tooles and O'Mayles.[340]

In 1540 there was further trouble in the south east as we find the new Deputy, Sir William Brereton, writing to Cromwell in May of that year: - "While I was at the said parliament, O'Connor, with a great number of horsemen and gallowglasses did burn in Bermingham's country. The Lord Chancellor and Master Treasurer were then in Kildare raising the country to 'keep upon' O'Toole, the O'Nolans, the Kavanaghs and O'Connor; but seeing Bermingham's country on fire, they went into O'Connor's country, burned divers towns and took some cattle. This caused O'Connor to return. I made haste to the borders and have concluded an hosting to go upon him. I desire that the bearers may return soon; they could never be worse spared out of this land than now. We have great need of horsemen and necessaries, as bows, strings, spears and powder. Sir Thomas Cusake has done diligent service."[341]

Edicts for the 'Reformation of Ireland' were issued in July 1541 a number of which appear as follows:-

(1) The King shall in future be reputed and acknowledged to be the King of Ireland, as in truth he always was...

(7) Every person committing a robbery beyond the value of 14d., for the first offence shall lose one of his ears, for the second the other ear and the third time shall suffer death.

(8) No horseman shall keep more than one servant or groom for each horse.

(9) No gentleman or any other shall retain horsemen or footmen called kerne, unless their lord is willing to be bound for their honesty and fidelity.

---

[339] The inhabitants of the Glen of Imaal - A.K.
[340] Carew MSS No.113 ; State Papers Vol. 602 pg.162
[341] Carew MSS No. 146

(11) Every gentleman having lands and free tenants shall answer to the King for himself and his followers.

(21) No lord or nobleman shall have in his shirt beyond 20 cubits of linen cloth; no vassal or horseman more than 18 cubits; no kerne or Scot more than 16 cubits; grooms, messengers or other servants of lords 12 cubits; husbandmen and labourers 10 cubits. None of the aforesaid shall use embroidered shirts on pain of forfeiting such shirt and 20s.

Chapter 14

The 16th. Century Part II

A part of Fr. Nolan's history seems to be missing and so I propose to try and fill in the missing years - about 1540 to 1603- as best I can, in keeping with the general thrust of Fr. Nolan's draft.

Prior to the reign of Henry VIII Ireland was a country which had almost become entirely Gaelic again. In the preface to the Calendar of State Papers the author had these important observations to make: "The power of the English in Ireland had so much decreased in the time of Henry VII that the old Irish system of Government in clans or separate small nations had revived and was in full force throughout the greater part of the land.[342] The wars of Henry VIII, Mary and Elizabeth reveal the whole strength and weakness of the system and show how the superior combination of the English, supported by continual supplies of men and money from home, prevailed over the craft and daring of the native chiefs."

Although they didn't know it the Gaelic lords and their people were entering a critical phase leading to the demise of the old Gaelic order as it had stood for thousands of years.

The system of government in Gaelic Ireland was dynastic in the sense that each sept and was ruled by a member of a special family known as the Derb Fine. The sept itself was composed of a number of families most of whom were related. Land for the use of each family was allocated after the death of the Ri (king)[343] and upon the inauguration of the new ruler. This system of land distribution was called gavelkind. Under this system bards and brehons (law interpreters) were given the use of extensive lands as befitted their noble calling. Similarly near relatives of the king or chief were given lands befitting their station. In Ui Cheinnselaigh (Wexford, Carlow and South Wicklow) the

---

[342] As late as 1537 it was noted that "the McMurrough doth take Black Rent from the town of Gowran and the kernty of McMurrough have stolen two horses belonging to John Nashe out of the pasture of Reemore, beside Gowran." - Calendar of State Papers.

[343] In some parts of the country divisions took place annually or after a set number of years. In some areas the land was divided equally, in others they were parcelled out according to age and rank. The lands pertaining to the office of chief and tanaist were exempt from division. Women had no rights at all but illegitimate sons had. Gavelkind was abolished by a special law in 1606.

Mac Eochaidh's (Keoghs)[344] were the bards and the O'Dorans were the brehons and these professions were closed to other families.

In addition to the freeholders mentioned above there were workers who had no lands[345] but were attached to a particular family and there were slaves. In Ireland in the early Middle Ages the female slaves called 'Cumals' were worth one and a half milch cows and appeared to be of more value than male slaves. Slaves were captured in raids as were cattle. Slavery seems to have died out in Ireland before the end of the Middle Ages c.1500. but there was still a class of labourer who continued to be called 'sclabhai' and who worked for their food.

The King's duties were laid down by the Brehon law. He himself had no part in the making of the laws but he was the law enforcer. In time of war he was the supreme commander.   He was given sufficient resources to enable him to keep a sizeable retinue of soldiers and was also entitled to coyne and livery. It was his duty to defend his subjects. In common parlance the duty was called 'spend me and defend me'.

The Brehon Law was the law of the whole island where Irish septs lived. The Dorans were the Brehons in Ui Cheinnselaigh. The making of a brehon was a long and arduous course. A young man had to spend twenty years studying laws before he could be admitted to the court of judges. Brehon Law

---

[344] The Mac Eochaidhs were said to be descended from Eochaidh the son of Enna Cinnsealach a 3rd. century King of Leinster. In his notes on the parishes of Co. Carlow, O'Donovan, the great antiquarian, wrote an account of the capture and escape of Eochaidh. Following some famous poetic contest a dispute arose between Eochaidh and the poet of Niall of the Nine Hostages. Eochaidh who was equally famous for his prodigious strength slew his opponent. The High King pursued Eochaidh into Leinster, laid waste the province and forced the Ui Cheinnselaigh to hand over Eochaidh. He carried off his prisoner to Ath Fathad - Aghade - in Carlow, on the banks of the Slaney and there left him chained by the neck. The end of the chain was put through a hole in a huge rock and secured by an iron bar. As Niall headed northwards nine of his champions returned to put an end to Eochaidh. When he saw them coming he put forth all his great strength, gave a sudden jerk and seizing the iron bar attacked and slew the champions. Encouraged by this feat the Ui Cheinnselaigh rallied and pursued Niall's army overtaking them near Tullow and inflicting a heavy defeat on them. O'Donovan also noted that there is an ancient fort near the north end of the parish and 16 chains from the S.E. of the fort and one a half chains from the east side of the Clonegal -Carlow road there is a long stone 12 ft. by 5ft. having a hole six inches in diameter near the top. It is called Cloghafile (Poet's Stone) from time immemorial and is said to be the stone to which Eochaidh was bound.

[345] These people were described as ' a purely menial labouring class', who felt no loyalty to the Gaelic aristocracy and even looked upon Cromwell as a deliverer - Ed. McLysaght in *Irish Life in the 17th. Century* pg. 85

covered all aspects of intertribal and interpersonal relationships in much the same way that the law is applied today in civilised countries. Many of the great Norman magnates such as the Fitzgeralds and the Butlers insisted on the use of the Brehon Law in their own districts.

One such law was the law of 'cin comhfocais' which made the ruler responsible for the misdeeds of any of his clan who broke the peace or transgressed the law. Another law was the law of Restitution, whereby a chief had to return goods stolen by any of his subjects, with interest. Other laws dealt with transhumance or the movement of flocks and herds to high ground in summer and back to winter quarters in the autumn. In the course of transhumance practically all the tribe moved and only the old and sick were left behind with their carers. This system was known as 'booleying'.[346]

The institution of Kingship was very archaic and carried with it the idea that the King was a sacred personage who was responsible for the fertility of the land and abundance of fish in the rivers. If famine prevailed or any other natural calamity occurred he was held to be responsible. The Kingship did not devolve upon the son or nephew as of right. In the case of the Kavanaghs, for example Art Bui the King of Leinster, who died in 1519 was succeeded by his brother Gerald and he in turn was succeeded by his brother Maurice or Muiris. He then was succeeded by Cahir McInnycross an illegitimate relation.

There were often bloody feuds over the chieftaincy[347] and in 1543 after the death of Cahir McInnycross when Murtagh the son of Art Bui became the McMurrough, the position of Tanaist was disputed. One group led by Gerald McCahir a grandson of Moriertagh Og of Garryhill was opposed by another group led by Cahir McArt of Polmonty (the ancestor of the Borris Kavanaghs).[348] A full scale battle was fought at Hacketstown in 1545 where over two hundred men lost their lives. One family suffered enormously. They were the Ballytiglea[349] Kavanaghs who supported Cahir McArt. Seven of the sons of Donell Reagh Kavanagh of Ballytiglea were killed. This battle resulted in Cahir McArt becoming Tanaist, but it also meant that there was much feuding and inter-sept rivalry for the next three decades. One such incident was

---

[346] In the preface to the Calendar of State Papers the author says that 'most of the wild Irish led a nomad life, tending cattle, sowing little corn and rarely building houses, but sheltered alike from heat and cold and moist and dry by the Irish cloak.'

[347] Another example of this occurred in Wicklow where the Tanaist of the O'Tooles - a son of Art Og from Castle Kevin - was killed in a bitter inter tribal war which considerably reduced the power of the O'Tooles in Wicklow.

[348] Cahir McArt was responsible for the murders of Cahir McMoriertagh Og of Garryhill and his mother Maeve in 1526 - see page 268

[349] Now spelled Ballyteiglea - about a mile and a half south of Goresbridge

the murder of Donell the eldest son of Gerald McCahir by one of the Ballytiglea Kavanaghs in 1570.

The towns and cities of Ireland were developed by the Vikings first and later the Normans. Trade between the native Irish and the Vikings was at best a begrudging type of intercourse but trade there was in skins and wool. The Irish bought cloth, wine and other exotic goods from the townsmen. The existing town were rapidly developed by the Normans and trade was expanded. Inland towns such as Carlow, New Ross, Leighlin, Kilkenny and Enniscorthy only came into being in the 13th. century and at first they were purely military fortresses. Even by the year 1500 these towns were relatively small and populated only by the English burgesses brought over by the English clergy and officials.

The rest of the south east - apart from the Viking towns of Wexford, Waterford and Arklow was literally a wilderness. What roads there were clung to the sides of hills as most of the lowland area was covered with forest. Even as late as 1600 there was considerable forest in Idrone[350] in Carlow and we may presume in the rest of it as well.

As we have seen from Fr. Nolan's history, the descendants of the early Norman lords had succeeded in carving out great estates for themselves and by the early 1500s the Fitzgeralds and the Ormondes were very powerful indeed. So much so that they regarded themselves as the de facto rulers of Ireland. They intermarried with the Irish, they spoke Irish, they used the Brehon laws, they practised fostering, they dressed in the Irish manner and they employed Irish bards.[351] But they differed from the Irish in that they never used gavelkind[352] and they practised primogeniture, thus ensuring the power of their families into the future. But, as we have seen, towards the end of the 15th. century and right through the first decades of the 16th. there was a power struggle between the Fitzgeralds and the Ormondes even though they were connected by marriage during those years.

The Gaelic clans of Leinster became embroiled in this feud and suffered because of it. The O'Connors of Offaly and indirectly the O'Moores of Laois were related to the FitzGeralds and gave them their support. The Kavanaghs and the O'Nolans were connected with both parties and while they acknowledged the lordship of the Fitzgeralds they also acknowledged the unique position of Piers Roe Butler the 8th. Earl of Ormonde whose mother, a

---

[350] As is evident from the map of the Idrone.

[351] In 1537 the Jury of the Commonalty of Kilkenny complained that Piers Roe and his wife and family were using 'coygn and livery' at will in the lands under their control. - Calendar of State Papers

[352] An English term used to describe the Brehon system of land division

Kavanagh, had been married to O'Nolan before her marriage to James Butler.[353]

During the rebellion of Silken Thomas the Kavanagh- O'Nolan loyalty was given to the Fitzgeralds mainly because Cahir McInnycross, the McMurrough was intimately connected with the Fitzgeralds. However Piers Roe succeeded in winning over the loyalty of the Kavanagh-O'Nolan alliance.

Another complication in this period was the stance taken by Lord Leonard Grey, the Deputy, who was a brother-in-law of Gearoid Oge the 9th. Earl of Kildare and therefore an uncle of the unfortunate Silken Thomas. As soon as it became apparent that the Fitzgeralds were leaning towards rebellion he sided with Piers Roe as the champion of English interests. However he tried everything in his power to avoid having to arrest his kinsmen. [354]

A more serious development which knelled the end of Gaelic power in Leinster was the introduction of cannon guns. This new technology gave the Deputy massive fire power against which no castle could stand. Hitherto, the Gaelic Lord in his castle or the Geraldine in his keep was secure from all but the longest of sieges. And this new technology was accompanied by even more sinister developments that really spelled disaster for the Leinster Gaels - O'Nolans, Kavanaghs, O'Moores, O'Connors, O'Byrnes and O'Tooles.

Among the many diverse and complex evolving forces which combined to bring about the demise of the Gaelic way of life were : the determination of Henry VIII (and later Elizabeth I) and his ministers to bring Ireland under English rule and under English law; the emergence of a breed of adventurers who were calculating, ruthless and ambitious, and who sought to advance their fortunes at the expense of the native Irish, whom in the main they despised as being almost sub-human and fit only for exploitation or even genocide; the clash of cultures which were totally at variance in their concepts of justice, morality and religious beliefs; the inordinate difficulties of communication between peoples who spoke such different languages; the calibre of the government officials from the highest to the lowest in both Ireland and England who were in the main amoral, corrupt, degenerate, avaricious and deceitful.

Cahir McArt of Polmonty became the McMurrough in 1547 when Murtagh McArt Bui died. He was pressurised into renouncing the title of King

---

[353] See footnote on page 271

[354] The soft footed approach taken by Grey towards the rebels eventually led to his being tried, convicted and executed for treason. He was also implicated in the escape to France of Gerald Fitzgerald, the heir to the Geraldine lands and titles who eventually came back to Ireland in 1547, where he was welcomed by the Kavanaghs, the O'Moores and the other Gaelic chiefs of Leinster. He was partially successful in pursuing his claims and in 1589 the Queen restored much of his patrimony. - CSP

of Leinster in Dublin but was given the title of Baron of Ballyann. He also had to give his son, Donough, as a hostage. 1548 seems to have been comparatively peaceful for the O'Nolans and Kavanaghs even though there was trouble in Leinster. For example the O'Connors of Offaly were in rebellion and were crushed by William Seyntloo[355] who 'killed many of them and their *slaves* who carried their victuals'. Three of the O'Nolans were pardoned as of Imaal in this year. They were Murrough McGerrot Duffe, Tirelagh McFiach and Thady. Tirelagh was the son of Fiach O'Nolan of Kilbride, and grandson of William of Kilbride, while Thady was the son of William of Kilbride. I was unable to place Murrough in the genealogy.[356] Other O'Nolans of Rosslee were pardoned also - Donald McDonough and Morgan his brother, also of Rosslee[357].

Cahir McArt didn't keep the peace for very long as he seized Ferns castle in 1549 from Arthur Butler, a son of James the 9th. Earl of Ormonde.[358] There must have been further trouble also as five of the O'Nolans were pardoned in this year. They were Donal McDonough of Rosslee and his son Morgan, Charles McLesagh of Ballytrane (might have been a grandson of William of Kilbride), Ross McEdmond of Kilknock and his son William McRoss.

Whatever troubles there were led to the invasion of Ui Cheinnselaigh in 1550 by Brabazon, the Deputy. Cahir mobilised the forces of the area,

---

[355] Seyntloo was one of Henry VIII's captains who was appointed Seneschal of Wexford in 1541. In 1539 he had been granted a huge area of land in South Wexford for life at no rent but fealty only. By 1561 he had been knighted and was given grants of lands in Meath and Westmeath. (Fiants)

[356] In 1544 a Murrough McArt O'Nolan gave a grant to J. Swetman and L. Blanchville - to the use of the Earl of Ormonde - of messuages (sites for dwelling houses), lands etc., in 'Ballintrane & Ballincrea in Fodyrt'.

[357] See chapter on O'Nolan families.

[358] It is significant that in the same year Anthony Colclough was instructed to repair the Castle of Leighlin. Early in the year he sent a reply to Dublin to say that he had arrived there and had begun to work a very good quarry of slate 'which will be useful for Carlow as well as Leighlin'. He sent a request for 6 pickaxes, 20 shovels, some ordnance, powder and money. He then went on to say that ' the country will be glad to show the utmost of their powers in furthering these works. CSP
At this time also Brian Jones or Johns met Cahir McArt at Leighlin where the latter complained that Sir Richard Butler and Art Boy (this was Art Bui of Clonmullen who was murdered by Heron in 1562- the grandson of Art Bui, King of Leinster) were following old and unjust actions against him. Later in the month Jones wrote to Bellingham the Lord Deputy, saying he had not heard from Sir Richard Butler or Cahir McArt 'concerning the wheat'. CSP - For more information on Heron, Jones etc., see the chapter about the adventurers later in this book.

including many of the O'Nolans, but Brabazon's guns and cannon ensured their dispersal. Many were killed and Donough, the hostage, was executed. Cahir was forced to go to Dublin once more and make his submission. The Council members included the Earls of Desmond and Clanrickarde, Thomond and Tyrone and the Lords Mountgarret[359] (Richard Butler), Cahir and Ibracan. The McMurrough had to give further hostages and also give up much of the territory to which he had laid claim. In addition Cahir had to accede to the pressures from the Deputy and the Council to proceed with the division of clan lands.[360] In doing so he acquired for himself and his successors the lordships of St. Mullins and Ballyanne and these lands formed the preponderance of the property of the house of Borris Idrone in later years. This division of property was carried out in many parts of Ui Cheinnselaig in the succeeding years and so it happened that many of the O'Nolans were given grants of huge properties for themselves and their descendants in Forth O'Nolan.

From the Patent Rolls of 1603 we learn the names of some of the O'Nolans who were given lands. Edmond O'Nolan[361] whose son Callough McEdmond O'Nolan was slain in rebellion was given the lands of Kilgreny; Dermot O'Nolan[362] was given the lands of Ballykenny[363] and his grandson Donel Enass McDermot O'Nolan was slain in rebellion ; Donough Duffe O'Nolan[364] was given Killmoglish and Lisgra ; Kilbride was the estate of Roderick O'Nolan's father Dowry O'Nolan[365]. Roderick himself was slain in rebellion; a daughter- in - law who owned part of Kilbride, Marrogh Ny Dowry O'Nolan was attainted of felony; the old castle of Ballytrarney, Ballytrarney, Raheen, Killean, Aclare and Ballymogue were the lands given to Donough

---

[359] He was the 2nd son of Piers Roe and his estates were near New Ross.

[360] "In Cahir McArt's time, his country having been first completely conquered and devastated, all the lands of the clan were divided among the different septs and families by order and authority of the Crown, and hereditary succession and English feudal tenure were established. For the maintenance of this division of the lands, so necessary for the English conquest, but so fatal to the Irish practice of gavelkind, English Captains were stationed in various districts of the Kavanagh (and O'Nolan) country, whose duty it was, not only to maintain this and other enactments, but to win over the whole district as well as they could to English obedience." - Hughes (*The Fall of Clan Kavanagh* pg. 286)

[361] He was the son of Shane Duff who was the son of Cahir O'Nolan of Ballykealy, living in the mid 1500s.

[362] He was a brother of Edmund of Kilgraney

[363] Ballykeenan

[364] He was the son of Owen and grandson of Cahir of Ballykealy. He was a first cousin of Edmund and Dermot mentioned above.

[365] Dowry was in fact Maurice ne dower who was a son of William O'Nolan of Kilbride. William may well have been a brother of Cahir of Ballykealy.

O'Nolan[366] whose son was Cahir McDonagh O'Nolan of Ballytrarney gent; part of the lands of Ballykealy were in the possession of Lisagh O'Nolan[367] whose son Donough McLisagh O'Nolan was killed in rebellion; Balligilbert was the land of Thady,[368] the father of Terence or Tirlagh Ballagh O'Nolan (who was attainted of felony).

The foregoing list of the O'Nolans who were in occupation of their ancestral lands in the latter decades of the 16th. century represents only a small fraction of the actual number, but those were the only ones mentioned in the Patent Rolls. For a more complete picture of the 16th. century dynasties of the O'Nolans see the chapter on O'Nolan families later in this book.

In October 1553 Queen Mary issued instructions to the Lord Deputy, St. Leger and others of the Council for the government of Ireland; to restore the old religion, survey the revenues, regulate the army and reduce Leinster; Cahir McArt to be made a Baron[369]; lands in Leix and Offaly to be granted in fee simple and garrisons to be reduced to 500 men.[370]

Cahir McArt died in 1554 and he was succeeded by Murrough of Coolnaleen as the McMurrough (and Baron of Coolnaleen). At this time John Fitzthomas Fitzgerald[371], now the claimant to be the Earl of Kildare, tried to lay claim to large territories in Wexford, South Carlow and in O'Byrne's country in Wicklow. Driven almost to despair the Kavanaghs and O'Byrnes aided by their staunch allies the O'Nolans decided to carry the fight to the enemy and invaded the southern part of Dublin county, taking cattle and burning houses. The military, aided by the citizens of the city, after great slaughter drove the rebels to Powerscourt where they surrendered. Seventy five of them were hanged and the rest pardoned.

Murtagh, the McMurrough was captured shortly afterwards and was hanged, drawn and quartered at Leighlin, together with 24 of his chief men. It is unclear who became the McMurrough after the death of Murtagh , but it may well have been contended for by Brian McCahir of Polmonty, Careduff (Cahir Duff) Kavanagh of Clonmullen and Moriertagh Og Kavanagh of Garryhill.[372] As the decade wore on it seemed that Brian McCahir was the acknowledged leader.

---

[366] Donough was in fact a son of Cahir of Ballykealy and a brother of Shane Duff.

[367] Lisagh or Leasagh was a son of William of Kilbride.

[368] Thady was the son of Tirelagh More, who was the son of Fiach O'Nolan. Fiach was the eldest son of William of Kilbride.

[369] He was made Baron of Ballyann

[370] CSP

[371] He may have been an illegitimate son of Silken Thomas.

[372] At the time a contemporary English official noted that there were only three men of note of the Kavanaghs (mentioned above) and there was enmity between them.

Bowing to the pressure the Gaelic leaders sought to alleviate the hardships being endured by their people by agreeing to surrender their lands to the Crown and have them regranted. In addition they agreed in principle to ensure a division of the lands among the occupiers after the fashion of the English and to introduce primogeniture. This agreement was not implemented for some years because of the opposition of many of the septs and the sheer difficulty of trying to explain to a very independent people, who for the most part were unlettered, the ramifications of such a social and economic upheaval resultant from the change.

In 1556 orders were given for the plantation of Laois. The O'Moores were to live in the part 'beyond the bog'. The chief of every sept was to appoint how many of his sept he would answer for; they were to hold their lands of the fort and answer the laws of the realm 'as the English do'. The freeholders (English planters) to cause their children to speak English, marry English blood, keep open the fords, destroy the fastnesses and cut the passes. The number of planters to be 160 including men who had already got grants there such as Harpole, Eustace - a brother of the Viscount Baltinglass,[373] Hugh Jones and William Cantwell.

The success of the plantation of Laois encouraged the administration to proceed with the plantation of Offaly, on the same terms. As soon as Elizabeth ascended the throne in 1558 the her resolve to settle Ireland with English planters soon became evident.

The way was now clear for the wholesale confiscation of church lands and Crown lands. The efforts of the adventurers intensified and the Butlers were seriously involved in expanding their dominions. They had gained control of Tullowphelim by the end of the century where Theobald Butler was ensconced by Thomas the 10th. Earl of Ormonde, his uncle, after he married Elizabeth, the Earl's only daughter.[374] Theobald was created Viscount Butler of Tullowphelim and Governor and Lord of the Lordship of Carlow in 1603. As we shall see later in this book, the Ormondes finally gained control over a

---

[373] The Eustaces were descended from one Sir Eustace Le Poer and their war cry was Poeragh - aboo. They were big landowners in Kildare where Lord Portlester - Roland Eustace - was the lord of Kilcullen. By marriages to heiresses they acquired lands in Offaly and they got 4 knights fees in Kildare from a Fitzgerald heiress whose father was Baron of Naas. Roland was created Viscount Baltinglass. James the 3rd. Viscount, who was later attainted because of his religious revolt, owned half of Naas manor and received chief rents from the Eustace relations, the St. Los, Flattisburys, Suttons and Misset's lands and Clinton's court. - S.P. (A.K.)

[374] Theobald died in 1613 and Elizabeth married a Scotsman, Sir Richard Preston, Lord Dingwall, by whom she had one daughter, Elizabeth. This woman, Elizabeth Preston married her first cousin, the 12th. Earl and 1st. Duke of Ormonde (1610 - 1688)

considerable portion of Forth O'Nolan when Thomas the 10th. Earl (Black Tom)[375] was given huge grants of lands in the area.

In a similar way the lands of the Kavanaghs were diminished in both Carlow and Wexford. The O'Byrnes and O'Tooles fared no better in Wicklow.

For example in 1562 Heron was granted the Abbey lands of Ferns. This led to confrontation with the Kavanaghs, the O'Nolans and the O'Byrnes. Heron who was also Seneschal of Wexford, treacherously murdered Art Bui of Clonmullen and this led to grave unrest in 1563 when the Irish went on the rampage in the area attacking the farms and homes of the English planters. Four of the prominent O'Nolans received pardons for their part in the disturbances. They were four sons of William of Kilbride - Fiach, Leasagh, Maurice ne dower and Thady and the four of them had been involved in the capture of Harvey[376] and Davells[377]. It may well be significant that in the previous year the Earl of Ormonde had been given a huge grant of lands in Forth.[378]

To add to the general confusion in the area "Henry VIIIs surrender and regrant policy was giving rise in the second generation, to a rash of succession disputes and of questions about the earlier or current surrenders. This was partly because of its comparative success, which had extended the area in which central government could function, if in a limited way. There was also now an incursion of opportunists taking up half-forgotten claims to lands granted in the distant past and subsequently lost, through absenteeism or otherwise, to the resurgent Irish. There were specialists in discovering such claims - a Wexford lawyer named Synott, for example, who traced the titles of Leinster lands derived from William Marshall through heiresses, was able to advise pleasantly surprised gentlemen in England that they could learn something to their advantage in Ireland."[379]

---

[375] Black Tom was educated at the court of Queen Elizabeth, to whom he was distantly related, and became a royal favourite. He was made the Queen's commander in Munster and later during the Nine Years War (1594 - 1603) he was appointed Lieutenant General of Ireland. It was as a result of this favouritism that he was given the grants of land in Forth in Carlow.

[376] Very little is known about George Harvey except that in 1578 he was granted the office of Constable of Maryborough, Co. Laois and this office was granted to him again in 1583 and in 1598 it was again granted to himself and his eldest son Philip. He was probably a very young soldier in 1563, when he was captured with Davells.

[377] For more information on Davells see pages 323 - 327

[378] See pages 320 - 322

[379] The Peoples of Ireland - Liam de Paor pg. 128

In this way Sir Peter Carew, a knight from Devon, a descendant of the Carews[380] who had been granted lands in Carlow in the 13th. century, now claimed his lands (some three hundred years later). The lands in question were mainly in Idrone and were in the possession of five septs of the Kavanaghs, namely the septs of Garryhill, Ballyloughan,[381] Ballyloo,[382] Polmonty[383] and the Rower.[384] Most of the lands were bounded by the Barrow, the Burren River and the Blackstairs mountains. The case was fully examined by the Chancellor, Lord Weston in 1568, who found that the Kavanaghs could offer no proof of title. Carew took up residence as an officer of the Crown, in Leighlin castle, for a short time and endeavoured to get possession of the disputed territories. However, instead of using coercion he tried to use diplomacy and persuasion, offering the Kavanaghs the option of continuing as tenants. This offer was apparently accepted though somewhat reluctantly.

Carew's claim caused a rift between the Ryans and the Kavanaghs because the Ryans now discontinued paying their rents to the Kavanaghs and sought to pay them directly to Carew. One outcome of this dispute was the granting of Borris Idrone, formerly a Ryan stronghold, to Morgan McBrian Kavanagh, the descendant of Cahir McArt, in 1600. After this many of the Ryans moved westwards into Tipperary which was under the protection of the Earl of Ormonde.[385]

Carew met with fierce resistance to his claims from an unexpected quarter. Sir Edmund Butler, brother of the Earl of Ormonde (Black Tom) went into rebellion because of the loss of some of the lands in the Carew claim. The lands in question had been granted to Piers Roe, the 8th. Earl of Ormonde by the Kavanaghs earlier in the century.[386] They included some thirty townlands in the area of Leighlinbridge. Carew was ordered to put down the rebellion and in 1568 he attacked Clogrennan castle, occupied by Sir Edmund Butler. The rebels

---

[380] See page 123

[381] About six miles south east of Bagenalstown

[382] Two miles west of the Fighting Cocks Crossroads

[383] On the Wexford Border two miles south of St.Mullin's Abbey

[384] A couple of miles west of New Ross in Co. Kilkenny

[385] In fact it would appear that the Ryans attempted to convey away much of their lands to the Ormondes in exchange for new tenancies in Tipperary. Certainly in 1549 they had approached Lady Joan Butler, in Callan, who was administering the estates of her late husband (James the 9th. Earl who had been poisoned in London in 1544 by his enemies, possibly St. Leger the Deputy). This was reported to the then Deputy, Bellingham, by Walter Cowley who declared that 'it would be evil taken if they should now cloke Irishmen's lands against the King, when he was ready to set foot there.' He states then that 'the Ryans have since resorted to Cahir McArt Kavanagh'.

[386] See page 258 - footnotes.

(Butlers, Kavanaghs, O'Nolans and Ryans) went on to Kilkenny and mobilised a large force for the defence of that city. Carew attacked it and defeated the rebel forces killing four hundred of them. Butler was arrested but was released almost immediately on the orders of his brother the Earl, who enjoyed considerable favour at court, where he had been reared.

The following year 1569, Edmund Butler was again in rebellion and was joined by discontented elements of the O'Nolan - Kavanagh -Byrne faction.[387] In an attack on Leighlin seven of the defenders of the castle were killed. The rebels then attacked Enniscorthy during the annual fair which was held on the 15th. August 1569, and robbed and pillaged the traders from Wexford town who had travelled up to Enniscorthy by boat. Many people were killed in the affray. As a result of this attack Edmund Butler was again arrested along with his brother and both were lodged in Dublin Castle. Due to the influence of Black Tom, who protested that their actions had been provoked by the unjust claims of Sir Peter Carew, both were acquitted and by way of mitigation the Earl declared to the Council that Sir Edmund Butler was insane.

That incident was in fact part of the Desmond Rebellion which was sporadic and occurred for two periods 1569 - 1573 and from 1579 - 83. Among the leaders of the rebels at Enniscorthy were James FitzMaurice Fitzgerald (the captain general of the 14th. Earl of Desmond's private army), the son of Sir Morish Fitzgerald (the White Knight), McCarthy Mor (late Earl of Clanrickarde), the Butlers, Sir Edmund and Piers, Sir Edmund's sons James and Piers.

What is perhaps most interesting about this episode is the fact that for the first time in the region (apart from the rebellion of Silken Thomas in the 1530s) discontented elements from the old Gaelic order and those from the Old English came together to oppose the government on the question of land ownership. This gelling of the two sides which hitherto had been mortal enemies was further evidenced in the Baltinglass rebellion of 1581 and the alliance of the Old English Catholics of south Wexford with their Gaelic neighbours in opposing the imposition of religious change, and the disposal of church and royal lands.

The Baltinglass revolt seems to have been a purely religious revolt, but land may well have been a factor also. James Eustace, Viscount Baltinglass, who was a major landowner in Kildare, Carlow[388] and Wicklow seems to have

---

[387] Details of the O'Nolans involved will be seen in the appendix detailing the list of O'Nolan pardons taken from the Fiants of the Tudor Monarchs.

[388] He owned lands in Forth O'Nolan at this time - Ballyvendon (probably Ballyvolden, a small townland near Aghade), two third parts of Balliochill and two third parts of Ballivickfinn.

tried to involve Gerald,[389] the 11th. Earl of Kildare and his son - in- law, Christopher Nugent the 14th. Baron Delvin as well as Fiach McHugh O'Byrne. Kildare and Delvin rebuffed his advances. He was more successful with Fiach McHugh who enlisted the help of the O'Toole, O'Nolan, Kavanagh faction. The new Lord Deputy - Grey de Wilton[390] - decided to oppose the rebel force and he sent half his army under George Moore to the Wicklow retreat of Fiach, at Glenmalure. In the ensuing battle Moore and a large number of his men were shot and killed including Sir Peter Carew Jnr., who had inherited Idrone from his uncle Sir Peter.

Grey's knee-jerk reaction to what he perceived as a great Popish plot resulted in the Earl of Kildare and Delvin being sent as prisoners to London. William Nugent, Delvin's sixth son went into revolt and his innocent great uncle, Nicholas, Chief Justice of the Common Pleas was suspected of complicity also. Nicholas was tried and executed. Delvin and Kildare were freed and Delvin later so impressed Queen Elizabeth with his loyalty that she granted him vast estates of lands confiscated in Cavan and Longford.

Grey himself with his entire army moved against the rebels and although any major actions were avoided by the rebels the burnings and seizures of cattle and horses soon reduced their support. By mid summer of 1581 Fiach was sufficiently subdued so that garrisons could be placed in strategic locations such as Castledermot, Wicklow and Arklow. The revolt effectively petered out. William Nugent made his escape to the continent with Viscount Baltinglass.[391] They escaped via Wexford town but there were casualties. Walter Gallde Kavanagh, who was a prominent rebel of his time was captured and hanged at Wexford. Others implicated in the escape of Baltinglass were the four Wexfordmen who were canonised as saints in 1992.[392] Another to suffer death for the same reason was Criomthainn McMurrough Kavanagh (another of

---

[389]This was Gerald the young brother of Silken Thomas who with the help of Grey (his uncle) and the O'Tooles was spirited away to Rome and was restored to some of the family properties by Queen Mary. Gerald was very much in favour at Elizabeth's court and in 1589 the Queen made an order that Sligo Castle and lands were to be given to the Earl in exchange for the Castle and lands of Carlow. In addition the Deputy was instructed that he was to be restored to the lands and rents of his ancestors.

[390] Not to be confused with Lord Leonard Grey who was executed in 1541.

[391] Baltinglass was attainted and his properties seized for the Crown. The discontented Eustaces became part of the rebellious movements for the next twenty years. Lady Baltinglass, however, who had stayed behind, was given the Church lands of Killerig in Carlow as an estate in 1589.- State Papers

[392] Matthew Lambert (a baker), Robert Meyler, Edward Cheevers, Patrick Cavanagh and two others whose names were not recorded. These were beatified on 27th October 1992. July 5th is the Feast of the Wexford Martyrs.

Fiach's accomplices), the second son of Murtagh the McMurrough who was executed in 1557.

Carlow seems to have quietened down somewhat after the Butler rebellion had been put down. All the people of Idrone with the exception of the Tallons of Nurney[393] and the Kavanaghs of Garryhill became Carew's tenants and paid their rents. As one writer says "the Kavanaghs of Garryhill, with the pride of the senior race of the Kavanaghs could hardly be brought to acknowledge Sir Peter's claim and always resisted it when opportunity was given."[394]

Prior to this (in the 1550s) there had been large scale disruption in the general area when the government tried to dispossess the O'Connors and the O'Moores in the Plantation of Laois and Offaly which were then dubbed

---

[393] The Tallons (an old Anglo Norman family) went to law with Sir Peter. They brought him before the Star Chamber and Council Board. Sir Peter died before the suit was ended. The Tallons in fact owned one eight of a knight's fee in Ballynakill, in eastern Idrone and in 1290 Henry Tallon witnessed a charter of Earl Roger Bigod to New Ross. In 1301 Richard Tallon was named as one of the magnates of Ireland and held the barony of St. Mullins in Idrone from Earl Roger. He was killed in 1307 by Maurice de Cantiton. In 1314 Hugh Tallon founded the house of Austin Friars at Tullow endowing it with 3 acres of land in the vill of St. John near Tullow which he held of the Knights Hospitallers. In the reign of Henry VIII Nicholas and Hubert Tallon complained that, (in a suit against the Kavanaghs) their father and grandfather and all their ancestors who had been seised of certain lands in Idrone were kept from them by the Kavanaghs. In 1568 Sir Peter Carew complained of entry into his lands by the Kavanaghs and Tallons. William Tallon later held his lands from Sir Peter Carew and when he died in 1584 his lands of Agha were left to his son James who alienated them in 1604. (E. St. J.Brooks) - A.K.

[394] This resistance continued when the Carew lands were bought by the Bagenals in the 1580s. Dudley Bagenal, a rash young man, confronted Moriertagh Og of Garryhill, following a cattle raid by the Irish (1586). He accused Moriertagh and when the latter protested his innocence he was promptly shot by Bagenal. Moriertagh's sons, with Walter Reagh Fitzgerald of Glassealy, (a son in law of Fiach McHugh O'Byrne and great grandson Gerald the 8th. Earl of Kildare) lost no time in stealing more of Bagenal's cattle and when he went in pursuit with a band of soldiers they were ambushed and Dudley and sixteen of his men were killed while the remainder fled. The feud between the Bagenals and the Kavanaghs continued until the end of the Nine Years War. In one incident, following the submission of the Kavanaghs and Walter Reagh to the Lord Deputy Perrott, Walter Reagh was attacked, in Dublin, by Ralph Bagenal, a brother of Dudley who was killed. Bagenal was restrained and imprisoned for a time. Walter was also accused of badly wounding two sons of Sir Edmund Butler and of killing 8 of Ormonde's 'chief followers and servants', while lurking in the woods of the Leverocke and Shillelagh (on the borders of O'Nolan country). - S.P.

King's county and Queen's county.[395] As a result of the rebellions of the O'Moores and O'Connors the plantation was initially largely unsuccessful. However in 1563, when Sussex was the Deputy, he gave grants of lands to 29 of the more warlike O'Moores and O'Connors while at the same time giving fresh grants to 44 English soldiers[396] and 15 to Old English colonists. Far from being appeased the O'Moores and O'Connors, especially those who had been dispossessed, continued on the rampage and the remainder of the century saw frequent raids and counter - raids in the area.[397]

All this activity had a disquieting effect on the whole region and by the end of the century the O'Nolans, O'Byrnes, O'Tooles and Kavanaghs had all been sucked into the maelstrom. They took an active part in what has been called the Nine Years War[398] and many paid a harsh penalty as is evident from the number of forfeitures by those peoples in the early 1600s following the defeat of the Irish at Kinsale.

However the conquest was long and painful on all sides. The sporadic attempts at seizing Church and Royal lands and putting English planters in the

---

[395] The King in question was King Philip of Spain who married Queen Mary, Henry VIII's daughter by Catherine of Aragon. Mary succeeded the sickly King Edward who died in 1553. Mary, a Catholic, tried to repeal anti - Catholic legislation and was said to be responsible for the execution of some 300 Protestants for which she became known as 'Bloody Mary'. She died in 1558.

[396] Robert Harpole made his first appearance in Ireland as a grantee of lands in the Plantation of Laois and Offaly. He later played a prominent role in the subjection of the O'Nolans.

[397] In 1567 Christopher Nugent, Baron Delvin, who was married to Mary the daughter of Gerald the 11th. Earl of Kildare, was given a royal commission to extirpate the O'Moores, sons of Ferrasc McRosse and their followers.

[398] See Chapter 17.

farmsteads met with stoic resistance. There are many records of attacks on such settlements, by the native Irish. For example, Sir Francis Knollys writing about the exploits of Donal Spainneach Kavanagh of Clonmullen itemised over thirty raids, which included murders, committed between 1577 and 1579.

As can be seen from a perusal of the Fiant Data, the O'Nolans were very much to the fore in all the rebellious wars of the 16th. and early 17th. century fighting alongside the Kavanaghs, O'Byrnes, O'Tooles, and Butlers.

Chapter 15

The Nine Years War

As we have seen the 16th. century was most turbulent. The O'Nolans and the other Gaelic families of the south east were embroiled in all the major disturbances that occurred- the rebellion of Silken Thomas (1536), the Butler rebellion (1568/69), the Browne incident (1572)[399] and the Baltinglass revolt (1580). While there was no major war in the 1580s there was much unrest and the O'Byrnes, Kavanaghs and O'Nolans under the leadership of Fiach McHugh O'Byrne and Donal Spainneach continued their relentless harassment of English tenants and officials. Between 1578 and 1580 the Kavanagh/O'Nolan[400] faction were involved in more than fifty attacks on the tenants of English settlers, particularly those of Thomas Masterson, who was the constable of Ferns. Masterson was especially targeted because as early as 1566 he was responsible for the deaths of Muiris Kavanagh of Coolnaleen and 24 of his chief men and in 1578 he was the man who arrested Gerald, a brother of Muiris and brought him to Dublin where he was executed. Then they were

---

[399] This incident resulted from the harassment of Matthew Furlong, by Robert Browne of Mulrankin, Co. Wexford. Browne, a member of a prominent Anglo Norman family, was married to a daughter of Sir Nicholas White, an important government official. According to Hore, Browne's sister had been murdered by some of the Furlongs and Matthew was being held responsible, though he was not the actual murderer. Matthew Furlong complained of Browne's actions to Brian McCahir Kavanagh, who retaliated and burned some villages in Browne's territory. In one of the skirmishes Browne himself was killed. The gentlemen of Wexford and Sir Nicholas Devereux, his uncle, 'rose in arms'. Brian McCahir appealed to his in-law, Fiach McHugh O'Byrne and the Furlongs, and they gathered a sizeable army which included many O'Nolans, particularly Murrough Ne Dower O'Nolan of Kilbride (Fiach's kinsman). A pitched battle was fought near Dunbrody, Co. Wexford and the 'gentlemen' of the county were defeated losing thirty of their number. It is possible that Heron was killed in this battle and Masterson barely escaped with his life. Henry Davells was also involved in the incident. Some notable men lost their lives in the battle including brothers of Fiach McHugh and Muiris an Iarainn Kavanagh of Coolnaleen. When White, who had been in England, returned, he became infuriated with the news of the murder and placed Brian McCahir and his allies 'beyond the pale of pardon'. This resulted in further depredation by the Irish on the tenants of the new landlords which continued for a further twelve months.

[400] During this period from 1594 to 1601 there were more than 80 individual O'Nolans pardoned (for being in rebellion). See Appendix 2 for details.

also involved in the Baltinglass rebellion in 1580/81. Masterson further enraged the Kavanaghs when, in 1580, he killed 40 of them, 'very bad people'[401] but Donal Spainneach escaped. He complained to the Earl of Ormonde who was so enraged that he sought to have Masterson hanged for the offence.

In 1581 more trouble came in the form of the new Lord Deputy, Grey, who 'visited' the area and left substantial reinforcements with Masterson. 17 of Donal Spainneach's people were killed by Masterson in 1581 and Later in the same year Masterson claimed to have killed 200 people whom he had come across in the forest.[402] Sometime during the same year he was involved in another skirmish with them and killed many more. In June 1581 Richard Synnott with a band of soldiers killed 54 more men while in October Donal Spainneach's forces lost another 50 while trying to ambush Masterson.[403]

Another group of Kavanaghs with men in pay, seem to have been active in the pursuit of Walter Eustace, a brother of the Viscount Baltinglass, who was also in rebellion with his brother. They were pardoned in 1583 for help in the capture of Walter. It is probable that they were in the pay of the Earl of Ormonde.

In the following years Fiach McHugh was in the wars with the officials in Wicklow and on one occasion attacked Wicklow. He was repulsed with the loss of 30 men. This attack followed an incursion into O'Byrne country by Harrington and Sir W. Russell which resulted in the loss of 1000 cattle 'preyed' from the O'Byrnes.

In 1583 Donal Spainneach's father, Donal, was captured and executed by Sir Nicholas White and in the following year the owner of the lands of the Leverock in the Kilbride/Clonegal area, Murrough Leigh McCahir Kavanagh was captured and executed at New Ross along with his brother.

Donal Spainneach's uncle, Cahir Oure McCahir, of Clonmullen, was slain, in 1585.

Moriertagh Og Kavanagh of Garryhill, an elderly man at the time, was murdered by Dudley Bagenal in 1586 and Bagenal himself was murdered by the Kavanaghs shortly afterwards. In the same year Fiach McHugh's son escaped from Dublin castle along with Red Hugh O'Donnell, one of the Kavanaghs and others. They were being held there as hostages for good behaviour. Some of the hostages were recovered in Wicklow, but Fiach had to give more hostages

---

[401] It would seem that these soldiers were in fact under protection having served in Munster with the Earl of Ormonde - Carew MSS.

[402] Only 50 of these people were armed. - S.P.

[403] In the same year Viscount Baltinglass (with his allies) burned Clondalkin.

including two of his sons and his wife's brother.[404] He secured their release by sending in six thieves' heads.[405]

This unrest in Carlow after the murders of Moriertagh Og and Bagenal led to the Lord Deputy declaring that 'much of the lands in counties Carlow, Wexford and Kilkenny were waste and uninhabited of English tenants'[406] Despite this he also stated in 1588 that the south east 'stands in reasonable good terms for quietness, save stealths and robberies sometimes committed in Carlow, Kilkenny and Wexford.'[407]

As the century wore on the Irish clans came under more and more pressure which culminated in the last big effort to win some kind of local autonomy.

In order to see what happened in the south east of Ireland, in perspective, it might be well to look at the bigger picture first and summarise what happened during the period from 1593 to 1603 which was known as The Nine Years War.

The MacMahon lordship in Monaghan was targeted for plantation and conquest by the Lord Deputy, Sir William Fitzwilliam, who was just as corrupt as St. Leger. His treacherous dealings with the clan leaders in 1593 set alarm bells ringing in Tyrone.

Hugh O'Neill the 2nd. Earl of Tyrone reacted by covertly organising resistance to the English presence in Ulster. He recruited his son-in-law Red Hugh O'Donnell and they commenced a series of raids and attacks on the English garrisons which prompted a response from the Lord Deputy who sent a relief army in 1594, to Enniskillen, which was being besieged. The relief army was surprised when crossing a ford on the River Arney. In the hasty retreat the English forces abandoned their supplies and the encounter became known as the battle of 'the ford of the biscuits'.

In the following year O'Neill organised another attack and defeated an English relief force at Clontibret. The English force had been returning south after bringing supplies to a garrison in Monaghan. They were commanded by Henry Bagenal, the son of the late general Sir Nicholas Bagenal. O'Neills generalship and his well trained troops won the day and Bagenal's army lost 31 killed and 109 wounded. O'Neill was immediately declared a traitor.

---

[404] A list of hostages in Dublin Castle at that time included sons of Shane O'Neill, Crimthinn Kavanagh (sent in by Donal Spainneach, his first cousin), Donough O'Nolan, sent in by Captain St. Leger, Fiach's hostages - Redmond and Brian McFiach and Hugh O'Toole and Walter Reagh's hostage Kedagh O'Toole (his nephew).

[405] State Papers - Two years later he sent in 26 heads - belonging to the O'Moores and other 'loose people' coming into his country!

[406] State Papers

[407] Despite the excitement caused by the Spanish Armada

His early successes led to the spread of the war into Leinster, where he was supported by Fiach McHugh and Donal Spainneach Kavanagh, the two foremost local military commanders.

On-off negotiations and partial peace treaties ensured that the war was protracted. O'Neill constantly strove to build up his army which consisted of native Irish, some English mercenaries, Scots mercenaries and some Spanish soldiers sent to help him, following entreaties to the monarch of that country.

In 1598 O'Neill achieved the most comprehensive defeat of an English army on Irish soil, when he defeated Bagenal at the Battle of the Yellow Ford. As a result of this battle the English had to abandon the garrisons in Armagh and on the Blackwater. Bagenal himself and 800 of his men perished.

Queen Elizabeth replied by sending over Robert Devereux, the Earl of Essex, a kinsman of the Devereux family of Ballymagir in Co. Wexford, with an army of 16,000 men. This army was to have been transported to the north in shipping but this failed to materialise and Essex decided to head south. His exploits in the south east will be dealt with later. He had some successes and got submissions before heading back to Dublin. He was ordered to go north but fearing that his position at court was being undermined he decided to leave his command and go to London. There he was placed under house arrest. In the following year he attempted to organise a rebellion or coup and being discovered he was tried for treason and executed in 1601.

His successor as Lord Deputy was George Blount, Lord Mountjoy. The new Deputy changed tactics and refused to parley with O'Neill. In addition he set up 25 small but strong garrisons in Ulster and others in Leinster which had the effect of producing near famine conditions in both provinces.

Following the arrival of the Spaniards at Kinsale in 1603, O'Neill and O'Donnell led a forced march through Ireland only to be defeated by Mountjoy. This defeat spelled the end of Irish resistance to English rule and local chieftains all over the country sought terms for themselves and their septs.

This brief history of the period sets the scene for the events that happened in the south east during the period.

The Gaelic clans of the area rallied themselves under the leadership of Fiach McHugh O'Byrne and Donal Spainneach Kavanagh of Clonmullen. The O'Nolans, O'Moores and O'Connors of Offaly threw in their lot with their more easterly neighbours.

Whether they were being tutored by O'Neill or following his example, the Gaelic leaders of the south east began applying for surrender and regrant. The years from 1590 to 1593 were relatively calm, but it would seem that they were building up their forces for the coming confrontation. The pardons issued in 1592 were part of this surrender and regrant procedure. Donal Spainneach, like many of his Kavanagh relatives applied, was pardoned, his surrender accepted immediately and he was given a pension of 2s. 6d a day ' for his better encouragement' as the Queen herself so aptly put it.

Four prominent O'Nolans also applied for and were given pardons. They were Callogh McHenry O'Nolan of Carrickslaney, Donal (Daniel) McHugh McDonal of Shangarry, Gerald of Kilmaglush (whom I suspect was Gerald McCahir originally from Ballykealy) and Phelim McCahir of Ballykealy. There is no record of any further transactions with the O'Nolans.[408]

Fiach McHugh himself even applied to the Lord Deputy, Fitzwilliam, for pardon but the English spies were busy reporting on Fiach's warlike preparations and his overtures were refused. At the same time that he applied for the pardon he had called on all the men of his country aged between 16 and 60 to meet him with armour and any weapons they could find. He was also supported by the O'Moores as his sister was married to Rory O'Moore. In the north, O'Neill mounted a public relations campaign against Fitzwilliam, sending a large volume of complaints about him to the English officials which had the result of Fitzwilliam being recalled in 1594.

One of the little known causes of the eventual downfall of Fiach was the attack on the castle of Sir Piers FitzJames FitzGerald, at Ardrye on the Barrow, near Athy.

Walter Reagh[409] with three of his brothers and three sons of Fiach and twenty more men burned the castle at daybreak. Sir Piers and his wife perished in the attack and also his wife's two sisters and two soldiers. The raiding party then drove off the FitzJames cattle. Sir Piers was attacked and killed because of his allegiance to the Crown.[410] This attack was denounced at all levels, especially because of the deaths of the three women who were daughters of Sir Maurice Fitzgerald and therefore closely related to the Earl of Kildare. It would

---

[408] Not all the O'Nolans 'misbehaved'. Thomas Nolan, of Galway, whose descendants owned huge areas of land in the west in the next two centuries, was corresponding with the Lord Deputy about the activities of the Burkes and O'Flahertys in 1589. In 1585 the O'Nolan of Galway was one of 67 signatories from Connaught who surrendered their Irish names and customs of inheritance and received their castles and lands by patent to them and their heirs in English succession.

[409] He was the son of Maurice FitzWalter Fitzgerald of Glassealey, Co. Kildare. The family were known as 'the bastard Geraldines'. His mother was Honora O'Toole of Powerscourt and Walter himself was married to a daughter of Fiach McHugh. Fiach's wife was Rose, a sister of Honora.

[410] A Piers FitzJames was involved in the slaying of Coollen McDavy (one of the leaders of the McDavy More Kavanaghs, who gave their names to the Macamores in Wexford) and 20 of his followers, in 1582. In that incident FitzJames was accompanied by Captain Mackworth, Captain Hungerford and Captain Thomas Wingfield. According to the State Papers Piers FitzJames had twenty five horsemen 'in pay'.

seem that the women could have been saved but for the intransigence of Garret, a brother of Walter Reagh, who refused to allow them to escape. Because of this terrible atrocity the Lord Deputy was compelled to act against the O'Byrnes and their allies.

Fiach applied to the new Deputy, Sir William Russell, for a pardon but Russell wrote to the Privy Council stating it was reported to him that 'Fiach had three or four spanyards cum in to him out of Brittayen with great complottes and a seminary priest with them. Whereupon Fiach immediately sett all ye axemen hee could gett to worcke to make a great store of pykes and smyths to make hedes for them. He also sends his raskalls to enter by day as well as by night all ye villages and undefensible houses in those countries adjoining to take away all ye arms and warlyck furniture they can meet withall.' Naturally the pardon was refused and the Deputy, in fact, recommended the 'extirpation' of Fiach and his followers

Murtagh Og Kavanagh of Garryhill surrendered to Russell[411] in December of that year, but that too was only lip service. The plan appeared to be that the O'Nolans and Kavanaghs would keep the peace, but would act as a shelter to Fiach and his men if they came under pressure, by taking in their horses and cattle etc. This ploy was later used in reverse during the 1598/99 campaign of Donal Spainneach.

The pressure came in January 1595 when the Deputy, Russell, made an expedition against Fiach and captured his stronghold at Ballinacor. Fiach managed to escape, but at some stage his wife Rose was wounded in the breast.[412]

A further expedition was undertaken in February and a parley was arranged. Fiach seemed to be willing to surrender but his second in command Walter Reagh Fitzgerald had opposite opinions. Nothing came of the talks. The Crown forces remained a month in the area and in numerous skirmishes with Fiach and his men they claimed to have killed and wounded many of them, including brothers of Walter Reagh and a brother of Fiach called Redmond McHugh. A price of £100 was offered for the head of Fiach and £140 if captured alive.

Fiach and Walter Reagh retaliated by killing many settlers near Dublin and burning their houses.

But there was dissension among the compatriots of Walter Reagh who conspired with the English to have him captured. His first cousin and trusted

---

[411] According to a recent article in the Irish Times, which dealt with Fiach McHugh, following the unveiling of a plaque to commemorate him in Rathdrum, Sir William Russell had a fixation with capturing or killing Fiach, whom he described as being 'of far greater ability than the Earl (Hugh O'Neill)'

[412] State Papers

adviser, Dermot McPhelim Reagh plotted with Mortagh Teig Og O'Byrne[413] and Harrington[414] to bring about his capture. Walter was wounded during the course of his capture and brought to Dublin where he was hanged in chains for 24 hours, before being 'examined'. After his 'examination', when he informed his questioners about the O'Neill/ O'Byrne dealings, he was executed.

Fiach was harried and hunted for the next two months (Spring 1595) by the Lord Deputy who killed about 40 of his dwindling army. It was declared that only the agility of his men saved them or many more could have been killed.[415] The Deputy renewed his efforts in May, having sent for reinforcements from England, who duly arrived in Waterford. In one encounter Fiach himself was badly wounded but managed to elude his pursuers.[416]

The Lord Deputy left many troops in the area before his departure to Dublin, in the various forts including Ferns, Ballymore, Monney, Arklow, Williamstown near Baltinglass, Castle Kevin[417] and Ballinacor.

Fiach and his band survived to apply for pardons but only succeeded in getting protections and days of 'respect' to enable him to send in hostages.[418] However through the good offices of Harrington and because of pressures

---

[413] This was Morogh McTeig Og O'Byrne of Blind Wood. He was pardoned four times during the reign of Elizabeth, almost always in company with his six brothers and with Cahir McWilliam O'Nolan of Kilbride, as part of the company, on one occasion. It is significant that he was padoned in 1597, the year of Fiach's murder by the English. It is quite plausible to suggest that he was acting on the orders of Fiach in this business as Fiach probably felt threatened by the independent minded Walter Reagh.

[414 414] Sir Henry Harrington - an adventurer of similar qualities to Masterson, Heron etc. He was the 'captain' over the O'Byrnes and O'Tooles and was based at Newcastle. He was responsible for the building of Carnew Castle whence the name Carnew - Carn Nua (it was also called Cloghnua in the State Papers). After the final defeat and death of Fiach, Harrington (who was acquitted, of the charges) was accused of aiding and abetting him - and so it would appear. It was noted in the State Papers of the time (1595) that Harrington made a plea to the Government to have Fiach accepted on a surrender basis. As part of his argument he cited the horrendous cost to the government in having him pursued and quietened, while at the same time implying that the troops were worse needed for duty in the north.

[415] State Papers

[416] His wife Rose was captured in May 1595 and the L.D. seems to have put Harrington in charge of her. Harrington was also accused of harbouring traitors and especially Rose, Fiach's wife. Rose was eventually taken prisoner and was sentenced to be executed on 3rd. July 1597.

[417] Near Annamoe.

[418] Fiach even offered his own nephew Owny O'Moore as his hostage.

coming on the Government from the O'Neills and O'Donnells, Fiach managed to survive the winter of 1595/6 and even succeeded in building up his forces once more.[419] Many of the warlike men of the O'Moores, O'Connors and O'Nolans enlisted in his army with the blessing of their own chieftains. It was noted in a letter from the Lord Deputy to Burghley, the Queen's Chancellor, that Owny O'Moore (the son of Rory Og) had passed over the bridge of Carlow to join Fiach. He and his little army must have passed through Forth on the way and were joined, no doubt, by the warlike sons of the O'Nolans. He also noted that Piers Butler (the son of Sir Edmund Butler and nephew of the Earl of Ormonde) had sworn great friendship with Donal Spainneach and that James Butler, Piers's brother, was to marry a sister of Owny O'Moore.[420] He further stated that Fiach McHugh was promised 200 gunmen out of the north.

Even in February 1596 Fiach was in contact with the government officials. That month the Lord Deputy and Council had 'intreated Her Majesty's mercy to Fiach McHugh' and later in the month Fiach sent in his hostages to Sir Henry Harrington. He also applied to have his goods restored or be given a warrant to take meat and drink without breach of his protection.

In March 1596 the spies were busy and the Lord Deputy got word that the Connaught rebels, with the Scots intended going down through the midlands and joining up with Fiach. The Deputy marched against them and defeated them in McCoughlan's country (near Banagher, Co. Offaly). Most of the rebels escaped back to Connaught.

During the summer of 1596 Fiach and his allies were petitioning for surrender and regrant, but were also in close contact with the Earl of Tyrone and were compounding their own plots.[421] The correspondence between Fiach and Tyrone was generally intercepted.

By August things were hotting up in Wicklow and a Captain Parkins complained that James Butler had treacherously hanged 6 of the garrison at Ballinacor. He intimated that Fiach must have been party to the killings. In

---

[419] In Nov. (1595) Fiach submitted on his knees before the Lord Deputy and Council and petitioned to be received into Her Majesty's mercy. As a result of this supplication his protection was renewed for three months. - S.P.

[420] Both of these Butler brothers were later executed for their part in the rebellion. Their surviving brother Theobald was made Viscount Butler of Tullowphelim in 1603 and he married his first cousin, the only daughter and heir of Thomas Butler (Black Tom), the 9th. Earl of Ormonde.

[421] In June, it was reported that there was an assembly in the Briskillo (possibly the Brecklaghe - the Myshall area of Carlow, see chapter on Land Divisions) of Phelim McFiach, Owny O'Moore, Gerald McMoriertagh Kavanagh and his brother Murtagh Og with 100 more. Gerald McBrien and his brother Muiris Kavanagh were sworn to Fiach. - S.P.

September 1596, Fiach and his army now numbering about 300 were intercepting the munitions being sent to Ballinacor and they burned and spoiled right up to the city of Dublin.[422] They captured the fort of Ballinacor and took Parkins prisoner. The Lord Deputy and council were wary about moving against Fiach as they feared that Tyrone (who was in an uneasy peace) would then begin to move against them and that all Leinster might become sucked into the conflict.

After much prevarication the Lord Deputy marched against Fiach and Ballinacor was retaken in late September. Captain Lee[423] was left there in charge of the fort, but within a short time he was complaining that the Butlers had raided his estate and stolen 500 cows from his tenants, while burning six villages. The Earl of Ormonde, meanwhile, left garrisons in the castles of Tullowphelim and Clogrennan.

The Earl of Ormonde also arrested his brother, Sir Edmund Butler and one of his sons, presumably in order to put pressure on the other two sons, who were supporting Fiach, to withdraw that support. At this juncture Donal Spainneach 'joined himself with Fiach by oath' despite the fact that he had just received a pardon.

The winter dragged on with sporadic raids being made on Fiach's country. For example in November (1596) Sir Edward Bowe's men went into the glens. They killed many cattle and almost captured Fiach and Rose. Fiach's army had now swelled to 700 which included men from the north, the Butlers, two brothers of the Earl of Kildare and presumably some forces from the O'Nolan/Kavanagh area. The Lord Deputy himself also campaigned that month and camped at Tullow. He claimed to have dispersed Fiach's 'rabble'.

Because of the tense situation in the north, the Queen offered Fiach a pardon, on condition he would send in hostages etc., but he refused this offer saying that he would only accept O'Neill's peace. Tyrone was not too overjoyed with this response and intimated that if Fiach refused to accept a pardon he would withdraw his support.

Raids and counter raids continued into the new year (1597). Captain Lee killed over 30 rebels in Fiach's country[424] and Thomas Ball received £15 for bringing in the heads of seventeen of Fiach's men. In February the Lord Deputy moved to Carlow to prevent any rising in O'Nolan/Kavanagh country.

---

[422] State Papers

[423] In 1583 Lee had been granted a lease of church lands and tithes in counties Carlow (Rathmore) and Kildare. He was sent to prison in Nov. 1595 for killing Kedagh O'Toole and also wounding Dermot McPhelim O'Toole. He seemed to have got an early release as by the following March he was soldiering up in the north.- S.P.

[424] This happened as Lee was ambushed bringing victuals to the fort at Rathdrum from Wicklow. - S.P.

With the advent of Spring Lee was ordered to use all possible means to prosecute Fiach. He was supplied with ample men and arms for the purpose. His energetic and continuous harassment of the people led to near famine in the area and many of Fiach's men melted away to their own areas. By the month of May his numbers had dwindled dramatically and there was much distrust among even his family and close followers. As late as April (1597) O'Neill was making desperate attempts to have Fiach included in parleys with Sir John Norris.[425] He complained bitterly that the fact that the government did not offer pardon to Fiach was a breach of faith.

On May 6th. the Lord Deputy sent a force to rendezvous with Lee's men at Rathdrum. Early the following morning they made a concerted forced march through the glens until they came to the cabin where Fiach was sleeping.[426] He had three or four swordsmen with him. They were surprised in their sleep and all in the cabin were killed. Captain Lee[427] was credited with having been responsible for the killing.

Fiach's death effectively put an end to the threat of further rebellion by the O'Byrnes. The theatre of war now switched to Wexford/Carlow and the leadership of the southern rebels devolved upon Donal Spainneach.

Spies reported that the Kavanaghs (and therefore the O'Nolans) had 400 foot and 60 horse in readiness to support Phelim McFiach, who took over his father's mantle as the leader of the O'Byrnes.

In March 1598, O'Neill met with the chief men of the Kavanaghs, O'Nolans, O'Moores and O'Connors and on their behalf Donal Spainneach agreed to act with him. Donal now styled himself the McMurrough and King of Leinster.[428]

Although supposedly observing the truce that O'Neill had with the English, the armed men of Leinster were forced to resort to coyne and livery to supply their needs. This led to conflict between them and Henry Wallop's garrison at Enniscorthy backed up by Richard Masterson (the eldest son of Thomas Masterson and Seneschal of Wexford). The O'Moores of Laois backed up by the O'Nolans and Kavanaghs moved through Carlow into Wexford, collecting booty on the way from the tenants of the loyalists and Englishmen. Masterson was able to raise a force of about 600 consisting of his

---

[425] Fiach himself was afraid of treachery and offered to send his wife, Rose. O'Neill, accordingly sought permission from the officials to allow her to come in Fiach's place. - S.P.

[426] Fiach was obviously betrayed by someone who knew his exact whereabouts.

[427] Lee was very active in the war but was killed at the Battle of the Yellow Ford in 1598 - Hayes McCoy (Irish Battles)

[428] Hore's History of Wexford Vol 6 pg.104 & State Papers

own men, Wallop's forces and two companies of levies from Picardy. A battle ensued and was fought on the 18th. May 1598 near Enniscorthy.[429]

Due to the good generalship enjoyed by the Leinstermen, who kept a force in reserve until the crucial time, the combined English force was severely mauled losing most of their soldiers and many of their officers. Masterson himself barely escaped. On the Irish side only four or five men lost their lives. This remarkable victory was celebrated in Carlow that night.

Shortly afterwards the Earl of Ormonde, who was Lord Lieutenant General, sent his nephew, Sir James Butler, with an army to subdue the O'Moores. In a battle fought in Co. Laois the English forces were again defeated with heavy losses and Butler himself was killed. Brian O'Moore was also killed.

After O'Neill's great defeat of the English at the battle of the Yellow Ford (August 1598) the Gaelic clans of Leinster became the dominant forces in the area. The O'Moores subdued almost the whole of Laois and Donal Spainneach with his O'Nolan allies 'wasted with fire and sword a great part of Meath, because it had not joined the confederacy in defence of the Catholic faith against the English.'[430] In addition to giving Meath some attention, the English tenants of Wexford and Carlow suffered from preys being taken and premises burned.

By November of 1598 there were two Irish armies in Leinster. One was under the command of Owny O'Moore and the other under the command of Donal Spainneach, who had suspended for a time his title of King of Leinster and had accepted the title of General of that part of Leinster and of the mountain men (the O'Byrnes) and the bastard Geraldines of Kildare. He had under his control 2,500 foot and horse.[431]

The winter of 1598/99 seems to have been relatively quiet but hostilities resumed in the Spring of 1599. Robert Devereux, the Earl of Essex arrived in Ireland with the biggest army ever seen. He had with him 20,000 men and 2000 horse. Because of bungling by the officials in London the shipping needed to transport the troops to Lough Foyle never materialised and Essex decided to march south. He was harried by the combined forces of the Leinster men and in Co. Laois a detachment of his men was soundly defeated. In the course of the rout, his soldiers left behind them many plumed helmets and the place became known in local folklore as 'The Pass of the Plumes'.

---

[429] Garret Og of Clonmullen, a first cousin of Donal Spainneach was one of the foremost captains in this battle. He was captured shortly afterwards and executed on the 19th. June.
[430] An tAthair S. De Bhal in his book "Buncloidi" pg. 27
[431] State Papers

Harrington went into O'Byrne country with a considerable force, of 500 foot and 60 horse, but met with fierce resistance which resulted in a defeat and serious losses.

The Earl of Ormonde, on the other hand, met with more success, as in this year he took the Mountgarret[432] castle of Ballyanne which was manned by Ulster and Connaught men. All except nine of the defenders were put to death. He also destroyed two other Mountgarret castles.

In June, Essex decided to move his army, then camped at Waterford, into Wexford. He commandeered what shipping he could and moved the troops over to Ballyhack. He himself with a large contingent spent a night at Ballymagir in the house of his kinsman, Sir James Devereux. It is said that Sir James had to sell a townsland to pay for the entertainment. Essex moved his army northwards towards Enniscorthy and Ferns and ordered the villages of north Wexford to be fired, if Donal Spainneach was to be seen attending his passage. He then moved on to Gorey and Arklow. All along his route he was tracked by the Leinster forces and many small skirmishes took place. At Arklow Rock and Smithy Rock, a mile or so south of Arklow, a more serious engagement occurred in which the Leinstermen lost over 100 men and five of their chief commanders[433], the enemy possibly losing as many or more. They sued for peace but Essex refused to meet them. He proceeded on to Dublin and the Leinstermen gave up the pursuit and returned home.

Essex was ordered to go north but instead of marching his army to fight O'Neill he met him on his own and patched up a truce. As already noted he suddenly left his command, returned to England, was imprisoned and was executed in 1601.

His replacement, Charles Blount, Lord Mountjoy, was made of sterner stuff. After his arrival in February 1600 he refused at first, to treat with the native chiefs, but Phelim McFiach submitted 'upon his knees' to the Council.

Mountjoy's plan was to place strong garrisons in strategic places. These garrisons would have the effect of reducing each area by taking cattle and by 'pursuing rebels', in their areas.

Between the time of his arrival and his visitation to Wexford it is said that Donal Spainneach and his allies completely devastated the southern half of Wexford with an army of 1200. The Crown forces, which were much depleted, amounted to only 300 foot and 40 horse. They retired to their own castles and fortifications to mind their own holdings.

According to Richard Roche in an article about Forth and Bargy, 'Mountjoy overran the territory of the McMurrough Kavanaghs in the

---

[432] Edmund Butler, 2nd Viscount Mountgarret, a fist cousin to the Earl of Ormonde who was protected and pardoned 14 times during his life. He died in 1602.

[433] See Appendix 3 for a full account of this battle as recounted in Hore Vol VI

summer of this year'. Phelim McFiach again submitted and Donal Spainneach was pardoned but had to give up a son as a hostage and another son was compelled to attend school in Dublin. This effectively ended Donal's (and the east Leinstermen's) participation in the Nine Years War which came to an end with the Spanish fiasco at Kinsale early in 1601.

The formal pardon was not issued to Donal Spainneach until May 1601. This pardon included a very large number of named persons. Over thirty of these have been readily identified as O'Nolans, while as many as thirty more may have been O'Nolans.[434]

A number of O'Nolans were described as having been slain in rebellion and it is likely that they lost their lives in the battle with the Essex army near Arklow, as that was the last major action in the Nine Years War in which the Wexford/Carlow men were involved.

These included Rory O'Nolan of Kilbride, the son of Murrough and grandson of William of Kilbride; Donough the son of Leasagh and grandson of William; Callogh McEdmond McShane Duff who was the great grandson of Cahir O'Nolan of Ballykealy; Donal McEnass McDermot McShane Duff who was a great grandson of Cahir of Ballykealy; and possibly Cahir McDonough McCahir a grandson of Cahir of Ballykealy.

---

[434] See Appendix 2 for the list of O'Nolans pardoned (in the Fiants)

Chapter 16

The Adventurers

While perusing the Fiants of the Tudor Monarchs the same names of English grantees and officials keep cropping up. From the time of Henry VIII until the end of the reign of Queen Elizabeth the people who had most influence on affairs in Co. Carlow, at ground level, were Nicholas Heron, Sir Peter Carew, Anthony Colclough, Robert Harpole, Henry Davells, Francis Randall, John Barry, Edmund Lyne, Brian Jones, John Rowe, Humphrey Mackworth[435] and to a certain extent the Bagenals and Robert St. Leger. Neither the Bagenals or St. Leger appear to have been de facto officials of the administration (of course Sir Walter Bagenal was a general in the Army) but they were speculators.

Others who exercised great influence on events in the area were the Eustaces of Baltinglass and Sir Edmund Butler of Clogrennan Castle, the brother of the Duke of Ormonde. These men all had small armies under their command and it was these small armies that whittled away at the Gaelic structure. Placed in strategic locations they could impose their wills on isolated groups of natives and compel their compliance to English law. In addition to using force these unscrupulous men tricked and cajoled the Irish and exploited their naiveté.

Robert Sentleger or St. Leger was the first of those to get lands in Carlow. Of course his father was Sir Anthony St. Leger, who was Lord Deputy for three periods, 1540 - 1548, 1550 - 1551 and 1553 - 1556. Sir Anthony proved to be more avaricious than most and when the Church lands were offered to speculators like him he was first in line to buy them up at very cheap prices and sell them afterwards at huge profits. Sir Anthony was charged with corruption in 1556 and was dismissed as Lord Deputy and fined a large sum of money. Robert, too benefited from the hand outs and in 1545 he was granted a lease of Church lands in Co. Carlow, for a very low rent. He was given the manor or preceptory of Killerig and lands in Friarstown, Court of Killerig, Russelstown, Tullaghphelim and Maganey. In addition he was granted the

---

[435] Capt. Mackworth, who had been responsible for a great slaughter of the O'Moores and O'Connors in 1582, was killed by Cahil O'Connor (of Offaly) sometime before 1585. O'Connor escaped to Spain and was seen in Lisbon by a Luke Plunkett c. 1589. He was in the company of Edmund Eustace the son of the late Viscount Baltinglass. - S.P.

rectories of Killerig and Kilmakayll (?). In the same year he was granted the church lands of Kill, Co. Kildare to hold forever. He sold the Kill lands to Richard Aylmer of Lyons in 1550.

In that year he seems to have moved to Carlow as he got three leases of lands in Kilkenny and Laois in that year and was described as being 'of Carlow'. After his father's demotion St. Leger seems to have moved to Co. Kilkenny and the only other notices of him in the Fiants are pardons issued in 1561, 1571 and 1578. While the grants to St. Leger in Carlow did not impinge on the lands of Forth, his willingness to take Church lands in such a precarious area seems to have encouraged others.

The next grant of land in the general area was to Brian Johns or Jones who was granted a lease of a huge amount of land on the Laois Carlow border in 1549. Again this did not unduly upset the O'Nolans but it was devastating for the O'Moores whose territory seemed to have been earmarked for colonisation from an early date. The terms of the lease are most interesting and give an idea of the perilous nature of such landgrabbing. The amount of land was very extensive and his rent for the first year was only one penny. For the second year his rent was £10, for the third year £20 and £30 for the fourth year. It was to be £33. 6s. 8d. for the remaining sixteen years of the term. In the event he cashed in his chips in 1552 and sold his interest to Walter Peppard who was later the occupant of Kilkea Castle.

By that time Jones was Constable of the Castle of Carlow and seems to have remained in that post until 1557, when the reign of Philip and Mary (who made some attempt to reinstate the Catholic religion)came to an end. He was a member of two commissions given the power to govern the county in that year and to enquire into the whereabouts of church vestments, bells, chalices etc., which had been removed during the reformation under Henry VIII.

The real crunch for the O'Nolans came in 1550 when huge amounts of their territory were granted to two men - John Barri or Barry and Edmund O'Lenye or Edmund Lyne as he was also called, who were given a joint grant.

John Barry may well have been a member of an offshoot branch of the famous Barrys of Cork whose scion was to become the Earl of Barrymore.[436] It is also possible that a direct descendant of John Barry was in fact the James Barry who became the owner of much of the Forth lands in the early years of the 17th. century and who gave his name to Newtownbarry.[437] While Barry did

---

[436] In 1548, in the reign of King Edward VI, John Barre, of Freerton (Co. Kildare), was given a pardon along with men who were either his brothers or sons. They were David, Nicholas, Redmund and Robert. (Fiants) Redmund as a Christian name occurs quite frequently in the pedigree of the Barrys of Barrymore.

[437] Now called Bunclody.

not appear to hold any official title he was certainly heavily involved in the security of the region.

Edmund Lyne was Constable of the castle of Castledermot, in 1548 and he seems to have had either his brothers or his sons there as soldiers. In that year he received a pardon along with Thomas and Connor Lyne (or O'Loyne as they were described in the Fiant).

In practically all the Fiants dealing with security, such as commissions to execute martial law or commissions to be justices of the peace, he is always in company with his friend and business partner Barry. These men were invariably in the company of such noted adventurers as Randall, Heron and Harpole.

The land grant given to the two men was almost identical to the grant later given to the Duke of Ormonde in 1562,[438] leading one to speculate that they sold their interest to him. The rent they paid for the land was quite small - less than £14 per annum with a similar sum being paid to the castle of Carlow in lieu of customs. Edmund Lyne seems to have left the scene in the late sixties as the last notice of him is a pardon, in 1566. He is described as being 'of Rathvilly' and he was pardoned, as part of a large group, along with William Lyne of Rathmore, Donough Lyne of Brynston and Teig Lyne of Rathvilly, who may well have been sons or nephews.[439] Another sub-group consisted of four O'Nolans - Murrough of Kilbride, a horseman, Murrough of Ballinvalley, a horseboy, Gerald of Killenclonboley and Shane McGerald of Rathrush.

Nicholas Heron was the professional soldier sent into Carlow as constable of the castle of Leighlin, a very important and strategic crossing on the

---

[438] See sketch map in previous chapter.

[439] It would seem that when it suited them some of the 'establishment' people sided with the Irish in local land disputes. A prime example of this was the behaviour of Thomas Stukely, an adventurer who got grants of lands on the Wexford/Carlow border (the Leverock and the Abbey of Downe lands). In 1569, when the Butlers went into rebellion with the Munster Geraldines, in pursuit of a claim against Sir Peter Carew, he threw in his lot with them. Stukely was an uncle of Anthony Peppard (who was married to Maeve Kavanagh of Coolnaleen, the daughter of Murrough, the McMurrough, who had been executed in 1557). Peppard was a large landowner in Wexford, also, who had judiciously married a very important lady. Stukely, because of his connection was able to take possession of his granted lands. However when the Kavanaghs (and O'Nolans) sided with the Butlers he had no option but to join them. Stukely was captured and spent 18 weeks in jail. He was later pardoned, but was involved in other rebellious acts. In 1572 he went to Spain, to fight against the Moors. He brought Donal Kavanagh of Clonmullen with him and when the latter returned to Ireland some four or five years later he was called Donal Spainneach.

Barrow. The castle had been repaired by Colclough in 1549 and Colclough seems to have been the constable there until Heron's arrival in 1552. Colclough was given a pardon in 1549, presumably for overstepping his remit, and in 1550 he was given a grant of lands in Laois, part of the territories of Patrick O'Moore who was declared a traitor in 1547/8. After 1552 Colclough seems to have dropped out of circulation but he is mentioned again in 1558 when he was appointed to execute martial law in Wexford.[440]

Meanwhile in Carlow Heron was very active. In the year of his appointment he was pardoned along with Colclough and Gabriel Bleck (Black), who were described as captains, and John Mone, Richard Woode, Matthew Skelton and Henry Davells who were described as gents. These people were generally pardoned for overstepping the mark in their military dealings with the native Irish, but no explanation is given in the Fiant.

Heron was mentioned in the Fiants six times between 1556 and 1558. He was pardoned once in 1557 along with Davells, Harpole, Masterson and Egidius Hovenden. On the other five occasions he was appointed to execute martial law or to be a justice and keeper of the peace.

He was granted a lease of the castle and town of Ferns with the manor lands at a rent of £10, in 1558 and came into conflict with the Kavanaghs almost immediately.[441] This resulted in his murdering Art Bui Kavanagh of Clonmullen in 1562. He received further commissions to execute martial law in Carlow between 1558 and 1560. After that time he seems to have moved to Wexford, where he got the grant of lands. He was dead before 1573.

As was mentioned earlier Robert Harpole[442] was to the O'Nolans what Richard Masterson was to the Kavanaghs of North Wexford. The following brief study of his career will give us some insights into how such adventurers helped to reduce the native Irish.

Robert Harpole or Hartpole was an adventurer who was in Ireland during the years of the reign of Queen Elizabeth. According to Fr. Kavanagh in his

---

[440] He may have remained in the Wexford area during the next ten years and he bought the Tintern lease in 1568 and had it granted to him by the Queen. He bought the lease from Thomas Woode, gent., who was given the lands in 1552 by Edward VI. Woode too was an entrepreneurial adventurer whose son Richard seems to have been Sheriff of Carlow from 1569 - 1573.

[441] It is significant that this appointment was made one year after the execution of Murrough Kavanagh of Coolnaleen (Ferns), the McMurrough, with 24 of his chief men, at Leighlin, where Heron was constable.

[442] The name is spelt in different ways. On his tombstone which was discovered at Castle hill in Carlow in 1809 it is spelt Hartpole. The effigy on the tombstone is of man fully clothed in armour with his head resting on his helmet and a bloodhound at his feet. It gives the year of his death as 1594.

article ' The Fall of the Clan Kavanagh, Harpole made himself rich at the expense of the inhabitants of Forth. It is likely that they were the people who had to victual and supply the Castle of Carlow following an agreement between the Kavanaghs and the Lord Deputy for the victualling and supply of provisions to the castles of Carlow, Leighlinbridge and Ferns.

Harpole seems to have come to Ireland during the reign of Philip and Mary as the first notice of him is in a Fiant of that period when he received a pardon, along with Nicholas Heron, Captain and Constable of the Manor of Leighlin, Henry Davells, Thomas Masterson of Kilkenny and Egidius Hoveden of Levedston, Co. Kildare, gentlemen and soldiers. Harpole and Davells were noted as being of Leighlin and we must assume that they came to Ireland with Captain Nicholas Heron and formed part of his garrison in the castle of Leighlin.

Nothing more is heard of him until 1563 when he was given a grant of lands in Co. Laois (along with his friend Davells)[443] then being planted as Queen's County. In the following year he was given a grant of further lands there. The usual conditions for planters was included in his grant - e.g. he could only let the lands to people of English birth and he couldn't sell or alienate his property without licence from the Crown.

In 1564 he was pardoned along with Davells and one Oliver Shortall FitzRobert - "in consideration of their services against the Irish rebels and in execution of martial law, during which they may have offended, without malice, against the rigour of the laws"

Harpole & Davells were, like all their ilk, ambitious and ruthless men, and in 1565 they obtained a lease of the Monastic lands of Baltinglass Abbey which were beside the Barrow in Idrone. The lands were Ballibar, Clonmelsh, Chapleston and Powerston, together with the customs of the tenants.

The following year Harpole and Davells, along with Anthony Colclough[444], Francis Randall,[445] Nicholas Heron (later appointed Constable of

---

[443] He must have been a very active soldier in this period as rewards such as those grants were only given to men who had worked hard in the cause of the reformation and the subjugation of the native Irish.

[444] This is the famous Anthony Colclough (pronounced Coakley) who got a grant of Tintern Abbey in south Wexford and was ancestor of a very famous dynasty which lasted right up to the 20th. century. He is first mentioned in the State Papers in 1548 when he was a Crown Officer in Carlow and he also received a grant of lands in Laois. He was involved in the submission of Cahir McArt to Bellingham the L.D.

[445] Randall was a sheriff in Co. Carlow in 1566 and in the eight years prior to that he was numbered among the justices and keepers of the peace who were commissioned to execute martial law at various times e.g. 1558, 1563, 1564 and 1566 (Fiants). He does not appear to have been a landowner in Co. Carlow.

Ferns Castle and leasee of the Duffry) and John Sankye[446] (the under Marshal for the whole realm - Nicholas Bagenal being the Marshal) were given a commission to execute martial law in the county. The powers given to them were sweeping and wide. They were empowered "to search out all disorders committed in the county and on finding any persons to be felons, rebels, enemies or notorious evil-doers, to punish them by death or otherwise. This power not to extend against any having 40s. a year freehold or £10 in chattels or any of honest name unless taken in the act or duly convicted. With power also to treat with rebels and enemies and for that purpose to grant safe conducts and to conclude good order with them under the instructions of the Lord Deputy."

In 1567 Harpole was granted the office of Constable of the castle of Catharlaghe with six armed footmen for its defence. He was given a fee of £20 annually and was allowed 6d. a day to pay each footman. In addition he was to receive such other profits as Francis Randolf had.

In the same year he must have been over-zealous in performing his duties as he was pardoned along with his cronies - Davells and Thomas Masterson and Henry Masterson. Masterson of course was later appointed Constable of the Castle of Ferns and proved as much of an entrepreneur as his good friend Harpole - at the expense of the Kavanaghs who lived in the area.

Davells went on to Wexford (1574) and took over the lease of the Duffry when Nicholas Heron died. He didn't last too long in Wexford and by 1575 he had moved back to Dungarvan. He was given a lease of extensive lands in Cork in that year and the next year he got an even more extensive lease of lands in Tipperary valued at £40. 1s 1d. per annum.

Harpole was quite active in quelling the 'Butler Rebellion' and in August 1569 he was in the company of the Viscount Baltinglass and John Eustace on the borders of Carlow because of the "rising out", but they were too weak for Piers Butler "then in the woods of the Dullagh and Slewmargy". A week later the same gentlemen wrote to the Lord Chancellor concerning Edward Butler 'who had burnt Lyttle North in Kildare and taken Tully (Tullow).' They had withdrawn to Carlow where they found the footmen who were supposed to be defending the castle there had defected to the rebels.[447]

In 1571 the State Papers noted that depositions were taken from the inhabitants of Forth O'Nolan, Rathvilie and Clonmore, declaring the extortions of Robert Harpole, Sheriff and W. Begg, sub-sheriff of the County of Carlow, taken before Walter Archer Jnr. and Pat Goughe by virtue of

---

[446] Sankye was Sheriff of Offaly in 1566 - Fiants.
[447] State Papers

letters from the Earl of Ormond.[448] No action seems to have been taken against Harpole as he was still in office the next year.

Harpole and Davells got a Commission to muster and array the inhabitants of Co. Carlow in 1572. In this they were joined with the Bishop of Leighlin, James Eustace of Friarstown, John Rowe[449] the Sheriff of Co. Carlow and John Barry, gent. They were charged "to assemble before them all the inhabitants, of whatever degree of the Co. of Carlow and the crosses and marches of it, to assess and array, according to their property, the numbers of horse and foot which they should supply (to the Deputy in a hosting) and to make separate musters of the men of each barony making a return to the Lord Deputy before July 1st."[450]

Again in 1572 Harpole, Davells, Francis Cosby, Anthony Colclough, John Barry, John Wodd, Richard Gorsse and Mathew Lynt (Lyne), gentlemen, were "to make enquiry of the ancient boundaries of the barony of Idrone, the lawful inheritance of Sir Peter Carew and to certify same to Chancery."

In 1573 and 1574 orders came for similar musters as mentioned above, except that in 1574 Davells was omitted from the list of scrutineers, having been moved to Wexford, where, no doubt, he had to perform similar duties.

Like his Irish neighbours Harpole was subject to Surrender and Regrant and in 1576 he had to surrender all his lands in Laois and Carlow to the Queen but he received them back again in the same year but instead of leases he was now given his Laois lands forever. The family set themselves up in Shrule Castle where they continued down to the 18th. century and then died out.

During the same eventful year (1576) Harpole was a commissioner with the other important Englishmen of the province with the task of discovering

---

[448] Unfortunately, I found this document (a copy of which is on microfilm in the National Library) to be mostly illegible (to me at any rate), as the copy itself is quite poor and the quality of the penmanship somewhat appalling.

[449] Not much is known about John Rowe. He seems to have been an Elizabethan official who pardoned in 1566 and he was described as 'John Rowe, of Ballynabranagh, gent.' In this pardon he was in the company of many others including Edmund Butler of Clogrennan, Purcells, Byrnes(sic), numerous Brennans, William O'Nolan of Kilbride and Gerald O'Nolan of Killinclonboley. In 1570 his address was Kellistown and he was pardoned especially for the forfeiture of a recognisance of £500 by him. The following year he was Sheriff of the county and was commissioned to execute martial law with Davells who was described as the Captain of the Kavanaghs. Again in 1572 he was given a similar commission. - Fiants.

[450] Taking muster gave rise to many abuses of crown money - the officials claiming for many more men than were actually in service. Many Anglo Norman lords benefited enormously from these frauds and disliked the measures taken to counteract them. - S.P.

by inquisition the concealed lands of monasteries and attainted persons.[451] (Lands were concealed by conveying them away to relatives or acquaintances who received remuneration for their part in the deception).

The following year Harpole was mentioned in despatches. It was during this year that the massacre of Mullaghmast happened in Co. Laois. Representatives of the seven septs of Laois[452], numbering some hundreds, were invited to the fort of Mullaghmast by the planters under the guise of a parley. While there most of the men were murdered by bands of soldiers controlled by Harpole, Cosby, Hovenden, Piggott and Bowen. Only a small number of the Irish escaped. Rory Og retaliated by capturing Harrington and Alexander Cosby. Harpole was the man who organised the rescue of Captains Harrington and Cosby and other prisoners who had been captured by the O'Moores. When the rescue party attacked the house where the prisoners were being held they killed all the rebels who were there except Rory Og O'Moore who made good his escape. Rory's wife was killed in the action also. Rory, in retaliation burnt and spoiled Carlow.[453]

Harpole was rewarded with a grant of Monksgrange in the Queen's Co. to hold forever for the one twentieth part of a knight's fee at a yearly rent of 40s. 8d. In this year also he renewed his lease on the Castle and Manor of Carlow.[454]

In 1578 he was required to act on a Commission to discover concealed lands. In this year, too, he was pardoned for not appearing in court with a Thomas Dorres alias Baker of Catharlaghe. It may have been significant that Gerald McMoriertagh Kavanagh of Garryhill was pardoned at the same time, but it is not known why.

Three years later Harpole was pardoned along with his son William, and he was described as Robert Harpole, late Sheriff of Catharlaghe. In the next

---

[451] State Papers
[452] O'Moores, O'Kellys, O'Lalors, O'Devoys, Macaboys, O'Dorans and O'Dowlings.
[453] State Papers - Rory was the son of the Rory O'Moore who was made Captain of Leix in place of his brother Kedagh in 1542. Donal McCahir Kavanagh (a grandson of Moriertagh Og of Garryhill), who slew Kedagh O'More, was attainted, thereby forfeiting to the King, according to Brian Jones
[454] Ibid.

year, 1582, his sons William and Thomas with others, were pardoned at the behest of Robert Harpole and during this same year Robert with his son William received a lease of the Manor of Catharlaghe for 21 years.

In 1583 Robert and William Harpole were pardoned along with Gerald McMoriertagh Kavanagh of Garryhill.

By the year 1587 Robert Harpole was again Sheriff of Carlow, as he was instructed along with Edmund Butler, William Harpole, Joshua Mynce and James Grace of Ravillie, gent., to take muster and array of the inhabitants of Co. Carlow. In this year, his son Walter was granted the Deanery of Leighlin. It was in this year also that another Walter was giving him plenty to worry about. This was Walter Reagh Fitzgerald to whom we have already alluded. Walter had killed followers of the Earl of Ormonde in 1586 and one of the men they despoiled was a man called Archdeacon.[455] He gathered a company of 'chief kern' and pursued Walter Reagh and his band (comprised of his brothers and cousins and O'Nolans, Kavanaghs, O'Moores and O'Byrnes). A skirmish was fought and Archdeacon's men were defeated and he himself captured. He was held to ransom and a herd of 35 cattle had to be brought to the woods of Shillelagh to secure his release. Being sheriff of Carlow it is certain that Harpole was ordered to assist in the efforts then made to arrest Walter Reagh and his band.[456] At this stage he must have been a man in his mid to late fifties with very little stomach left for such arduous tasks.

The next year, 1588, William and Robert Harpole got a lease of the Manor of Catharlaghe for 21 years. It is noteworthy too that in that year a man called John Stoughton was instructed to take the muster of the ward of

---

[455] Now called Cody - A.K.

[456] In an effort to bring Walter Reagh to heel the Lord Deputy ordered the arrest of Walter's father and mother and they were brought captive to Dublin. A brother of Walter, who was being held hostage, following his pardon in 1586 was executed. Edmund Butler was given licence to scour the countryside to find Walter Reagh but despite his best efforts for 3 months he failed. Then his son Piers was given 25 kern and ordered to find the stolen 'prey' and to protect Ormonde's tenants. Sir Nicholas White got in on the act and released 25 of Captain St. Leger's company to assist Piers Butler. It was all to no avail, except that Conal McKedagh O'Moore was killed in a skirmish and his head displayed on a spike at Dublin Castle.

Captain Lee (whose company finally killed Fiach McHugh O'Byrne in 1597) laid a plot to capture Walter Reagh. He tried to bribe one of Walter's followers to betray him. Lee used his own wife, an Irishwoman, as the interpreter with the would-be 'traitor'. The traitor inveigled Walter Reagh to go to Lee's house, but when he entered the room the woman told him it was a trap. Walter Reagh killed the 'traitor' and escaped. Lee banished his wife for this act. Shortly after this Walter Reagh was allowed to surrender and his parents were released. - State Papers

Carlow. This was the year of the Spanish Armada and the English purse was fairly empty because of the cost of the defences. Ireland too held its breath and waited for the result.

Nothing more is heard of the Harpoles until 1593 when William was the recipient of a grant of lands in Forth from the Earl of Ormonde.[457], and in 1594 Robert got a licence to alien Monksgrange in the Queen's Co. to his son Walter, the Dean of Leighlin and also to John Hovenden of Ballyfile and Robert Bowen of Ballyadam, together with the tithes, to be held to the use of Grane, his wife with the remainder to his heirs. His star was in the ascendant that year because his son William was appointed as Constable of the Castle of Catharlaghe with ten footmen for its defence and a fee of £20, with 8d. a day for each footman.

Since he had come into the country in the mid 1550s he must have been a man of about 65- 70 years old by 1594 the year he died. In those days that would have been considered very old indeed. His son William appears a few times after that. In 1596 he got a licence to be absent in England for six months and in the following year he was pardoned with other gentlemen including Gormagans and Gerald Mc Cahir Kavanagh. In 1602 William was pardoned along with very large number of men - gentlemen, yeomen and soldiers. In this group also were Robert, Thomas, John and Edmund Bowen of Ballyadam, who were possibly in-laws of the Harpoles. Sir William Harpole was Constable of Carlow Castle in 1611.[458]

We are sure that Robert Harpole had one daughter, Helen, as her husband Francis Cosby was slain 'in the Queen's service'[459] with his father, Alexander Cosby and she and Dorcas, the widow of Alexander were granted dowers to enable them to marry again. Dorcas got a dower of £5. 4s .9d., while Helen only got £3.16s. 6.,[460].

These adventurers were in Carlow during the most turbulent period of its history vis a vis the destruction of the O'Nolan clan. While they as the Crown

---

[457] Hayes -(possibly the lands that had been granted to Gerald McMoriertagh Kavanagh, Owen O'Gormagan and Cahir MacGerald McTeig (O'Nolan?)in 1585.- A.K.) According to the State Papers he got a 21yr. lease of the Castles and lands of Forth O'Nolan. In return he had to supply 12 couples of rabbits every week to the Earl's castles at Gowran, Kilkenny and Dunmore.

[458] Carew MSS Book VI pg. 26

[459] Fighting against the O'Moores. This was the famous battle at Stradbally where Owny O'Moore overcame the Cosbys and their soldiers. Father and son were killed that day. Both were shot at the bridge. The wives were watching the fight and when the men were killed Helen turned to Dorchas and said "since my husband was the last to be killed he must be deemed to be the owner of the estates and so I am claiming my third or dower."

[460] CSP

officials whittled away at the foundations of clan life, Ormonde, by then one of the most powerful men in Ireland, nibbled away at their lands. By the time the Nine Years War had ended most of the O'Nolan chieftains were either dead or attainted. The clan way of life had been irrevocably changed and only a few of the leaders continued into the next century as landowners.

Chapter 17

The 17th. Century

(Fr. O'Nolan's commentary continued)

After Tyrone (O'Neill) had defeated Sir Henry Bagnal in 1598 he proceeded to stir up insurrection in Munster "Upon this all the undertakers in that province who had come out of England, and were unequal to the work of a plantation, forsook their Castles and dwellings, before they were so much as attacked or had sight of the rebels."[461]

This is a concise commentary on the quality of the English Settlers, who had been encouraged to come over, and take possession of the lands from which the Irish septs had been driven. The mere rumour of an Irish rising sent them scurrying, like rabbits to their holes. If such were the class of settlers expected to hold their lands against the Irish clansmen, it is no wonder the latter clung so tenaciously to their original territories and were still after four and a half centuries, the dominant factor in the country outside the radius of the fortresses of the pale. The descendants of those who came over with Strongbow held steadily to the principles of their progenitors and annexed every stray acre on which they could lay hands by fair means or foul, but the later settlers had not the hardihood or grip and proved a costly bargain to the state.

Contemporary records of the O'Nolans are very few about this period, but in searching through the State Papers a few have been unearthed.

On the 5th. December 1606, among a list of those who were granted a general pardon we find the name of Teige McShane O'Nolan.[462]

Inquisitions were as common during this century as parliamentary commissions are today and about equally as helpful to the Irish people.

In the Chief Remembrancer's Office, in the Exchequer Court in Dublin we find the record of one held at Rathvilly on 13th. September 1605, concerning Donough McLisagh O'Nolan,[463] one held at the Sessions House, Carlow in June

---

[461] Cartes Ormonde C. VIII

[462] This man, who was from Boherduff (near Fenagh) was a grandson of Cahir of Ballykealy and he had been pardoned in 1601 in company with Donal Spainneach. On this occasion too, he was pardoned with Donal Spainneach and other Kavanaghs and Ryans.

[463] see chapter re O'Nolan families - Kilbride O'Nolans

1617 concerning Daniel O'Nolan and one held at the same place in 1623 concerning Donal O'Nolan.

In an Inquisition held at Carlow in 1625 Thadeus O'Nolan of Ballykealy claimed one third of Kilbride. And in another one held in Carlow in 1628 Murrough O'Nolan of Garanpursin, gentleman, deceased was proved to be the owner of twelve acres (great county measure, each acre being equal to fifteen Irish Acres) in the barony of Forth O'Nolan. He died in 1624 (13 September) leaving a son and heir, Patrick O'Nolan who was married at the time. The lands were held of the King by Knight's service - a form of tenure of which the Irish were very fond as it did not require them to do homage, or take the oath of supremacy. The Earl of Ormonde claimed a rent of eight pence an acre out of Forth O'Nolan.

Cahir O'Nolan of Ballykealy was seized of twenty one acres (like measure) in Ballykealy. He died on the 15th. January 1592 and was succeeded by his son Teig O'Nolan, who was married at the time of his father's death. The lands were held by Knight's service.

Brian O'Nolan was seized of the town and lands of Lauraghteigue[464], containing fifteen acres (like measure) arable land and so died on the 23rd. of March 1626. He left a son and heir Tadeus O'Nolan who was aged twenty and half years and was married at the time of his father's death.

Captain James Nolan held command of a detachment of the Catholic forces stationed at Clonmullen Castle, then still in the possession of Sir Morgan Kavanagh, the son of Donal Spainneach. In the course of an excursion from that garrison (during the 1641 wars) his company was said to have killed Patrick O'Nolan and to have hanged James Curwen, servant to Thomas Bagenal. Captain Nolan went to Spain in 1652 where he served in the army of the King for about ten years. Upon his return he found that his little patrimony had been appropriated by the Duke of Ormonde. He brought suit before the Privy Council for its restitution but the Ormonde influence was much too strong in that court for any 'mere' Irishman to have a chance of success. Charges of murder, based on the excursions of his command from Clonmullen and illegitimacy were made against him and needless to add the Council did not require much evidence to decide against his claim. Though accused of having killed Patrick O'Nolan in the earlier stages of the case, in the later stages it was alleged that Patrick O'Nolan[465] was living and would be called as a witness to prove the invalidity of James's claim.

---

[464] Now known as Laragh - a townland just south of Ballon. - A.K.

[465] It would appear that this was a different Patrick. In addition to those killings Captain James was alleged to have killed a Thady Nolan in 1669 after his return and had fled to England to escape prosecution. - A.K.

Ormonde's defence to the action resolved itself into a panegyric of his own merits and a statement that his agent - Walsh - had informed him Nolan had no claim to the lands in dispute. As probably Walsh had been the instrument used in acquiring possession of the lands no other statement could be expected of him.

In the patent Rolls about this time (1603-4) we find many grants of Irish lands[466] to the English garrison. The lands of Forth O'Nolan shared the common fate as we learn from the following:- "Grant from the King to Sir Oliver Lambert, Knt.,[467] and privy councillor; After others, Carlow County: the fourth part of the town and fields of Kilgreny[468] in Foert O'Nolan, containing five acres small county measure; the lands of Callough McEdmond O'Nolan of the same, gent., slain in rebellion; rent two shillings: one third part of Ballykenny[469] in Foert, containing six acres small measure; the lands of Donel Enass McDermot O'Nolan of the same, gent., slain in rebellion ; rent two shillings and three pence. Killinclonboly in Foert, containing 9 acres small measure; the lands of Gerald Killin of the same, attainted of felony, rent three shillings- the moiety of Killmoglish[470] in Foert containing sever acres small measure - two thirds of Lisgra[471] in Foert containing six acres in like measure and the moiety of Templepedder in Foert containing 10 acres in like measure; the lands of Gerald McDonough Duffe O'Nolan; rent six shillings and eightpence - two thirds part of Ballyvendon[472] in Foert containing four acres small measure and two third parts of Balliochill in Foert containing eleven acres like measure and two third parts of Ballivickfinn in Foert, containing six acres like measure; the lands of James Eustace, late Viscount Baltinglass, attainted; rent six shillings - the third part of Kilbride[473] in Foert containing twenty six acres small measure, the estate of Roderick O'Nolan of the same gent., slain in rebellion; rent six shillings - another third part of Kilbride, containing twenty six acres small measure; the estate of Marrogh Ny Dowry O'Nolan of the same gent., attainted of felony; rent six shillings and four pence - the old castle of Ballytrarney in Foert and two third parts of the

---

[466] According to Donal Moore in his thesis on the McMurroughs, Carlow Castle and Manor with a large area of land in the Barony of Forth (Myshall area) were granted to Donough O'Brien the Earl of Thomond in 1606.[466]

[467] See the note about Sir Oliver Lambert on page 262

[468] Kilgraney near Kilbride in the east of the county. - A.K.

[469] Might be Ballykealy, - A.K.

[470] About a mile east of Fenagh. - A.K.

[471] This might be Lisgarvan - a mile east of Kilmoglish

[472] Ballyvendon, Balliochill and Ballyvickfinn are not known to me but Ballyvendon may well be Ballyvolden.

[473] About three miles south east of Ballon village

following towns, Ballytrarney twenty acres, Rahin seven acres, Killean[474] six acres, Aghclare five acres, and Ballivoige six acres, containing in all forty four acres small measure; the lands of Cahir McDonagh O'Nolan of Ballytrarney gent., dead without heirs; rent ten shillings and eight pence - in Ballykely in Foert, a messauge and four acres; the lands of Donough McLisagh O'Nolan of the same gent., dead in rebellion; rent one shilling and two pence- two third parts of Balligilbert[475] in Foert containing forty acres small measure; the lands of Terence or Tirlagh Ballagh O'Nolan of the same, attainted of felony; rent nine pence; together with all their appurtenances of whatever kind . To hold for ever in free and common soccage, by fealty only for all rents, services and demands whatever; in consideration of his good, true and acceptable services to Queen Elizabeth.

Other lands in Forth were granted to Thomas the Earl of Ormonde as follows:- in the quarter of the said lordship Sleight Sheain, the third part of Kilbride viz., twenty acres arable, six and a half pasture and mountain, one acre wood - the third part of ? containing six acres arable - the like of Ballybohell[476] containing six acres arable - the like of Carrickenislane[477] containing five and a half acres arable and one acre moor, and one slang? of wood - the like of Kilnocke, containing twenty acres arable and ten acres pasture; thirty acres - the like of Balligilbert containing seven acres arable; the third of Ballivendon, otherwise Garrinlyne[478], containing two acres arable - the like of Ballekillie[479] viz., six and a half acres - the like of Barragh[480] viz., one and half acres pasture and one and a half acre wood; three acres - in the quarter of the said lordship Sleighmorrogho, the third part of Ballynowric and Killmorric viz., thirteen arable acres; the moiety of Grange - Snyddocke otherwise Graignshiddock or Grange - peddocke[481] viz., one and a half acre wood - the third part of Templered and Cloughmaghronin viz., eleven and a half acres arable - the like of Ballemore otherwise Ballemorge[482] viz., three

---

[474] These are Raheen & Killane about a mile north east of Fenagh. I suspect Ballytrarney Castle was in the same area. The townland is now called Ballintrane and is about a mile north of Raheen/Killane - A.K.

[475] Now called Gilbertstown

[476] Possibly an old name for Altamont - A.K.

[477] Carrig on Slaney, about four miles south east of Tullow. -A.K.

[478] Garreenleen - north east of TemplePeter -A.K.

[479] Ballykealy

[480] Near Kildavin in the east of the county

[481] Graiguenaspideog a mile from the Fighting Cocks Cross Roads on the main Carlow - Wexford road. - A.K.

[482] This is either Ballaghmore or Ballymogue. - A.K.

acres and a half arable - the like of Ballytrahin[483] and Kilbrickan[484] viz., ten and a half arable, four acres pasture and three acres wood; seventeen and a half acres; the like of Kilbea otherwise Kilkaa[485] viz., two acres arable and one acre moor; five acres - the like of Killean viz., three acres arable and two moor; the like of Ollard[486] viz., two acres arable and one acre and a slang of wood; the moiety of Kilmoglish five acres two acres moor and one acre wood; eight acres; the third part of Kilshegaroon viz., two acres arable and one and a half wood; three and a half acres; in the quarter of the said lordship called Slightcoyne, the town of Rathoroth[487] viz., twenty arable acres; the third part of Ballyvalden[488] and Balligodenan[489] viz., four acres arable; the like of Radowgin viz., three acres arable; the like of Rathbrege and Rathragh[490] viz., four acres arable; the like of Ballin viz., five acres arable, and four acres mountain, nine acres; the like of Keppagh[491] viz., two acres arable and one acre and a stang wood; the like of Mornex otherwise Morney viz., two acres arable and three stangs of wood; the like of Ballelion[492] viz., two acres arable one acre and a half wood and two and a half acres mountain, six acres; in the quarter of the said lordhship called Pubbledrome[493], the third part of Ballefright otherwise Ballefirish and Balledonnogh[494] viz., four acres arable; the moiety of Balletemple[495] viz., six acres arable; the third part of Ballyclaneboy otherwise Killinclonboy viz., two acres arable and one and a half wood, three and a half acres; the moiety of Ballynowe[496] viz., six acres arable; the like of Shraghsellic otherwise Straighshelle[497] viz. six acres arable; the like of Ballinhombin[498] otherwise Ballihomilin viz., six acres arable; in the quarter of the said lordship

---

[483] Ballintrane - A.K.

[484] Adjacent to Ballintrane (see note on previous page) - A.K.

[485] Now called Kilkey adjacent to Kilbrickan & Ballintrane. - A.K.

[486] Ullard about two miles east of Fenagh. - A.K.

[487] Possibly Rathtoe two miles north of Ballon - A.K.

[488] Ballyvolden near Aghade - A.K.

[489] Possibly Ballygarret near Aghade - A.K.

[490] Ratheeragh in the north east of the Barony - A.K.

[491] Near Ballykealy

[492] Near Cappagh and Ballykealy

[493] Probably lands above the Slaney

[494] Maybe Caledon - a corruption of Ballydonagh - near Ardattin - A.K.

[495] Ballintemple about six miles S.E. of Tullow (The Butler's Estate)

[496] Ballynoe on the north side of the Slaney about four miles south of Tullow. - A.K.

[497] Possibly Ballynastraw near Ballintemple - A.K.

[498] Unknown.

called Breeklagh[499]otherwise Bresklagh, the moiety of Ballinbeale[500] viz., fifteen acres; the third part of Mogishell[501] and Birragh[502] viz. two acres arable; a stang of wood and one acre and a half mountain; the moiety of Ballinrush viz., three acres and two of wood; the third part of Rossacloie[503] viz., two acres arable and one acre and a half wood; the moiety of Kilavy and Shanganie[504] viz., six acres arable; the like of Kileere otherwise Killeor and Tyroline[505] viz., six acres arable; the like of Shian[506] viz., two acres arable and one acre and a half of wood; the like of Cowldonnogh, Kittagh, Coilte Henrie and Garrin-pursin, and the town of Cowlwilliam McDonnogh otherwise M'Onogh and Boghan Oneill[507] otherwise Donill viz., six acres arable and three acres pasture; granted to him and his heirs male by patent dated 13th. September in the 5th. and 6th. of Philip and Mary to hold by the 20th. part of a knight's fee and the rent of forty nine pounds three shillings and nine pence Irish. To hold forever, by the 20th. part of a knight's fee, for all other rents, services and demands whatever. [508]

The honesty of the grantees is open to question. They were receiving from their King grants of forfeited lands as a reward for services to the State, of what nature is not disclosed, and in the very grants, so made, advantage is taken of the want of knowledge on the part of the King, or the venality of his ministers, to cheat the state. We will not analyse each item of the grants but take a few which lend themselves to ready identification:- "The fourth part of Kilgraney containing five small acres" - the townland of Kilgraney contains 324 acres so that instead of five acres Lambert got 81 acres: "The moiety of Kilmoglish containing seven acres" - Kilmoglush contains 335 acres half of which is 167 and a half acres: "The third part of Kilbride containing twenty six acres" - Kilbride contains 750 acres, one third of which is 250 acres: Ormonde got the "third part of Ballykille containing six and a half acres" - He was found at the passing of the Act of Settlement in 1666 to hold at Ballykealy 760 acres statute. A wonderful increase in sixty one years!

---

[499] This old division is now unknown but probably referred to lands around the Myshall area. - A.K.

[500] Might be Bealalaw

[501] Myshall

[502] Unknown today. It is not Barragh as that has already been referred to.

[503] Rosslee about two miles SE of Fenagh

[504] Shangarry near Rosslee

[505] Might be Turtane near Rosslee and Kilmaglush

[506] Sheean adjacent to Garryhill cross roads

[507] Possibly Boggan north of Kilbride

[508] Ryans History of Carlow pages 117 - 120

In the grants themselves intrinsic confirmation of the fraud is forthcoming from the fact that the original owners are described as 'gentlemen.' This word bore at that period a very definite signification so different from the loose use of the term today, and the idea of describing as a 'gentleman' persons whose estate consisted of six small acres, rent two shillings and three pence, would be laughable if it were not so tragic.[509]

England's panacea for all Irish ills at this period was transplantation - clear away the Irish and so pacify the land. That portion of Leinster inhabited by the Kavanaghs, O'Morchoes, O'Nolans, O'Byrnes and O'Tooles was always a thorn in the side of the English garrison. By their situation and the strength of their position they cut asunder the King's forces of Dublin and Waterford and rendered intercommunication difficult and sometimes impossible.

Fr. Nolan goes on to give a description of the Wexford plantation of 1613 which is not entirely relevant to this work except in so far as the movement of some of the dispossessed population from Wexford was towards the mountains then under the control of Donal Spainneach Kavanagh of Clonmullen. There many Murphys and Hanricks found refuge. He then goes on to outline the transplantation of 289 families from Leix, including O'Moores, O'Kellys, O'Nolans, O'Dorans, O'Lalors and O'Dowlings. They were moved to Kerry at the behest of Patrick Crosby. The O'Nolans in question were the descendants of Lucius O'Nolan who had been dispossessed of his lands in Forth O'Nolan in 1550 and had moved to Stradbally where he married the daughter of the local chieftain there- O'Lalor. All the Nolans or O'Nolans from Kerry and Limerick are descended from Lucius. The following is an abridged version of the transplantation from Laois.

Having obtained estates in Co. Kerry, Patrick Crosby, an Elizabethan adventurer, undertook to induce or compel natives of Laois to transfer to that county. It would appear that the administration wanted to prove that transplanting of peoples was possible so that the world would see that such a policy could work in Ulster.[510]

Crosby obtained the seignory of Tarbert, beyond the mountains of Slievelogher, in Co. Kerry, with an abatement of royal rent from £55 to £3.15s. a year, reserving three quarters for his own demesne. He was to grant terms for the residue of the seignory at reasonable rates, so that the people of

---

[509] Another grant, according to Ryan's History, given at this time (1604) was that to Sir Henry Brunker, President of Munster, which had been formerly granted to William and Robert Harpole and had reverted to Sir Robert Napper of lands in Ballinastraw, Aghade and Killenure. - A.K.

[510] O'Leary - *History of the Queen's County.*

the seven septs, being provided with sufficient lands might have no cause for returning to those places whence they were to be driven.

On the 26th. January 1607, Sir Arthur Chichester notified to the Earl of Salisbury that it was then in hand to "remove the Moores and septs out of Laois, who had always been ringleaders in rebellion, and the most notable disturbers of the peace in the Kingdom, shooting at the recovery of their lands, taken from them for their rebellion and bestowed upon the English in the time of Queen Mary. Since that time they have been charged with having been eighteen times in rebellion, which was only suppressed with great charge and loss of men." He went on to say that it would be better of begin the process at once rather than wait until the Moores went on the offensive. If they refused to depart by fair means, he would ask the King's permission to attempt their removal by force. He then proposed to do likewise with the O'Connors of Offaly.

In April of the same year the Lord Deputy and Council urged the King to consider the urgency of 'removing' the old inhabitants of Queen's county, so as to remove the chief cause of former disturbances.

Patrick Crosby made further serious representations in June to the same effect while the O'Moores likewise made representations begging to be allowed to stay in their own lands which they now hold by lease. Naturally the appeal of the O'Moores fell on deaf ears and in August the King granted his approval for the scheme.

Crosby now tried to induce the natives to go with him but they refused and both parties went before the Council in January 1608, where the native chiefs steadfastly refused to budge unless they were given the freehold of the estate at Tarbert for £40. The Council agreed to this and the Irish were sent home to prepare for the departure.

Crosby was appointed the organiser of the exodus by the invitation of the chiefs who felt unequal to the task. They promised to depart with him, some to Tarbert and others farther into the land of Kerry, wherever he should dispose of them. A formal agreement was drawn up as follows:-

'That he (Crosby) shall give six ploughlands of Tarbert, of the ten ploughlands there, to the six persons subscribed and their heirs, they paying him and his heirs £6 sterling chief rent, with other services and rising out; and for the rest of the six septs he shall place them in the Abbey of O'Dorny, Coishcassan, and upon the Plountaine in his other lands and shall divide amongst them twelve ploughlands, upon long leases, giving them such freedoms and for such rents as the Lord Bishop of Kerry and John McMurtagh shall set down; and they both, from time to time shall end all controversies that shall arise between Mr. Crosby and any of the septs who shall depart with Mr. Crosby at Midsummer's Day next.

That the septs and their heirs for ever shall be faithful, loving and obedient to Mr. Crosby and his heir Piers and their heirs forever."

Despite the agreement the septs of Laois bickered among themselves and it was found very difficult to persuade them to go. Force was threatened and eventually the planned exodus took place in 1609. Some were planted in Thomond and others went into Connaught while most went into Kerry with Crosby.

Lucius (Luke) O'Nolan's descendants went to Kerry with the Lalors to whom they were related. Lucius, it will be remembered left Forth in 1550, probably following some internal tribal dispute, or to escape the attentions of the authorities for rebellious acts. In Laois, Lucius married a daughter of the chief of the O'Lalors and he and his followers settled there.

In the Royal Irish Academy there is a manuscript said to have been written in 1610, by one of the O'Moores who had been exiled, in which he states that banishment and extirpation of all the survivors of his sept - men, women and children - was then finished. During a whole week the governor and sheriff of Laois had been employed in destroying the people remaining there, in seizing their cattle and all they possessed, while a savage order had been issued to hang any them found in their ancient principality.

Fr. Nolan continued with an account of the war of 1641 and the formation of the Confederate Catholics. He attributes the formation of the Confederates largely to the efforts of a remarkable man, Roger(Rory?) O'Moore of Ballyna in Leix, the last of the great O'Moores to lead his people in war.

He finally mentions the coming of Cromwell but does not continue beyond that.

Chapter 18

The O'Nolan Families

The purpose of this chapter is to try and give an indication of how the O'Nolan families evolved over the centuries commencing in the 16th. century. The reason for this starting date is because the first trickle of data began to appear only as the conquest progressed. Up to that time English officials had no way of finding out any information or very little about the O'Nolans or the other Gaelic families for that matter. As in the case of the Kavanaghs it has been very difficult to try to trace the descent of any of the Nolans from the Tudor period down to modern times. However, because of the work done by Edmond (Eddie) Nolan, who lived in Ballinrush House until the early 1920s it has been possible to trace the descent of some of the families and these accounts will serve as an illustration. The reason it is possible to trace these is because of the family connection with the same lands for long periods of time. In the case of the 'Morgan' Nolans it would seem that not alone was the sub sept living in the same area for all those years but they kept the name of their 16th. century ancestor as well.

It has not been possible to include a mention of all the Nolan families living either in Forth or Carlow and I must stress that the families I have selected have been chosen mainly because they seem to have lived in the same areas, of Forth, for very many generations. The families being detailed here will serve as examples of how different families could be traced. The information is as accurate as I could make it and if there are errors I beg the reader's pardon.

The Ballykealy, Kilbride, Rosslee and Kilknock O'Nolans descended from Donough and Edmund O'Nolan[512] who were alive in the early to mid 1500s. Edmund had a number of sons and when the English imposed the division of lands on the Gaelic clans in the mid 1500s he seems to have settled his sons in large holdings in Co. Carlow. He settled his son Cahir in Ballykealy, William in

---

[512] Edmund must have been the successor to Murrough 'ne dowre' O'Nolan who was the Captain of his Nation in 1518, according to the Fitzgerald rental book. It would also seem from this that Murrough was the father of William O'Nolan of Kilbride as the name 'ne dowre' occurs there. One of William's sons was called Murrough ne Dowre. The sobriquet 'owre' or 'ower' means swarthy.

Kilbride and Rosse in Kilknock. Donough seems to have had two sons at least, Donal of Rosslee and Hugh of Shangarry.

It would seem that Cahir of Ballykealy had ten sons, all of whom were born during or before the middle of the 16th. century. They were, Gerald, Brian, Teig, Donough, Edmund, Muiris, James, Phelim, Shane Duff and Owen. He may also have had a son Cahir who may indeed have been the father of Donough mentioned above and possibly James, Teig, and Brian. We can assume he had daughters too but since women didn't figure to any extent in the Tudor data I have been unable to trace any. In any event all these men, with the possible exception of Edmund, Brian and Shane Duff, were in rebellion at various times right down to the end of the Nine Years War. Since the sons of chieftains were bred for warfare it is not surprising. The fact that neither Edmund, Brian or Shane Duff were mentioned as having been pardoned does not mean that they were inactive. It simply means that they were not caught in the act of rebellion. It could be inferred also that they died at a relatively young age, perhaps in battle. Shane Duff for example, had six sons - Edmund of Kilgraney, Dermot, Mortagh, James, Teig and Melaghlin Duff, all of whom were in rebellion at various times, in the company of the Clonmullen or Garryhill Kavanaghs and also the O'Byrnes. It is noteworthy that Edmund of Kilgraney was also in rebellion with the Purcells. His son Callough McEdmund was slain in rebellion and he does not appear to have had any other sons. A great grandson of Dermot seems to have been the man who survived to the lands of Shane Duff, which may have been the lands of Kilgraney. He was the son of Donal McEnass McDermot McShane Duff O'Nolan and in 1617 an inquisition of his lands was held in the Sessions House in Carlow and another in 1623.

A great great grandson of Brian McCahir of Ballykealy, seems to have been Tadeus who was married by the year 1626. In addition to Ballykealy he claimed ownership of one third of Kilbride. It may well have been a son of his who was the last chief of the O'Nolans and who according to O'Flaherty died in the later decades of the 17th. century.

It would seem certain that the Kilbride O'Nolans descended from Murrough 'ne dowre' O'Nolan as one of William's sons was called Murrough Ne Dowre in the Fiants. William must have been married to a daughter of Fiach McHugh and one of his sons was called Fiach - a name that is unusual in the O'Nolans. Nearly all of William's sons fought with Fiach McHugh during the turbulent latter decades of the 16th century. They were Fiach, Cahir, Leasagh, Maurice ne Dower, Thady, Murrough ne Dowre and Dermot. It is purely speculative to suggest that Maurice ne Dower, was married to an O'Moore of Laois as in 1578 William was in rebellion with that sept and in addition Maurice had a son who was called Rory - a name that seemed to have been non-existent in the O'Nolans prior to then. Rory was the owner of

Kilbride at the time of his death, when he was slain in rebellion, probably with the O'Byrnes or Kavanaghs in the early 1600s. A great grandson of Murrough ne Dowre, Patrick, was the son of Murrough of Garrypurseen (Craanpurseen surely) who according to an inquisition in 1628 held his lands from the King by part of a knight's fee. Patrick's father, Murrough, died in 1624.

While the Kilbride and Ballykealy O'Nolans were populous the Kilknock O'Nolans were very sparse. Rosse McEdmond the progenitor of the Kilknock line seems to have had only one son, William McRosse who was in rebellion in 1549 as was Rosse himself. William's son Edmund McWilliam McRosse was in the wars in 1571 and again in 1584. His son Donough McEdmund was in rebellion with Donal Spainneach Kavanagh in 1601.

There were other branches of the O'Nolans too. In Bealalaw, Fyrr O'Nolan had four sons - Morrogh, Patrick, Phelim and William all of whom were in rebellion with the Kavanaghs of Garryhill. It is possible that Fyrr was a brother of William of Kilbride as the Christian names of Morrogh and William appear in both families. The only other place I have seen Fyrr is in connection with the O'Byrnes. One Owen McFyrr (M'Fir) O'Birne of Busherstown gent. was pardoned in 1584 and again in 1601 (as of Ballybrat - Ballybrack?)when he was in rebellion with the Kavanaghs.

There were a number of other families of O'Nolan that emerged from my study of the Fiants of the Tudor monarchs. They included the O'Nolans of Rathrush, Tullowphelim and Carrickslaney. There is mention of Donough McEochaidh O'Nolan of Rathrush. who was in rebellion with Donal Spainneach in 1601 and was in rebellion with the Kavanaghs & Butlers in 1602. In 1571 Teig O'Nolan of Tullowphelim was in rebellion with the Butlers and in 1588 he was again in rebellion with the Butlers aided by Kilkenny and Tipperary rebels. He had at least one son James who was in rebellion with Cahir Duff Kavanagh in 1575 and with Brian McCahir Kavanagh in 1577.

Henry O'Nolan of Carrigslaney was in rebellion with the Kavanaghs of Garryhill in 1584 and his son Callogh McHenry was a member of a large company of men pardoned with Donal Spainneach in 1592 and with the Kavanaghs of Garryhill in 1597.

There is also a mention in the Fiants of Morrogh McGerrot Duffe who received pardon in 1548.[513] He was in rebellion with the O'Byrnes and may well have been a cousin of William of Kilbride. A Charles McLesagh of Ballytrane(Ballintrane) is also mentioned receiving a pardon in 1549. It is possible that he represents another sub sept of the O'Nolans. The only other

---

[513] It would seem that in that year Cahir McArt Kavanagh and Hugh McShane O'Byrne had agreed to 'make a prey' and with it get silk, saffron and cloth in Kilkenny. However the writer, Oliver Sutton, a sheriff, declared that Hugh McShane was very glad to 'come in' to the L.D.

family in which Lesagh appears is in the Kilbride family. It may be that Lesagh was in fact a brother of William, and Charles of Ballintrane was his nephew. A Lysagh McMurgho O'Nolan of Ardristan was pardoned also in 1549 and he may have been the father of Charles. Patrick O'Nolan of Ardristan was a grandson of William of Kilbride but he may have just been fostered there. It is possible too that he inherited Ardristan.

Yet another family must have been in possession of Rathoe, as Gerald Duffe O'Nolan of Rathoe was paying some form of rental to the Fitzgeralds in 1518. He may well have been the tanaist to Murrough Ne Dowre, the chieftain, who was paying the rent to Fitzgerald at the same period.

The O'Nolans of Ballykealy

Cahir O'Nolan of Ballykealy described as a gentleman, was born about 1520-30 and he died in 1592. He had ten sons:

1. **Teig**, who was noted as being a freeholder in 1608 was pardoned in 1600 for being in rebellion with the Kavanaghs of Garryhill. He was married twice and had, by his second wife, Onora O'Byrne, two sons Tadeus and Gerald. Tadeus died without issue and was succeeded by his brother Gerald. Gerald was succeeded by a son Garret. Garret's descendants were in possession of lands in Ballykealy until the middle of the 18th. century, (according to Burke's Landed Gentry) which the writer noted was a prime example of 'ancient and continuous territorial possession'.

Garret, born c. 1670, was married twice. By his first wife Elinor Warren, he had a daughter who married a man called Grimes, mother of "the celebrated Marcus" and other sons.[514] By his second wife Anastacia Wall he had three sons the eldest of whom John Nolan Esq. was also married twice.

John Nolan Esq. born c. 1710 married Mary Whelan of Laragh House by whom he had a daughter, Mary who married William McDarby Esq. and by his second wife, Mary Delahunty he had several sons most of whom died young except his third son James.

James Nolan Esq. born c. 1758 married Mary Moore and had two daughters and six sons one of whom died in infancy. The remaining sons were:

a. John who was born in 1792 and married Catherine Walsh leaving two sons and a daughter. He died in 1824.

b. Edward who was born in 1793, the Right Rev. Dr. Nolan, Bishop of Kildare and Leighlin who died in 1837.

c. Thomas from whom the line continues.

---

[514] *Visitation of Arms*

d. Patrick born in 1797 graduated as an M.D. from Trinity College in Dublin and died at Rome in 1841.

e. Daniel Francis who was born in 1806 became a priest, who served in the diocese under the authority of his brother Bishop Edward.

f. Thomas Nolan Esq. was born in 1795 and married Juliana Blount of Oxford by whom he had only one child - a daughter - Julia who died in 1845. Juliana died in 1875.[515] Juliana was, effectively, the last of the O'Nolans of Ballykealy that we know about for definite. This of course begs the question of what happened to Catherine Walsh (who was married to John Nolan the eldest son who died in 1824) and her two sons and daughter. An Edward Nolan of Ballykealy is noted in the Index to Leighlin wills as of 1814. He must have been a descendant of Garret Nolan. It is possible that many of the Nolans living in and around Ballykealy/Ballon are descended from the sons of John Nolan who died in 1824.

2. **Gerald** who was pardoned in 1566 and 1571 for being in rebellion with the Butlers and in 1572 and 1600 for being in rebellion with the Kavanaghs of Garryhill and finally in 1592 for being in rebellion with Donal Spainneach Kavanagh. He had at least one son Edmund.

Edmund O'Nolan was pardoned in 1597 for being in rebellion with the O'Byrnes. He had one son at least.

Gerald McEdmund O'Nolan who was noted as being of Killane was attainted of treason, for being in rebellion. Gerald may have had a family and many descendants but there is no way, that I know of, of finding this out. The same is true of the other sons.

3. **Brian** pardoned in 1601 for having been in rebellion with Donal Spainneach had at least one son.

James pardoned, like his father, in 1601. James had a son

Tirelagh O'Nolan of Laraghteigue who was pardoned in 1597 for having been in rebellion with the Kavanaghs of Garryhill and in 1601 with Donal Spainneach. He had a son

Brian McTirelagh who was also pardoned for rebellion in 1597 and in 1601. He must have been quite a young boy at the time as his grandfather was pardoned in the same year. Boys were brought along as part of their martial training to look after horses etc. Brian had a son -

Tadeus who was born in 1606 was married by 1626 and was the subject of an inquisition in 1625 where he claimed ownership to one third part of Kilbride. Thady who made a will in 1703 may have been his grandson or great grandson.

---

[515] Burkes Landed Gentry. (Edward of Ballykealy, who made a will in 1814 may have been descended from one of these).

231

4. **Donough**, pardoned in 1601 for having been in rebellion with Donal Spainneach. He was the man who was sent in as a hostage in 1593 by Captain St. Leger who seems to have been the officer charged with 'ordering' the O'Nolans at that time. Donough had two sons

> (a) Shane pardoned in 1575 for being in rebellion with the Keatings and in 1601 for being in rebellion with the O'Sullivans of Cork. He had a son

> Patrick McShane of Ballintemple a freeman in 1608.

> (b) Cahir the owner of Ballintrane, Aclare and Ballymogue. He was the father of Art, Edmund and Gerald all pardoned in 1601 for having been in rebellion with Donal Spainneach. It is possible that the Charles (Cahir) Nolan, gent., of Ballykealy, who is the only one of three Carlow Nolans mentioned in the Prerogative Wills of Ireland, as of 1690, was the son or grandson of one of those men - Art, Edmund or Gerald. We do not know if Charles was married, but an examination of his will would be most illuminating.[516]

5. **Muiris** who had a son Thomas pardoned in 1601 for having been in rebellion with Donal. Thomas himself had a son Gerrot also pardoned in that year.

6. **James** pardoned in 1567 with the O'Tooles, in 1570 with the Butlers, in 1573 with Brian Kavanagh and in 1601. James had three sons Tirelagh, Murrough and John who were all pardoned at various times for having been in rebellion with the Kavanaghs, the Purcells and the O'Tooles and O'Byrnes.

7. **Shane Duff** who had six sons as follows:-

> (a) Edmund of Kilgraney who was pardoned in 1600 for having been in rebellion with the Kavanaghs of Garryhill, the O'Byrnes and Purcells and in 1601 with Donal Spainneach. He was father of Callough McEdmund O'Nolan who was slain in rebellion.

> (b) Dermot pardoned in 1600 with the Kavanaghs of Garryhill and the Byrnes. He had a son Enass who was father of Donal McEnall O'Nolan described as the owner of Ballykeenan and Cappagh in 1641. He was slain in rebellion and an inquisition was held to enquire into his lands in 1617 and another in 1623.

> (c) Murtagh pardoned in 1601 with Donal Spainneach had two sons Gerald who was pardoned in 1597 and Donough pardoned in 1601, a freeholder of Carrickslaney in 1608. Gerald had one son Murtagh McGerald of Myshall, a freeman in 1608 and Donough had a son Shane McDonough who was pardoned in 1601.

---

[516] Unfortunately the will, like very many others was destroyed in the fire at the Four Courts during the Civil War. It is vaguely possible that copies of wills may be in the possession of families still living today.

232

(d) James pardoned in 1585 for being in rebellion with Donal Spainneach and in 1597 with the Kavanaghs of Garryhill.

(e) Teig pardoned in 1601.

(f) Melaghlin Duff pardoned in 1602 for being in rebellion with the Wexford rebels.

8. **Phelim** pardoned in 1592 and 1601 with Donal Spainneach. He had a son Cahir pardoned in 1566 (probably a very young horseboy).

9. **Owen** pardoned in 1571 for being in rebellion with the Butlers. He had two sons:-

a)Donell Duff who was pardoned in 1600 with the Purcells and in 1601 with Donal Spainneach. He was the father of Rory McDonell Duff O'Nolan of Kilbrickan who was pardoned in 1601 with Donal Spainneach and Gerald McDonell Duff of Kilmaglush, Lisgra and TemplePeter. Rory was the father of Charles of Kilbrickan mentioned in the Book of Settlement as the owner of lands there.

b)Donough pardoned in 1598 for being in rebellion with the Butler in Tipperary, in 1599 he was out with the Fitzgeralds and Tallons, in 1600 he was out with the Purcells and in 1601 he was pardoned with Donal Spainneach. He had a son Donal McDonough Og who was pardoned in 1601.

10. **Edmund**

It can be seen from the above that information about the various sons and their descendants is very sparse. It may well be the case that between 1601 and 1641 they and their families continued on in parts of their lands at least but certainly by the time Cromwell had come and gone most of the O'Nolans had lost their grip on their holdings. According to my findings the only Nolans to hold on to anything were the Ballykealy O' Nolans and the Shangarry O'Nolans.[517]

The O'Nolans of Shangarry
(Knockendrane & Ballinrush)

The Shangarry O'Nolans descended from Hugh. Hugh may in fact be the Hugh Roo who was pardoned for aiding and abetting a robbery (see Fiant details). Hugh had a brother Morgan of Rosslee (pardoned in 1549) and Donald McDonhe pardoned at the same time may have been their father. The 'Morgan Nolans' of Ballaghmore and Rosslee are descended from Morgan.

Hugh[518] had four sons Cahir, Donal, William and Hugh. Donal appears to have been married twice. By his first wife he had a son Edmund who was the

---

[517] This begs the question of the will of Charles, gent., of Ballykealy, who made a will in 1690.

[518] Hugh and his son Donal appear to have both died in 1647.

father of Captain James Nolan, who fought against the Cromwellians in Colonel Daniel Kavanagh's Clomullen regiment. By his second wife, Anastace Byrne he had another son Patrick who seems to have inherited the Shangarry lands. Patrick was dispossessed and forced to take lands in Connaught. The Lawrence Nolan, gentleman, who was the owner of the Shangarry lands in the early part of the next century must have been a son or grandson of Patrick. Patrick was born around the year 1600 and his grandson, Lawrence, seems to have been still in possession of substantial lands in the latter decades of the 1600s (he was born c. 1670). Because of the work done by Fr. Nolan and his relative Eddie, I have been able to establish family trees (descending from Patrick) for the Nolans of Ballinrush (the last of whom sold out his farm in the early 1900s and moved to Dublin) and the Nolans of Knockendrane one of whom, James, a captain in the 1798 rebellion, died in 1857 aged 112 yrs.[519]

It is tempting to speculate that the Shangarry O'Nolans were connected with the Purcells of Tipperary through marriage (as they were in rebellion with the Purcells at various times).

1. **Cahir** was pardoned in 1601 and 1602 for being in rebellion with Donal Spainneach. As already noted he had a son Edmund by his first wife who was the father of Captain James Nolan and by his second wife he had a son Patrick who was born c. 1600. I will deal with Patrick's descendants shortly.

2. **Donell** who was in rebellion in 1592 and again in 1600 and 1601 was born c. 1561 and had two sons Donough[520] and Dermot, both of whom were in rebellion in 1597 and 1601, but nothing more is known about that family.

3. **William** was in rebellion with the Purcells in 1600.

4. **Hugh** was also in rebellion with the Purcells in 1600.

Patrick who succeeded to Hugh's lands in Shangarry was noted in the Book of Settlement as being the owner of lands in Shangarry and Ballinrush. I assume he had two[521] sons Lawrence and **John**[522] who in turn was father of **Lawrence**,

---

[519] I think this may be an error. There is no date of birth on the tombstone in Drumphea, which states that he died in 1857 aged 112 and that his wife (nee Barry) died in 1827 aged 60 yrs.

[520] This is probably the Donough of Ballaghmore who was a freeholder in 1608.

[521] He may in fact have had three sons as a James of Tinnaclash whose will was proved in 1742 must have been a relative of Luke the son of Lawrence, the gentleman of Shangarry, mentioned above. This would explain how the name James became so predominant in the Tinnaclash family and also it would explain how they came into possession of that house and lands.

[522] This must be the John who in 1700 claimed and was allowed the estate for lives in the lands of Shangarry and Ballinrush forfeited by Lawrence Nolan. (see King James Irish Army List) by Dalton. He is also probably the John Nolan who is buried in TemplePeter

described as a gentleman, of Shangarry the man who had land dealings in the latter part of the 17th. century and into the 18th. as detailed in the Land Registry offices in Dublin and alluded to later.

Lawrence[523] had three sons, Lawrence, John and Luke of Tinnaclash. In 1713, the year his eldest son was born, he sold 200 acres of land in Shangarry[524] to a Mr. Quill. I assume he moved to Lisgarvan at that time.[525]

1. **Lawrence** of Lisgarvan was born in 1713. He married Anne Wright (d.1776), a Quaker who turned Catholic, of Lisconnor, Fenagh. They had four

---

in the Tinnaclash burial plot. He was born in 1677 and died in 1770 aged 93 years. If this is so it would seem that John went to live at Tinnaclash with his son James.

[523] It would seem from correspondence that Fr. O'Nolan received from an E. O'Leary of Portarlington, that Lawrence had a brother who had a son Matthew. This Matthew was living at Kilconnor. He died in 1793 aged 78 yrs. Mr. O'Leary stated categorically that Matthew was a first cousin of the Ballinrush Nolans. Matthew's eldest son, also John, was evicted by the Watsons and died at Rathvinden, near Leighlinbridge in 1835, aged 84 yrs. Father and son were buried in Temple Peter. John of Rathvinden had a son Jacob, who died unmarried in 1860. He was buried in Newtown, Bagenalstown. Jacob's sister was married to a Kehoe and Robert Kehoe succeeded to Rathvinden, where his son John Kehoe J.P. was the owner in 1919. Matthew had three other sons who married and had families, but there are no details of them. He also mentions the extended families of a daughter which included a Rev. Patrick Doyle and a Rev. Matthew Lalor and a Rev. James Lalor. On the Keogh side Robert had a brother Rev. John Kehoe P.P. and a nephew Rev. Matthew Treacy P.P.

[524] The Nolans are represented in Shangarry today by Peter and Kathleen Nolan (nee Nolan) both of whom are descended from old Nolan families, Peter's from Shangarry and Kathleen's from Coolasnaughta/Knockendrane. Peter's great grandfather was Andrew Nolan, a schoolmaster born c. 1830, a son of James Nolan who died in 1840. Andrew's sons included Peter (who inherited the farm), James, Andy and John and four sisters, two of whom were teachers, Ellen in Myshall and Mary in Grange . Peter and James went into business in Dublin where they acquired three public houses, one of which is the present Palace Bar in Fleet Street. When they sold out their properties they came home and Peter went to farm Shangarry. James bought Upton House, Fenagh, where he lived for a considerable time, and a farm at Lasmaconly. James had five sons three of whom married (John, Francis and Edward). Peter had eight sons and one daughter Rose (now Sister Sarto in Kilkenny). The sons were the late Andrew of Shangarry, James (dec.), Fr. Tom (dec.), Fr. P.J. (dec.) Sean (dec.), Fr. Joseph (dec.), Michael and Patrick (my kind informant), are both retired businessmen, living in Dublin and both are married with families.

[525] Eddie O'Nolan stated that John the first and his son Lawrence moved from Shangarry to a farm at Lisgarvan (where John died) on the expiration of the lease. Lawrence himself seems to have died c. 1746/7 as a Lawrence Nowlan is mentioned in the Index to Leighlin Wills as having had his will proved in 1747.

sons and two daughters - Anna born in 1761 who married a Sinnott of Buntawn, Co. Kildare and Mary who married Patrick Byrne, of Ballyragget.[525] The sons were James, Edmund, Lawrence and John. In 1760, according to the Eddie O'Nolan mss, the family was evicted from Lisgarvan and moved to Knockendrane where Lawrence had sometime previously bought 400 acres of land from Lord Duncannon for £550.

2. **John**, of Ballinvalley, was born about 1714 and had two daughters. According to family tradition one of them married a Beaumont of Hyde Park in Wexford, but this does not appear in the Burke account of the Beaumont family. The other daughter, Anne who was born in 1740 married Brian O'Brien of Ballinvalley. He died in 1813 and she predeceased him in 1797. If Eddie O'Nolan of Ballinrush is correct in his pedigree this John Nowlan was called 'John the Poet'. Eddie also infers that he delivered a speech in Myshall in an 'Address from the Roman Catholics of Myshall'[526].

The sons of Lawrence of Lisgarvan were:

a) James, of Knockendrane who was given one fourth of the lands for his use. He became a Captain in the United Irishmen and led the Myshall rebels during the 1798 rebellion.[527] He married Elizabeth Barry and they appeared to have had five sons and four daughters. They were Anne who married John Fenelon and emigrated to America, Catherine who died in 1866 aged 61 yrs., Mary who died in 1882 aged 72 yrs. and Ellen Tyrell who died in 1886 aged 85 yrs. His sons were:-

    1. John b. 1794 who died in 1832 aged 38 yrs.

    2. Lawrence b. 1795 who died in 1884 aged 89 yrs.

    3. Robert b. 1801 who died in 1893 aged 92 yrs.

    4. Edward b. 1802 who died in 1843 aged 41yrs.

    5. Richard who died in 1899. [528]

---

[525] Mary's grandson was Rev. George Byrne who died in Carlow - Graigue. A note in the margin of a copy of a letter states he was a Protestant Priest!

[526] These Addresses were common in the climate of the times. The idea was to appease the Government party and the Protestants who suspected that there were United Irishmen under every roof in the parish.

[527] According to Eddie Nolan this man was born in 1745 and died in 1857 aged 112 yrs.! See the Chapter about Famous Nolans for more information about James. I imagine the proper date of his birth was 1754 since Anne Wrigth, his mother was only born in 1732.

[528] Richard left some of his land to Luke Nolan, a relative, who was the great grandfather of Jimmy Nolan of Knockendrane, the present owner. The Nolans are still well represented in Knockendrane as there is another family of the name in ownership of lands there- Jim Nolan brother of Michael of Coolasnaughta, the late Tom of Knockdramagh and Pat and four sisters, Anne, Kitty, Mary and Margaret wife of John Foley of Garryhill.

b) Lawrence of Knockendrane and Ballymartin, Borris, who died in 1808 aged 44 yrs. This was probably the Lawrence Nowlan who, with Sir Richard Butler, went bail for Patrick Doyle who was accused of being a United Irishman in 1797. Lawrence had one son who left Knockendrane and went to live at Ballymartin. This man is not named in the Eddie Nolan Mss and he had two other sons.

> 1. Rev. Dr. Nolan P.P. of the united Parishes of Gowran, Dungarvan, Clara and Pitt(?). He was at the same time President of the Ecclesiastical College of Kilkenny. He was one of the most eloquent preachers of his time in Ireland and was styled 'the Silver Tongued Priest'.
>
> 2. John who married a Miss Lyons settled at Leighlinbridge where he started a hotel called 'The Swan'. He had three children:-
>> Lawrence, who died unmarried.
>> Mary, who died unmarried.
>> Ellen, who was a nun in Portarlington in the early part of the 20th. century.

c) John (born c. 1765) lived on his portion of Knockendrane and married. He had three sons, Samuel, Charles and William. After some time he acquired a farm at Ballytore or Coolcarrigeen in Co. Kildare where he and his sons Charles and William went to live.

> 1. Samuel of Knockendrane married a Miss Clowery and they had three daughters. After Samuel's death his widow married a man named Sheridan and the farm passed out of Nolan ownership. Samuel's daughters were:
>> Mary who married a McAssy who owned a farm near TemplePeter.
>> Bridget and Amelia who went to live with Mary after their mother's second marriage. Both died unmarried and are buried in TemplePeter in the old Knockendrane burial plot.[530]
>
> 2. William died unmarried in Co. Kildare.
>
> 3. Charles (born c. 1800), of Ballitore married and had a son :
>> John (born c. 1835), known as 'Amnesty John'[531]

d) Edmond who was born in 1755 left Knockendrane and purchased the residence and farms of Ballinrush and Shangarry. He married Elizabeth Doyle who came with the townland of Craan, Co. Wexford, as her dowry. Edmond

---

[530] This is situated at the north western side of the sanctuary of the ruined Church. It is a large plot enclosed by a wall about three feet high. It is divided in the centre by a smaller wall. The far half is the burial ground of the Tinnaclash Nolans. The grave has a Latin inscription and a coat of arms.

[531] See the chapter dealing with some famous Nolans. Charles had at least one other son also - Fr. Patrick Nolan who was P.P of Ballon and who died in 1894 aged 55 yrs.- A.K.

held Craan until the expiration of the lease in 1844. Elizabeth died in 1832 and Edmond in 1847 and both were buried in Myshall.[532] Edmond had four sons and six daughters. His daughters were:

1. Johanna who married a Byrne was the grandmother of Rev. John Maher of Cloneslee in Co. Laois and of the Rev. William Maher of Ballyloughan.[533]

2. - married to a man called Lawlor

3. Bridget married to a Kavanagh.

4. Elizabeth married to a Kearny.

5. Maria married to a Kinsella. She was the mother of the Rev. John Kinsella P.P. of Edenderry in Offaly.

6. Matilda married a Burke and was mother of Mons. Edward Burke P.P. of Bagenalstown, (d. 1916) a former President of Carlow College and from 1897 he was Domestic Prelate to Pope Leo XIII.

Ballinrush House - Courtesy Seamus Lalor

[532] His daughter Elizabeth Kearny, who died in 1835 aged 28 yrs. and his granddaughter Elizabeth, eldest daughter of Luke Nowlan of Raheenwood are also buried in the grave.

[533] Rev. W. Maher was a close correspondent of Fr. O'Nolan (the co-author of this book), but his notes seem to have disappeared. Only about ten letters survive.

The sons of Edmond were:

1. Rev. Thomas Nolan born in Ballinrush in 1792. He was ordained in Carlow and went to teach in the College, but being of a very delicate constitution the Bishop (J.K.L.) sent him home as a curate to Myshall. He recovered his health and was appointed Administrator of Tullow, where he was responsible for the construction of the Gothic Tower and Spire on the Church. In 1838 he was appointed P.P. of Abbeyleix and built a church at Ballyroan[534]. During the Repeal Agitation he stood on many a platform with Daniel O'Connell. He was a close friend of Lord and Lady de Vesci and then Wm. Gladstone visited those people he met Fr. Nolan and requested his blessing. Fr. Thomas died in 1886.

2. Rev. John Nolan who was born at Ballinrush in 1808 was ordained in Carlow College and appointed Curate of Baltinglass. He was responsible for building the Catholic Church there. An orator of note he is said to have been the man who styled O'Connell 'The uncrowned King of Ireland' at a Monster Rally at Mullaghmast Co. Kildare in 1843. He was appointed P.P. of Killeigh in Co. Kildare in 1867 and while in that county was responsible for building the Convent of Mercy at Rathdangan and the schools in Kildare town. He died in 1880.

3. Luke Nolan who was born at Ballinrush bought Raheenwood where he lived for most of his life. However at some time he bought a farm at Derrymore, Co. Westmeath and moved there. In 1815 he married Elizabeth Kavanagh, daughter of John McMurrough Kavanagh of Myshall, and had 19 children most of whom died young. Three sons and seven girls survived. The girls were:

   1. Johanna entered St. Brigid's Convent, Tullow in 1856 and celebrated her Golden Jubilee in 1918. She was called Sr. M. Francis Assisi.

   2. Bridget, d. 1898, married Patrick Dunne of Grangeford. They had four daughters - Nannie and Josephine who were unmarried, Teresa who married Michael Nolan of the Lodge, Garryhill and Catherine who married Patrick Nolan.[535]

   3. Catherine married Denis Dunne of Painestown.

   4. Maria married John Hill of Bogtown, Co. Westmeath and they had one son Henry.

   5. Anna, unmarried, died at Raheenwood in 1872.

---

[534] He also built a tower and spire on the church in Abbeyleix.

[535] This family moved to Donegal. He was a son of Henry Nolan of Garryhill. She died shortly after her marriage and was buried in Rathoe. Henry Nolan seems to have had at least one other son Edward who died in 1916. James of Garryhill who died in 1915 may have been another son of Henry.

6. Teresa, d. 1913, married Edward Burke of Barronstown Co. Wicklow, and had two children Teresa who married McDonnell of - Park, Carlow and Joseph.

7. Charlotte died unmarried in 1908.

Luke's three sons were:

1. John of Raheenwood, who also had a drapery business in Dublin. He married Bessie Molony of Thurles and lived at Rathgar Rd. in Dublin. He had two sons - Luke who became a solicitor but who died young (in 1899) and Thomas, an engineer who worked in India. Thomas was married and had a son and daughter (in the 1900s) John died in Dublin and was buried in Glasnevin Cemetery near Parnell's Grave.

2. Robert (d. 1887) lived in Derrymore and married Marianne Hannon. They had three children - a son Luke and two daughters, Elizabeth and Annie.[536]

3. Richard who died in 1863.

Raheenwood House - Courtesy Linda and Stewart Donald

---

[536] Robert was a member of the Mullingar Board of Guardians. He died accidentally when his car overturned in his own avenue. The local papers of the time paid him glowing tributes as a true friend of the poor.

4. Edmond Nolan who was born at Ballinrush in 1803 married Mary Heffron (Heffernan?) of Dublin and was father of nine children two of whom died in infancy. He died in 1887. His surviving children were seven sons and three daughters. The daughters were: -

1. Sophia who died young became Sister M. Evangelist and was one of the first nuns in the Convent at Gort in Co. Galway.

2. Anne Elizabeth married Lawrence McLaughlin J.P. of Clonybacon House, Co. Laois. She died without issue in 1909.

3. Teresa was educated in Rathfarnham Convent in Dublin and spent some years in the U.S. before marrying R.J. Rowe. They lived in Rathgar, Dublin.

The sons of Edmond were as follows:-

1. Edmond who married Miss Tuite of Dublin, lived at Ballin House, Co. Laois. He was imprisoned during the Land League days and died in the U.S. He had no family.

2. Eugene who was born in 1844 became a Fenian when he was studying Medicine. He took part in the 'Rising of Tallaght' (Co. Dublin) but escaped arrest. After further escapades with the Fenians he became an M.D. and was M.O. of Castlecomer. He was married to Mary Molony but they had no family. He died from fever aged 28 yrs at the residence of his uncle Rev. John Nolan who was a P.P. in Co. Kildare and his wife died two years later. They are both buried in Myshall graveyard.

3. John who was unmarried died at Ballinrush in 1887 aged 20 yrs.

4. James, unmarried, emigrated to the U.S. but died at the Isthmus of Panama, aged 20 yrs in 1883.

5. Thomas who married Margaret Cantwell went to live in the 'residence and demesne' of Ballynook, Co. Wicklow, which was bought for him by his father. He had three children - Edmund (married in the U.S. and had two children Eugene and Mary), Eugene and Linda. Linda died at Ballinrush in 1887. Eugene became the Director of the Boston Stores in Chicago and of the Surf Hotel. He married Gladys - Samms. Thomas himself died in the U.S. at the residence of his son Eugene in 1916. His wife who died in Ireland was buried in Baltinglass where there is fine monument to her memory which was erected by her children.

6. Joseph qualified as an M.D. and was appointed to Tullow Hospital in 1873 and twenty years later he won the coronorship of the county with over 600 votes to spare.[537] In the same year he

---

[537] It is said that there were bonfires lit on all the hills of south Carlow on the night of his victory.

was appointed a Commissioner of the Peace. A keen sportsman who hunted the Carlow hounds, he contracted a fever and died in 1914 aged 63 yrs. He was married to Catherine Kelly and had five surviving children - Edward (of Kilconnor House - a great sportsman and winner of many Hunt Races - joined the Dublin Fusiliers in 1914 and served in the Dardanelles in World War 1. He later contracted malaria and was invalided home and died in Dublin), James (a Medical Student joined the Navy as a probationary surgeon and was killed in action in the Mediterranean aged 21 yrs.), Mary (married John Cahill, Capt. in the Royal Irish Regiment who was killed in France in 1916), Irene (married R.J. Keogh of Park Carlow and had four children) and finally Eugennie who was a Volunteer nurse in France and England during the War.

7. William a J.P. who was formerly of Ballinrush House moved to Dublin in the early 1920s. He had been an extensive landowner, an enterprising farmer and a popular nationalist. He was a Commissioner for the Peace in 1893 and was a County Councillor for Myshall at the inception of the Local Government Act. He married Catherine McLaughlin of Stradbally, Co. Laois in 1892 and they had two sons. One, Eugene died an infant and the other son was Edmond or Eddie Nolan who compiled most of the Pedigree.

The Nolans are represented today in Ballinrush by Jim and Breda Nolan[537] who have a family of six boys and six girls. Jim Nolan's mother was an O'Neill of Ballinrush.

The O'Nolans of Ballaghmore, Cappawater & Rosslee

The 'Morgan' Nolans of Ballaghmore, Cappawater and Rosslee,[538] are, in all probability, descended from Morgan McDonal McDonough O'Nolan, who,

---

[537] Jim, a retired farmer is the well known composer and reciter of ballad and verse and a very accomplished amateur actor in his younger days. Jim's great grandfather came back to Ballinrush from Co. Wexford. Jim was an only son and his sisters are Kathleen (Tracey) dec., Peggy (Donohue) dec., Mary (Mulooly) and Bridie (Phelan).

[538] There is another family of Nolans whose ancestors have been in Rosslee/Kilmaglush for many generations. They are the Nolans of the Tailor's Cross. Today the family is represented by Tom, Edward, John, Michael and Henry Nolan and their four sisters. Jim's sisters were Mrs. Browne (dec.) whose family now reside in Slyguff and Mrs Kavanagh of Raheenwood (mother of Ritchie the famous singer and composer). Jim's brothers were Tom d.s.p, Ned d.s.p., and Jack of Tullow, still living. Their father, Tom, one of four

as we have seen, featured in the pardons being so liberally granted in the reigns of the Tudor Monarchs. In the 1608 list of Gentry and important people in the county, Donough O'Nolan of Ballaghmore was noted as one of the significant men (being, in fact, a Constable). I have no proof, but the evidence is very strong and points to the fact that Donough must have been Morgan's son.

According to the grants of 1604 the lands of the O'Nolans in Ballaghmore and Rosslee went into Ormonde ownership. It would seem that the former lords now became the tenants, but they always kept the name of their ancestor Morgan to distinguish the family.

The next one of the family to emerge was Michael Nolan of Ballaghmore who died in the 1830s. His son was Matt Nowlan of Ballaghmore who was a tenant in the mid 1800s of a farm leased from Butler & Watson. Matt Died in 1852. Matt had at least one son, Michael who was probably born in the second decade of the 19th. century and who inherited the farm. He was the father of Matt and John (for whom their father bought or leased Cappawater). We will deal with the Ballaghmore Nolans first.

Matt of Ballaghmore was married to a Miss Clowery and they had two sons (one of whom Matt went to America) and one daughter Catherine. She married a Nolan from Rosslee[541]. Matt's eldest son was Michael Nowlan, a noted cyclist in his time.

Michael, who married Lucy Vize of Wexford, had three sons and two daughters, Teresa d.s.p. and Mary who married John Torpey. The sons were:-

    1. Matthew Nolan B.A. a teacher in Newbridge College from 1938-1977. Matthew who died in 1977 was the father of Lt. Col. Michael Nolan and Mary FitzSimons, a teacher, of Blessington.

    2. James of Ballaghmore who died unmarried.

    3. Frank who married and had three daughters. One of his daughters, Mary, married Dan Jordan and they now own Ballaghmore.

John Nolan of Cappawater, brother of Matt (from whom descended the Ballaghmore Nolans) was the ancestor of one of the present Nolans of Rosslee,

---

brothers who emigrated to America came home to the family farm in the early decades of the 1900s.

[541] Her husband was in fact Patrick Nolan, of Myshall, who inherited Rosslee from his mother Matilda (widow of Bernard Nolan of Rosslee). He was the father of the late Bernard Nolan of Myshall. Bernard was married to Mary (Babby) Kavanagh, of Myshall, and their two sons are Patrick and Desmond. Patrick of Rosslee also had thee other sons - Matthew d.s.p., Patsy d.s.p and Michael who died following an accident. His daughters were Teresa, dec., (married to Thomas Doyle of Kildavin), Dolores Kavanagh of Moanmore, Matilda Brophy and Anna Mary.

represented today by Matt Nolan of Rosslee, who bought lands there in his own lifetime. The late Tom Nolan T.D., and the only Government Minister ever from Carlow, was Matt's brother. The descent of this family is as follows:-

John, of Cappawater, (m. Margaret Nolan of Kilmaglush - the Grassyard), had four sons and two daughters, one of whom died young. The other daughter, Hanna, married Ml. Murphy of Ballyellis, Gorey, but that family died out. The fours sons were Matthew, Michael, John and Edward. The three youngest all emigrated to America in the latter decades of the 19th. century. All three married but only John (married to a Miss Carney), had a family - one daughter, Catherine who died in the latter decade of the 20th. century. Matthew married and had five sons and four daughters - Margaret, Josie, Bridget and Catherine. Margaret is married to Edward Kennedy of Kilballyhue[542] and Bridget married Peadar McMahon of Baldoyle. Matthew's sons were :-

1. John d.s.p.

2. Tom (the late T.D. and Minister) married Margaret Doran. They had six sons and four daughters namely - Breda (Principal of the R.T.C. in Borris), Margaret, Colette and Marie. Tom's sons are M.J. (former T.D. and sitting County Councillor), Enda and Tom (both sitting County Councillors), Eamonn, Michael and John. M.J., Enda and Tom seem to have set a record in that, this would appear to be the first time three brothers were elected County Councillors at the same time in Ireland.

3. Matthew (now of Rosslee), married Kathleen Fenelon of Curracruit and has three sons and two daughters - Bridget and Mary Frances. Their sons are:- Joseph, Martin and Fergus.

4. Edward married a Miss Moore and they have one son, Brian and two daughters, Aine and Jane.

5. Joseph d.s.p.

---

[542] Edward Kennedy gave me the following information about a Nolan family who lived in Kilballyhue from sometime in the late 18th. century up to the later part of the 19th. century. A John Nolan/Nowlan from Ballyloo leased the lands from Eustaces of Castlemore in the later 1700s. He may have been a son of Thomas Nolan of Ballyloo whose will is mentioned in the Index of Leighlin wills as of 1779. There was clause in the lease that specifically mentioned that the tenant was to be compensated for improvements. John Nolan built the magnificent four storey house but Eustace was unable to compensate him. The land was made over to Nolan in lieu. John had a son, also John, who was Justice of the Peace and he had a daughter, who was a nun in Carlow. John the J.P. died in 1863. He was married at the time and some years later his widow (a Dublin lady) and family moved to Dublin. When the Eustace lands were taken over by the Land Commission the Nolans took legal action for compensation but appear to have failed in their action.

Kilballyhue House - Courtesy Edward Kennedy

The O'Nolans of Kilbride

Like most of the O'Nolan septs very little is now known about the Kilbride O'Nolans. Again what information is available came from the Fiants.

William of Kilbride was the owner of large estates in the mid 1500s. It was he who sold Ballintemple and other lands across the Slaney to the Butlers in 1564. He was pardoned in 1559 and in 1566 for having been in rebellion with the Butlers. In 1578 he was pardoned for having been in rebellion with the O'Moores. He had seven sons and we do not know of any daughters. His sons were Feagh, Cahir, Leasagh, Maurice ne dower, Thady, Murrough ne Dowre and Dermot.

1. **Feagh** was pardoned for his rebellious activities in 1563 when he was a party to the capture of Harvey and Davells.[543] He had two sons that we know of Tirelagh More (pardoned in 1548 for being in rebellion with the O'Byrnes and in 1575 with Cahir Duff Kavanagh) and Donough (pardoned in 1601 with Donal Spainneach. He was a freeman of Carlow county in 1608).

---

[543] For details of these adventurers see the chapter devoted to Adventurers.

a) Tirelagh More had a son Thady pardoned in 1597 for his rebellious actions with the O'Byrnes and Kavanaghs of Garryhill. Thady had a son Tirlogh Ballagh of Ballygilbert who was attainted of treason.[544]

b) Donough had three sons - Dermot (pardoned in 1597 with the Kavanaghs of Garryhill), Shane (pardoned in 1575 with the Keatings and in 1601 with the Sullivans of Cork) and Tirelagh (pardoned in 1601 with Donal Spainneach). Shane had a son Teig who was in rebellion with Donal Spainneach in 1601.

2. **Cahir** was pardoned in 1584 with the O'Byrnes and in 1601 with Donal Spainneach. He had one son Donal McCahir of Brekenagh gent.

3. **Leasagh** was pardoned in 1563 with the O'Byrnes, in 1576 with the Kavanaghs and in 1601 with Donal Spainneach. He had one son Donough who owned part of Ballykealy and who was slain in rebellion.

4. **Maurice ne dower** (meaning the swarthy) was pardoned in 1569 and 1572 with Fiach McHugh. He was attainted of treason. He had two sons Rory and Patrick. Rory was pardoned in 1598 when in rebellion with the Kavanaghs and O'Byrnes and he was slain in rebellion. He was noted as the owner of Kilbride. Patrick of Ardristan was in rebellion with the Butlers in 1571.

5. **Thady** was pardoned with the O'Byrnes in 1548 and in 1563 he was involved in the capture of Harvey and Davells.

6. **Murrough ne dowre** was pardoned in 1569 with Fiach McHugh and again in 1572. He had one son Brian pardoned in 1601 with Donal Spainneach.

7. **Dermot** was pardoned in 1569 and 1572 with Fiach McHugh. He had two sons Gerrot and James. Gerrot was pardoned in 1583 with the Kavanaghs and O'Byrnes and in 1602 he was pardoned in Co. Westmeath with various rebels. He may have had two sons Cahir and Owen both pardoned in 1601. Dermot's other son James was pardoned in 1597 with the Kavanaghs of Garryhill.

The Nolans of Tinnaclash

I have some information on the Tinnaclash Nowlans but I know from the correspondence of Fr. John O'Nolan that he was in contact with that family in the early 1900s with a view to finding out more about them. However nothing seems to have come of it. We do know of course that they descended from Luke, a brother of Lawrence of Lisgarvan (later of Knockendrane) and that many of them are buried in TemplePeter. When Fr. Patrick Nolan P.P. of

---

[544] A Terlagh Nowlan made a will in 1680. He may have been a son or a grandson of Tirlogh Ballagh. It is possible, too, that Turlough Nowlan, of Herbidas in Co. Kildare, part of the manor of Kilkea, who leased lands to his sons William and Henry, in 1733, may have been a son of Terlagh.

Ballon died in 1894 there were two Nolans named as chief mourners. They were Dr. Nolan of Tullow and Mr. James Nolan of Tinnaclash, both described as cousins. In the Index to Leighlin Wills, James Nowlan of Tinnaclash had his will proved as of 1742 and another James had one dated 1829.

Tinnaclash House - Courtesy Michael Eustace

The following is a tentative pedigree of the Tinnaclash Nolans.

Luke the son of Lawrence of Lisgarvan inherited Tinnaclash from an uncle James. It would seem from the gravestones in Temple Peter that Luke's grandfather John was living in Tinnaclash at the time. John was born in 1677 and died the same year as Luke in 1770.

Luke was born in 1704 and died in 1770 aged 66 years. He appears to have married late and his son James was born in 1743. James died in 1828 aged 85 years. His will was noted in the Index to Leighlin Wills as of 1829. His wife Johanna died in 1811. He seems to have had three sons at least:-

1. Luke, who was born in 1788, was married and had at least one son James. Luke died in 1848.

2. Joseph who was born in 1784 died in 1844. It would seem that both brothers may have died from some of the diseases prevalent during the famine times.

3. Richard Nolan the son of James Nolan of Tinnaclash died in 1809 aged 18 yrs.

247

James the son of Luke above was probably born around 1820 and survived the ravages of the famine years. It would seem that he did not get married until late in life, due to the unsettled times he lived in. He had at least one son James, who died in 1920 aged 58 yrs.

This James had three sons:- Bertie, Luke and John. Bertie was a veterinary surgeon and the other men farmed Tinnaclash. Bertie and John were bachelors and they died in the first half of the last century.[545] Luke was married and had two children, a son, who died young and a daughter, Maeve (now deceased) who married Michael Eustace[546] of Castlemore. Luke died in 1945.

The Tinnaclash Nolans were gentlemen farmers, like their relatives in Knockendrane and Ballinrush and they were also middlemen. I understand that some of the rental books of the Tinnaclash Nolans are still extant.

The Nolans of Kilconnor who were known as the Counsellor Nolans are a very old family too and they are represented today by Edward (Noel) Nolan of Kilconnnor House. He is the son of Nicholas Nolan whose father Thomas was born c. 1830. Thomas's father was Edward who would have been a young man prior to 1798.

Kilconnor House - Courtesy Noel and Mrs. Nolan

---

[545] I am indebted to Noel Nolan of Kilconnor House for the last piece of information.
[546] The Eustaces, of course, have had a long association with Castlemore. Michael's wife Maeve Nolan is now deceased. They have three daughters - Ann m. to Jim Kennedy of Clogrennan, Elizabeth and Mary.

While examining Indexes to wills and Marriage Bonds a few other Nolans or Nowlans appeared which would indicate that there are other branches of the sept not accounted for in this book. In the chapter dealing with the 19th. century these are mentioned in detail. It is possible that there were sub septs of the clan in Linkardstown, Grangefort, Borris, Kilmaglush, Ballyloo, Ballyryan, Augha and Tinryland.

While examining the tombs in Temple Peter I came across an interesting site which is the burial ground of the Nolans of Craanaha and Ballybromell. The fine railed burial site would indicate that they were people of consequence.

The Nolan papers (i.e. the collection of papers I was given containing drafts of Fr. O'Nolans chapters and correspondence) include a small selection of letters from an O'Nolan family of Rathanna, though this family died out in the male line in the 1900s. The John O'Nolan who corresponded with Fr. O'Nolan used embossed paper which was unusual in the early 1900s.

I would like to stress once more that this book is not and never purported to be a book detailing the descent of all the Nolans. The examples I have given above are a chance selection in the sense that some of the material was readily available.

The O'Nolans of Galway

When Thomas Nolan of Ballinrobe castle died in 1628 he left his widow and a son and heir Gregory. Hardiman who wrote a history of Galway in 1820 had this to say about the Nolans. 'This family was formerly of the first rank and opulence and is still wealthy and respectable. Thomas Nolan Esq., of the town and castle of Ballinrobe died June 18th. 1628, was possessed of most extensive landed possessions, to which his son Gregory succeeded and out of which his widow Agnes Martin had dower. This property was confiscated in the civil war of 1641, but a considerable part still remains in the families of Loughboy, Ballinderry and Ballybanagher. The tomb of the ancient family of O'Nolan of Loughboy is situated in the centre of the Franciscan Friary Churchyard in Galway and bears the following inscription - " This tomb was first erected in the year of our Lord 1394, by the O'Nolans of Loughboy and is now rebuilt and ornamented by Michael O'Nolan, Galway, one of the representatives of the said family." A terrible conflagration took place in Galway in June 1473, by which the town was nearly destroyed. This misfortune was soon overcome by the exertions of an industrious and already opulent community, the chief amongst whom were the fourteen tribes also Nolan, Port, Coine, Cuin and Tully are particularly noticed.'

If Michael O'Nolan is correct in stating that the ancient tomb of the O'Nolans dates from 1394 then the original group of O'Nolans who went to Galway must have gone west from Carlow before then, possibly as early as 1170 after the Norman invasion when they opposed the Norman/McMurrough alliance. What is certain is that there was a very powerful family of O'Nolans in Co. Galway and they were situated in the Ballinrobe region. Another branch of the family set up in the Loughboy area of Mayo. In 1628 Thomas Nolan, who died, was the owner of Ballinrobe castle and he had at least one son Gregory, by his wife Agnes Martin. Gregory's son was John Nolan of Ballinderry and John's son was Patrick, who married a Browne of the Neale (Brownes were the ancestors of Lord Kilmaine). He had several children but his heir was John Nolan of Ballinderry who was born c. 1680. This John married Ellis Brabazon of Co. Mayo in 1709 and their son was Thomas. It is probable that Gregory Nolan who was party to many land transactions in the early 1700s was John's brother. Thomas had three sons - John, Anthony and Brabazon. Nothing much is known about them except that they were all involved in land dealings. John succeeded to the Ballinderry estates. He married an heiress, Margaret French of Port a Carron. His grandson John, married Mary Nolan of Loughboy, Mayo, in 1836 and they had six sons and one daughter Elizabeth. The sons were:-

> John Philip who was the heir to Ballinderry;
> Walter of Claremadden, Co. Galway;
> Francis, a barrister;
> Philip who was in the Indian Civil Service;
> Sebastian;
> Edward a lieutenant in the British Army.

John Philip was an Army Officer and later an M.P. for Galway North and a J.P.

There are about 200 Nolan families in the Galway/Mayo area today and they are descended from the Nolans who went to Galway in the 12th. century. Many may be descended from the Nolans I have written about above.

As we know many of the Nolans spread from Co. Carlow into the neighbouring counties of Wexford, Kilkenny, Kildare and Wicklow in the 17th., 18th., and 19th. centuries. Fr. Meehan, the P.P. of Ballindaggin, in Co. Wexford, writing to Fr. O'Nolan in 1919 stated that there were 25 families of Nolan/ Nowlan in his parish and that their ancestors had been very active in 1798 when they were noted as 'great fighting men'.

Chapter 19

Land divisions in Forth

The Barony of Forth, at the present time encompasses all of the lands between the Burren river and the Slaney, a more or less quadrilateral area running on a north-west/south-east axis. There are a few townlands on the Idrone side of the Burren which are in Forth (Craanaha, Clonbulloge, Moanmore, Kilkey, Kilbrickan, Ballintrane, Clonmacshane, Graiguealug and Graiguenaspiddeog). On the north-west the barony is bounded by Kellistown West and Kellistown East and on the north by Roscat and Castlemore townlands. In the south and south-east the barony is bordered by St. Mullins Upper (which includes Clonegal, Monaughrim etc.) and by the modern border of Co. Wexford. There are a few townlands of Forth across the Slaney on the north-east side (Ballintemple, Ballinastraw, Craans, Ballynoe, part of Aghade, Ardattin, Ratheeragh, Rathvarrin and Newtown)

The total area of the barony is close to 38,000 acres. There are 12 civil parishes in the barony or in some cases parts of parishes e.g. part of Fenagh and part of Nurney. In the table below we see the names of the parishes and the area of that parish that is in the barony of Forth.

It is not clear how an area came to be called a barony but most scholars believe that the Normans so described the existing divisions they found in place when they conquered Ireland in the 12th. century.

The parishes and areas of each parish mentioned below do not necessarily reflect the sizes and denominations of the parishes as they may have existed in the middle ages but in general they probably do.

Parishes in Forth and the area of that parish in the barony.

Aghade	1370
Ardoyne	3476
Ballon	3825
Ballyellin	771
Barragh	11717
Fenagh	1380
Gilbertstown	2979
Kellistown	1739
Myshall	8637
Nurney	142
TemplePeter	986
Tullowmagimma	702
Total	37724

There are 104 townlands in the barony. Like the baronies the townlands were old Gaelic divisions which the Normans found useful for administrative purposes. In most cases the names of the townlands are Gaelic in origin but some have been totally anglicised e.g. Sherwood, Deerpark and Altimont. While the origin of the names of townlands is outside the scope of this work, it might be appropriate to mention a few of them.

As in most counties the most frequently occurring names are those beginning with Bally or Ballin. Both of these are really the old Irish 'Baile' meaning originally the dwelling or place of habitation and later meaning townland. In the case of these names the second part is probably the most interesting because it gives much more information. Ballinvalley is in fact Baile an Bhealaigh or in translation *the dwelling at the pass,* while Ballyshancarra (in the barony of St. Mullins Upper) is Baile Sean Cuire or *the dwelling of the old warrior, or the dwelling of Sean the warrior,* although O'Donovan states that this is Baile Sheain Charraig - *the rock of Scabby John!* Ballykealy is most likely Baile Coille or the townland of the wood.

Many names also begin with Kil, as in Kilbride. This is the old Irish word Cill meaning a Church and Kilbride means the Church of St. Bridget. Kilknock, I assume means the Church on the Hill, while Kilbrickan means the Church of St. Bricin.

Names beginning with Knock generally mean a hill and so Knockdramagh is really Cnoc druim an Ath or *the hill beside the hump backed ford,* while Knockbrack is really Cnoc Breac or *the Speckled hill.*

Occasionally we find the names of people as in Clonmacshane. This is Cluain Mac Sheain or *the meadow of John's son* and Ballygarret may well be Baile Gearoid, or *Gerard's dwelling.*

In the early 16th. century the O'Nolans probably occupied most of the barony as they had done since the recovery of the lands from the Normans in the 14th./15th. century. Like their neighbours the Kavanaghs they were a somewhat nomadic people. Their wealth was in their flocks and herds and they practised transhumance or the movement of the entire population of the sub-sept, to upland pastures, in summer. Undoubtedly, there was some tillage work done, as places existed where there were mills for grinding corn, e.g. Milltown near Garryhill and Milltown near Kilbride.

Under the Brehon laws the lands were divided among the clan members according to strict rules and in the sixteenth century we find that the larger divisions (and probably the smaller ones) were still extant.

The Barony of Forth at that time (according to the Fiants) was divided into 'quarters'. These were called in the Fiants by the anglicised names of 'Sleight Shean, Sleight O'Morhoo, Sleight Coyne, Pubble Dromo and Brecklaghe'. These names give us some insight into the nature of the divisions at that time. 'Sleight Shean' is really Sliocht Sheain or (the area occupied by)the descendants of Sean. The Sean in question was undoubtedly Sean, the Tanaist, who became the O'Nolan following the slaying of his chief in 1399, while fighting against the army of Richard II.

Sleight O'Morhoo is a corruption of Sliocht O'Murrough or the 'tribe of the descendants of Murrough'. Murrough as a Christian name occurs in the O'Nolan families of Ballykealy, Kilbride and Bealalaw but we have no idea who the original Murrough was, who gave his name to the land division Sliocht O'Murrough.

Sleight Coyne may be a corruption of Sliocht Coinn or the tribe of the descendants of Conn, but if this is so none of the 16th. or 17th. century O'Nolans bore the name Conn. It is possible that the name was of very ancient origin and it could have been the case that some of the descendants of Conn of the Hundred Battles settled in the region. At any rate it seems that Conn's brother Eochaidh Fionn was given the 'seven Fotharta of Leinster' as his patrimony and he may well have called one of his sons Conn after his brother, the famous Conn of the Hundred Battles.

'Pubble Dromo' might be Pobal Druim or the 'people of the hill', and refers to that hilly area of Forth across the Slaney including Ballintemple, Ardattin, Ballynoe and Ballynastraw. It might also mean ' the hilly part belonging to all the people'. As it is the only area of really high ground in the Barony with the exception of the more southern part which seems to have been in the possession of the Kavanaghs, it is likely that this was the area used by all the people for their summer movement when cattle were brought to high pastures.

The most puzzling of the names is that of Brecklaghe. It seems to refer to the area in and around the village of Myshall as most of the lands mentioned in the Fiat which were granted the Earl of Ormonde lands in 1562, lie in that area.

The people, mostly O'Nolans, who lived in these districts generally lived and worked within the confines of their own areas. The ruling classes of the O'Nolans, including their bards and brehons would not have been restricted in their movements. Only members of the ruling classes and their retinues were allowed to carry arms. Most of the sons of the local rulers were bred to arms and knew no other kind of work. Many would have been fostered with kinfolk in different parts. A few of them are mentioned in the Fiants as being from Imaal or Clonmullen and were described as 'kern'. Kern were young foot soldiers who fought with a sword and with lances. The near relatives of the rulers graduated as horsemen. In some cases independent bands of kern were formed and hired themselves out to the overlords such as Fiach McHugh O'Byrne or Donal Spainneach Kavanagh.

Relationships between the various sub septs was not always idyllic. The position of clan chieftain was much coveted, because of the prestige it gave the successful claimant and because of the wealth he and his family enjoyed. While it is not known if there were battles among the O'Nolans for the position of chieftain, it is well documented that serious disturbances occurred among the Kavanaghs. While all this feuding was taking place the insidious English administrative machine was relentlessly pursuing its goal of total domination.

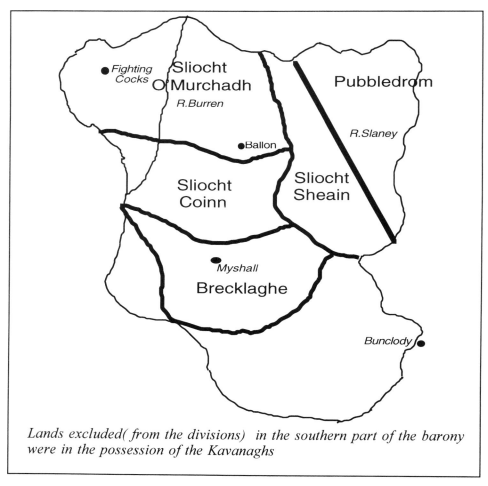

Lands excluded(from the divisions) in the southern part of the barony were in the possession of the Kavanaghs

Land divisions as they appeared to be in the Barony of Forth
prior to 1600 A.D

254

Old Royal titles were discovered and long forgotten claims to Irish lands were resurrected. In addition church lands, long held by Gaelic families were granted away to ravening adventurers who were urged and encouraged to take up their lands by force if necessary and settle among the Irish.

From 1536 onwards there was much turmoil in Leinster and the inhabitants of Forth did not emerge unscathed. The eighteen years from 1536 to 1554 were the years in which the Gaelic way of life, as it had existed from time immemorial, came under sustained attack and while it lasted in a modified way into the next century, the death knell of a unique way of life was sounding.

The destruction of the House of Kildare with the killing of Silken Thomas and his uncles combined with the relentless closure of the monasteries and the usurpation of their lands by Henry VIII, who leased the lands out to his minions, paved the way for the conquest.

In Co. Carlow or Catharlaghe as it was called, the earliest known grants by lease, from Henry VIII, were the 1541 grants[546] to James the Earl of Ormonde and a joint lease to Christopher Dowdall, Oliver Werdon gents. of Co. Louth and Jenico Chamberlayne of Drogheda, merchant. Since all these grants were conveyed by English officials it is unlikely that the inhabitants of Forth were immediately aware of their significance. The leases in question were all of Church lands. Some of these Church lands were indeed in the possession of clerics but some would appear to have been abandoned for centuries and were in the possession of the natives.

The lease to the Co. Louth men, was of the preceptory or manor of Killerig together with the lands of Killerig, Russelstown, Moygane, and 'Courtt' of Killerig and Tullefelme (Tullowphelim) and the rectories of Killerig, Kilmkaill and Powerstown. The lease was for 21 years and the rent was £4 per annum. In addition the leasees had to pay the late preceptor £25. 4s 7d yearly. While the rent was small for what we assume was a considerable collection of properties yet the total annual payment was quite sizeable.

It was, in fact, astronomical in comparison to the rent required of the Earl of Kildare a few years previously when he rented the lands of Ardristan, Rathoe, Roscat and Templemurry from Thomas Everarde, the then prior of St. John the Baptist, 'without' the Newgate of Dublin. He leased the properties in question for 31 years and the rent was one grain of corn for the first six years and 13s. 4d per annum for the remainder of the period. Of course the implication here is that the lands were completely under the control of the native Irish, most likely the O'Nolans, as the barony of Forth at one time stretched right up to the town of Carlow. Even the Earl of Kildare must have thought it a formidable task to wrest the lands back from the occupiers.

---

[546] Fiants of the Tudor Monarchs

In 1543 the lands were granted to Thomas Luttrell of Luttrellstown along with many other properties formerly belonging to Hospital of St. John the Baptist. Those lands were later granted away by lease to William Brabazon (a high English official) and Richard Delahyde, in 1546 or 1547 to hold for 21years at an annual rent of 3s. 4d. The lands mentioned above must have been part of the lands of the Knights Hospitallers, who had huge grants of lands in various counties.

It is obvious from these contrasting cases that the Killerig properties were occupied and controlled by state officials and their tenants and were capable of paying the rents.

The grant of a lease to the Earl of Ormonde[547] in 1541 was for a large number of rectories in various counties and included Kellistown, part of the possessions of the late monastery of Kenlis, Co. Kilkenny.

In another grant in the same year the Earl was leased the site of the monastery of Carmelites of Leighlinbridge and the site of the monastery of Augustinian Friars of Tullowphelim[548] and their appurtenances i.e. tithes, rents and customs. For both of these properties he was asked to pay annual rents. For the Leighlinbridge property the rent was 46s 8d and for the Tullowphelim lands it was 26s 8d. Leighlinbridge, of course with its castle and garrison was much more lucrative than Tullowphelim, a very rural area.

The Lord Deputy, St. Leger, was given a lease in 1542 of the Priory of Grane,[549] together with the rectories of Castledermot, Kiltegan, Kilpipe, Hacket and many others in the general area. In addition he got the leases of rectories in Co. Wexford and Co. Cork. His annual rent for these was 66s. 8d. This would lead one to believe that those lands were all in the possession of the natives also.

---

[547] This was James the son of Piers Roe. In the previous year James had granted the castle and lands of Tullow to his mother, the Dowager Lady Ormonde (nee Fitzgerald) for her own use. It is probable that these lands were part of the dower of the Dowager as her father claimed to own those lands. James's grandmother (the mother of Piers Roe) had been married to O'Nolan. It is quite likely that the O'Nolans accepted the status quo.

[548] In 1546 the Vicarage of Tullowphelim was granted to Robert Johns, who was probably the father of Brian Johns or Jones, following the death of Gerald McMortagh. (Possibly an O'Nolan or a Kavanagh) - Fiants.

[549] Formerly in Co. Carlow but now in Co. Kildare. In 1538 Egidia Wale the Abbess was given a pension of £4 per annum and in the same year the Lord Deputy Grey was granted a lease of the Priory of Graney with its appurtenances. The only other reference I came across was in Wicklow History and Society where it is mentioned in an article by Linzi Simpson. Also see page 137 re the Charter to the Numery of Graney. It would seem that Walter de Riddlesford, an early Norman, granted some lands in the Bray area to the nunnery of Graney.

In 1544 James Bathe[550] was the recipient of the lease of the rectories of Fenagh, Drummin, Barragh, Kylrosnarryn, Ballykealy, Drumphea and Castlemore with the tithes and a carucate of land, property of the late priory of Tullaghfelym - parcels of the possessions of the Abbey of St. Thomas Court by Dublin. He received these lands along with many more grants in various counties.

During the reign of Kind Edward VI in 1550 a huge grant of lands in Forth were made to Edmund O'Leyne and John Barri of Freerton, gent. This was exactly the same grant which was made to the Earl of Ormonde later on in 1562[551]. At that time the rent was £13. 16s 8d. with a yearly sum of £13.6s. 8d. payable to the Constable of the Castle of Carlow in lieu of Customs. What is perhaps remarkable about this grant is that there was no explanation for the availability of the lands. They were not Church lands so the implication is that they were assumed to be King's lands. For the huge amount of land in question the rent was relatively small leading one to surmise that the O'Nolans were still in possession but may in fact have been paying some kind of annual rent.[552]

In 1551 Brian Johns (or Jones)[553] was the Constable of the Castle of Carlow and two years later Edward Randolf gent.[554] was granted the lease of the Manor and Castle of Carlow for 21 years at an annual rent of £23. 3s The

---

[550] He held the office of Chief Baron of the Exchequer and continued so during the reigns of Edward V1 and Philip and Mary. He was confirmed in office by Queen Elizabeth in 1559 and in 1560 he took the Oath of Supremacy. He received grants of lands in other areas including Crumlin and Ballybough which was adjacent to his residence in Drumcondra. The office was worth £67.10s. p.a.

[551] For full details of this grant see the section dealing with the grant to Ormonde later in this chapter.

[552] See next chapter for more information on Barri and Leyne (Barry and Lyne)

[553] The last mention of Johns in the Fiants is in Fiant 180. He was commissioned to execute martial law in Kilkenny in company with the Earl of Ormonde and his brother Edmund Butler. Under the same Fiant Nicholas Heron, the sheriff of Co. Carlow was to execute martial law in Co. Carlow.

[554] Randolf seems to have become the Constable of the Castle of Carlow in 1553 and continued in this office right up to 1566 when he was either retired or dead as he was succeeded by Robert Harpole. In 1558, 1561, 1563 and 1564 he was joined with others in the execution of martial law in the county. (Fiants Eliz. Nos. 53, 381, 542, 682 and 953) Some important names continually recur during those years, as his co- officials. Nicholas Heron, Roland the Viscount of Baltinglass, the Earl of Ormonde and his brother Sir Edmund Butler, John Barre or Barry, and Edmund O'Lyne. Later on we shall see the names of Barry and Lyne appearing as owners of lands in Forth pre 1641. See next chapter re the adventurers.

manor lands lay on the Laois side of the Barrow and in comparison to the extent of lands granted in Forth they were minuscule. But because they lay in a protected area the lands yielded a very high rent. Johns seems to have been in the area for some time as he was commissioned in 1557 to govern the county in the absence of the Lord Deputy who was on expedition against the Scots. He was joined in this commission with the Bishop of Leighlin, Nicholas Heron, John O'Barre and Edmund O'Layne. In the same year Johns and the first two mentioned above were commissioned to "enquire of all chalices, ornaments, bells, houses and lands belonging to Parish churches and chapels and in whose hands they now are."

It would seem that Philip (of Spain) and Queen Mary were making some attempts to undo the reformation imposed by Henry VIII. But of course their efforts were short lived as Elizabeth was on the throne by 1558 and she immediately began to reimpose the reformation that her father had started.

It was during the reign of Elizabeth that Ireland was transformed. The adventurers[555] who had come into Ireland as a trickle during the reign of Henry VIII now began to come in torrents and combined with the non compromising officialdom that was then in place completed the rape of a nation in less than thirty years.

So the next stage was set for the alienation of Irish lands, in general, and O'Nolan lands in Forth, in particular. Queen Elizabeth, who was possibly the most successful British Monarch ever, granted lands in Forth to Thomas, the Earl of Ormonde and Ossory. Among church lands in counties Kilkenny, Wexford, Tipperary, Kildare and Waterford she granted certain 'parcels in the Lordship of Foert' in Carlow. In her Fiant No. 504 dated 1562 A.D. she granted him the following:-

'In the quarter called Sleight Shean, a third part of each of the following, Kylbride, the wood of Garryncoyllcoyll, Kylbreny, Ballymolyn, Ballyvehell, Carricknislane, Kylnocke, Balligilbert, Ballyvenden, Ballykeylle and Barragh;

   In the quarter called Sleight O Morhoo, a third of Ballynourye, and Kylmorye, half of Grangespiddocke, half of Grangeluge, a third of Templeped and Cloughmasonyn, a third

---

[555] See next chapter for details of many of the adventurers

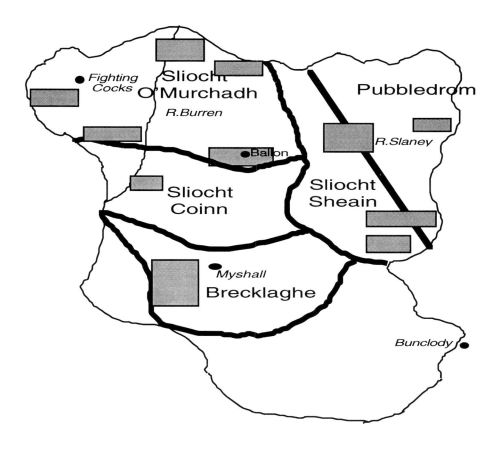

Representation of the Elizabethan Grant of 1562 to the Duke of Ormonde

of Ballymoge, a third of Ballytrahin and Kylbryckan, a third of Kylkaa, a third of Kyllean a third of Ollerde, half of Kylbuogles, a third of Lyshegarnen;

In the quarter called Sleight Coyne, Rathowth, a third of Ballyvalden and Balgodeman, a third of Radowgin, a third of Rathbrogue and Rathraghe, a third of Ballyn, a third of Keppaghe, a third of Mornex, a third of Ballylyon;

In the quarter called Pubble Dromo, a third of Ballyfreight and Ballydonnaghe, half Ballytemple, a third of Ballyncloneboy, half Ballyenowe, half Sraughesteel and half Ballynhoinbin;

In the quarter called Breckelaghe, half Ballybeall, a third of Mogisshill and Birraghe, half Ballynrusshe, a third of Rosseloy, half Kyllavie and Shangarrie, half Kyll(ieen) and Tyrolme, a third of Tartancaple, a third of Lysnecrlce and Koyllehenry and Garrynpursin, the town of Cowlwillm Mc Onoght and Bogghan Onyll. To hold the possession of Athasshill for ever, by the service of a twentieth part of a knight's fee, for all demands. And to hold the remaining premises in tail male, by the like service, at a rent of £49. 3s. 9d.'

While this did not amount to a granting away of a third of the entire patrimony of the O'Nolans it was a considerable grant on paper. The implications of this grant were not felt by the O'Nolans at the time, as they were still in possession of the lands and were most likely unaware of the process and its significance.[556] They had more to do at the time in trying to contend with the mind boggling changes that were now part and parcel of the time in which they lived; the impositions being forced upon them by the Constable of the Castle of Carlow, who claimed that they and the inhabitants of Rathvilly Barony were obliged to supply victuals to the garrison of the castle; trying to implement the divisions of lands ordered by the Lord Deputy; attempting to cope with Inquisitions into the ownership of Church lands; trying to understand the demands being made on them to accept a new religion which denied the Pope his title as Head of the Church; coming to grips with the idea of 'surrender and regrant' whereby Irish chiefs were encouraged to come in and surrender their lands, abandon the rule of the Brehon laws of land distribution , give up their Irish titles and acknowledge the British Monarch as their Queen, and accept English law.

In this connection the grant made in 1564 to Sir Edmund Butler,[557] by William (Roo) O'Nolan (of Kilbride) of all his possessions in Ballintemple is

---

[556] In 1562 Cahir, Gerald and John McDonagh O'Nolan made a grant to Arthur Kavanagh and Nicholas Tywe - to the use of Sir Edmund Butler - of the town of Kilmurry in exchange for lands in Ballintrane and Raheen. They were grandsons of Cahir O'Nolan of Ballykealy (Hayes). The Arthur Kavanagh mentioned was probably Art the son of Moriertagh Og of Garryhill. At the same time they made a 'quit claim' to Ballynunnery. In this year also a grant of lands etc., was made to the same two men by Owen O'Nolan, 'also to the use of Sir Edmund Butler of the town of Leighlin and half his lands in Killenure' (Hayes)

[557] Sir Edmund also benefited from a 'quit claim' to the manors and castles of Clogrennan, by Donal Kavanagh, in 1568. Donal may have been a grandson of Gerald 'Sutton' Kavanagh (5th. son of Murrough Ballach, King of Leinster who died in 1511).

most significant.[558] It should be noted that William was pardoned for being in rebellion with the Butlers in 1559 and 1566.[559]

Another very interesting grant was made in 1573 to Owen O'Gormagan[560] of all the castles, lands etc, in Forth,[561] belonging to the Earl of Ormonde. This grant was made by Richard Shee, a solicitor, the Earl's agent. O'Gormagan, and his wife Onora Ne Dhonal,[562] got a further grant the following year of the manor of Rathethe.[563]

---

[558] Hayes

[559] Fiants

[560] The O'Gormagan's were natives of Co. Carlow. They later changed their name to O'Gorman. Owen O'Gormagan was pardoned on three occasions - in 1565 as of Grangeforth and described as a husbandman; in 1571 as a horseman, he was pardoned along with his sons John and Hugh and one William Barry; in 1585 he was pardoned as of Grangeforth, his pardon not to extend to intrusion in crown lands or debts to the crown. In that same year he was given a further grant of lands in Forth by the Earl. In this same grant Gerald McMoriertagh Kavanagh was also mentioned as was Cahir McGerald McTeig (O'Nolan ? of the Ballykealy branch). (Hayes). Owen O'Gormagan is mentioned again in the 1589 Queen's grant of church lands in Killerig and other places in Co. Carlow, to Mary Travers (widow of the late Viscount Baltinglass), now married to Gerald Aylmer, where the Viscountess was given the right to redeem her lands out of the hands of Owen O'Gormagan and others. (Fiants)

[561] According to the maps of the Down Survey there were seven standing castles in Forth in 1654. They were Kilbride, Ballyvolden, Rathoe (ruin), Kilknock (ruin), Ballintrane, TemplePeter and Fenagh (ruin).

[562] She was probably the daughter of Donal Kavanagh of Ratheadan, mentioned earlier as having quit his claim to Clogrennan Castle.

[563] This must be Ratheadan

Chapter 20

The Barony of Forth in the 17th. century

The critical years from 1500 to 1600 saw the conquest of Ireland almost completed. The great Gaelic families lost their grip on their lands which were now flooded with the new English or Anglo Irish landowners and their tenants. As a result of the wars the country was devastated. For example, in 1600 an Edmund Coldhurst, farmer of the castle and manor of Lysfynny, Co. Waterford, applied to the Earl of Ormonde to rebuild the town of Tullow.[564]

The vast estates of Southern Leinster, occupied for centuries by the O'Nolans, Kavanaghs, O'Moores, O'Connors, O'Tooles, O'Ryans and O'Byrnes, were lost. Some of the ruling families of those names managed to hold on to considerable lands for a while longer[565] but in the main they succumbed to the extreme diverse pressures and simply sold off their holdings or became tenants of the new owners.

In Carlow the Kavanaghs of Borris, who had become Protestant, at least nominally, succeeded in surviving both the rebellion of 1641 and the Cromwellian holocaust. Despite being involved with the Jacobites (the Catholic followers of King James) in 1690 they still managed to survive as considerable landowners into the 18th. and 19th. centuries.

The Carew manuscripts give the following details about Co. Carlow, including the barony of Forth, for the year 1608. The persons of note in the county were Theobald, Lord Viscount Butler of Tullagh,[566] Thomas, Lord

---

[564] Hayes (Manuscript sources for the history of Irish Civilisation)

[565] This would include the various O'Nolans as mentioned by Fr. Nolan in the previous chapter. Donal Spainneach Kavanagh also managed to hold on to much of the land in and around Bunclody.

[566] Theobald, at this time, was granted with other Ormonde lands, half a mart land in Kilbride, Kilgraney and Kilkele, a quarter of a mart land in Kilmurry and Ballymogue, a twelfth of a mart land in Cappagh and all of Pubbledrom. In addition he was granted a

Bishop of Leighlin and Ferns and the following knights and esquires: Sir Thomas Colclough, Sir Richard Masterson and Sir William Harpole, Morgan McBrien[567], Henry Davells, William Wale[568], George Bagenal,[569] Oliver Eustace[570], Gerald McMortagh[571], Donal Kavanagh, Nicholas Harman, George Harpole and Brien McDonough[572].

Among the constables were Rory O'Nolan[573] of Kilbrickan and Thomas O'Nolan of Ballymogue, who were constables in Forth. The freeholders in Forth were named as: William Barry of Rathrush, Murrough Birne[574] of Straugh (Sraugh), Teig Nolan of Ballykealy, Donough Nolan of Ballaghmore[575], Murtagh McGerrott[576] of Myshall, Donal McHugh[577] of Shangarry, Donal Nolan of Killane[578], Donough Morrogh[579] of Carrickslaney, Patrick McShane[580] of Ballintemple, Donough Roe[581] of Kilbride and William Cooke of Kilcoole.

---

licence to hold Saturday markets and two fairs annually, on the vigils of the feasts of St. Peter and St. Luke at Tullowphelim.

[567] Morgan McBrian McCahir Kavanagh of Borris

[568] William Wall

[569] George was granted a large part of Idrone to hold for ever. Another part of Idrone, around Garryhill was granted to the Earl of Kildare. The parcel was part of the lands owned by Donough and Gerald Kavanagh who had been attainted (grandsons of Moriertagh Og who was killed by Bagenal).

[570] A descendant of the Viscount Baltinglass

[571] Gerald McMoriertagh Kavanagh - a grandson of Moriertagh Og (killed by Bagenal in 1586)

[572] Brian McDonough Kavanagh of the sept of Ballyloughan. He was sheriff of Carlow in 1608.

[573] A great grandson of William of Kilbride. He was the son of Donal Duff and grandson of Owen.

[574] In the Book of Settlement and Distribution this man's descendant is called Tirlogh Line.

[575] Possibly a grandson of Hugh of Shangarry - see that family in chapter 15 or a son of Cahir of Ballykealy who had been given as a hostage in 1593, but most likely the former.

[576] Might be an O'Nolan - possibly Murtagh McGerald McMurtagh McShane McCahir (of Ballykealy).

[577] The father of Donough of Ballaghmore.

[578] He may have been the Donal who was described as the owner of Ballykeenan and Cappagh in 1641. If so he was a Ballykealy O'Nolan.

[579] Probably Donough McMurtagh O'Nolan, a grandson of Shane Duff of Kilbride.

[580] This man was Patrick McShane McDonough McCahir O'Nolan of the Ballykealy sept.

[581] Donough McFeagh McWilliam of Kilbride. He was a brother of Tirelagh More whose grandson Tirelagh Ballagh of Ballygilbert, was attainted.

The O'Nolans were still grimly hanging on. But the overlordship of the barony of Forth was taken over by the Ormondes, and the surviving O'Nolans had to pay them some kind of rent. It was said that they had to pay 8d. per acre to the Ormondes.[582]

In 1616, possibly in an effort to help the old owners Brian Kavanagh of Borris, a great grandson of Cahir McArt, managed to secure a lease of the entire barony for 21 years.[583] But that arrangement didn't last long and in 1621 the barony was leased to a Sir T. Roper for a number of lives.

If the Deputy - Strafford - is to be believed, the lot of the common people improved somewhat under English rule. This is what he wrote in 1637:-

"The people, in general, are in great quietness, and, if I be not much mistaken, well satisfied and fast delighted with His Majesty's gracious government and protection, it being almost sure that, the lower sort of Irish subject, hath not, in any age, lived so preserved from the pressures and oppressions of the great ones, for which I assure you, they bless God and the King and begin to discover the great and manifold benefits they gather under the shadow of and from their immediate dependence upon the Crown, in comparison of the scant and narrow coverings they formerly borrowed from their petty, yet imperious lords."

Hore and Graves who quoted Strafford in their book *The Social State of the Southern and Eastern Counties*, were of the opinion that he was correct in his assessment.

The O'Nolan grip on their own lands was almost broken and by the year 1641 they only owned 2,335 acres of their original patrimony. The following table shows the area of land, in acres, owned by the different proprietors in Forth in 1641.

Sir Thomas Butler	6807
Earl of Ormonde	5954
Kavanaghs	5617
O'Nolans	2335
Oliver Eustace	1857
Patrick Esmonde	1593
Tirlough Line	1215
O'Neills	1211
John Barry	1179
Henry Warren	975
Henry Gormagan	923
Sir Wm. Reeves	756
Edmund Bryan	470
E. Percevall	372
Alderman Kennedy	331

[582] Ryans history of Carlow.
[583] Hayes

Dr. Thomas Arthur	324
Owen Birne	231
Edward Wall	140
Sir Theobald Butler	63
Edmund Eustace	40
Edward Harman	40
William Cooke	28
Church Lands	573

This shows a total area of 32,926 acres but in the Griffith's Survey the lands of Forth were said to measure almost 38,000 acres.[584]

The O'Nolan ownership was divided between twelve owners as follows:-

Patrick Nowlan, Shangarry	413
Patrick Nowlan, Ballinrush	380
Garret Nowlan, Ballykealy	344
Patrick Nowlan, Craanpurseen	222
Garret Nowlan, Tindclane	175
Garret Nowland, Cunnygar	151
Garret Nowland, Ballon	145
Charles Nowlan, Kilbrickan	144
Patrick Nowlan, Ballinrush	120
Daniel Nowlan, Ballykeenan	108
Philip Nowlan, Ballydrom	100
Dermot Nolan, Cappagh	33

As can be seen from the table there were two Patrick Nowlans in Ballinrush, a Patrick of Garrenpurseen and a Patrick Nowlan in Shangarry. The Patrick who owned Ballinrush and Shangarry was probably the one and same person. As already mentioned he must have been the ancestor of Lawrence Nolan (born c.1670 - 90) who was evicted from Shangarry in the early 1700s. Lawrence was described as a gentleman and he was the ancestor of the Knockendrane and Ballinrush Nolans.

The Garret Nowlans (also Nowland) might have been just one person and the owner of several farms. I have identified this man as the Gerrot O'Nolan who was the grandson of Teig O'Nolan of Ballykealy. His great grandfather was Cahir of Ballykealy.

The Charles Nowlan of Kilbrickan must have been a son or a nephew of Rory O'Nolan of Kilbrickan and was therefore a great great grandson of Cahir of Ballykealy.

Daniel Nowlan of Ballykeenan was Donal O'Nolan, who was still regarded as the titular owner of Ballykeenan, although he had been slain in rebellion,

---

[584] The size of the acre was different - in 1641 an acre was a 'Plantation acre' which was somewhat larger than the acre of the 19th. century.

probably at the famous battle of Arklow Rock already alluded to. He was a great great grandson of Cahir of Ballykealy also. Inquisitions to enquire into the amount of lands in their ownership were held on Donal and his son in 1617 and 1623.

Dermot Nowlan of Cappagh, was, in all probability, either a son of Donal or a cousin.

The question then arises as to what happened to the other O'Nolans. Like their Kavanagh counterparts many of the landowners either forfeited their lands because they were in rebellion or simply sold them off to the entrepreneurs and merchants from Dublin who saw the opportunity to acquire cheap land. The former owners then became tenants of the new owners and began to adapt to the rapidly changing environment.

The huge forests that had been the hiding places of the erstwhile rebels and a refuge for the women, children and aged and sick were targeted and the process of clearing them began. The Wallops in Enniscorthy became very wealthy from the oaks that grew profusely in the Slaney Valley. Many of the dispossessed O'Nolans and Kavanaghs and others (such as the Keoghs, Dorans, Ryans, O'Byrnes and O'Tooles) became the labourers and tradesmen for this huge industry.[585]

In addition to the felling of timber and the work of getting the trees to the river to be floated down to Enniscorthy the work of clearing the lands began in earnest. In addition many ironworks were set up in the south east which required oak to make the charcoal necessary for the process. A man called Bacon set up more than fifty of these ironworks mainly in the south Wicklow area. The vast tree stumps left had to be removed and ditches were built. For the first time fields began to appear in many areas. It is likely that all this industry brought a measure of prosperity to the area that insured relative calm, though this happy situation seems to have deteriorated rapidly following the onset of the rebellion in 1641.

Despite the frenzied felling of trees the forests were still quite formidable up to the latter decades of the 17th. century.

While the descendants of the old Gaelic owners felt aggrieved at their losses and pursued every legal channel they could to repossess their lands, the generality of the landless people seem to have accepted the passing of the old order.

There appears to have been a period of uneasy peace in Ireland in the period from 1601 to 1641 but it was no doubt a turbulent period with much lawlessness and crime. For example coyne and livery, which was made a

---

[585] Thus the descendants of ancient chieftains had to work on the lands once owned by their clans, and now owned by the stranger. This was the origin of the saying, which has a great element of truth in it, that every Irish peasant considered himself a descendant of kings.

criminal offence in the early 1600s was practised sporadically by the remnants of the Gaelic gentry for many decades afterwards. Cattle stealing was widespread in Ireland in general and we have no reason to believe that the O'Nolans and Kavanaghs abstained from the practice.

The Plantation of Ulster, too, was a catastrophe which led to deep unrest in that province. In Wexford the Plantation of much of the north of the county, in the second decade of the 17th. century, had a similar effect, with the displacement of people, who had been in possession of their lands from time immemorial. It was a similar case in the midlands where the Plantation of Laois and Offaly was continued and strengthened.

The barony of Forth in Carlow suffered because of the Plantation of Wexford, in that many of the dispossessed fled to the Mountains, then still under the control of Donal Spainneach, if not in his actual possession. Many of the Murphys, formerly of Oulart, along with Kavanaghs, Hanricks and Keoghs, from various parts of the county, moved into areas like Clonmullen, Barragh, Kilbranish and Myshall. This movement of people put pressure on the native population then in situ.

It was the discontent of the native chiefs who had lost so much in so short a time that led to the next great war - the war that lasted from 1641 right up until the mid 1650s when Cromwell devastated the country. Although it was the likes of Rory O'Moore[586] and Sir Phelim O'Neill[587] (the main instigators) who started the rebellion,[588] many very complex events occurred, which turned it into the most catastrophic episode ever to befall the Irish.

These occurrences included: the massacres of Protestants in Ulster and their equally sanguinary retaliations; the wildfire effect of the bloodshed in the north which engulfed the whole country and led to the wholesale dislocation of the Protestant population; the war between the Parliament and the Monarchy in England, which spilled over into Ireland; the interference of the Papal Legate, Rinuccini in Irish affairs, which led to a civil war being fought just prior to the Cromwellian invasion and the Cromwellian invasion itself which

---

[586] Rory O'Moore survived the wars of the entire decade 1641-51 and was on Inishbofin when it was surrendered to General Reynolds in 1652. It is said that he escaped to Ulster and lived in the guise of a fisherman until his death.

[587] Tried and convicted of Treason and executed in Dublin in 1653.

[588] The rebellion followed immediately after a meeting held in Dublin which was attended by over eighty persons including O'Moores, O'Byrnes and Sir Christopher Plunkett (who was married to a Bagenal). Sir Morgan Kavanagh was to have attended the meeting but didn't arrive. The meeting was held on the 22nd. October 1641. Government, through their spies, became alerted to the intended rebellion and the conspirators had to fly the city. The rebellion began almost immediately.

resulted in the most complex displacement of people and the most disastrous economic turmoil ever seen in Ireland.[589]

Carlow, so near to Kilkenny, the seat of the Confederacy, couldn't escape the general disturbances. Sir Morgan Kavanagh of Clonmullen, the son of Donal Spainneach, became an important leader in the rebellion and consequently many of the O'Nolans became involved. We only know of one, Captain James Nolan, who has been written about elsewhere. He managed to survive the entire period, but, as we have seen, upon his return to Ireland after the Restoration, he became embroiled in serious litigation with the Duke of Ormonde in trying to establish his right to lands in Shangarry.

It would seem appropriate at this juncture to mention some of the events of the war that must have had a profound effect on the people of Forth and adjoining districts.

In Carlow, as elsewhere, the rebels, which now included the remnants of the O'Moore, Kavanagh, O'Byrne and O'Nolan fighting men, (but led by Mountgarret[590] and Preston[591]), took over the castles and strongholds of the English administration. Carlow, Leighlinbridge and Tullow castles were seized and garrisoned by the rebels. It would seem that some atrocities were committed if the people quoted in Ryan's History of Carlow are to be believed. Some English people were killed and others driven out of their holdings.

The confederates declared themselves royalists but the Council in Dublin didn't see it that way. They impressed upon the king (Charles I) the necessity of bringing the revolt under control. He appointed the Duke of Ormonde as his Deputy and commander-in-chief.

One of the first actions of Ormonde was to march south to attempt the recovery of the town of Ross which was held by the rebels under the command

---

[589] The human suffering at this time, because of the awful trauma of the wars, coupled with the brutality inflicted upon the innocent, was unparalleled in Irish history. The visitation of the Cromwellians (following so closely on that of the Elizabethans) using all their calculated barbarity, ensured that the consequences of their cruelty and greed would reverberate right down to modern times. The accounts of the savagery of Cromwell's minions in Prendergast's *"Cromwellian Settlement of Ireland"*, would draw tears from a stone.

[590] Richard Butler, the 3rd. Viscount Mountgarret, who was elected the President of the Confederacy.

[591] He was the 2nd. son of the 4th. Viscount Gormanston. He was a professional soldier who fought in the Spanish Army with Owen Roe O'Neill. He fought in several engagements in the rebellion and he was in command of an army defeated by Cromwellians in 1647. He was made Viscount Tara by King Charles II (in exile), and in 1652 he escaped abroad to join the King. The title Visount Tara ceased upon the death of his grandson who was killed by the Blundells of Offaly in 1674.

of Captain Arthur Fox. The town was ably defended and Ormonde decided to raise the siege and return to Dublin. A few miles north of New Ross, at a place called Ballinvegga, he met the rebel forces under the command of Preston. It is said that the latter managed to 'snatch defeat from the jaws of victory'. Ormonde's forces were on the point of breaking, having been shocked by a furious charge from the rebel horsemen, but Preston refused to commit further troops and Ormonde had time to rally his men. In the counter-attack the rebels were routed and their baggage captured. It is said that over 600 rebels died in the battle.

The heroic charge was led by one of the Butlers and Sir Morgan Kavanagh who was most likely accompanied by his sons, Colonels Daniel[592] and Charles, and Captain James Nolan. Butler and Sir Morgan were killed in the battle, which took place on the 18th. March 1642.

Colonel Daniel, Charles and Captain James must have been involved in the next battle fought in the south east. It occurred in 1648. This was one of the civil war battles.

Lord Antrim had assembled a force of Scots near Wexford town under the command of Colonel Glengarry, his cousin. They were joined by the O'Byrnes and Kavanaghs. This group was loyal to Rinuccini, who, by his intransigent policies had split the confederates, but was supported by O'Neill.

The remnants of the Supreme Council ordered Lord Thomas Esmonde, who was now commander-in-chief of the Leinster forces, to attack them. He was supported by Lord Fleming of Slane and Colonel Pierce Fitzgerald.

The Glengarry/Kavanagh army moved towards Enniscorthy pursued by their enemies, who overtook them at Davidstown. There a battle was fought which resulted in the complete defeat of the Glengarry army which suffered losses of over 300 killed and 80 taken prisoner, including Glengarry himself.

It would seem that most of the Kavanagh/O'Byrne/Nolan faction escaped and lived to fight another day.

They appear to have escaped Ireton's attentions when he attacked and captured the castles of Leighlinbridge, Carlow and Tullow in the summer and autumn of 1650. These forts were then garrisoned with bands of Cromwellian soldiers who kept the area quiet.[593] It would seem that the stronghold of Clonmullen and the adjacent Duffry, still provided the Carlow/Wexford rebels with a safe sanctuary for a time.

---

[592] Daniel was ransomed about this time - he was being held as a hostage and was attending school in Dublin (probably Trinity College).

[593] Keeping the area 'quiet' included such actions as the destruction of Catholic churches. It is known for example that Barragh and Myshall Churches were destroyed at this time and only a few ruined walls remain today. The new chapel in Myshall was built c. 1776.

Their next important offensive was undertaken in the Spring of 1651. Cromwell[594] had left a Colonel Cook in charge of affairs in Wexford and Cook had placed a strong garrison in Enniscorthy and another in Ferns.[595] Early in 1651, because of the continued opposition of the Kavanagh/O'Nolan/O'Byrne faction a decree was passed excluding Wicklow, north Wexford and parts of Carlow from the 'protection of the Parliament'. In effect this gave a licence to the garrisons to kill anyone they pleased. On the 1st March they were given licence to 'take preys and booties'. In the first week of March the rebels moved against them and ambushed a party of soldiers at Scarawalsh, killing 50 of them. They then attacked and pillaged Enniscorthy.

Cook's response was immediate and painful. He moved into the area with a large company of soldiers and spent four days burning, looting and pillaging. He then moved up into Wicklow to continue his depredations.

Within a very short time many of the rebels took ship and went abroad.[596] It was estimated that as many as 40,000 young men, the remnants of the rebel armies, went abroad from all Ireland in this period, to seek service in Spain and France. The population was seriously diminished. The Cromwellians sent as many as 100,000 people to the Barbados to work the sugar plantations there. Starvation and disease accounted for over another half a million people in the twenty years from 1640 to 1660. In that time the

---

[594] Following the execution of King Charles I in January of 1649, Oliver Cromwell was appointed Commander-in-chief of the Army and Lord Lieutenant of Ireland. He landed in Dublin in August and sacked Drogheda in September, killing over 3000 people. He then moved to Wexford in October and when that town was captured (over 1000 killed), he moved on to New Ross which capitulated. From there he moved into Munster and became ill with malaria. He rested in Youghal until early in 1650 and then proceeded to mop up the rebel resistance groups. He captured Kilkenny in March. In May 1650 he went back to England leaving the army under the control of his son-in-law, Major General Ireton.

[595] According to local tradition a garrison was also placed in Huntingdon Castle in Clonegal. This, combined with the Carlow garrison, which was 600 strong, would have been utilised to keep the O'Nolans in check.

[596] Hore - History of the Town & County of Wexford Vol. 6 pg. 497 - it would seem that only one of the Kavanagh brothers went abroad as Charles was a prisoner in 1652. Daniel's property which included Clonmullen, Kilbranish, Barnahask and Barragh were confiscated following his attainder. It appears he went to Spain and was accompanied by Captain James Nolan and one Daniel Farrell who had been instrumental in the capture of Enniscorthy castle from its first Cromwellian commander Captain Todd. Charles must have obtained his release as he managed to hold on to Carrigduff by various means as we shall see later.

population sunk from one and half millions to about 500,000[597]. If one compares the present population of Carlow (c. 40,000) with the population at that time on a pro rata basis, it would seem that the population of the entire county was about 15,000 in 1640 and not more than 5,000 in 1660.[598]

As was mentioned, not all the rebels chose to go abroad and those that remained formed small groups of guerrilla fighters who took to the woods, making occasional forays against the soldiers and settlers. They became known as Tories. According to Berresford Ellis in his book To Hell or Connaught, "a plan was adopted to subdue the Tories by seeking to destroy their means of subsistence. No smiths, harness makers or armourers would be allowed to ply their trade outside the English garrisons. No beer, spirits or wine were to be sold, nor fairs or markets held, beyond garrison limits. A new Pale, the district within which the English held power, was to be formed from the Boyne river to the Barrow river.

The counties of Wicklow, parts of Dublin, Kildare and Carlow, where the Tories were particularly active, were to be excluded from 'protection' so that anyone found in arms in those areas after February 1652, was to be killed."

Cromwell's army had almost completed their work all over Ireland by the end of 1652 and then the business of considering how to distribute the confiscated lands began in earnest.

Dr. William Petty (portrait across) was appointed to carry out a survey of the entire island so that an equitable distribution could be made. This work became known as the 'Down Survey'.

It was a monumental work, requiring enormous skill and organisational ability. The actual work was not commenced until 1654 and then it took two years to complete.

In the meantime the Cromwellians began the work of revenge. Wild stories of hundreds of thousands of Protestants having been murdered in the

---

[597] "Hell or Connaught" - Berresford Ellis. Later historians have disputed these figures and it is thought that as many as a million people may have survived.

[598] In view of the above it was probably nearer to 10,000

1641 rebellion were believed and retribution was promised. Anyone who had been party to the killing of Protestants or Englishmen was to be tried and executed. One of the first men to be tried and shot was Colonel Walter Bagenal,[599] of Dunleckney, who had been a Royalist officer in the Confederacy and who had sentenced William Stone (a spy) to death, in 1642.

Dunleckney Manor

The work of trying to remove the landowners from their estates was now commenced also. The lands of all who had been in rebellion were declared confiscated. Some people managed to hold on to their lands by declaring themselves as 'innocents' i.e. they could prove that they had taken no part in the rebellion or they were too young at the time to be participants. All

---

[599] He was the grandson of Dudley Bagenal who had murdered Moriertagh Og Kavanagh of Garryhill. His estates were confiscated but when Charles II was restored to the monarchy Walter's son Dudley was reinstated in his lands and house. However his financial circumstances deteriorated very rapidly and by 1678 his debts were colossal, so much so that in the early decades of the 18th. century he was forced to sell off a lot of property in Dublin and Meath to the Earl of Shelburne for £30,000 (Land Registry Mss. Book 67 pg. 475)

landowners who were not guilty of murder were ordered to leave their lands and move into Connaught.

In the barony of Forth practically all the land owned by the O'Nolans and Kavanaghs was declared forfeit. A few managed to hold on. Many of the dispossessed joined the Tories. Colonel Lawrence stated that the areas in which the Tories were most active were Wexford, Kildare and Carlow where new landowners were often assassinated.

Major Charles Kavanagh, of Carrigduff, offered to combat the Tories in counties Wexford, Carlow, Kilkenny and Wicklow, in return for exemption from transplantation. He was given leave to select thirteen fellow Irishmen to form his band. He established his headquarters at Aghadagh[600], in an old castle. There he was well positioned to protect Leighlinbridge where convoys going from Kilkenny to Carlow were often ambushed by Tories. Captured Tories were either executed or sent to the West Indies.

In January 1654 the Governors of Carlow, Kilkenny, Clonmel, Wexford, Ross and Waterford had orders to arrest and deliver to Captain Thomas Morgan, Dudley North and John Johnson, English merchants, all wanderers, men and women, and such other Irish within their precincts as should not prove they had such a settled course of industry as yielded them a means of their own to maintain them, all such children as were in hospitals or workhouses, all prisoners, men and women, to be transported to the West Indies. In the course of four years they had seized and shipped about 6400 Irish men and women, boys and maidens.[601]

In Wicklow the O'Byrnes and the O'Tooles still held out in the mountains, but in 1656 they suffered a severe defeat at the hands of the Cromwellians, in an engagement near Dublin city, which effectively finished their resistance.

The Down Survey details for Co. Carlow compare in almost all details with the Books of Settlement and Distribution[602] which were drawn up after the Restoration of Charles II. These books give the grants of the Down Survey but with the modifications consequent to the Acts of Parliament granting reversions. So the names of all the grantees who were nominated to get lands in the Down Survey are not all included, but in the main they are very similar.

The native owners, meanwhile, were being pressurised into moving to Connaught. A Patrick O'Nolan of Shangarry was the only O'Nolan we know about who, according to Ryan in his History of Carlow, actually moved to lands in Connaught. It would seem that Sir Arthur Savage was the adventurer

---

[600] Agha - a townland about three miles east of Leighlinbridge

[601] Prendergast - *Cromwellian Settlement of Ireland.*

[602] See later in this chapter for the details of the grants as outlined in the Books of Settlement and Distribution dealing with the Barony of Forth.

who took over the lands in the area. The deadline for moving was extended from May 1654 to March 1655. Those who didn't join the Tories and who didn't wish to move to Connaught, chose to stay in their native country accepting roles such as labourers and ploughmen.

The Tories continued to be active and in 1659 after the death of Cromwell and seeing the increasing likelihood of Charles II being restored, they became even more of a threat. So much so that Garret Kinsella, a well known Tory leader in Co. Carlow was offered an amnesty if he changed sides and became a Tory hunter. When he refused, Colonel Pretty, who was the commander for the Carlow region was given permission to employ twenty Irishmen for the purpose and was given leave to arm them with guns and ammunition.[603]

The priests were harried and hunted and shared the same fate as the Tories i.e. execution or banishment.[604]

Dr. Dempsey who had been appointed Bishop of Leighlin on March 10th. 1642, died in Spain in September 1658 aged 56 years.

Between 1658 and 1678 (when the diocese was amalgamated with Kildare) it was under the care of Vicars.

In 1662 the Vicar General for the Diocese was Dr. Charles Nolan.[605] In 1657 Fr. Agapitus of the Holy Ghost order, who was running the affairs of the Carmelite Order was in Dublin. He reported that there were about 12 priests in Dublin who ministered to their flocks in disguise. Fr. Agapitus had several narrow escapes and once in the company of Dr. Charles Nolan he just managed to escape from pursuing troopers by running into a wood and hiding.[606]

Ormonde, as the owner of much of the Barony of Forth, had his estates confiscated,[607] but a sizeable portion of his property was in his wife's name and she, as an 'innocent' and a Protestant did not have to forfeit her lands. In any event after the Restoration the Earl of Ormonde (created Duke of Ormonde in 1661) was immediately granted back his lands.[608] By 1670 he and

---

[603] 'Hell or Connaught' - Berresford Ellis

[604] At a public Mass in the Square in Tullow, in 1929, a Mass Stone was used which had been in use in Penal Times. It was in the possession of Mr. Garret Moore.

[605] Probably either a Kilbride or a Ballykealy O'Nolan. Charles was a loose Anglicisation of Cahir.

[606] 'Hell or Connaught' - Berresford Ellis

[607] It would seem (from Ryan pg. 204) that the adventurer who was granted the Duke of Ormonde's lands was Sir Arthur Savage whose son Philip is mentioned in the Book of Settlement as the purchaser of certain lands in Forth at the end of the century.

[608] In 1661 the members of the Irish Parliament petitioned that the soldiers and adventurers who were removed from the Duke of Ormonde's lands be given other confiscated lands in

his third son, Richard, who became Viscount Tullagh and Earl of Arran, seem to have acquired the ownership of most of the Barony of Forth and the former owners the O'Nolans now became tenants on small holdings.

It is interesting to see how tenancies were granted. As I have no knowledge of any document relating to the granting of lands to an O'Nolan, by the Earl of Arran, I will use the following as an example.

In 1668 the Earl of Arran, Richard Butler, granted a lease of Ballykealy lands to Michael Smith on the lives of himself and his son Joseph at a rent of £49 sterling and in 1722 Joseph Smith let the lands[609] to his son Michael, of Ballyneskeagh, Co. Meath, for a period of 71 years and in the same year the lands were let to Caroline Gill of Dublin, who was probably another merchant banker, for £130.

Sometime after 1668 the Smiths borrowed money from Mark Bagot and his son John Bagot and mortgaged the property to them, but the property seems to have been redeemed by 1710.

The Smiths, of course, were middlemen, and they in turn let the lands to smallholders in return for rents which must have been paid either in money or in kind - i.e. by giving animals or crops. Many of their tenants must have been O'Nolans.

Sometime during the Cromwellian period, a law was passed compelling the Irish to dwell in towns and villages. It is probable that clusters of primitive houses began to appear at that time in places such as Ballon, Ballon Hill, Boggan, Kilbride, Myshall, Raheenleigh, Clonmullen, Kilbranish, Aghade, Ardattin and many more.

The Restoration of Charles II was perceived by many of the Irish as the dawning of a new era where wrongs would be righted and religious persecution would become a thing of the past. But this was not to be. Of the thousands of people all over Ireland, who petitioned to have their lands restored, less than 900 succeeded and in many instances these cases dragged on for years. The new Cromwellian owners clung tenaciously to what they were granted. In 1641 Catholics accounted for 60 per cent of the landownership in Ireland. This had shrunk to less than 9 per cent in 1659 and after the Restoration it revived to only 20 per cent. In the barony of Forth, the situation was a curious one, since virtually the only people to be reinstated were the Duke of Ormonde[610] and the Butlers who were theoretically Protestants.

Carlow and if sufficient lands were not available there they urged the king to grant them lands in other counties. This request was embodied in a later Act of Parliament.

[609] Excepting the Quaker burial ground.

[610] It is most likely that Piers Roe, the 8t. Earl of Ormonde and his son James were Catholics or perhaps lukewarm Protestants. However Thomas, the 10th. Earl (Black Tom) was very definitely a staunch Protestant as he had been educated in the court and was a

The ownership of lands by the Catholic families of Forth had dwindled to almost nothing during the Cromwellian epoch and there was little or no change during the Restoration period. While there were many claims lodged in Chancery Courts in the period up to 1690 many of them were never settled and under the new regime, in the aftermath of the Jacobite wars, they were quietly dropped. Judging by the land transactions of the early 1700s only a couple of O'Nolans owned any land at all at that stage and this will be dealt with in the next chapter.

If we examine the data detailing the owners of lands as recorded in the Book of Settlement & Distribution we see that the Catholic ownership of lands amounted to just over 50% of the 32,353 acre total, while the Protestant ownership excluding the Butler/Ormonde lands was quite small indeed at about 10%.

Name of Proprietors 1641	
Kavanaghs	5617
Nowlans	2335
Tirlough Line	1215
O'Neales	1211
Henry Gormagan	120
Edmund Bryan	470
Owen Birne	231
Patrick Esmonde	1593
Oliver Eustace	1857
John Barry	1179
Ald Kennedy	331
Edward Wall	140
Total Catholic	**16299**
Henry Warren	975
Henry Gremack	803
Dr. Thomas Arthur	324
E. Percevall	372
Sir Wm. Reeves	756
Total Protestant	**3230**
Earl of Ormonde	5954
Sir Thomas Butler	6807
Sir Theobald Butler	63
Total Butler	**12824**

If we contrast this with the ownership of the lands finally granted we see that the Catholic ownership was now at zero though upon examination it can be seen that some of the old Anglo Irish families had managed to retain their

---

favourite of Queen Elizabeth, to whom he was related. Walter the 11th. Earl (a nephew of Black Tom and son of John Butler of Kilcash) and his son James may well have been more inclined towards the Catholic religion as they were close adherents of King Charles.

lands by having their sons change their religion as in the cases of Francis Eustace and Sir Lawrence Esmonde whose father and brother respectively were Catholics. It is noteworthy that none of the old Gaelic owners are listed here, though it would seem that they did in fact manage to hold on to some small amounts of land as in the case of Lawrence Nowlan, who owned lands in the early part of the next century. These may have been accounted for in the miscellaneous section entitled 'Undesignated lands' or they may have been claimants when the Act of Settlement was repealed in 1689.

Grantee	Transferred
Sir Richard Kennedy	2630
Duke of Ormonde	6102
Philip Savage	2071
Francis Eustace	1874
Henry Warren	1354
Earl of Anglesey	1994
Earl of Arran	324
Ml. & Ann Barry	471
Sir Lce. Esmonde	843
Thomas Piggott	808
Wm. Draper	423
Ulick Wall	127
Wm. Reeves Prot.	292
Earl of Kildare	330
Wm. Cooke of Rathrush	28
Richard Warburton	144
George Sandfield	30
James Stopford	30
Grantees in 1654	7984
Protestant Land	4325
Undesignated Lands	5453
Total Lands	**37637**

The actual transfer of the lands is interesting in itself. The following table shows the owners, lands and grantees in 1666.

Owners 1641	Grantee 1666	Townland	Acres
	Protestant Land	Fenagh & Myshall	126
	Warren Henry	Ballon Hill	52
Arthur Dr. T.	Arran Earl of	Newtown	324
Barry Ann	Barry Ann	Kilbride	144
Barry Ann	Barry Ann	Kilpatrick	40
Barry John	Barry Ml.	Rainesh	600
Barry John	Barry Ml.	Milltown	173
Barry John I.P.	Barry Ml.	Arbon	66
Barry John I.P.	Barry Ml.	Torman (pt. of)	48

Barry John I.P.	Duke of Orm.	Ballykealy	61
Barry John I.P.	Eustace Fra.	Kilknock	12
Barry Thomas	Grantee in 1654	Ardbearn	35
Birne Owen	Draper Wm.	Coolroe	231
Birne Tirlogh		Boggan	54
Birne Tirlogh	Duke of Orm.	Ballymogue	184
Birne Tirlogh	Duke of Orm.	Carrickslaney	200
Birne Tirlogh	Duke of Orm.	Carrickslaney	341
Birne Tirlogh	Duke of Orm.	Myshall	438
Bryan Edmund	Duke of Orm.	Shraugh	346
Bryan Edward	Duke of Orm.	Kilcoole	124
Butler Lady	Butler Lady		28
Butler Lady	Prot. land	(Mahone)	1350
Butler Lady	Prot. land	Barragh par.	320
Butler Lady	Prot. land	Mahone td. in ?	238
Butler Lady	Protestant Land	Shangarry	1017
Butler Lady	Prot. land	Barragh part of	209
Butler Lady	Protestant Land	Ballon - a bog	567
Butler Sir Theobald		Cappagh+Ballon	68
Butler Sir Thomas		Lisgarvan	30
Butler Sir T.	Grantee in 1654	Ardagheen	52
Butler Sir T.	Grantee in 1654	Bainasragh?	103
Butler Sir T.	Grantee in 1654	Ballintemple	395
Butler Sir T.	Grantee in 1654	Clonacona	102
Butler Sir T.	Grantee in 1654	Knockatubbrid	80
Butler Sir T.	Grantee in 1654	Knockbarragh	112
Butler Sir T.	Grantee in 1654	Knockbrack	60
Butler Sir T.	Grantee in 1654	Levebrie	5000
Butler Sir T.	Grantee in 1654	Newtown	198
Butler Sir T.	Grantee in 1654	Raheenardagh	148
Butler Sir T.	Grantee in 1654	Ratheeragh	72
Butler Sir T.	Grantee in 1654	Rathvarrin	140
Butler Sir T.	Grantee in 1654?	Ballinacrea	100
Butler Sir T.	Grantee in 1654?	Ballaghmore	138
Butler Sir T.	Grantee in 1654 ?	Lasmaconly	48
Butler Sir T.	Grantee in 1654?	Ullard - pt. of	29
Byrne Gerald	Grantee in 1654	Ballyleen	108
Churchlands	Eustace Fra.	Garreenleen	133
Churchlands	Eustace Fra.	Gilbertstown	143
Churchlands	Wall Ulick	Killane (pt. of)	11
Cooke Wm. of Rathrush		Ullard pt. of	28
Esmonde Patk.	Esmonde Law.	Clonegal	339
Esmonde Patk.	Kildare Earl of	Clonogan	389
Esmonde Patk.	Esmonde Sir L.	Farrenoneile Wood	147
Esmonde Patk.	Esmonde Sir L.	Barragh Wd.	446
Eustace Edmund		Garreenleen	40
Eustace Oliver		Gilbertstown	50
Eustace Oliver		Kilcoole	25
Eustace Oliver		Kilknock & Ballyveal	520
Eustace Oliver		Lisgarvan (pt. of)	30
Eustace Oliver		Ullard	40

Eustace Oliver	Duke of Orm.	Killinaglasse	48
Eustace Oliver	Eustace Francis	Ballynunnery	114
Eustace Oliver	Eustace Fra.	Ballymogue	74
Eustace Oliver	Eustace Fra.	Beddingstowne	240
Eustace Oliver	Eustace Fra.	Bendenstown	23
Eustace Oliver	Eustace Fra.	Kilknock	722
Eustace Oliver	Eustace Fra.	Knockaymoy	19
Eustace Oliver	Eustace Fra.	Lisgarvan	21
Eustace Oliver	Eustace Fra.	TemplePeter	12
Eustace Oliver	Eustace Fra.	Turtane	85
Eustace Oliver	Eustace Fra.	Killinaglasse	48
Eustace Oliver	Grantee in 1654	Bendenstown	100
Eustace Oliver	Wall Ulick	TemplePeter	133
Gormagan Henry	Duke of Orm.	Ballygarret	350
Gormagan Henry	Duke of Orm.	Ballykealy	408
Gormagan Henry	Duke of Orm.	Ballyvolden	45
Gormagan Henry	Grantee in 1654	Ballygarret	120
Harman Edward	Grantee in 1654	Ballybeg	40
Kavanagh Art	Grantee of 1654	Knockshane	450
Kavanagh Art	Reeves Wm. Prot.	Cranemore	292
Kavanagh Danl.	Anglesey Earl of	Carrickduff	162
Kavanagh Danl.	Anglesey Earl of	Clonmullen	353
Kavanagh Danl.	Anglesey Earl of	Kilgraney	257
Kavanagh Danl.	Anglesey Earl of	Kilgraney wood	85
Kavanagh Danl.	Anglesey Earl of	Wd & Mountain	673
Kavanagh Danl.	Butler Eliz.	Myshall / Shangarry Woods	102
Kavanagh Danl.	Eustace Fra.	Ullartmore, wood of	51
Kavanagh Danl.	Warren Henry	Ullartmore	109
Kavanagh Danl.	Anglesey Earl of	Barragh	126
Kavanagh Murtagh	Grantee in 1654	Ballintrane Lower	120
Kavanagh Murt.	Grantee in 1654	Ballymogue	100
Kavanagh Murt.	Kennedy Sir R.	Ballaghaderneen	32
Kavanagh Murt.	Kennedy Sir R.	Ballaghaderneen Wood	812
Kavanagh Murt.	Kennedy Sir R.	Ballyleagh & Rathleagh	571
Kavanagh Murt.	Kennedy Sir R.	Clony (Clonee)	276
Kavanagh Murt.	Kennedy SirR.	Glasgrany	114
Kavanagh Murt.	Kennedy Sir R.	Knockdramagh	175
Kavanagh Murt.	Kennedy Sir R.	Shane	163
Kavanagh Murt.	Sandfield Geo.	Myshall & Rusleagh	576
Kennedy Ald.	Kennedy Ald. Pr.	Ballmoardy	131
Kennedy Ald. Ir. Papist			22
Kennedy Ald. I.P.	Kennedy Ald. Prot.	Ballintrane	178
Nolan Dermot	Grantee of 1654?	Cappagh	33
Nowlan Charles	Warburton Rchd.	Kilbrickan	144
Nowlan Daniel	Warren Henry	Ballykeenan	108
Nowlan Garret		Tindclane	175
Nowlan Garret	Grantee in 1654	Ballykealy	344
Nowlan Patrick	Duke of Orm.	Ballinrush	120
Nowlan Patrick	Duke of Orm.	Ballinrush	380
Nowlan Patrick	Duke of Orm.	Shangarry	413
Nowlan Patrick	Duke of Orm.	Cronepurseen	222

Nowlan Philip	Grantee in 1654	Ballydrom	100
Nowland Garret	Warren Henry	Ballon	145
Nowland Garret	Warren Henry	Cunnygar	151
O'Neale Donough	Draper Wm.	Owlert	192
O'Neale Don.	Piggott Thomas	Kilcarry	313
O'Neale Don.	Piggott Thomas	Monaghrim	272
O'Neale Don.	Piggott Thomas	Monaghrim Hill	90
O'Neale Hugh	Piggott Thomas	Ballyredmond	223
O'Neale Hugh	Piggott Thomas	Ballyredmond pt. of	121
Ormonde Earl of	Duke of Orm.	Kilbride	539
Ormonde Earl of	Duke of Orm.	Kilbride & Boggan	86
Ormonde Earl of	Duke of Orm.	Kilgraney	115
Ormonde Earl of	Duke of Orm.	Kilgraney	215
Ormonde Earl of	Duke of Orm.	Kilkeele	127
Ormonde Earl of	Duke of Orm.	Kilkeele Wood	357
Ormonde Earl of	Duke of Orm.	Rathoe	350
Percevall E.	Prot. land	Gravens (Mahone)	372
Reeves Sir Wm.		Cranemore Mountain	293
Reeves Sir Wm.		Mountain nr. Mt. Leinster	463
Wall Edward	Wall Ulick	Claneshannon	116
Wall Edward	Wall Ulick	Grange Pedowe	24
Warren Henry	Grantee in 1654	Ballintrane Upper	100
Warren Henry	Warren Henry	Aghclare/Coolnachegan	110
Warren Henry	Warren Henry	Ballinvalley	32
Warren Henry	Warren Henry	Laragh	44
Warren Henry	Warren Henry	Raheenkillen	52
Warren Henry	Warren Henry	Killane & Garriarte	148
Warren Henry	Warren Henry	Ballykeenan	70
Warren Henry	Warren Henry	Graiguealug	120
Warren Henry	Warren Henry	Aclare	269
Warren Henry	Warren Henry	Ullard pt. of	30

By analysing the data[611] we can see for example that the Barrys managed to hold on to most of their lands which seem to have been transferred from John Barry, who is described, interestingly enough, as an Irish Papist,[612] to his son Michael Barry who is described in the original document, as a Protestant.

Tirlogh Birne and Edmund Bryan both lost out to the Duke of Ormonde and it is likely that in the Cromwellian grant that Sir Arthur Savage was the recipient.

The lands of Patrick Esmonde, an Irish Papist, were all granted to Sir Lawrence Esmonde, a Protestant. They were brothers and were both sons of Sir Thomas Esmonde, a Confederate leader in 1646.

---

[611] I have put in the modern spelling of townslands where possible.

[612] He was the descendant of John Barry who was the recipient of a huge grant of lands in 1550 which has already been alluded to.

Oliver Eustace was also described as an Irish Papist. He was a lateral descendant of the 1st. Viscount Baltinglass. His lands were, in the main, transferred to his son Francis Eustace who became a Protestant, though his involvement in the army of King James, in 1690 would seem to belie his acceptance of the state religion.

The Earl of Anglesey seems to have got most of Daniel Kavanagh's lands and Sir Richard Kennedy appears to have got most of Murtagh Kavanagh's[613] lands, while George Sandfield got almost 500 acres, plantation measure, in the Myshall area. Alderman Kennedy took the precaution of turning Protestant and so secured his lands.

The O'Nolans fared no better than the Kavanaghs and the Duke of Ormonde became the owner of Patrick Nowlans Shangarry/Ballinrush lands[614] - later disputed by Captain James Nolan. Henry Warren[615] was another who benefited from the destruction of the O'Nolans and Sir Arthur Savage, the unsettled Cromwellian grantee, was given small parcels of lands in Carrickslaney, Boggan, Ballymogue, Ballinvalley and Laragh.[616]

Thomas Piggott who got most of the O'Neale lands may have been one of the Raheenduff (Co. Laois) Piggotts or he may have been a Cromwellian adventurer or soldier as probably was Wm. Draper.

The evidence would seem to indicate that the Duke of Ormonde, either personally or through his agents and in total agreement with his cronies Sir Richard Kennedy, Henry Warren and the other grantees, accomplished the final rape of the native Irish clans.

In the matter of religion, during the Restoration period, the penal laws were relaxed somewhat but in the main Catholics received little or no reprieve from the hardships imposed during the Cromwellian period.[617] With the accession of James II, who succeeded his brother Charles II in 1685, matters improved and priests could move around the country unmolested.

---

[613] Murtagh was a descendant of Moriertagh Og of Garryhill.

[614] The O'Nolans must have successfully reclaimed some of their lands during the Restoration as Lawrence Nolan was the owner of considerable lands in Shangarry in the early 1700s.

[615] Possibly a descendant of Captain Humphrey Warren who came to Ireland in the mid 1500s. Humphrey's son, Henry, was an English official who had a direct meeting with the Earl of Tyrone in 1595. Henry was married to a daughter of Adam Loftus and was made Sir Henry at a later date. It is probable that Henry Warren who had the lands in Forth was a son of his. The Warrens also had lands in Cork, Meath and Kildare at one time or another.

[616] Ryan's History of Carlow

[617] From the time of Henry VIII up to the time of the Restoration over 300 clerics were killed in Ireland by government forces.

The thirty years between 1660 and 1690 were relatively trouble free, in the sense that there was no Irish rebellion, but the dispossessed native Irish gentry and their descendants, who had got no satisfaction from their claims to be reinstated in their lands were still most aggrieved and many joined the dwindling ranks of the Tories who continued to hide out in the woods making forays against the unwary planters.

It was a period of relative prosperity when the new landlords began to apply themselves to improving their estates and building suitable houses. A road network was begun which formed the basis of the modern roads system. Hedgerows began to appear and more and more land was reclaimed from forest and bog.

Because most of Forth was now owned by the Duke of Ormonde it would appear that no big houses[618] were built in the barony during the remainder of the century, with the possible exceptions of Kilconnor, Ballintemple and Ballykealy. It is likely also that the Warrens built a house in the area. Ormonde of course spent lavish amounts of money on his Kilkenny, Carrig-on-Suir and Dunmore properties which at the time were much talked about because of their grandeur and style.

Ballintemple - burnt accidentally in 1917

---

[618] Substantial houses as opposed to grand houses were built by the tenantry - for example Millpark House in Kilbride was built in the early part of the century for a daughter of Rev. Henry Echlin, the Bishop of Down and Connor and it came into the possession of the Tomlinson family around 1670 - see *The Carlow Gentry* by Jimmy O'Toole

The descendants of the dispossessed Irish chieftains, who still held lands in 1641 were given great hope when in 1689 the Irish Parliament convened by the Duke of Tyrconnell[619] decided to repeal the Act of Settlement. Under the terms of this Repeal they (along with all the other dispossessed) were given liberty to take steps to recover lands lost during the Cromwellian Confiscations. Of course they were given very little time to commence their litigation as the Williamite Wars overtook and overshadowed all other events. The Ulster Protestants were the first to resist and the resultant siege of Derry was quickly followed by the defeats of the Boyne and the disastrous one at Aughrim (Co. Galway). The treaty of Limerick negotiated by Patrick Sarsfield, which in theory safeguarded the rights of Catholics was quickly forgotten when Sarsfield and his army were shipped to France. But the Catholic landowners of Connaught seem to have benefited from the treaty insofar as their rights to lands were preserved if they could show that they were not proactive on the side of James II during the war. In this way the O'Nolans of Galway managed to survive into the 18th. century and beyond as considerable landowners.

We do not know how many O'Nolans enlisted in the Irish Army of King James II but it is highly likely that many of them did. We do know that Colonel Charles Kavanagh of Carrigduff, the Tory hunter of earlier times, who must have been a man in his sixties at the time, was commissioned to raise an infantry regiment in the area. This regiment participated in the siege of Derry and later went to Waterford. When that city surrendered they were allowed to go to Cork. It was at Cork that the regiment surrendered to the Williamites and Charles Kavanagh along with his fellow officers, twenty six of his men and his son Morgan were imprisoned on a warship - the Breda - which blew up in the harbour killing many on board including Charles. His son Morgan was blown into the sea but escaped unharmed.[620]

With the defeat of the Jacobites and the forced emigration of the Irish - Catholic armies the country was left to the conquerors. The refugee Protestant - English planters returned and claimed the lands once again . The descendants of the chiefs of the O'Nolans, O'Byrnes, O'Moores, O'Tooles and Kavanaghs either left the country or accepted tenancies where they could. Many were forced to migrate to the towns and villages that sprung up in the early part of

---

[619] Richard Talbot (of Malahide), a Catholic, who had fought the Cromwellians in 1649 and who was restored to his lands after the Restoration, was made Lord Deputy in 1687 and Commander-in-Chief of King James's Irish Army.
[620] *Buncloidi - A History of the District* by An tAthair S. De Val.

the 18th. century. There they took up work as tradesmen and labourers[621]. Very few managed to hold on to land.

Very little land in Carlow was forfeited as a result of the Williamite wars. According to Simms in his book The Williamite Confiscations only four landowners in Carlow forfeited land. They were Dudley Bagenal 403 acres, Charles Byrne 150 acres, King James II 768 acres and John Warren 260 acres. The lands were sold and the new owners were Catherine Johnson, Sir Wm. Robinson, Walter Stephens, Richard Tighe, Walter Weldon and Richard Wolseley[622].

Three Nowlans are mentioned as owners or occupiers of lands in the closing decade of the century. They were John Nowlan who claimed he had a lease of three lives on part of the lands of Shangarry and Ballinrush. By a lease dated 1669 Richard the Earl of Arran leased the lands to Thomas Bagenal to hold in trust for the claimant - John Nowlan.[623] I think this John Nowlan was the son of Patrick O'Nolan who had been dispossessed by the Ormondes earlier in the century. He must then have been the father of Lawrence Nowlan, gent., who carried out numerous land transactions in the early part of the next century.

Edmond Nowlan had a 21 yr. lease of Cappawater dating from 1686 from the late proprietor John Warren and Margaret Nowlan, spinster, had a lease dating from 1687 from John Warren for 200 acres in Aclare and Coolnasheegan.

Apart from these three claimants subsequent to the Williamite wars we must assume that the O'Nolans had almost entirely disappeared in the barony of Forth as the landowning elite that they once were.

The large landowners in Forth at the close of the 17th. century were the Ormondes, the Earl of Arran, the Warrens in the person of Maurice Warren who claimed the lands of John Warren (attainted in the Jacobite war), the

---

[621] Very few seem to have moved out of the area in the period 1650 - 1690 as in the Carlow town census of 1669 there were only six or seven Nolans living in the town and in the Hearth Money Rolls for Dublin there was only about the same number.

[622] He bought the lands near Tullow which became known as the Wolseley estate or Mount Wolseley. According to Jimmy O'Toole the family owned over 2000 acres in Co. Carlow and as much in Co. Wicklow. The most well known people in the family were Sir Garnet Wolseley who was Commander-in-Chief of the British Army in the last decade of the 19th. century and his younger brother Frederick after whom the Wolseley motor car was named by his friend and business partner Herbert Austin, Austin Car Manufacturer.

[623] From this evidence we can see that the Catholic landowners tried every subterfuge possible to conceal their ownership of lands and they were accommodated by the likes of the Earl of Arran and the Bagenals.

Eustaces, the Butlers in Ballintemple and the Baggots in the person of Mark Baggot, who managed to salvage much of the estates of John[624], his father.

New names began to appear such as Doyne, Wolseley, Burdett and Paul. Doyne was an offshoot of the Doynes of Wells in Co. Wexford and Burdett was an English Protestant who took up a lease on Garryhill (from Viscount Duncannon) and went to live there where he was noted as a notorious bigot who was disliked by many of his fellow landlords[625].

---

[624] John Baggot was the 'receiver' in the county prior to the Jacobite war but was noted as a Catholic 'rebel'. He and his son Mark were two of the first freemen of Carlow town under the charter granted by James II. Mark Baggot went to live in Dublin around the close of the century, but was still involoved in his land holdings in the early decades of the next century. They came originally from Bagotstown in Co. Limerick. John Baggot married Helen the daughter of William Cooke of Painestown (Oak Park) and Mark was his son. Mark (who married Ann Hudson) was the father of John Baggot the first of the family to settle at Castle Bagot near Rathcoole in Co. Dublin. Mark's son John died in 1792 and his son James John Baggot died in 1860. He was buried with his father John in Newcastle Lyons Churchyard. They continued as landlords in Forth down to that time. In 1847 J.J. Baggot wrote a letter of sympathy to his tenant Edmond Nolan on the death of Edmond's father - the first of the Knockendrane family to settle at Ballinrush.
[625] Jimmy O'Toole - *The Carlow Gentry*

Chapter 21

The O'Nolans in the 18th. century

After 1690 the numbers of Catholics applying to the courts to have their lands returned diminished dramatically. From that time onwards the land was settled on the landlords some of whom continued in ownership right up to the 20th. century. Many of those owners were descendants of Cromwellian grantees and others were grandee tenants of the Ormondes[626] and their ilk such as the Annesleys who owned much of North Wexford and were the owners of Barragh in Forth. As already mentioned the large landowners in Forth at the close of the 17th. century were the Ormondes, the Earl of Arran, the Warrens in the Eustaces, the Butlers in Ballintemple and the Baggots in the person of Mark Baggot. The Whaleys[627] of Castletown seem to have acquired ownership of considerable lands in the Myshall area during the 18th. century which they sold or leased to Robert Cornwall. Others to grace the scene were Doynes, Wolseleys, Burdetts and Pauls. Ten of the original Cromwellian planters in Carlow were Quakers (four of them were ex-soldiers) but five of the Quaker Cromwellians had left the area by 1700.

Minor players such as Robert Lecky and John Watson who were Quakers[628] had purchased or leased lands in and around Fenagh prior to 1678 when the first Meeting House (of Quakers) was established at Kilconnor. According to Jimmy O'Toole Watson was imprisoned for a time and his land forfeited as Quakerism was as much frowned upon as Catholicism. Kilconnor became the centre for Quakers in Co. Carlow and in the next twenty years 33 Quaker families from different parts of Ireland moved into the Fenagh area. They were leased small farms by Lecky and Watson. Lecky had purchased or leased 548 acres in Ballykealy and 335 acres in Ballinadrum while Watsons owned 354 acres.

The Quaker tenants included Wrights, Bornes (from Wicklow), Boles (from Tipperary) , Burtons (from Laois) and Malouns (Malones). By 1839 the

---

[626] Some were purchasers of Ormonde lands.

[627] Whaleys were closely related to the Cromwells and benefited considerably from the Confiscations and distribution of lands. They owned Castletown and 4000 acres of land in the county. Richard 'Burn' Chappell Whaley was a notorious priest hunter who died in 1769. Fortunately for the county the Whaleys only came to Carlow in 1763.

[628] Watson was not a Quaker but his grandson became one. Watson had an only daughter who married Robert Lecky. It was Robert Lecky's son - John Watson III who became a Quaker and who built the Meeting House.

Quakers had been absorbed into the general community and had almost disappeared as a minor religion in the area.

There were other minor players too such as John Swift an uncle of Dean Swift who owned an estate in Ballynunnery.

The century must have been one of breathtaking change. It was during the 1700s that field enclosures became the norm. Estates were laid out and houses built.[629] The road system was put in place and many bridges were built.

It would seem from new evidence now appearing that the Penal Laws were not enforced as rigorously during the 18th. century as they were in the Cromwellian period. Certainly by 1730 there was serious relaxation of the laws as they applied to property. If one were to go by the strict letter of the law Catholics could own very little, but the sheer volume of memorials of deeds transacted by Catholics gives the lie to this.

Between 1708 and 1785 there were over 400 recorded memorials of deeds involving Nolans, Nowlans or Nowlands. As the century progressed the numbers increased, indicating that more and more Catholics were being allowed to transfer properties.

Quite a large number of these transactions involved Nolans etc., living in Dublin where the properties being leased, sold or transferred were houses. Some of the memorials refer to Marriage Settlements, others to mortgages and one to the discovery of Catholic lands[630]. However a good number of the transactions involved Nolans or Nowlans or Nowlands in other parts of the country including Carlow, Galway, Mayo and Cork.

Lawrence Nolan, gentleman, of Shangarry, Co. Carlow, was involved in a transaction concerning 200 acres in Shangarry in 1713. He and Gregory Nolan of Dublin, gentleman, sold or leased the land to Jeremiah Quill. The land was 'late in the possession of John Butler'. The lands described thus: - part of Shangarry mearing on the one side to the lands of Shangarry owned by widow Elizabeth Nolan, on another side Ballinrush and on the other side Myshall & Lasmaconly. It would seem that the Nolans had a 30 year lease on the lands. Mark Baggot was mentioned in the sale. He was to get £60 annually and Nolan was to get 1s. It would seem that Baggot had financed Nolan and held the lease as security.

A Lawrence Nolan, gentleman, of Clonleagh[631] in Co. Carlow was a party to a transaction involving land in Co. Meath in 1730. It would seem from the memorial that Walter Bagenal mortgaged the lands for £175. The parties to

---

[629] For example Myshall Lodge was built by Robert Cornwall and Hollybrook House by Henry Feltus during the 18th. century.

[630] It would appear from the deed that a Thomas Nolan from Tralee was involved in the discovery of concealed lands in Co. Kerry in 1754. (No. 117924)

[631] Probably Clonee which is adjacent to Shangarry.

the agreement were; Samuel Cotton of London, Edward Foley of Dublin and Lawrence Nolan of Clonleagh in Co. Carlow, gentleman, of the first part and Henry Earl of Shelburne of the 2nd. part, William Martin of Lincoln's Inn, Middlesex and James Macullock (a gentleman of his Majesty's Privy Chamber) of the 3rd. part and Alex Hamilton of Dublin of the 4th. part.

In 1733 Lawrence Nolan of Clonleagh in Co. Carlow was a party to a sale of land in Knockduff, Scarawalsh Barony, from a Mr. Camack to Arthur Gore. Again in 1736 Lawrence was involved in a transaction of Lease and Release to Michael Boote of Dublin. It would seem that Lawrence Nolan owed Boote £400 (a very considerable sum of money in those days). He seems to have sold him his interest in the following lands :- "All that and those the town and lands of Cronrus with its commonage and appurtenances, likewise all that part of Shangarry of which is the real estate of the said Lawrence Nolan which was not purchased by the late Earl of Arran formerly and commonly known and distinguished by the name of Ticullum, Ardbearn, Mortallunarin and Killavee with their appurtenances situate in the barony of Forth, Co. Carlow and which said granted premises contain by confirmation 300 acres more or less. To have and to hold the said granted property and every part thereof in as full and ample a manner as Lawrence Nolan and his under tenants then held and enjoyed, the same to the said Michael Boote, his heirs and assigns from thenceforth for ever with a covenant for peaceable enjoyment of the same also a proviso for redemption upon said Lawrence Nolan, his heirs and assigns, on payment to said Michael Boote, his heirs or assigns, such sum of money as shall on a fair account appear to be due to Michael Boote. That then the said granted and sold premises shall be returned to the said Lawrence Nolan his heirs etc., and then the Deeds of Lease and Release shall be null and void which Deeds are witnessed by John Nolan, eldest son and heir to Lawrence Nolan, and James Loughlin caretaker and apprentice to the said Michael Boote..."

This Lawrence Nolan would seem to be the man who was married to Ann Wright, a Quaker, of Kilconnor, Fenagh. According to the notes about this family written by Eddie Nolan in the 1920s Lawrence Nolan was 'evicted'[632] from his Shangarry lands and bought 400 acres in Knockendrane (Barony of Idrone) from Lord Duncannon.[633] He was the ancestor of a large number of families about whom more will be written later.

---

[632] It is more than likely that his holding in Lisgarvan was a leasehold and that the lease had expired.

[633] Brabazon Ponsonby the 2nd Viscount Duncannon and 2nd. Earl of Bessborough (Co. Kilkenny). William Ponsonby, his grandfather was a Cromwellian officer who acquired considerable lands in Ireland after 1654 by buying up debentures from his fellow officers and soldiers.

John Nolan of Bahana gave a 21 yr. lease to Paul Nolan of Shangarry of lands in Shangarry in 1746, called Brettace and Tycollum and also part of Ardbearn at an annual rent of 7s. 9d. per acre. John Nolan must be John the eldest son of Lawrence mentioned above. It is not clear why he was living in Bahana. He may have married a lady in that area.

Lawrence Nolan of Whitenhall, Co. Kilkenny was party to a marriage contract made between himself and his daughter's husband, Ebenezer Warren of Kilkenny city and Viscount Mountgarret and Folliott Warren of the third part in 1766. The latter two were to act as executors to see that the contract was fulfilled. It seems that Lawrence Nolan paid a sum of £800 as a dowry for his daughter, Mary, and Ebenezer agreed to provide her with £80 per annum should she survive Ebenezer. In order to make sure of the £80 Ebenezer paid over £400 of the money he received to the Viscount Mountgarret and in addition he paid a sum of £1000 out of his own pocket. Piers Byrne of the city of Dublin, gent., was the witness. From this we might assume that Ebenezer was in fact somewhat elderly.

The Warren contact with the Nolans did not end there as some time afterwards William Warren leased lands at Tinnaclash to a Michael Nolan which were assigned to Lawrence Nolan of Knockendrane. Lawrence, himself, then assigned the lands to Luke Nolan of Tinnaclash. Others mentioned in the convoluted memorial were Norbert Graham who was owed money and Cuthbert Feltus who ' took four notes' (valued at £32. 4s. 6d.) from Luke Nolan.

At about the same time (1770s) a Graves Chamney rented lands from Richard Nolan and others. The lands included Bendenstown, Gilbertstown, Garreenleen and part of Kilknock, formerly the estate of Edmund Eustace the Elder. Robert Warren was also involved in this deal. It is possible that the estate was sold as an encumbered estate.

Another Nolan to loom large in the land dealings that occurred during the early part of the century was Gregory Nolan. This man, who was domiciled in Dublin, had contacts with Galway, Carlow and Tipperary. On the balance of evidence he may well have been a Galway Nolan.[634] His first transactions were

---

[634] When Thomas Nolan of Ballinrobe castle died in 1628 he left his widow and a son and heir Gregory. The Gregory mentioned above was in all probability his grandson. Hardiman who wrote a history of Galway in 1820 had this to say about the Nolans. 'This family was formerly of the first rank and opulence and is still wealthy and respectable. Thomas Nolan Esq., of the town and castle of Ballinrobe died June 18th. 1628, was possessed of most extensive landed possessions, to which his son Gregory succeeded and out of which his widow Agnes Martin had dower. This property was confiscated in the civil war of 1641, but a considerable part still remains in the families of Loughboy, Ballinderry and Ballybanagher. The tomb of the ancient family of O'Nolan of Loughboy is situated in the centre of the Franciscan Friary Churchyard in Galway and bears the following inscription -

done in Tipperary with the Butlers. Prior to 1710 he loaned money to Colonel Thomas Butler of Kilcash[635] and got a lease on lands for a period of 21yrs. at an annual rental of £40. 7s.[636] and in that year, 1710, he sold his leasehold interest to a man called Carroll for £116 sterling with the proviso that he could redeem his interest after 5 yrs. upon repaying his debt.

Two years later, in 1712, Gregory was named as the only surviving executor of a will of a man called Walter Blake. Other parties named in the document were Juliana Blake the widow, James Blake of Galway and Richard England of Ennis, Co. Clare who paid the two Blakes £90 each on foot of a land transaction in Co. Clare where 240 acres of the Burren changed hands. In the following year Gregory (as the executor of Walter Blake) and James Blake sold 58 acres in Co. Clare to Brigadier General Francis Gore of Clonrone. In the same year Gregory and Lawrence Nolan of Shangarry, gentlemen sold 200 acres in Shangarry to Jeremiah Quill as detailed above.

Gregory seems to have redeemed his Tipperary lands from Carroll as in 1716 he sold his interest in Kilcash to John Osborne for £550 and in the same document it was noted that he received arrears from Colonel Thomas Butler of £428. Gregory may well have been a banker. In the next year, 1717, he released and sold lands in Galway to Edmund Fitzpatrick for £200. In 1721 a Gregory Nolan, a parson, of Middlesex, made his will. It is possible that he was the same man involved in all the above transactions, as being a parson he would have been socially mobile.

In 1732 Felix Nowland and his sons mortgaged lands in Doneraile in Co. Cork to William Smith of Co. Kildare - a number of townlands and properties in and around Doneraile which had been leased to them for a number of lives in 1725. In the same year Felix Nowland let a farm near Doneraile for 5s. for one year and shortly afterwards he rented 800 acres from Lord Doneraile for 5s. a year. In 1736 Felix sold houses and yards etc. to Sir John St. Leger and in the same year sold houses to William Smith for £100 sterling. Again in 1736 Felix sold his interest in some Doneraile lands to Hon. Hayes St. Leger for £740. This sale was witnessed by Samuel Nolan of Killbreak, Co. Cork, gentleman. In

---

" This tomb was first erected in the year of our Lord 1394, by the O'Nolans of Loughboy and is now rebuilt and ornamented by Michael O'Nolan, Galway, one of the representatives of the said family." A terrible conflagration took place in Galway in June 1473, by which the town was nearly destroyed. This misfortune was soon overcome by the exertions of an industrious and already opulent community, the chief amongst whom were the fourteen tribes also Nolan, Port, Coine, Cuin and Tully are particularly noticed.'

[635] He fought in the army of King James II. His son, John, became the 15th. Earl of Ormonde upon the death of Charles, Earl of Arran and 14th. Earl of Ormonde - his third or fourth cousin.

[636] This was a very substantial amount of money in those days.

1742 Felix Nowland of the city of Cork, tallow chandler, and his son William let lands in Cork to a man called Beale for an annual rent of £15.

The Nolans of Ballabanagher, Co. Galway were involved in quite a considerable number of land dealings during the century beginning with Thomas Nolan. It would appear from the memorial dated 1730 that there was a dispute between Thomas Nolan[637] and Arthur French over £300 rents due to Nolan for lands. Nolan himself had mortgaged lands to a man called John Vesey, the Archdeacon of Kilfenora for £1000. The lands in question were the Castle, lands and town of Ballabanagher.[638] The following year Thomas sold lands including Carrownecrossy and Ballabanagher to George Staunton of Dublin. He sold him twenty messauges, 20 cottages, ten lofts, 10 gardens, 150 acres of land, 50 acres meadow, 150 acres pasture, 40 acres of furze and heath, 40 acres of wood, 30 acres of moor and marsh and the castle and town of Ballabanagher and other lands in Galway.[639]

Later in the century Thomas's sons John, Brabazon and Anthony Nolan was involved in numerous land deals. Land was sold in Galway and Mayo in 1752 for over £4,000 . They sold land in Mayo for £1039 in the late 1770s and again in 1780 more land was sold in Mayo for £700.

In Dublin a man called Michael Nolan, gentleman, carried out numerous transactions which involved the sale of houses and city properties mainly and later in the century, in the last two decades, his son Redmond was party to over twenty property deals.

Another case worth mentioning is that of Thomas Nowland. He and a man called Thomas Marriott, both domiciled in England, made a deed in 1718 giving ownership of lands in Ireland to an English gentleman, Joseph Gardner, his wife, and two daughters. The total extent of these lands were c. 1500 acres in Co. Meath and 730 acres in Co. Wexford. In another later deed he, Marriott

---

[637] He seems to have been a stepson of Richard Burke of Ballabanagher.

[638] In the Nine Years War the Nolans defended the castle against the Burkes and the Flahertys to the number of 500 or 600 who tried to rescue a son of Edmund Burke who was being held hostage there. As a result the boy was to be hanged but was spared by the entreaties of his grandfather, William Burke of Shrule. One of the Galway Nolans - Thady - was in the pay of the Government and was a 'pursuivant' or state messenger who in 1596 was ordered to bring certain persons to Dublin. Bingham, the Governor of Munster ordered the Mayor and Sheriff of Galway to assist Thady in his duties. The Nolans survived the Nine Years War, the Rebellion of 1641, Cromwell and the Williamites which in itself was testimony of their sagacity and tenacity. It is significant that in 1585 O'Nolan of Galway was one of 67 signatories from Connaught who surrendered their Irish names (they dropped the O and Mac) and customs of inheritance and received their castles and lands by patent to them and their heirs in English succession.

[639] Memorial no. 47021

and the Gardners leased all the lands in question to the Hon. John Rochfort[640] of Dublin. No sum of money was mentioned in the deed.

I found 30 Nolans/Nowlans mentioned in the Index to Prerogative Wills of Ireland, compiled by Sir Arthur Vicars. These wills were made during the 18th. century with a few having been made in the late 1600s. What this implies is that these people were all people of some substance. In the main they were domiciled in Dublin with only three mentioned for Co. Carlow. The Carlow Nowlans were Charles, gent., of Ballykealy who made a will in 1690, Edward, a merchant whose will was dated 1764 and Daniel of Mount Pleasant who made a will in 1794. In the Index to Leighlin Wills twenty one Nolans/Nowlans made wills. Five of the wills were dated in the late 1600s. They were:

1. Terlagh Nowlan whose will was dated 1680.
2. William of Grangfort, will dated 1687.
3. Robert, will dated 1691.
4. Daniel, will dated 1692
5. Joan, nee Gosse, of Laragh, 1693.

Laragh House - undergoing reconstruction - May 2000

---

[640] Hon. John was the grandson of Prime Iron Rochfort, a Colonel in Cromwell's army who was executed in 1652 for killing a fellow officer in a duel. Hon. John Rochfort was the first of the Rochforts to settle at Clogrennan.

Nine of the wills were dated in the 18th. century with most occurring before 1750. Lawrence Nowlan crops up again and I suspect that this was Lawrence of Shangarry who moved to Lisgarvan. These are the nine I have mentioned:

1. Thady Nowlan, will dated 1703.
2. James Nowland of Carlow, 1713.
3. James Nowlan of Tinnaclash, 1742.
4. Thady Nowlan of Linkardstown, 1743.
5. Lawrence Nowlan, 1747.
6. John of Ballyryan, 1749.
7. William of Borris, 1754.
8. Thomas of Ballyloo, 1779.
9. James of Paulville, 1781.

The Nolans/Nowlans whose wills were dated in the 1800s. were:

1. Edmund Nowlan of Ballinacarrig, 1803.
2. Bridget of Park, Carlow, 1805.
3. Edward of Ballykealy, 1814.
4. John of Augha, 1828.
5. James of Tinnaclash, 1829.
6. (unnamed) of Kilmaglush 1827.[641]
7. John of Tinryland, 1833.

It can be seen from the above examples, that, while the O'Nolans had lost most of their original patrimony in Forth O'Nolan, even as late as the end of the 18th. century a few of their number were still regarded as belonging to the gentry.[642]

In the case of the Kavanaghs, during the same period, only the Kavanaghs of Borris are mentioned as part of the gentry.

The 18th. century, in general, seemed to be a period of relative calm. The population doubled during the century with most of the growth occurring during the last 25 years. This explosive growth has been attributed to the ready availability of cheap food in the form of the potato as it was possible to feed a family of six with the potatoes grown on one acre of land. Another cause was the custom of people getting married at a very young age. Housing, too, was no obstacle as a cabin could be built in one or two days from sods and stones and timber with a thatched roof.

---

[641] This man was probably the father of Edward Nolan of Kilmaglush.

[642] In the 1886 edition of Burke's Landed Gentry there is a section devoted to the Galway Nolans.

According to William Farrell the Co. Carlow rebel captain the years prior to 1798 were happy years in Co. Carlow. Here is what he had to say - 'We had, to be sure, a great deal of poverty on the one hand, but, if we had, we also had a great deal of wealth. Working tradesmen and labourers in general had but a small allowance for their labour but provisions were cheap in proportion, while the generality of employers of every description were comfortable and wealthy and able to keep them constantly in work...There was no such thing known as men, willing and able to work, obliged to starve for want of it; and if anything was wanting to show the easy circumstances of the people it would be found in the numbers in every town and in every part of the country that could afford time to practice all the manly exercises so well known to Irishmen, as hurling, football, cudgelling, tennis or handball, leaping, wrestling and throwing the sledge or bar or grindstone.'

It is interesting to note, too, that there was a proliferation of schools in the latter decades of the century, with accelerated growth in the early decades of the 19th. century. Most of these schools were described as 'hedge schools' even though many of them were in houses or barns and most of them were undenominational. For example in Newtownbarry (Bunclody) there were five schools in the town by 1826 and one of these was taught by John Nowlan who had 64 Catholic and 12 Protestant children attending. At Boolynavoughran a man called Freeman taught 48 Catholic and 2 Protestant children. Fr. Doyle, writing to his Bishop (J.K.L.) in 1824 stated that there were 19 Hedge Schools in the Kilbride - Kildavin - Clonegal area at that time, including one at Ballykeenan, one at Kilbride/Kilgraney, one at Lackabeg, one at Cranemore and one at Barnahask. We know that there was a school at Ballon which was well attended. Ballon townland was owned by a Mr. Marshal in 1815. He built the National School there which had 150 pupils in 1839. Most children attended in the summer but very few in the winter. The school had two teachers. We can assume that the educational needs of the people of Myshall and Garryhill were catered for by similar men to John Nowlan who worked for as little as £18 per annum. The salaries of the teachers were paid by the parents of the pupils and the parents also paid for the upkeep of the schools.

Like all the counties of Ireland, Carlow was targeted by the United Irishmen and the Society flourished there. According to Ryan (History & Antiquities of the Co. Carlow) there were over 9,000 members in the county. If this is the case there must have been large numbers of men (and perhaps women) in the Society in every town and village in the county. Following accusations that men from Myshall had gone to Tullow to recruit people to the United Irishmen the alarmed citizens decided to repudiate this charge. John

Nolan of Ballinvalley (John the Poet)[643] was the orator who delivered the Address. In the course of the address it was noted that "a most wicked and malicious report has been spread abroad that several inhabitants of this town did assemble near Tullow with an intent to administer an unlawful oath ... such an accusation tended to asperse our loyalty to our most gracious Majesty and much beloved Sovereign" . The Address was delivered to Robert Cornwall of Myshall Lodge.

The introduction of the Orange Society (which was begun to combat the United Irishmen) in Carlow was attributed to John Staunton Rochfort of Clogrennan. This had a further disquieting effect on the whole county with nightly patrols of yeomen by Rochfort and Cornwall Brady of Myshall. According to Ryan in his history of Carlow Captain James Nowlan was one of the leaders of the group of rebels who attacked Leighlin and Borris on the night of the 24th. May 1798. This attack coincided with the attack on Carlow town, the night which the Directory of the United Irishmen had designated as the night the rebellion was to commence. As we know the attacks on Carlow and Borris were failures and the Carlow rebels suffered the most severe loss of any battle in the entire rebellion with losses of over 600 men killed, apart from many more caught and executed after the battle. Captain James Nowlan seems to have escaped any retribution and lived out his life in Knockendrane until his death in 1857 at the reputed age of 116 yrs.

While information about the O'Nolans (or Nowlans as they were generally called by the end of the 18th. century) is scarce enough we do know that a few were arrested after the 1798 rebellion and were transported to Australia. I know of only two who emigrated to America during the century. I found the names in a Ship List. They were James Nowlan who travelled to America in 1762 with 70 other people and Eleanor Nowlan who travelled there in 1766 on the brig 'William'.

We know also that some rebels from Forth were hung in the grounds of Robert Cornwall's estate at Myshall and many more were compelled to build a road known to this day as 'The Croppies Road'. It is said, too, that Cornwall at this time burnt the 'Cross of Myshall' which had been in the area for a long time. The Nowlan convict list of persons sent to Australia is quite interesting. It contains the names of eight Nolans, six of whom were convicted for their parts in the 1798 rebellion and 2 who were part of the Emmet Insurrection of 1803. The six men involved in the 1798 rebellion were two James Nolans, one of whom was sentenced at Gowran, John, also sentenced at Gowran, William sentenced in Co. Kilkenny and William and Thomas sentenced in Dublin. There are no details of their circumstances nor of the length of their sentence.

---

[643] John the Poet was most likely well aware of the involvement of his nephew Captain James Nowlan who was in all probability one of those recruiting at Tullow.

The two men convicted in 1803 were Michael Nolan from Naas who was sentenced at Kilmainham and William who was sentenced in Dublin. Michael had a widowed sister and four children to support and William had a wife and three children. Both were sentenced to 7 years transportation.

Another Nowlan, Timothy, was found guilty of administering the United Irishman's oath at Ballon in March of 1798 and at the Carlow Assizes he was sentenced to Transportation for life. Three men who were accused of conspiracy to murder Robert Cornwall of Myshall got bail. One of them James Dougherty was bailed by Michael Nolan of Killane. A James Nolan was bailed by Henry Whalley while a Patrick Doyle was bailed by Sir Richard Butler and Lawrence Nowlan. Nolan and Doyle were accused of being United Irishmen.

Myshall Lodge - burnt 1922

Chapter 22

The Barony of Forth in the 19th. century

The terrible trauma of the events of 1798 was closely followed by a wave of persecution of the Catholic people. In Wexford this took the form of Chapel burning. By December of 1798 sixteen chapels had been burned and by December of 1799 as many more. However the same bitter animosities did not seem to be as apparent in Co. Carlow and by the time the numerous trials had finished in Carlow town, with their consequent grisly executions, life began to return to normal in the county. The nightly patrols of yeomen probably continued for some time.

It would seem that the Act of Union was opposed by the majority of the people (though the Catholics had no say since they had no vote) but as we know it was passed in 1801.

The Penal Laws were relaxed even more in the early decades of the century culminating in the passing of Catholic Emancipation in 1829. By that time considerable numbers of schools had been founded and though they might still be Hedge Schools or Pay Schools the fact that they were tolerated is a testimony to the gradual relaxation of the laws taking place. But the people in general lived in extreme poverty. Fr. Doyle writing to the Bishop (J.K.L.) of Kildare & Leighlin, in 1824, stated that 'by far the greater number are not able to pay the masters, or clothe the children, and even vast numbers of those sent to school pay nothing...I consider the people well disposed to educate their children if they only had the means to do so.'[644]

The so called Tithe War of the early decades of the century had some repercussions in the area because of the incident known as 'The Battle of the Pound' which occurred in Newtownbarry (Bunclody).

The Catholic population were compelled to pay Tithes in the form of money to the Protestant rectors in the various parishes, in addition to

---

[644] This depressing statement with its inference of abject poverty is at variance with the Bishop himself commencing the work on Carlow Cathedral in 1828 and work being carried out on Tullow church where the spire was added by Fr. Nolan a little later in the century, not to mention the building of St. Patrick's College in 1793 and the Court House in 1830. There was, undoubtedly, some kind of depression following the Napoleonic Wars. For example during that period (1810-17) wheat was fetching prices of 2 guineas a barrell while in the late 1820s the price had dropped to £1.11s. 8d. Cows which had been selling for 14 guineas dropped to £7 and cattle fell from a high of £12 to £5.

supporting their own church and clergy. Bishop J.K.L. was a vehement opponent of the Tithe system which he saw as clearly unjust.

In 1831 a dispute arose between the people of Newtownbarry and district (St. Mary's Parish) and the Rector, Mr. McClintock, an amiable and inoffensive gentleman.[645] The people maintained that the Tithes were being demanded before they were due. The total amount of money due to the Rector was about £370. The authorities decided to make an example and seized three cattle, two of them belonging to a Mr. Doyle of Tombrack and one belonging to a Mr. Nowlan. The cattle were brought to the pound field in Newtownbarry (where John Nolan's filling station is now situated) on the 17th. June, the Fair Day, to be sold at auction.

Trouble was expected and the local magistrates Irvine, Graham and Derenzy sent for Yeomanry corps from Myshall and Enniscorthy to supplement the Newtownbarry force. A crowd of people congregated at the pound. At the suggestion of Adam Feltus, the Myshall magistrate, it was agreed that, in order to defuse the situation, that the dispute as to whether tithes were due or not should be left to four gentlemen to decide. Two men were nominated to represent the parish and Feltus went into the town to get Mr. McClintock. Before he left Feltus addressed the Myshall yeomen and said "Myshall men, I rely on you being steady. Bear everything. If stones are thrown don't mind, but on no account drag a trigger!" Before he and McClintock had time to get down to the pound field the battle had begun.

After Feltus had left, the crowd had become very noisy and tension mounted. Graham who was in command of the local yeomen told the people to disperse or violence would be used. It was then decided to bring the cattle into the town and they were brought out on the road. The yeomen formed up behind them but the people pressed in on them. The yeomen used their bayonets to keep the crowd back. Stones were thrown and then Graham gave the order to fire. The people fled in all directions and the yeomen fired three volleys hitting some of their own comrades as well as killing fourteen people and wounding twenty three others. Thomas Murray of Kilknock, a Myshall yeoman was shot in the heel.

An immediate inquiry was called for and a letter was sent to the Lord Lieutenant. It was signed by twelve of the principal inhabitants of Newtownbarry including the two Catholic clergymen. Another signatory was Darby Nowlan.

After the inquiry was completed charges were brought against Graham and others for unlawful killing but their cases never came to court being postponed from one Assizes to another and with the passage of time all charges were left in abeyance.

---

[645] Letter of Canon Doyle in *Irish Catholic* 1896.

There were other instances of Tithe resistance in the south east at Graiguenamanagh and Carrickshock in Co. Kilkenny where a process server and twelve policemen were killed by rioting protesters.

Meetings were held all over the country in the wake of these events with a view to having the Tithe system abolished but to little effect. The meetings in Co. Carlow were generally orderly affairs. For example the meeting in Tullow was presided over by Paul Carter, a local Protestant. As the decade progressed resistance to the payment of Tithes seems to have become centred in Rathvilly but this may have been because of local antipathy towards the Rev. John Whitty arising out of an incident in the 1798 Rebellion.[646] In 1832 cattle were seized on Whitty's instructions and a forced sale was organised in Carlow. Horns were blown in Castledermot[647] at the fair there (which coincided with the day of the forced sale) and 5,000 people marched into Carlow and despite a huge police presence carried off the cattle. P.J. Kavanagh in his admirable article in Carloviana noted eleven incidents in all during which 'mobs' defied and in some cases attacked the police and bailiffs. There was also a noticeable move towards sectarianism with Protestant churches having their windows broken. There were other minor incidents at Hacketstown, Tullow and Grangeforth.

The death notice for Fr. Thomas Nolan P.P of Abbeyleix, who died in 1886 noted that he took part in the tithe agitation both in Co. Carlow and in Co. Laois when he was moved there. Fr. Nolan was one of the Ballinrush Nolans and there is more detail about him in the chapter about the O'Nolan families.

Some relief for Tithes was granted in an Act of Parliament in 1838 but people had to wait until 1868 before the Tithes were abolished.[648]

From 1838 until 1843 the county was gripped by Repeal fever. Daniel O'Connell (dubbed 'the uncrowned King of Ireland' by Fr. Rev. John Nolan who was born at Ballinrush in 1808 at a Monster Rally at Mullaghmast Co. Kildare in 1843) tried to have people elected who would vote for the repeal of the Union. In 1841 he made a determined but unsuccessful attempt to have his own nominees (including his son John) elected for Carlow. This election was marred by the intimidation of the voters by both parties. Voters were kidnapped and held in Kilkenny by the Repeal party and a 'mob' estimated at over 100,000 marched on Carlow town with view to having them vote for

---

[646] Rev. Whitty's manse at Arles was attacked in 1798 and twenty two insurgents were killed in the attack. Rev. Whitty's son David was also a Yeoman captain during the Rebellion. (P.J. Kavanagh M.A. writing in Carloviana)

[647] Apparently this method of warning the people of a tithe seizure or sale was widely used in the area at the time.

[648] From *Buncloidi* by An tAthair S.de Bhal.

Repeal. A sizeable army and police presence with artillery prevented the 'mob' from coming into the town. In the election which went on for four or five days the Tory party won the seats by the narrowest of margins when Bruen of Oak Park and Bunbury of Moyl were duly elected.[649]

During this period of unrestrained population growth there was much poverty all over the whole country so much so that a 'Poor Law' system was set up between the years 1838 and 1842. This resulted in the erection and opening of Workhouses. Each county was divided into Unions of Electoral Divisions with a Board of Poor Law Guardians for each Union. There was only one Workhouse in Carlow and that was built in Carlow town in 1844. It was built to accommodate 800 inmates. Other workhouses were built in Baltinglass, Shillelagh and New Ross. These catered for people who lived on the periphery of the county. In 1845 there were 250 people in the Carlow Workhouse and half of that number was children.

Co. Carlow fared remarkably well, in comparison, during the time of the Famine. From 1846 until 1851 only 28 people died of starvation in the county. The population of Carlow county was 86,228 in 1841 and this had dropped to 68,075 in 1851.[650] It is thought that over 11,000 people died in that period and almost 7,000 migrated or emigrated. Those who died (apart from the natural deaths), died from diseases related to the famine, cholera and typhus.

As in the rest of Ireland it was the poor who suffered most during the famine. Relief schemes were put in place which afforded some measure of alleviation of the hardships being endured. These took the form of public works such as road building, lowering of hills and filling of valleys and later in the decade they included works on the estates of the landlords, such as wall building, planting etc. In Ballon the 'new road' was laid down at a cost of £400. It was built around the hill.

It was the landlords in the main who bore the brunt of organising the Relief Schemes. When conditions got worse during the winters they organised Soup Kitchens. In Forth these were set up in Myshall, Clonegal, Kellistown, Barragh, Ballon, Rathoe, Tullow and Fenagh. John Lecky of Ballykealy was singled out as meriting great praise for his efforts on behalf of the poor. Others who were noted as having made very successful efforts to effect relief were Thomas Braddel (of Coolmelagh) in Clonegal and the Rev. Robert Cooper in Barragh.

---

[649] 1843 saw the end of the Repeal Movement when O'Connell backed down at Clontarf. He had organised a Monster Meeting with over half a million expected to attend, but the Government ordered that the meeting should not be held and O'Connell capitulated. He died in Genoa in 1847.

[650] The population of Co. Carlow in 1971 was about 40,000

There were near riots in some areas. In Leighlin a mob of over 200 people tore up the newly laid roads because there was not enough work for all. In 1846 a crowd gathered at Alexander's Mill at Milford and only dispersed when they were promised that the gentry would give relief to the poor. At Carnew, in Co. Wicklow, a crowd stole a rick of corn and brought it to the nearest cross roads where it was threshed and divided.

In December of 1846 the numbers of the destitute who were working on the relief schemes was 1,503 men, 6 women and 64 boys. By March of 1847 the number had swelled to 3005 persons.

The Workhouse in Carlow was filled to capacity in that year with 1,073 people being accommodated. Every effort was made to discourage people from going to the Workhouse. There were very stringent rules which were strictly adhered to. Families were segregated. No one could leave the house without permission. No visitors were allowed except once a week. No tobacco or drink could be consumed on the premises. In addition the fare on offer was worse than that offered in the gaol.[651]

It can be seen from the numbers above that Carlow fared not too badly during the period. One of the factors which contributed in no small measure to the migration/emigration from the county was the change in land occupation patterns. In 1841 there were 4,290 holdings of between one and fifteen acres. By 1851 these had shrunk to 2,098. This resulted in consolidation of holdings and a flight from the land, of smallholders.

Emigration from Carlow was not as severe as in other counties but it must have been considerable enough during the hundred years between 1750 and 1850. In Manchester alone there were 100,000 Irish born people before 1840 and the numbers in Liverpool may have been higher.[652] Many of the Famine emigrants from Carlow must have found their way to America/Canada[653] on what were known as 'the Coffin Ships'. In the American Civil War[654] (in the

---

[651] Thomas O'Neill in an article about the Famine in *Carloviana* 1947

[652] In the 1851 census in England there were Nolans/Nowlans in more than 10 different English counties. I do not have the specific numbers of Nolans, but I suspect there were many.

[653] While the numbers of Nolans/Nowlans who emigrated to Canada are not fully known I found a list of over 70 who had lived there in the latter decades of the century. See www.ingeneus.com for details.

[654] Some Nolans had gone to America earlier and during the Revolutionary War ten Nolan/Nowlans were mentioned as having been participants fought with the American forces. One a Lt. Pierce Nolan got a grant of land in Virginia in the late 1790s. Two James Nolans were privates in Colonel Daniel Morgan's Riflemen, who were pivotal in the defeat of the English at the famous battle of Sarratoga in 1777 (*Irish Settlers in America* by Ml. J. O'Brien)

1860s) no less than 873 young men called Nolan/Noland/Nowlan/Nowland were involved on both sides. On the Union side which fought the Southern Confederates, mainly on the Slavery issue, 820 Nolans were enlisted, a good few as officers, while only 53 opposed their brothers by fighting with the South. The vast majority survived the war and we presume went on to become the ancestors of the huge numbers of Nolans now citizens of the U.S.[655]

There was no significant agitation after the Famine period but a political movement known as the Fenians sprang up. The Fenian movement was founded in America by Irish emigrants who had been active in the Young Irelanders, notably John O'Mahony, Michael Doheny, James Stephens and T.C.Luby. Stephens came back to Ireland to grow the movement in Ireland and England. It was a largely urban based movement that got little support from rural people.

In the Myshall / Ballon area the Fenian organiser was John Nolan later known as John Amnesty Nolan. After the abortive Fenian Rising of 1867 he seems to have left the area.[656] His brother Rev. Patrick Nolan was very active in the Land League later in the century and was instrumental in the defeat of the Tory party in the 1880 elections in Carlow[657]. Three other Nolans were active in the Fenian movement too. John B. Nolan of Ballinrush (of whom later) was the prime organiser of the Fenians in Belfast, Andrew Nolan of

---

[655] See www.civilwardata.com. Another interesting site was the Chicago site which had noted the following deaths of Nolans which might be of interest.

John died Feb. 26, 1887 at the residence of his father, after a short illness of acute consumption, the youngest surviving son of Edmund Nolan, of Ballinrush, Co. Carlow. He was brother to Mr. Edmund Nolan, the well-known business manager of the Irish-American Club of Chicago. - March 19, 1887.

Matthew   aged 37 yrs., Oct. 17, 1884, native of Co. Carlow. Funeral from resid., 18 Hope st. to St. Patrick's Church to Calvary.

Michael   at resid., 3348 Auburn ave., husband of Julia, nee Moran, aged 53 yrs., native of Co. Carlow. Burial Calvary. San Francisco papers please copy. -July 19, 1890 Nolan, Michael of Carlow, married to Julia Moran of Westmeath. They were residents of Nativity parish prior to the Great Fire.

Nellie F.   Jan. 18, 1890, daughter of the late John and Ann Nolan, of Co. Carlow, aged 18 yrs. Funeral from her mother's resid., 2833 Vernon ave. to St. James Church to Mt. Olivet

[656] See the chapter about 'Famous Nolans' for details of this remarkable man.

[657] Arthur Kavanagh of Borris and Henry Bruen of Oak Park were the sitting Tory M.Ps who were defeated. It is said that it was this defeat and the sight of the bonfires lit by his tenants, in his native Borris, celebrating this defeat, that hastened the death of Arthur Kavanagh. This remarkable man, who had been born limbless, overcame his disabilities to become an excellent horseman, a fishermen, an able landlord and an M.P.

Ballinrush in Leinster and Eugene (Hugh) Nolan of Ballinrush (no relation to John B. or Andrew) was active in the organisation in Dublin where he was a student.

The Griffith Valuations of the later part of the century give us some indication of the economic standing of the remnants of the O'Nolans left in occupation of their ancient patrimony.

Nolans	Townland	Acres	Owner
Nowlan James	Rossacurra		Baggot James
Nowlan James	Rossacurra	100?	Baggot & Brady
Nowlan Edm.	Ballinrush	300	Baggot James
Nowlan Ml.	Ballinrush	77	Baggot James
Nowlan Pat.	Ballinrush	46	Baggot James
Nolan Felix	Craanpursheen	30	Baggot James
Nolan Ml.	Craanpursheen	40	Baggot James
Nolan Mary	Kilmurry	40	Baggot James
Nolan Felix	Sragh	231	Baggot James
Nolan Mgt.	Sragh	House	Baggot James
Nowlan Thomas	Shangarry	100?	Baggot James
Nolan Patk.	Shangarry	House	Baggot James
Nolan James	Shangarry	2	Baggot James
Nolan Rev. Ml.	Myshall	4	Baggot, Brady, Whaley
Nowlan James	Myshall	100?	Baggot & Brady
Nolan Rev. Ml.	Myshall	100?	Baggot & Brady
Nolan Lwce.	Myshall	House	Baggot & Brady
Nolan Wm.	Myshall	House	Baggot & Brady
Nolan Mary	Myshall	House	Baggot & Brady
Nowlan Ml.	Knockdramagh	31	Bessborough, Earl of
Nowlan Ml.	Knockdramagh	40	Bessborough, Earl of
Nolan Mgt.	Clonee East	House	Bessborough, Earl of
Nowlan John	Sheean	150?	Bessborough, Earl of
Nolan John	Aclare	9	Bonham Rev. J.
Nolan James	Ballykeenan	House	Bonham Rev. J.
Nolan Mary	Garreenleen	238	Browne Robt. C.
Nolan Robert	Garreenleen	17	Browne Robt. C.
Nolan Robert	Gilbertstown	142	Browne Robt. C.
Nolan Henry	Ballygarret	40	Browne Robt. C.
Nolan James	Ballygarret	40	Browne Robt. C.
Nolan Myles	Ballinastraw	House	Butler James T.
Nowlan James	Straduff	House	Butler, Borough, Wall
Nowlan Chas.	Straduff	House	Butler, Borough, Wall

Nowlan Edm.	Lasmaconly	145	Butler Wm. P.
Nowlan Edm.	Lasmaconly	159	Butler Wm. P.
Nowlan Matt.	Ballaghmore	90	Butler W.& Watson Jos.
Nowlan James	Ballaghmore[658]	61	Butler W. & Watson Jos.
Nolan Matt.	Commons	50	Cooke Mary & Brewster
Nowlan James	Rosslee	37	Courtown Earl of
Nowlan James	Rosslee	77	Courtown Earl of
Nowlan James	Rosslee	100?	Courtown Earl of
Nolan James	Craans (Ardattin)	20	Doherty Rt. Hon J. (reps)
Nowlan Eliz.	Knockbrack	House	Doyle Rev. Chas. M.
Nowlan Peter	Knockbrack	House	Doyle Rev. Chas. M.
Nowlan Ml.	Cranemore		Durdin Rev. Alex.
Nowlan Ml.	Cranemore	140	Durdin, Cooper, Newbold
Nowlan Ml. & Jas.	Milltown	28	Elliot Samuel
Nowlan Ml.	Milltown	House	Elliot Samuel
Nowlan James	Graiguenaspiddoge	50?	Elliot, Perkins, Carter
Nowlan Wm.	Graiguenaspiddoge	House	Elliot, Perkins, Carter
Nolan Henry	Aghade	2	FishbourneJ.Dowres Lord
Nolan Loughlin	Rathrush	117	Frankford late Viscount
Nolan Mary	Clonmacshane	40	Garret Wm.
Nolan Robert	Ballymogue	67	Haughton John
Nolan Mary	Ballymogue	60	Haughton John
Nolan Ter.& Ml.	Craanaha	188	Johnston Wm. G.
Nolan John	Knockdoorish		Keogh John H.
Nolan Luke	Boggan		Keogh John H.
Nolan Ann	Ballykealy	54	Lecky John J.
Nolan John	Ballykealy	House	Lecky John J.
Nolan Mary	Tinnaclash	37	Lecky John J.
Nowlan Catherine	Ballinadrum	10	Lecky John J.
Nolan Robert	Kilknock	84	Lecky & Brewster
Nolan John	Kilknock	10	Lecky, Brewster, Kepple
Nowlan James	Kilmaglush	24	Lecky, Elliot, Baggot
Nowlan Ed.[659]	Kilmaglush	49	Lecky, Elliot, Baggot
Nowlan Ed.	Kilmaglush	30	Lecky, Elliot, Baggot
Nolan Ed.	Ballon		Lecky & Stackpole
Nolan Peter	Ballon		Lecky & Stackpole

---

[658] There were 3/4 other families of Nowlan in Ballaghmore in very small holdings.

[659] Edward of Kilmaglush was the father of Thomas Nolan whose grandson Noel (Edward) Nolan is the present owner of Kilconnor house and lands. Nicholas Nolan, Noel's father bought Kilconnor from Dr. Joseph Nolan of Tullow (one of the Ballinrush Nolans) in 1919. Dr. Nolan had previously bought the property from the Watsons.

Nolan John (shoem.)	Ballon	House	Lecky & Stackpole
Nolan Felix	Ballon	House	Lecky & Stackpole
Nolan Martin	Ballon	House	Lecky & Stackpole
Nolan John (stonec.)	Ballon	House	Lecky & Stackpole
Nolan Patk.	Ballon	House	Lecky & Stackpole
Nolan Jas (Sandbrook)	Cunaberry		Lecky & Stackpole
Nolan Jas Jnr. (S.)	Cunaberry		Lecky & Stackpole
Nolan John	Cunaberry		Lecky & Stackpole
Nolan Anne	Cunaberry	3	Lecky & Stackpole
Nolan Mary	Ballintrane	150?	Lecky, Whelan, Garret
Nolan John	Barragh	130	Malcolmson H. (reps)
Nolan John	Kilknock	74	Nolan John
Nolan Cath.	Croanaleigh	House	Nolan Lwce.
Nolan James	Ballylower	House	O'Brien Catherine
Nolan Myles	Ballon	4 Hses.	Stackpole & Rev.W. K.[660]
Nolan Felix	Ballon	3 Hses.	Stackpole & Rev. W. K.
Nolan Thos.	Ballon	House	Stackpole & Rev. W. K.
Nolan Garret	Ballon	House	Stackpole & Rev. W. K.
Nolan James	Ballon	House	Stackpole & Rev. W. K.
Nolan Nicholas	Carrickslaney	House	Stackpole J. Browne Rob.
Nowlan John	Craan	2	Studdert, Downing, Smith
Nolan Robt.	Ballyleen	12	Tuthill, Wybrand, Symes
Nolan John	Ballyleen	House	Tuthill, Wybrand, Symes
Nowlan John	Craan		Studdert George
Nolan Ed.	Clonbulloge	4	Watson Thomas
Nowlan Jas.	Ballincrea	House	Whelan John (reps. of)
Nowlan Mgt.	Ballintrane	54	Whelan Pilsworth.
Nolan John	Cappagh	House	Whelan Pilsworth

It can be seen from the above data that while the Nowlans or Nolans did not actually own very much of their ancient heritage in Forth, they were, at least, in possession of over 2,300 acres if one allows about 50 acres for each blank above, as the acreage of each tenant.

The names of the landlords who had acquired the lands after the disintegration of the Ormonde estates are all listed above. Not all of those landlords were 'old' landlords and in fact we can plainly see that most of them were in fact relative newcomers.

Baggot, Butler and Lecky are in fact the only survivors from the 17th. century apart from the John Nolan who owned 78 acres in Kilknock and Lawrence Nolan who owned 180 acres in Croanaleigh, but admittedly those

---

[660] Rev. Wm. Kinsella

Nolans may have only become owners of their respective lands during the 18th. or 19th. centuries.

What of the other owners named as proprietors in 1641? The Kavanaghs who were the next largest landowners in Forth after the Butlers had almost disappeared. Thomas Kavanagh had about 120 acres in Boggan rented from John H. Keogh, J. Kavanagh had about 40 acres from Browne in Emlicon, - Kavanagh had about 200 acres in Ballinacrea from J. Whelan, Charles Kavanagh renting from Durdin, Newbold and Cooper at Cranemore had about 140 acres of mountain, and James Kavanagh was renting about 50 acres from Baggot in Croanruss. However Griffiths names a huge number of Kavanaghs as living in Raheenleigh on very small holdings. The Eustaces were still hanging on and Hardy Eustace and his mother Sarah still had Rathvarrin (434 acres), Ratheeragh (207 acres) and in Newstown they rented over 300 acres. In Myshall Oliver Eustace had 150? acres.

The new occupiers of lands in Forth are probably the forebears of many of the modern day citizens. They include people named Kelly, Kinsella, Byrne, Clowry, Prandy, Salter, Cummins, Coughlan, Flynn, Hogan, Rourke, Tracey, Roche, McClean, Fitzpatrick, Fenelon, Smith, Doran, Moore, Carty, Kepple, Collier, Phelan, Faulkner, Brophy, Smyth, Perkin, Doyle, Carter, Hughes, Townsend, Barton, Gorman, Corrigan, Neill, Leggett, Donohoe, Clarke, Lennan, Moran, Pierce, Bailey, McDonnell, Lee, Humphreys, Dawson, Foley, Maher, Hickey, Murphy, Brennan, Fox, Farrell, Conroy, Dowling, Swaine, Kealy, Kearney, Deegan, Rothwell, Levingestone, Moulton, Nugent, Robert, Jacob, Power, Rice, Barker, Hayden, Burgess, Devereux, Grennan, Stacey, Deacon, Redmond, Morris, James, Kennedy, Kehoe, Brien, Walker and Murray.

Undoubtedly many of the Briens, Kehoes, Neills, Murphys, Doyles and Gormans had lived in the barony long before Cromwell came and possibly others as well, but in the main those people mentioned in the Griffiths Valuations as tenants became the de facto owners after the land settlement bills were passed at the end of the century.

Finally in order to put everything written in this book into perspective, a little research was done into the numbers of Nolans living today in Forth. The total population of Carlow county in the 1990s was just over 40,000. The population of the barony of Forth is about 6,000 and this does not take into account the town of Tullow, which is on the border of Rathvilly barony. Out of the 124 electoral units in the barony there were Nolans living in just 58 of these. The total number of Nolan electors was 300. Assuming that this represents 150 families and assuming that each family unit consisted of 4 people this gives the numbers of Nolans in Forth as about 600. To further enhance the perspective there are over 1100 Nolan families living in Dublin while in the Kerry/Limerick/Clare area there are about 250 Nolan families.

I do not propose to extend this work any further as neither time nor resources will permit. The struggles of the Land League, Home Rule and the Fight for Independence are three enormous topics, not to mention the involvement of the people of the barony in World War One (where some Nolans found their way and lost their lives).

The final chapter in this book is devoted to giving some details about a few famous O'Nolans of the past. I leave the famous Nolans of the 20th. century (and there are many) to future historians.

Chapter 23

Some Famous O'Nolans

The O'Nolans or Nolans I have selected to remember in this last chapter more or less chose themselves. They are the men who contributed to the advancement of humanity in one way or another. I have not selected these men in any particular order, so the ordering of the merits of their contributions to society I leave up to the reader.

John 'Amnesty' Nolan

John Amnesty Nolan, was the son of Charles Nolan of Ballytore, Co. Kildare. His grandfather was John Nolan of Knockendrane, Co. Carlow. John Amnesty's grandfather, John, bought the farm at Ballytore sometime around the turn of the century. Charles had another son also. He was Patrick Nolan who later became P.P. of Rathoe. He went into business and became Acting Director of the great drapery establishment of Peter Paul McSweeney and Co. which later was better known as Clery & Co.[661] At some stage he joined the Fenian movement. Following the abortive Fenian rising of 1867 and the execution of the Manchester Martyrs, John Nolan, on his release from prison, began to work to secure the release of political prisoners from Irish and English jails. He came into contact with Isaac Butt (later the founder of the 'Home Rule' movement). Butt, a barrister, had represented many of the Fenian prisoners at their trials in 1867 and may in fact have represented John himself. Butt was elected President of the Amnesty Association and John was one of its most forceful and tireless organisers. As a direct result of the work of the Association there was a huge groundswell of public sympathy for the Fenians and for their ideals that resulted in the founding of the 'Home Rule' movement in 1870. According to Fr. Wm. Maher, John was 'the originator, the life and soul, the moving spirit of the Amnesty movement.'

It would appear that John Nolan went to America with the intention of mobilising American public opinion to further his aims of securing releases from English and Irish prisons. In this his efforts were successful and many prisoners were given early releases. One of these was Michael Davitt, who later became the founder of the Land League. After Davitt's release in 1877 John

---

[661] Fr. William Maher notes.

308

Nolan retired from political activities and went to work in Philadelphia. He worked with the firm of Sharpless Brothers, one of the largest firms in dry goods in America. He died in 1887 in New York, probably from T.B. He was buried in that city.

Michael Davitt had a monument erected to John Nolan in Glasnevin, at his own expense, in November of 1887. During the course of his speech, delivered on the occasion of the unveiling of the monument, to a crowd of several hundred, he said that some of them had come that day out of gratitude to the memory of a man who had remembered them when they were in prison. That he was sure they had assembled there to do reverence to the name of as true a soldier of Irish Liberty as any that had fought in the present generation. "Books had been written", he said, "about the history of the movement that had arisen in Ireland in the past twenty years, and one would search their pages in vain to find mention of John Nolan's name or any record of his work. Yet at one time there was no more familiar word in any household than John Amnesty Nolan." (cheers). "Under the leadership of Isaac Butt he marshalled the forces of Ireland to demand the liberation of political prisoners and to work for the freedom of Ireland from Castle Rule."

Michael Davitt went on to say that he himself thought it right and proper that although John Nolan's last remains were clasped in the friendly clay of freedom in America, that some humble record of his service and some memory of his name should be found there where so many true soldiers of Irish Liberty spoke to them from the tomb of service and sacrifice even unto death in the cause of Ireland (cheers) nor was it out of place that that little ceremony should take place on that day when Nationalists throughout the world were paying the annual tribute of love, reverence and devotion to the names of Allen, Larkin and O'Brien. Twenty years ago last Wednesday, those, their countrymen, offered up their lives freely and cheaply in Manchester for Irish Liberty; and twenty years had only deepened their affection for their memory. (cheers)

He then said that they had not the honour of having John Nolan in Ireland, because his friends in America objected to his remains being taken to anything but a free country. But whenever they came there he was sure that they would come to that monument and say a prayer for the eternal repose of John Amnesty Nolan, - another "ex criminal" like himself.

John Francis Xavier O'Brien then went on to say a few words. He said that he knew John Nolan better than anyone, and had worked closely with him. He ventured to say that he knew him even better than Mr. Davitt, who was responsible for the monument. John Nolan was a man who should be remembered in Ireland's long list of martyrs. Had he taken the course of simply minding his business he would have been one of the most prosperous merchants in Dublin. (hear hear). But he chose the service of Ireland and gave up his health and his prospects in her service.

Monument to John Amnesty Nolan in Glasnevin Cemetery

It would seem that a correspondent of the *Express*, a Dublin paper, had written an account of his death, but had incorrectly stated that John Nolan had died in poverty in America. Davitt immediately refuted this and a few days following Fr. Nolan of Rathoe wrote a letter to the Freeman's Journal and this is what he said:

"Dear Sir, I think it would ill become the only surviving brother of the late John Nolan, to remain in a state of silent indifference with regard to the honour done to his memory, both in word and deed, by Mr. Michael Davitt last Sunday at Glasnevin. I acknowledge that the feelings with which I read your account of Sundays' demonstration as far as related to my brother were those of gratified amazement. It is a prodigy of pure and disinterested friendship that Mr. Davitt should have erected that monument at his sole expense and unknown to all except the sculptor. I beg, through the medium of your paper, to give expression to Mr. Davitt of my deeply felt gratitude. I beg also to thank Mr. Davitt for his prompt contradiction of 'Aziola' in yesterday's *Express*.

My brother, in his last illness, was neither in want of money of his own nor of the solicitous care of true friends. Amongst those I would like to make particular mention of Mr. Phelim O'Neill, No. 10, St. Mark's Place, New York, who visited him nearly every day.

Until stricken down by his last attack of the lungs, my brother was on the staff of Sharpless Brothers, Eight and Chestnut Streets, Philadelphia. Ten years ago he voluntarily retired into obscurity, by ceasing connection with every political party both in Ireland and America.

If they would not occupy too much space and give you too much trouble, I would feel obliged if you publish this note and the enclosed from the Sisters of Mercy who attended him in his last illness. - Your truly,
Patrick F. Nolan. P.P."

" St. Vincent's Hospital, April 21st. 1887."
"Dear Rev. Father, - A friend of our deceased patient has requested me to forward any message left or expressed by Mr. John Nolan, during his last days while under our care at St. Vincent's.
I know it is sometimes the only consolation left the sorrowing ones; but though in Mr. Nolan's case there is really nothing to be transmitted to you of this nature, we have an infinitely more precious message. It is: he died a holy and consoling death, in the full possession of all his faculties and in perfect peace and resignation to God's holy will, as those sentiments he feelingly expressed when told by the sister of his evidently fast approaching end. His patience and uncomplaining silence during his trying illness was rewarded even here. He had the great happiness of receiving the Holy Viaticum a few hours

before his death. R.I.P. This Rev. Fr. is the account of his last hours, and few have been so privileged. - I remain very respectfully yours in our Lord.
Sister Ag. Per."

This is what Fr. Wm. Maher had to say about him. "He was tall, handsome and eloquent, and had he lived, would, in all probability, be not unworthy to rank among such imperishable names as Grattan, Flood, Fox and Curran."

Detail from Monument to John Amnesty Nolan

Philip Nolan

Philip Nolan was born in 1771 in Belfast , the son of Peter Nolan and Elizabeth Cassidy. According to the article written about him in the New Texas Handbook he received a good education. He was described as a " mustanger and filibuster" .

He seems to have gone to America in 1787 and obtained a post as bookkeeper and shipping clerk with General James Wilkinson of Kentucky the following year. According to the same authority he managed Wilkinson's business affairs in New Orleans from 1788 until 1791.

At that time ,Texas, which was very close geographically to New Orleans, was controlled by the Spanish. Philip soon realised the vast potential for trade with Indians of that region. Between 1791 and 1801 he made four expeditions into Texas from neighbouring Spanish Louisiana. These forays into unknown territory were regarded by early historians as filibusters - I suppose a filibuster might best be described as a primary expansionist move - and Gen. Wilkinson is supposed to have been the man behind these early forays into Texas which led eventually to the absorption of that state into the Union. Philip could have been described as an undercover agent.

His first expedition was the stuff of a real adventure. Wilkinson got him a trading permit from the Governor of Louisiana, Esteban Rodgriguez Miro. However when he arrived in the state with his wagons, his goods were confiscated and Nolan disappeared for two years. It seems he went to live with the Indians and began mapping the territory. He resurfaced again after the two years and arrived back in New Orleans with 50 mustang. He was greeted by the new Governor of Louisiana, Louis Hector, Baron of Carondelet in person, as "risen from the dead".

The next year again in 1794 Philip was back in Texas with a permit from the Baron to obtain horses for the Louisiana militia. By 1795 he had returned to Louisiana with 250 horses. As on the previous trip, he spent a lot of time surveying the areas he visited and aroused the suspicions of the Spanish authorities. These suspicions were further aroused when he went on a mapping expedition up the Missouri river with Andrew Ellicott, a boundary commissioner for the U.S.

By 1797 he seems to have won over the Spanish governor again and got another permit to find horses for the Louisiana militia. This time he took with him many wagon loads of trade goods, even though trade between Louisiana and Texas was strictly forbidden. During the course of this trip he seems to have tried to stir up the Indians against Spanish rule and so incurred the displeasure of some Spanish officials. He arrived back in Louisiana in 1798 with 1200 horses.

He married in 1799 and his wife was Frances Lintot, the daughter of a Louisiana planter. At this time Thomas Jefferson was in correspondence with Nolan about the huge numbers of wild horses in Texas, but the two never met.

He was unable to get another permit to go to Texas but despite this, he set out in 1800 with a large body of armed men. He moved into the interior of Texas and set up a small fort near the Brazos River and he and his men began rounding up horses. The Spaniards sent a force against the Irishman and his troops and in a battle fought there in March 1801 Philip Nolan was killed. Most of his men were captured and spent a long number of years in prison. His wife died shortly afterwards and his only son died in childhood.

He became famous as the first of along line of frontiersmen that eventually helped to free Texas from Spanish and Mexican rule. He was one of the first men to map Texas and in 1804 Wilkinson published a map of Texas based on Nolan's work.

Today Nolan county in west central Texas, and the town of Nolan also, are called after Philip Nolan. In addition there is Nolan's creek and Noland's River in Texas.

Amazingly the area of Nolan County was not populated with Anglos until well after the Civil War when buffalo hunters moved in. It was established as a distinct area in 1881 when Sweetwater, built by the Texas and Pacific Railway company, was named as the County seat. Settlers began arriving in big numbers after that and by 1910 there were 12,000 people in the county. Oil was discovered in Nolan county and was worth $100 million to the county in 1990. Nolan county is today largely agricultural. The farmers rear cattle, sheep and angora goats and they grow cotton, wheat and hay with potatoes, peaches, tomatoes, and watermelons.

Captain James Nolan

The information about Captain James Nolan is fairly scant, but it is interesting because of the claims he made regarding the Nolans. This information is contained in Carte's Life of the Duke of Ormonde. The events mentioned here occurred in the 1670s.

It would appear that after the restoration of the monarchy (1662)which occurred not long after the Cromwellian Confiscations many people who had their lands taken away applied to have them restored. A Colonel Richard Talbot attempted to make himself rich by assuring people he could get their lands back and charging them a hefty fee for his efforts if successful. A group of Lords - Westmeath, Mountgarret, Dungan, Netterville, Barnewall and Trimleston with forty five gentlemen signed a paper by which on behalf of the Roman Catholics of Ireland they appointed Col. Talbot as their agent for petitions (to get lands restored).

A committee was appointed by the king to look into the matter and when the committee met they called Col Talbot to present his cases. Talbot applied for time to bring in detailed accounts of individuals. The Duke of Ormonde, who was the de facto governor of Ireland at the time became alarmed that the real intention was to set aside the Acts of Settlement and this would throw the whole country into turmoil. However the committee did allow Talbot to be represented by a lawyer, who tried to imply that all the Catholics had been loyal in 1641 (which was clearly not the case). A long legal argument followed lasting several months and the upshot of it all was a report sent to the king outlining the forfeitures of lands and the distribution of lands in the aftermath of the Cromwellian invasion and after the restoration of the monarchy. In Ireland the people who had been granted lands - the soldiers, adventurers etc., became very alarmed, thinking that they themselves would be driven from their lands. They in turn now petitioned the king to leave things as they were.

The Lords in England were divided on the matter but the Duke of Ormonde stood in favour of allowing the Acts of Settlement to stand. His enemies then tried every means they could to prove that he himself was trying to hold onto lands he did not own.

Together with one Edmond Byrne of the Barony of Forth, Captain James Nolan became a witness in the case against the Duke of Ormonde. Cartes asserts that the Captain and Byrne were paid substantial sums of money to perjure themselves, the purpose being to discredit the Duke of Ormonde.

"The other witness produced was one Captain James Nolan, whose ancestor Hugh Nolan divided his little estate in Shangarry, in the same barony, containing ten acres Forth measure equally between his two sons ,Cahir and Daniel. The former left issue, and the latter marrying two wives, had by the first Edmond father of James Nolan. Daniel, on occasion of a difference with his son, declared that Edmond was born two years before wedlock, and by a feoffment made Sept, 1640, ready to be produced and proved, settled what land he had in Shangarry on Patrick Nolan, his son by his second wife Anastace Byrne, and his heirs ; so that captain Nolan could have no right to the land, which Patrick Nolan entered upon and possessed from his father's death, till he took lands in Connaught."

Captain Nolan joined the rebel forces in 1641 i.e. the Catholic side and he fought in Daniel Kavanagh's regiment. According to Cartes he was stationed at Clonmullen during the war and on one occasion he with some men had murdered five men in Co. Carlow, including Patrick Nolan and James Curwen a servant of Thomas Bagnall (whom he took out of his master's haggard at Ballynunnery) He survived the Cromwellian Wars and probably continued fighting in Daniel Kavanagh's regiment. In 1652 he went abroad with that regiment in support of the king who went into exile. He came back into Ireland sometime after the restoration in 1662. He served on a jury of ancient proprietors in 1664, before a court baron, which was enquiring into the extent of the lands of the Duke of Ormonde. At that court Shangarry was adjudged to belong to the Duke and Patrick Nolan, the ancient proprietor acknowledged this. Shangarry was never given to any adventurers or soldiers. Captain Nolan rented the lands until 1669 when he was alleged to have murdered Thady Nolan and to escape trial he fled into England.

Sometime in 1670 he approached the Duke of Ormonde for help, complaining that he had been turned out of his estate which had belonged to his ancestors and had been rented by himself. He went on to tell the Duke all he had done for him in securing his lands in the barony of Forth. The Duke gave him eight guineas and told him to go back to Ireland.

Nolan stayed on in London and soon became friendly with Talbot who urged him to pursue a claim to the Shangarry lands, by petitioning the king. Nolan did this and in his letter to the king explained how his grandfather was seized in fee of some lands in the barony of Forth on Oct. 29th. 1641 and had died in possession of those lands in 1647. His father died the same year. He said he followed the king abroad in 1652 and was in his service abroad until 1662, when he returned in the hope of having his lands restored. He then went on to say that the Duke of Ormonde, finding the lands in Shangarry etc. next to his and not occupied by adventurers or soldiers had taken possession of them without any manner of title. He further alleged that the Duke had agreed to restore his lands to him if he paid the Duke and his heirs 12 pence an acre. The Duke, however had reneged on the deal and he was now destitute with a wife and nine young children. He begged the king to refer his case to the commissioners appointed to look into those matters.

The Duke who was in the court heard the petition being read out and contacted Nolan. He told him that if he could prove that he was promised the land he could have it. Nolan said the Duke's agent Mr. Walsh had promised it before forty witnesses. Walsh when questioned by the Duke told him that Nolan had no claim on the land, which was occupied by Patrick Nolan who was ready to prove his title and former possession. The Duke felt compelled to write to the king about the matter and he wrote a very long and detailed letter explaining the whole matter, but indicting Captain Nolan.

Nolan was commanded to bring his witnesses and begged leave of the king to bring Colonel Talbot as a witness. Talbot however had to go to Ireland on business and was not available. Nolan then asked leave of the king to have his case heard in Dublin, but this was refused. The whole business of the Duke and Nolan took seven weeks. In his final summation Cartes said the object of the exercise was to try to take back the entire barony of Forth which was worth £1,500 p.a. (rents) and to get £14,000 of profits from the Duke.

We know that Captain James Nolan lost his case, (surprise, surprise) and that is all we know about him.

John B. Nolan

John B. Nolan[662] was born in Ballinrush in 1838. He went to the National School (Myshall) and then to a Secondary School in Tullow. Like many young men of the time he was 'prenticed to a grocer'. John B. Nolan went to Bagenalstown and worked in a shop there until he was about seventeen and then moved to Dublin. According to one report he entered "one of the most extensive establishments of that city where his abilities as a businessman soon procured him a most lucrative employment in Belfast."

In Dublin he joined the Irish Republican Brotherhood (the I.R.B.) and in Belfast he became one of the principal organisers of the Fenians there. James Stephens pressed him into resigning from business so that he could more fully do the work of organising the province. In March of 1866 Stephens and many of the Fenian organisers were arrested, but John B. managed to escape and went to London. While he was there he was very active in the Fenians and set up the Irish Directory, which was responsible for the raid on Chester Castle. He may well have been implicated in the Manchester affair which ultimately resulted in the hanging of Allen, Larkin and O'Brien - the Manchester Martyrs.

When things got too hot for him in England he went to America. In New York he was unhappy with the lukewarm attitude of the New York Fenians. He went to Chicago where he tried to have Northern Ireland worthily represented at the Chicago Fair, but without success.

His health must have deteriorated at this time and he seems to have moved about quite a bit. He was working for a Mr. Dunne in Peoria, then he moved to St. Louis and from that to Leavenworth and finally got employment in Kansas with Mr. James FitzPatrick. He stayed in FitzPatrick's house but T.B. eventually got the better of him and he died there on January 6th. 1870. It would seem that he had either founded a Fenian cell in Kansas or had become a key player in an existing one as on the Monday following his death a number of men assembled to decide how to pay tribute to John B. Nolan. These men included Captain McNamara, Thomas Haire, Major P. Shannon, Colonel R.H.Hunt, Captain M. Conlon, John Donnelly and M.A. Brady. One of the many resolutions of this body reads:

"Be it resolved that we shall ever cherish his memory with affectionate regard, and while the shaft of death has stricken him down suddenly in our midst, we regard him as much a martyr to the cause of freedom of his native

---

[662] He had a brother Andy who became a Commercial Traveller. I think they lived on the farm now owned by Jim Nolan of Ballinrush.

land as though his life blood was poured out on the gory field, in asserting her right to be free"

Another resolution read:

" Resolved - that while we bow with humble submission to the fiat of an Almighty God, we deeply deplore the loss of one who has proved himself an incorruptible patriot, ever true to his native land in her bitterest trials, filled with hope for her future; an earnest and zealous labourer in her cause; an ornament not only to her, but to the country of his adoption ; possessing all the qualities of mind and heart which endear man to his kindred and his kind."

The following from "Recollections of Fenians and Fenianism", by John O'Leary[663] appeared in the Irish Weekly Independent Saturday June 20th. 1896. 'Of John Nolan, who was mainly instrumental in spreading the organisation in the North, I, personally knew less than I did of Duffy, though, indirectly I heard and even knew a good deal about him, among other ways hearing him constantly in the paper. Judging from his work, which is the best test of most men, he must have had more than ordinary capacity in many ways, and most certainly he had more than ordinary activity and energy. There is no halo around his memory as there is around Duffy's but not the less was he a good man and true, doing in his day good work for Ireland and so deserving, at the least, such slight record of himself and his services as they get here.

John Nolan died, I understand not many years after the time of which I am now writing. Here, too, I may at least mention the name of Andrew Nolan, the brother of John, who then and long before, was one of our most energetic workers, but the seat of his activity was Leinster, not Ulster. They were both, I believe, Carlow men by birth and family, and both, I think, Commercial Travellers by profession. Andrew, I hear, is still living and I sincerely hope he is thriving and has thriven."

Bishop Edward Nolan

Edward Nolan was born in 1793 in Tullow, where his father James Nolan "occupied a position of respectability" according to Fr. Comerford in his Collections relating to the Diocese of Kildare and Leighlin. We know from the Ballykealy pedigree detailed above that James Nolan was descended in a direct line from Cahir O'Nolan of Ballykealy, who died in 1592.

James Nolan, the bishop's father was himself born in 1758 and was married to Mary Moore of Tullow in 1789. A very peculiar tale is related about Mary Moore. When she was just a girl, Dr. Keefe, the then Bishop, gave her an Episcopal ring, telling her to keep it for one of her sons who should be a

---

[663] Of Fenian fame

Bishop. Mary kept the ring, not mentioning the matter, except to her husband, and upon Dr. Keeffe's death, gave it to the Right Rev. Dr. Delaney, informing him of how she had come into its possession. Dr. Delaney accepted it in trust, and returned it before his death in 1814. This ring, according to Rev. Comerford was still in the possession of a member of the family at the time he (Dr. Comerford) was writing.

Edward became a pupil at Carlow College as did his brothers John, Thomas, Patrick and Daniel. Edward wished to become a priest and was sent to Maynooth. While he was there he had second thoughts and he was sent home, where he remained for two years. He returned to Maynooth in 1814 and was ordained in 1819, by Dr. Doyle (J.K.L.) who was then the Bishop of Kildare & Leighlin.

"Braganza" Bishops Palace, Carlow.

Braganza - the Bishop's Palace in Carlow

319

Edward was held in the highest esteem in the college and after attaining his doctorate in Philosophy he was offered a permanent post in the college which he declined. He went back to Carlow, where he was appointed a Professor in Carlow College occupying the chairs of Logic and later Theology. He was reputed to be a man of great gentleness and amiability. He led a saintly life of regularity, edification and devotedness to his many duties. He was held is such esteem by the Bishop, that he appointed him as his confessor.

One of his greatest moments was when he took part in the celebrated Bible Society debate in Carlow town. This was a huge event and admission was by ticket only. It was a defining moment in the history of Catholicism as the very essence of religion was being challenged in public debate. The Protestant side was represented by very able men - Hon. and Rev. E. Wingfield, Rev. Mr. Daly and Rev. Mr. Pope. The Catholic side was upheld by Rev. McSwiney, Rev. Clowry and Dr. Nolan.

The brunt of the entire argument from the Catholic viewpoint was maintained by Dr. Nolan, who gave an absolutely brilliant delivery that was most logical and lucid and refuted entirely the views put forward by the Protestant side.

During the course of his speech he delivered a withering condemnation of the Tithe System and of the Tory politicians whose sole object was to retain the status quo of the landlord system. He maintained the right of the Catholic clergy to place their weight behind the most suitable candidates in elections.

After the death of Dr. Doyle, JKL, he was appointed as Bishop of the Diocese in 1834. The consecration of the new Prelate took place in the Cathedral in Carlow, on the 28th. October. He was ordained Bishop by Archbishop Murray, assisted by the Bishops of Ossory and Ferns. But he was not destined to live a long life. After just a few short years Dr. Nolan caught typhus fever and died in October 1837. He was only 44 yrs old.

He had a huge funeral which was attended by people of all persuasions and he was buried next to Dr. Doyle in the Cathedral. A black marble monument over his grave bears the following inscription:

Here lie the remains of the
Right Revd. Edward Nolan,
Bishop of Kildare and Leighlin;
Consecrated, Oct.28th. 1834. Died, Oct. 14th. 1837,
Aged 44 years.
Ever from his childhood distinguished for his
Pure Piety, his Gentleness, and amiable simplicity of manners,
he was called from a life of beloved seclusion
Congenial to his humble and Retiring Disposition,
to watch over the Church of Kildare and Leighlin,

Which he Governed in Peace and Happiness,
Edifying all by his Saintly Example,
and Commanding the Cheerful Obedience of all,
More by the Influence of his Endearing Virtue
Than by the Authority with which he was Vested.
Requiescat in Pace.

Captain James Nolan
the '98 Rebel

For the information contained here I am indebted to Brother P.J. Kavanagh's excellent article in the Carloviana of Dec. 1997 entitled "James Nolan of Knockendrane, Captain of the Myshall Rebels 1798."

James Nolan was the son of Lawrence Nolan of Lisgarvan, and Anne Wright, formerly a Quaker of Kilconnor. In 1760 Lawrence was evicted from Lisgarvan where the family had been living since 1713. As has already been pointed out in the chapter dealing with families the Knockendrane and Ballinrush Nolans were descended from Hugh of Shangarry, living in the late 1500s and early 1600s one of a small number of ruling O'Nolan families and a princes of his sept.

Lawrence settled his four sons in Knockendrane, a farm of 400 acres which he had bought from Lord Duncannon in the late 1750s for some £550, subject of course to the yearly rent. He gave each son 100 acres. Like the Cloneys of Wexford and the Kellys of Killane many Nolans, including the Knockendrane and Ballinrush Nolans[664] were gentlemen farmers who leased other lands and sub let them to different tenants.

James was reputed to have been born in 1745 but this is probably incorrect as his mother was not born before 1730. His other brothers and sisters were born much later, Edmund in 1755, Anna in 1761, Lawrence in 1764, John in 1765 and another daughter, Mary, whose date of birth is not recorded in the data I have studied. I suspect James's date of birth may have been 1754.

He married Elizabeth Barry and they appeared to have had five sons and four daughters. The daughters were Anne who married John Fenelon and emigrated to America, Catherine who died in 1866 aged 61 yrs., Mary who died in 1882 aged 72 yrs. and Ellen Tyrell who died in 1886 aged 85 yrs. His sons were:-

    1. John b. 1794 who died in 1832 aged 38 yrs.

---

[664] Edmund, a brother of James bought Ballinrush. It is not clear what he did with his portion of Knockendrane.

2. Lawrence b. 1795 who died in 1884 aged 89 yrs.
3. Robert b. 1801 who died in 1893 aged 92 yrs.
4. Edward b. 1802 who died in 1843 aged 41yrs.
5. Richard who died in 1899. [665]

Fr. Swayne in compiling his *'98 in Carlow*, interviewed Peter Fox of Ballinrush[666] in 1972 about events in the Myshall area. Among other things he mentioned that "Myshall at that time was governed by Major Cornwall. He was the military officer for the district and the magistrate. The Myshall United Irishmen did not take part in the Battle of Carlow. They were commanded by Captain James Nolan and took part in the battles of Borris and the taking of Bagenalstown. They did not succeed in either of these but Nolan got his men back safely. There were informers in the camp and these gave the names of the insurgents to Cornwall. The parish priest, Fr. Brian Kavanagh knew that their fate would be the pitch cap or the hangman's rope so he went to Cornwall to plead for them. Cornwall said they would have to go to him to deliver up their arms; then he would grant them their lives, but on one condition, that they would enrol themselves in a labour corps and make a new road, ever since called the Croppy Road, and dig the pond."

Very little is known about James Nolan's career in the United Irishmen. Following accusations that men from Myshall had gone to Tullow to recruit people to the United Irishmen the alarmed citizens decided to repudiate this charge. John Nolan of Ballinvalley (John the Poet)[667] was the orator who delivered the Address. In the course of the address it was noted that "a most wicked and malicious report has been spread abroad that several inhabitants of this town did assemble near Tullow with an intent to administer an unlawful oath ... such an accusation tended to asperse our loyalty to our most gracious Majesty and much beloved Sovereign" . The Address was delivered to Robert Cornwall of Myshall Lodge.

A Militia unit was formed in the county, in the mid 1790s, as was done all over the country, because of the threat of a French invasion. Catholics, who up to this time were forbidden to carry arms could now do so as Militiamen. There was much opposition to the new Militia at first but when the balloting took place two hundred Myshall men turned up, although the allotted quota was only thirteen recruits for the parish. The remainder offered their services as substitutes for any draftees who didn't wish to be enlisted. The names of

---

[665] Richard left some of his land to Luke Nolan, a relative, who was the great grandfather of Jimmy Nolan of Knockendrane, the present owner.

[666] He was the owner of Ballinrush House and lands at the time, as the Nolans had sold out in 1920 and gone to Dublin. Seamus Lalor is the present owner of Ballinrush.

[667] John the Poet was most likely well aware of the involvement of his nephew Captain James Nowlan who was in all probability one of those recruiting at Tullow.

Monument to Captain James Nolan in Drumphea Cemetery

some Nolans/Nowlans appear on the Muster rolls of Major Newton's company of Militia. They included Patrick, James Snr., James Jnr., and James Nowlan. I would have no hesitation in saying that the James Nowlan mentioned or the other James Nolans were not Captain James. He was a middle aged man, married at the time, with a young family, and the men joining the militia were generally young men of no means.

Many of the officer class of United Irishmen in Wexford, men of James Nolan's ilk, had joined Yeomanry corps in their own localities and in this way they received military training and training in the use of firearms. Again it is purely speculative to suggest that James Nolan must have gained his experience in this way.

We do not know if he suffered any repercussions for his activities, but he continued living in Knockendrane until his death in 1858. This is what the Carlow Post had to say about him:-

' On Saturday morning the 17th. April, at his residence, Knockendrane, parish of Myshall, in this county, Mr. James Nolan departed this life at the very advanced age of 116 years. He remained in perfect possession of all his faculties till the day preceding his dissolution.

In personal appearance he was most commanding with good features, and fully six feet in stature. He was visited annually by his excellent landlord, the Earl of Bessborough, who delighted to hold converse with him on the many and varied incidents of which he was an eyewitness. His memory was excellent. The scenes of the memorable year of 1798 were related by him with the greatest precision and the most pleasing humour, and his recollection of the leading celebrities of the last century were most accurately and cheerfully reviewed by him. He was of good family and could trace his descent from the ancient princes of his country. The deceased had two brothers[668] Mr. Edward (Edmund) Nolan of Ballinrush in this county and Mr. John Nolan of Coolcargen (Coolcarrigeen) Co. Kildare, who lived to very great ages."

Brother P.J. Kavanagh rightly pointed out that by 1858 most Irishmen wished to forget 1798. 'This is well exemplified in General Cloney's Memoirs where he sought to distance himself from it. Hence the very vague reference in the Post to the part played by James Nolan in that event.' This is what is written on this tombstone:

Erected by Richard and Robert Nolan
of Knockendrane in affectionate memory
of their parents.

---

[668] The writer obviously did not know about Lawrence, of Ballymartin, who died in 1808 aged 44 yrs.

James Nolan who died April 21st. 1857 aged
112 years and Elizabeth Nolan, nee Barry
who died June 17th. 1827 aged 60 years and
of their brothers and sisters John died October
1832 aged 38 years.
Edward died April 13th. 1843 aged 41 years
Lawrence died Nov. 26th. 1884 aged 82 years
Anne Fenelon died in America
Catherine died August 15th. 1886 aged 61 years
Mary died Sept. 20th. 1882 aged 72 years
Ellen Tyrell died May 19th. 1886 aged 83 years
Their nephew John Fenelon died 184? aged 23 years.

Dr. Charles Nolan

Very little is known about Dr. Charles Nolan, but Comerford the ecclesiastical historian had this to say. "Dr. Dempsey was appointed Bishop of Leighlin on March 10th. 1642 and died in Spain in 1658 aged 56 years. From the death of Dr. Dempsey to the year 1678, when the Bishop of Kildare received its administration, the Diocese of Leighlin was under the care of Vicars. In a Propaganda Congregation held on the 12th. July 1661, a letter was read from the Archbishop of Armagh, stating that he had placed the Diocese of Leighlin under the Vicar -General of the deceased Bishop. From a report of the State of Ireland, presented in Rome in 1662, we find that the Vicar-General referred to was Charles Nolan. The following is the passage of this interesting document which relates to this Diocese:- 'In the Diocese of Leighlin I was acquainted with Dr. Charles Nolan, the Vicar-General, a most learned and holy man, who had undergone much suffering and exposed himself to many dangers on account of his flock, remaining constantly amongst them, surrounded by enemies and in circumstances of the utmost danger. He used to conceal himself in the woods and in mountain caves by day, and administer to his flocks by night."

Fr. Agapitus of the Holy Ghost order, who was running the affairs of the Carmelite Order was in Dublin. He reported that there were about 12 priests in Dublin who ministered to their flocks in disguise. Fr. Agapitus had several narrow escapes and once in the company of Dr. Charles Nolan he just managed to escape from pursuing troopers by running into a wood and hiding. We assume he was travelling through the country and had come to Carlow.

It is not known if Dr. Nolan lived until 1678 but there is no record of his death in the book of martryology.

Charles is the anglicised version of Cahir and Dr. Charles must have started out his life as Cahir O'Nolan. We have no idea which sup sept he was from, but we do know that he was a highly educated man and was, most likely, educated abroad. The name Cahir appears in the Ballykealy, Shangarry and Kilbride sub septs, so it would be safe to assume he came from the ruling family of one of those septs. As he was appointed Vicar General in 1661 it is safe to speculate that he was born between 1610 and 1620.

Professor John James Nolan

The obituary written about Professor Nolan by P.J. McLaughlin is simple, stark and unadorned, much like the man himself. He was very highly respected for his work in physics where he dealt with such topics as "The Electric Charge on Rain".

Born in Omagh, Co. Tyrone in 1888, he was the son of Martin Nolan of Roscommon and Bridget Owens of Fermanagh.

Whatever his father worked at involved moving residence fairly frequently, much like James Joyce's father. Young John James and his brother P.J. (later to become a Doctor) attended many schools including The CBS in Omagh, the National School at Stewardstown, Dromore and St. McCartans Seminary Monaghan and later St. Patrick's Academy, Dungannon, where he studied Italian.

He entered The Royal National University in Dublin which later became UCD in 1906 and was one of the few ever to hold a Bishop's Scholarship. (Another Professor Nolan - Thomas Nolans also held one). His future wife, a Miss Hurley was also in the same class.

In 1909 He graduated in Physics and Chemistry and was not alone top of the class but got the best ever marks in his exams. He was appointed Assistant in Physics in that year and in 1920 when the head of the Department died in 1920 John Nolan became Professor of Experimental Physics. He was renowned as a teacher and his research work in atmospheric electricity was closely studied by the important European Physicists - Mathias and Chaveau. Because of his international reputation as a scientist he was able to entice very famous men to come to Dublin to lecture, including Appleton, Thomson and Emeleus.

Professor Nolan was instrumental in founding the Institute for Advanced Studies and was at various times chief officer of the Royal Irish Academy and the School of Cosmic Physics.

As a man, Nolan never attempted to hide his antipathy to mediocrity, sham, insincerity, pretentiousness and self-seeking whether in academic or public persons. He had strong feelings about certain political events though he scarcely ever gave expression to them except among friends. He was well informed about people and he had a gift for summing them up in a witty word or phrase. His standards were high and he was not a man to temporise or waste words. Unsentimental, he refused to be distracted in the discussion of a question by the hard luck story or the emotional appeal. But everyone found that the man who looked inflexible was full of humanity, and students found him exact yet always fair and kindly. Friendship had a solid meaning for this cultured Irish Catholic scientist. He died in his own lecture theatre teaching his largest class, a circumstance not unbefitting a man so devoted to his profession.

Dom. Patrick Nolan

While researching Nolans in the National Library, I came across Dom Patrick Nolan. He was a Benedictine monk, who wrote two important works - one was A History of Irish Banking and the other was "The Dames of Ypres" (Macmine and Kylemore Abbey). In trying to find out a little more about him I came across a reference to his death in a publication called the Catholic Bulletin. This is what was said about him:

'We regret to have to record in this issue the death of two old and consistent friends of the Bulletin, the Rev. Dom Nolan, O.S.B., and the Rev. John Lennon, P.P. Of the work of Dom Nolan, a distinguished member of the Benedictine Order, there is detailed notice elsewhere in our pages. He was a deep thinker, a ripe scholar, a robust writer, a steadfast friend, a patriot of uncommon courage, a zealous, if modest churchman, whose sudden and unexpected death in Dorchester, Oxford, in the midst of ceaseless labours for the faith of his fathers and the land of his birth will be lamented equally as a loss to religion and to patriotic literature.'

In order to find out a little more about him I contacted Glenstal Abbey and Dom Mark Tierney sent me some further data, some of which was in French and was kindly translated for me by Deirdre Byrne of Knockainey.

It would seem that Dom Patrick Nolan was the son and heir of the Nolan side of the Brown and Nolan partnership, the Dublin publishers and booksellers. He was born in 1865 and received a University education. He desired to become a Benedictine, but as there were no noviciate in Ireland he opted to join the monastery in Maredsous in Belgium, where there was an Irish abbot - Dom Columba Marmion.[669] He brought with him a substantial sum of money, to be used to establish a Benedictine monastery in Ireland and this money was

---

[669] Dom Joseph Columba Marmion was abbot of the Belgian monastery of Maredsous when he died in 1923. He was born in Dublin in 1858 and was educated at Belvedere College, Clonliffe and at the Irish College in Rome. After his ordination he returned home and was a curate in Dundrum for a time. He was appointed professor of philosophy at Clonliffe and in 1886 he joined the Benedictine Order. In 1909 he was appointed the abbot of Maredsous. In 1999 he was declared "Venerable" by the Vatican.

left in Maredsous. He went there in 1894 but was transferred to Birmingham in 1895 and was ordained there in 1899.

He was in constant contact with Dom Marmion, and in 1914 Dom Marmion instructed Patrick to purchase a property. Patrick settled on Edermine, the former home of the Power family, whose last member Sir James Douglas Power was killed in the War in 1914. This house was to be used as a sanctuary for the young monks of Maredsous who were refugees in England. The money was provided by a wealthy aristocratic nun, the Marquise de Bizien du Lezard, who wished to see a Benedictine monastery and a convent established in Ireland.

However Dom Patrick seems to have been of an independent frame of mind and didn't get on very well with his Belgian colleagues or the Marquise. The abbot of Edermine wrote to Dom Marmion complaining about Patrick and asked for his removal from the monastery. It would appear that Patrick did things his own way and moved about in the local community and this was resented by the secretive monks. Fr. Marmion complied and moved him to another foundation called Erdington in England.

After the First World War Dom Patrick came back to Wexford and joined Fr. Sweetman at the Mount, near Gorey - incidentally the home of the infamous Hunter Gowan of 1798 infamy- where the Benedictines had established a college in the late 1800s. (James Dillon was one of the past pupils of the college)

In 1920 the Benedictines decided to close down Edermine, and Dom Patrick got his money from Maredsous where it had lain since 1894 and used it to buy Edermine. In 1922 he sold Edermine and continued to live at the Mount.

His superiors wrote to him on many occasions, castigating him for his disobedience in leaving his monastery at Erdington and for breaking his vow of poverty, but he always maintained he was not breaking any of his vows. He left the Mount in 1927 and tried to join Glenstal Abbey, a new Benedictine foundation, but he was not accepted. He then applied for a parish ministry and was accepted into Dorchester near Oxford. He died there, suddenly, in 1931 aged 66 yrs.

About half of his considerable estate was given to Glenstal, thanks to a compromise with his heirs.

Appendices - Appendix 1

Chronicles
of
England, France, Spain
and
The adjoining Countries

From the latter part of the reign of Edward II to the Coronation of Henry IV

by Sir John Froissart

Translated from the French Editions

With variations and additions from many celebrated MSS.

By Thomas Johnes, Esq.

To which are prefixed

A life of the Author, an essay on his works and a criticism on his History

In two Volumes.
LONDON

George Routledge and Sons, The Broadway, Ludgate.
New York: 416, Broome Street.
1874

At this period an expedition against Ireland was proposed in the English Council; for, in the truces King Richard had agreed to with France and her allies, young as he was, he had reserved Ireland from being included, as his predecessors had always claimed it as their right; and his grandfather, King Edward, of happy memory, had signed himself king and lord of Ireland, and had continued his wars against the natives notwithstanding his pressure from other quarters. The young knights and squires of England, eager to signalise themselves in arms, were rejoiced to learn that King Richard intended leading a large power of men-at-arms and archers into Ireland, and that he had declared he would not return thence until he should have finally settled everything to his satisfaction.......

After which he began to make most sumptuous preparations for crossing the sea, and taking possession of the duchy the king had invested him with. Purveyors were likewise busy in preparing, on a large scale, for the king's expedition to Ireland; and those lords who were to accompany him were ordered to make preparations of whatever things they might think necessary........

At this period the Lady Anne, Queen of England, fell sick, to the great distress of the king and her household. Her disorder increased so rapidly that she departed this life on the feast of Whitsuntide, in the year of grace 1394. The king and all who loved her were greatly afflicted by her death. She was buried in the cathedral church of London; ("On the 7th. June, queen Anne died at Shene in Surrey, and was buried at Westminster. The king took her death so heavily that, besides cursing the place where she died, he did also, for anger, throw down the buildings, unto the which, former kings, being weary of the city, were wont for pleasure to resort.")[670] But her obsequies were performed at leisure, for the king would have them magnificently done. Abundance of wax was sent for from Flanders, to make flambeaux and torches, and the illumination was so great on the day of the ceremony that nothing was ever seen like to it before, not at the burial of good queen Phillipa nor of any other. The king would have it so, because she was daughter to the king of Bohemia, Emperor of Rome and Germany.

He was inconsolable for her loss, as they mutually loved each other, having been married young. This queen left no issue, for she had never borne children.....there was no talk of the king's marrying again, for he would not hear of it. Although the expeditions to Ireland and Aquitaine were delayed by the queen's death, those lords who were named to go to Ireland did not fail continuing their preparations; and, as their purveyances were ready, they sent them across the sea to Ireland from Brisco and Lolighet in Wales; and conductors were ordered to carry them to a city on the coast of Ireland, called Dimelin, which had always been steadily attached to England, and was an archbishopric; the archbishop of which place was with the king.

Soon after St. John Baptist's day, King Richard left London, and took the road for Wales, amusing himself by hunting on the way, to forget the loss of his queen. Those ordered to attend him began their journey, such as his two uncles of York and Gloucester, with grand array, as did the other lords: the earl of Kent, half-brother to the king, Sir Thomas Holland, his son, the Earl of Rutland, son to the Duke of York, the Earl Marshal, the Earls of Salisbury and Arundel, Sir William Arundel, the Earl of Northumberland, Sir Thomas Percy, his brother, high steward of England, the Earls of Devonshire and Nottingham, with numbers of knights and squires. A considerable body remained at home to

---

[670] Stowe's Chronicle

guard the borders of Scotland; the Scots are a wicked race, and pay not any regard to truces or respites, but as it suits their own convenience.......

We will return to the King of England, who had with him full four thousand men-at-arms and thirty thousand archers. They were shipped at three different places, Bristol, Holyhead and Herford (from what follows I suppose this meant Haverford-West in Pembrokeshire, as it is pronounced Harford).

It passed over daily; but it was a month before the whole armament and their horses landed in Ireland. On the other hand, there was in Ireland a valiant knight, called the Earl of Ormonde, who, like his predecessors, held lands in that country, but they were disputed, and he had made similar preparations to his ancestors.

The Earl Marshal had the command of the van, consisting of fifteen hundred lances and two thousand archers, who prudently and valiantly conducted themselves. King Richard and his uncles embarked at Haverford in Wales, many at Holyhead and others at Bristol, and the whole landed without any loss. As they disembarked, by orders from the constable and marshals, they quartered themselves on the country, occupying a large uninhabited tract, of about thirty English miles, beside the city of Dublin. The army lodged themselves prudently, for fear of the Irish; had they done otherwise, they would have suffered for it. The King, his uncles and prelates were quartered in Dublin and near it; and I was told that, during the whole campaign they were well supplied with all sorts of provisions; for the English are expert in war, and know well how to forage and take proper care of themselves and horses. I will relate the history of this campaign of King Richard and what befell him, according to the information I received.......

It happened this same Sunday, after the King had received my book so handsomely, an English squire, being in the King's chamber, called Henry Castide, a man of prudence and character, and who spoke French well, made acquaintance with me, because he saw the King and lords give me so hearty a reception, and had likewise noticed the book I had presented to the King; he also imagined, from his first conversation, that I was an historian; indeed he had been told so by Sir Richard Sturrey. He thus addressed me: - "Sir John, have you as yet found anyone to give you an account the late expedition to Ireland and how four kings of that country submitted themselves to the obedience of the King?" I replied that I had not. "I will tell it you then," said the squire, who might be about fifty years old, "in order that, when you are returned home, you may at your leisure insert it in your history, to be had in perpetual remembrance." I was delighted to hear this and offered him my warmest thanks.

Henry Castide thus began:- " It is not in the memory of man that any king of England ever led so large an armament of men and arms and archers to make war on the Irish, as the present King. He remained upwards of nine months in Ireland, at great expense, which, however, was cheerfully defrayed by his kingdom; for the principal cities and towns of England thought it was well laid out, when they saw their king return home with honour.

Only gentlemen and archers had been employed on this expedition; and there were with the King four thousand knights and squires and thirty thousand archers, all regularly paid every week, and so well they were satisfied. To tell you the truth, Ireland is one of the worst countries to make war in or to conquer; for there are such impenetrable and extensive forests, lakes and bogs, there is no knowing how to pass them, and carry on a war advantageously; it is so thinly populated that the Irish, whenever they please, desert the towns and take refuge in these forests and live in huts made of boughs, like wild beasts; and whenever they perceive any parties advancing with hostile dispositions, and about to enter their country, they fly to such narrow passes it is impossible to follow them. When they find a favourable opportunity to attack their enemies to advantage, which frequently happens, from their knowledge of the country, they fail not to seize it; and no man-at-arms, be he ever so well mounted, can overtake them, so light are they of foot. Sometimes they leap from the ground behind a horseman and embrace the rider (for they are very strong in their arms) so tightly, that he can no way get rid of them.

The Irish have pointed knives, with broad blades, sharp on both sides like a dart head, with which they kill their enemies; but they never consider them dead until they have cut their throats like sheep, opened their bellies and taken out their hearts, which they carry off with them, and some say, who are well acquainted their manners, that they devour them as delicious morsels. They never accept ransom for their prisoners; and when they find they have not the advantage in any skirmishes, they instantly separate and hide themselves in bushes, hedges or holes under the ground so that they seem to disappear, no one knows whither.

Sir William Windsor, who has longer made war in Ireland than any other English knight, has never been able, during his residence among them, to learn correctly their manners, nor the condition of the Irish people. They are a very hardy race, of great subtlety, and of various tempers, paying no attention to cleanliness, nor to any gentleman, although their country is governed by kings, of whom there are several, but seem desirous to remain in the savage state they have been brought up in. True, it is, that four of the most potent kings in Ireland have submitted to the King of England, but more through love and good humour than by battle or force.

The Earl of Ormonde, whose lands join their kingdoms, took great pains to induce them to go to Dublin, where the King, our Lord, resided, and to submit themselves to him and to the crown of England. This was considered by every one as a great acquisition, and the object of the armament accomplished; for during the whole of King Edward's reign of happy memory, he had never

332

such success as King Richard. The honour is great, but the advantage little, for with such savages nothing can be done. I will tell you an instance of their savageness that it may serve as an example to other nations. You may depend on its truth; for I was an eye-witness of what I shall relate, as they were about a month under my care and governance at Dublin, to teach them the usages of England, by orders of the King and council, because I knew their language as well as I did French and English, for in my youth I was educated among them; and Earl Thomas, father of the present Earl of Ormonde, kept me with him out of affection for my good horsemanship.

It happened that the Earl, mentioned above, was sent with three hundred horse and one thousand archers to make war on the Irish; for the English had kept up a constant warfare against them, in hopes of bringing them under subjection. The Earl of Ormonde, whose lands bordered on his opponents had that day mounted me on one of his best horses, and I rode by his side. The Irish, having formed and ambuscade to surprise the English, advanced from it; but were so sharply attacked by the archers, whose arrows they could not withstand, for they are not armed against them, that they soon retreated. The Earl pursued them, and I, who was well mounted, kept close by him; it chanced that in this pursuit my horse took fright and ran away with me, in spite of all my efforts, into the midst of the enemy. My friends could never overtake me; and , in passing through the Irish, one of them, by a great feat of agility, leaped on the back of my horse, and held me tight with both his arms, but did me no harm with lance or knife. He pressed my horse forward for more than two hours and conducted him to a large bush, in a very retired spot, where he found his companions who had run thither to escape the English. He seemed much rejoiced to have made me his prisoner, and carried me to his house, which was strong, and in a town surrounded with wood, palisades and stagnant water; the name of this town was Herpelin. The gentleman who had taken me was called Brin Costeret, a very handsome man. I have frequently made inquiries after him, and hear that he is still alive, but very old. This Bryan Costeret kept me with him seven years, and gave me his daughter in marriage, by whom I have two girls. I will tell you how I obtained my liberty.

It happened in the seventh year of my captivity, that one of their kings, Arthur Macquemaire, King of Leinster, raised an army against Lionel, Duke of Clarence, son of King Edward of England, and both armies met very near the city of Leinster. In the battle that followed, many were slain and taken on both sides; but the English gaining the day, the Irish were forced to fly, and the king of Leinster escaped. The father of my wife was made prisoner, under the banner of the Duke of Clarence; and as Byran Costeret was mounted on my horse, which was remembered to have belonged to the Earl of Ormonde, it was then first known that I was alive, that he had honourably entertained me at his house in Herpelin, and given me his daughter in marriage. The Duke of

333

Clarence, Sir William Windsor, and all our party, were well pleased to hear this news, and he was offered his liberty, on condition that he gave me mine, and sent me to the English army with my wife and children. He at first refused the terms, from love to me, his daughter and our children; but, when he found no other terms would be accepted, he agreed to them, provided my eldest daughter remained with him. I returned to England with my wife and youngest daughter, and fixed my residence in Bristol. My two children are married: the one established in Ireland has three boys and two girls and her sister four sons and two daughters.

Because the Irish language is as familiar to me as English, for I have always spoken it in my family and introduce it among my grandchildren as much as I can, I have been chosen by our lord the King, to teach and accustom the four Irish kings, who have sworn obedience for ever to England, to the manners of the English. I must say, that these kings who were under my management, were of coarse manners and understandings; and, in spite of all that I could do to soften their language and nature, very little progress had been made, for they would frequently return to their former coarse behaviour.

I will more particularly relate the charge that was given to me over them, and how I managed it. The King of England intended these four kings should adopt the manners, appearance and dress of the English, for he wanted to create them four knights. He gave them first a very handsome house in the city of Dublin for themselves and their attendants, where I was ordered to reside with them, and never to leave the house without absolute necessity. I lived there three or four days without any way interfering, that we might become accustomed to each other, and I allowed them to act just as they pleased. I observed, that as they sat at table, they made grimaces that did not seem to me graceful nor becoming and I resolved in my own mind to make them drop that custom.

When these four kings were seated at table, and the first dish was served, they would make their minstrels and principal servants sit beside them, and eat from their plates and drink from their cups. They told me this was a praiseworthy custom of their country, where everything was in common but the bed. I permitted this to be done for three days; but on the fourth I ordered the tables to be laid out and covered properly, placing the four kings at an upper table, the minstrels at the one below and the servants lower still. They looked at each other and refused to eat anything , saying I had deprived them of their old custom in which they had been brought up. I replied, with a smile, to appease them, that their custom was not decent nor suitable to their rank, nor would it be honourable for them to continue it; for that now they should conform to the manners of the English; and to instruct them in these particulars was the motive of my residence with them, having been so ordered by the King of England and his council. When they heard this they made no

334

further opposition to whatever I proposed, from having placed themselves under the obedience of England, and continued good humouredly to persevere in it a long as I staid with them.

They had another custom I knew to be common in the country, which was the not wearing of breeches. I had, in consequence, plenty of breeches made of linen and cloth, which I gave to the kings and their attendants, and accustomed them to wear them. I took away many rude articles, as well in their dress as other things, and had great difficulty at the first to induce them to wear robes of silken cloth, trimmed with squirrel-skin or minever, for the kings wrapped themselves up in an Irish cloak. In riding, they never used saddles nor stirrups, and I had some trouble to make them conform in this respect to the English manners.

I once made inquiry concerning their faith; but they seemed so much displeased, I was forced to silence; they said they believed in God and the Trinity, without any difference from our creed. I asked which pope they were inclined to; they replied without hesitation, 'to that at Rome'. I enquired if they would like to receive the order of knighthood for the king would willingly create them such, after the usual modes of France, England and other countries. They said they were knights already, which ought to satisfy them. I asked when they were made; they answered at seven years old; that in Ireland a king makes his son a knight and should the child have lost his father, then the nearest relation; and the young knight begins to learn to tilt with a light lance against a shield fixed to a post in a field, and the more lances he breaks the more honour he acquires. 'By this method,' added they, 'our young knights are trained, more especially kings' sons.' Although I asked this, I was before well acquainted with the manner of educating their children to arms. I made no further reply than by saying this kind of childish knighthood would not satisfy the King of England, and that he would create them in another mode. They asked, 'In what manner?' 'In church with most solemn ceremonies,' and I believe they paid attention to what I said.

About two days after, the King was desirous to create these kings knights; and the Earl of Ormonde, who understood and spoke Irish well, as his lands joined the territories of the kings, was sent to await on them, that they might have more confidence in the message of the King and council. On his arrival they showed him every respect, which he returned, as he knew well how to do and they seemed happy at his coming. He began a most friendly conversation with them and inquired if they were satisfied with my conduct and behaviour. They replied, 'perfectly well; he had prudently and wisely taught us the manners and usages of his country, for which we ought to be obliged and to thank him.' This answer was agreeable to the Earl of Ormonde for it showed sense. And then, by degrees he began to talk of the order of knighthood they were to receive, explaining to them every article and ceremony of it, and how

335

great a value should be set on it, and how those who were created knights behaved. The whole of the Earl's conversation was very pleasing to the four kings, whom, however, as I have not yet named, I will now do. First Aneel the great king of Mecte (O'Neill the great king of Meath); secondly Brun de Thomond, king of Thomond and of Aire (O'Brien king of Thomond and Ulster); the third Arthur Macquemaire king of Leinster and the fourth Contruo, king of Chenour and Erpe (O'Connor king of Connaught). They were made knights by the hand of the King of England on the feast of our Lady in March, which that year fell on a Thursday, in the cathedral of Dublin that was founded by Saint John the Baptist.

The four kings watched all the Wednesday night in the cathedral; and on the morrow, after Mass, they were created knights, with much solemnity. There were knighted at the same time Sir Thomas Orphem, Sir Joathos Pado and his cousin Sir John Pado. The four kings were very richly dressed, suitable to their rank and that day dined at the table of King Richard, where they were much stared at by the lords and those present; not indeed without reason; for they were strange figures and differently countenanced to the English or other nations. We are naturally inclined to gaze at anything strange, and it was certainly, Sir John, at that time, a great novelty to see four Irish kings."

"Sir Henry, I readily believe you, and would have given a good deal if I could have been there. Last year I had made arrangements for coming to England and should have done so, had I not heard of the death of Queen Anne, which made me postpone my journey. But I wish to ask you one thing, which had much surprised me; I should like to know how these four Irish kings have so readily submitted to King Richard, when his valiant grandfather, who was so much redoubted everywhere, could never reduce them to obedience and was always at war with them. You have said it was brought about by a treaty and the grace of God. The grace of God is good, and of infinite value to those who can obtain it; but we see few lords now-a-days augment their territories otherwise than by force. When I shall be returned to my native country of Hainault and speak of these matters I shall be strictly examined concerning them; for our lord, Duke Albert of Bavaria, Earl of Holland, Hainault and Zealand, and his son William of Hainault style themselves lords of Friesland, an extensive country, over which they claim the government, as their predecessors have done before them; but the Frieslanders refuse to acknowledge their right, and will not by any means submit themselves to their obedience."

To this Henry Castide answered: "In truth, Sir John, I cannot more fully explain how it was brought about; but it is generally believed by most of our party, that the Irish were exceedingly frightened at the great force the King landed in Ireland, where it remained for nine months. Their coasts were so surrounded, that neither provision nor merchandise could be landed; but the inland natives were indifferent to this, as they are unacquainted with commerce, nor do they wish to know anything of it, but simply to live like wild beasts.

Those who reside on the coast opposite to England are better informed, and accustomed to traffic. King Edward, of happy memory, had in his reign so many wars to provide for, in France, Brittany, Gascony and Scotland, that his forces were dispersed in different quarters, and he was unable to send any great armament to Ireland. When the Irish found so large a force was now come against them, they considered it most advisable to submit themselves to the King of England. Formerly when Saint Edward, who had been canonised, and was worshipped with much solemnity by the English, was their King, he thrice defeated the Danes on sea and land. This Saint Edward, King of England, Lord of Ireland and of Aquitaine (this must be a mistake as Aquitaine was brought to the Crown of England by the marriage of Eleanora, the divorced Queen of Louis le Jeune, King of France, with Henry II) the Irish loved and feared more than any other King of England before or since. It was for this reason, that when our King went thither last year, he laid aside the leopards and flowers de luce, and bore the arms of Saint Edward emblazoned on all his banners; these were a cross patence or, on a field gules, with four doves argent on the shield or banner, as you please. This we heard was very pleasing to the Irish, and inclined them more to submission, for in truth, the ancestors of these four kings had done homage and service to Saint Edward; they also considered King Richard as a prudent and conscientious man, and have therefore paid their homage in the like manner, as was done to Saint Edward.

Thus I have related to you how our King accomplished the object of his expedition to Ireland. Keep it in your memory, that when returned home you may insert it in your chronicle with other histories that are connected with it."

"Henry," said I, "you have well spoken, and it shall be done." Upon this we separated ; and meeting soon after the herald March, I said :- "March, tell me what are the arms of Henry Castide; for I have found him very agreeable, and he had kindly related to me the history of the King's expedition to Ireland, and of the four kings, who, as he says, were under his governance upwards of fifteen days."

March replied, "He bears for arms a chevron gules on a field argent, with three besants gules, two above the chevron and one below."

All these things I retained in my memory, and put on paper, for I wished not to forget them.

337

Appendix 2

O'Nolan pardons according to the Fiants of the Tudor Monarchs

Date F.No.	Name	Address	Reason
1548 - 228	Morrogh McGerrot Duffe	Omale	with Feagh McHugh (in rebellion)
1548 -228	Tyrellagh McFyaughe	Omale	with Feagh McHugh (in rebellion)
1548-228	Thady	Omale	with Feagh McHugh (in rebellion)
1549 - 261	Donald M'Donhe	Roslowe	(in rebellion?)
1549 - 261	Murgan M'Donyll	Roslowe	with Lysagh McMurhgo (in rebellion)
1549 - 340	Charles McLesagh	Ballytrane	(in rebellion?)
1549 - 340	Rosse M'Edmond	Kilknock	(in rebellion?)
1549 - 340	William M'Rosse	Kilknock	(in rebellion?)
1552 - 1130	Hugh Roo		Accessory to Robbery of hides,goats
1553 - 1245	Margaret - a singlewoman-+	Yagoteston, co. Kildare	
1559 - 140	William	Kilbride	In rebellion with Edmund Butler
1562- 471	Murrough Ne Dowre	Kilbride	with McHugh McShane O'Byrne
1563 - 579	Feagh McWilliam (+Feagh)		for capture of G. Harvey & H. Davells
1563 - 579	Leasagh McWilliam		In Rebellion with Hugh McShane
1563 - 579	Maurice ne Dower Kilbride		In Rebellion with Hugh McShane
1563 - 579	Thady McWilliam		for capture of G. Harvey & H. Davells
1566 - 857	Cahir McPhelim Roe		In reb. with Cahir Carragh Kav.
1566 - 911	Gerald	Killinclonboley	In Reb. with Ed. Butler
1566 - 911	William	Kilbride	In Reb. with Ed. Butler
1567	James	In reb. with Dermot O'Toole	
1569 - 1345	Murrough Ne Dowre	Kilbride	In reb. with Feagh McHugh
1570 - 1617	James		In Reb with the Butlers
1571	Denis (with others) fined 5s.		Reb. with the Butlers?
1571 - 1868	Gerald		Reb. with the Butlers?
1571 - 1868	Owen (fined 5s.)		Reb. with the Butlers?
1571 - 1890	Teig (fined ?)	Tullowphelim	Reb. with the Butlers?
1571 - 2037	Patrick Fitz Maurice	Ardristan	? with 20 others one a Butler
1571 - 2043	Gillegrome McPhelan	Rathkenny??	?? fined 5s. with 30 others
1571- 1863	Edmund (a kern) with others	Carlow	Fined 10s
1571- 2066	Edmund (fined 5s - a kern)	Co. Carlow	Mercenary with Nic.Fannyng
1572 - 2103	Gerald Oge (kern)	Ballylower	In reb. with Moriertagh Og Kav.
1572 - 2202	Murrough	Co.Carlow	In reb. with Feagh McHugh
1573 - 2232	James (a yeoman)	Co.Carlow	In reb. with Brian McCahir Kav.
1574 - 2424	John (a cotter) with many	Kilkenny	In Rebellion?
1574 - 2424	Thomas, a cottener, + many	Kilkenny	In Rebellion?

338

1575 - 2609 Shan McDonough		In reb. with Keatings
1575 - 2610 Gerald Rua	Co. Carlow	In reb. with Cahir Duff K. of clonmullen
1575 - 2610 James McTeig	Co. Carlow	In reb. with Cahir Duff K. of clonmullen
1575 - 2610 Morgh McEdmund	Co.Carlow	In reb. with Cahir Duff K. of clonmullen
1575 - 2610 Tirrelagh More	Co.Carlow	In reb. with Cahir Duff K. of clonmullen
1575 - 2739 Dermot McWilliam	Foert	In reb.with the Fitz Olivers of Rathvilly
1576 - 2858 Tysoghe (horseman)	Co. Carlow	In reb. with Kavanaghs of Garryhill
1577 - 3155 James McTeig (yeoman)	Co. Carlow	In reb. with Brian McCahir Kav.
1578 - 3434 William (in co. with Laoismen)	Laois?	In Rebellion?
1582 Ferdoragh	Harristown Co. Kildare ?	
1583 - 4221 Garret ? ?		
1583 - 4221 James (in list with Garret) ?	?	
1584 - 4370 Edmund (a carpenter)	Kilkenny?	In reb. with Shees of Kilkenny?
1584 - 4441 Cahir McWilliam		In reb. with O'Byrnes
1584 - 4504 Henry	Co. Carlow	In reb. with the Kavanaghs of G'hill
1584 - 4504 Tirelagh McJames	Co. Carlow	In reb. with the Kavanaghs of G'hill
1585 - 4631 James Oge	Co. Carlow	In reb. with Donal Spainnigh K.
1587 - 5113 Felim McCahir (kern)	Co. Carlow	In reb. with the Kavanaghs of G'hill
1588 - 5244 Teig	Ballinwherey (Co. Kilk)	In reb. with Kilk/Tipp rebels
1591 - 5612 Brien	Co. Cork?	In reb. with the Desmonds?
1592 - 5788 Callogh	Carrickslaney	In reb. with Donal Spainnigh K.
1592 - 5788 Daniel	Shangarry	In reb. with Donal Spainnigh K.
1592- 5788 Gerald	Kilmaglish	In reb. with Donal Spainnigh K.
1592- 5788 Phelim	Ballykealy	In reb. with Donal Spainnigh K.
1597 - 6113 Brian McTirlagh	Co. Carlow	In reb. with the Kavanaghs of G'hill
1597 - 6113 Callough McHenry	Co. Carlow	In reb. with the Kavanaghs of G'hill
1597 - 6113 Dermot McDonough	Co. Carlow	In reb. with the Kavanaghs of G'hill
1597 - 6113 Dermot McOwen	Co. Carlow	In reb. with the Kavanaghs of G'hill
1597 - 6113 Donough McDonell	Co. Carlow	In reb. with the Kavanaghs of G'hill
1597 - 6113 Gerald McMorogh	Co. Carlow	In reb. with the Kavanaghs of G'hill
1597 - 6113 James McDermot	Co. Carlow	In reb. with the Kavanaghs of G'hill
1597 - 6113 James McShane	Co.Carlow	In reb. with the Kavanaghs of G'hill
1597 - 6113 John McJames	Co.Carlow	In reb. with the Kavanaghs of G'hill
1597 - 6113 Morogh McJames	Co. Carlow	In reb. with the Kavanaghs of G'hill
1597 - 6113 Thady Mc Tirlagh	Co. Carlow	In reb. with the Kavanaghs of G'hill
1597 - 6113 Tirelagh McBrien	Co. Carlow	In reb. with the Kavanaghs of G'hill
1597 - 6137 Edmund McGerald ?		In reb. with the Byrnes
1598 - 6219 Rory McMorough	Co. Carlow	In reb. with the Kavanaghs & Byrnes
1598 - 6232 Morogh McJames McShane	?	In reb. Byrnes and Tooles c. 400
1598 - 6232 Sherone (one of 400 or so p.)	?	In reb. with the Byrnes and Tooles
1598 - 6248 Donough (a yeoman)	Swinfin Co.Tipp ??	In reb. with Butlers, Byrnes, Ryans
1598 - 6248 Phelim ??		In reb. with Butlers, Byrnes, Ryans
1599 - 6323 Donough ???		In reb. with Fitzgeralds, Tallons etc.
1600 - 6408 Dermot McShane	Co. Carlow	In reb. with Kavs (G) and Byrnes
1600 - 6408 Donough McFeagh	Co. Carlow	In reb. with Kavs (G) and Byrnes
1600 - 6408 Edmund	Co. Carlow	In reb. with Kavs (G) and Byrnes
1600 - 6408 Fergenanim	Co. Carlow	In reb. with Kavs (G) and Byrnes
1600 - 6408 Gerald McCahir	Co. Carlow	In reb. with Kavs (G) and Byrnes
1600 - 6408 Morrogh McFirre	Co. Carlow	In reb. with Kavs (G) and Byrnes
1600 - 6408 Patrick McFirre	Co. Carlow	In reb. with Kavs (G) and Byrnes
1600 - 6408 Phelim McFirre	Co. Carlow	In reb. with Kavs (G) and Byrnes
1600 - 6408 Robert (a cottier)	Co. Carlow	In reb. with Kavs (G) and Byrnes
1600 - 6408 Teig McCahir	Co. Carlow	In reb. with Kavs (G) and Byrnes
1600 - 6408 William McFirre	Co. Carlow	In reb. with Kavs (G) and Byrnes
1600 - 6440 Donell McOwen (yeoman)	Tullow	In reb. with Purcells of Tipp.
1600 - 6440 Donough (yeoman)	Tullow	In reb. with Purcells of Tipp.

339

1600 - 6440	Edmund McOwen	Tullow	In reb. with Purcells of Tipp.
1600 - 6440	Hugh (yeoman)	Tullow	In reb. with Purcells of Tipp.
1600 - 6440	John (yeoman)	Tullow	In reb. with Purcells of Tipp.
1600 - 6440	Owen McArt (yeoman)	Tullow	In reb. with Purcells of Tipp.
1600 - 6440	Wm. McHugh (yeoman)	Tullow	In reb. with Purcells of Tipp.
1600 - 6447	Donough M'Yogho M'Yogho	Rathrush	In reb. with Kavanaghs & Butlers
1600 - 6447	Morogh	Ballyloughan	In reb. with Kavanaghs & Butlers
1601 - 6517	Brene McCahir	Ballykealy	In reb. with Kavanaghs (D.S)
1601 - 6517	Brene McMorogh	Kilbride	In reb. with Kavanaghs (D.S)
1601 - 6517	Brene McTyrlagh McBrene	Laraghteige	In reb. with Kavanaghs (D.S)
1601 - 6517	Cahir McHugh	Shangarry	In reb. with Kavanaghs (D.S)
1601 - 6517	Dermot McDonnell ?		In reb. with Kavanaghs (D.S)
1601 - 6517	Donell Duff McOwen McHugh	Ballykealy	In reb. with Kavanaghs (D.S)
1601 - 6517	Donell McHugh	Shangarry	In reb. with Kavanaghs (D.S)
1601 - 6517	Donell McOwen	Clonmullen	In reb. with Kavanaghs (D.S)
1601 - 6517	Donough McOwen	Clonmullen	In reb. with Kavanaghs (D.S)
1601 - 6517	Donough McCahir	Ballykealy	In reb. with Kavanaghs (D.S)
1601 - 6517	Donough McEdmund	Kilknock	In reb. with Kavanaghs (D.S)
1601 - 6517	Donough McKoghowe	Rathrush	In reb. with Kavanaghs (D.S)
1601 - 6517	Donough McMorogh	Ballykealy	In reb. with Kavanaghs (D.S)
1601 - 6517	Donough McMorogh	Ballykealy	In reb. with Kavanaghs (D.S)
1601 - 6517	Donough Oge McDonough	Co. Carlow	In reb. with Kavanaghs (D.S)
1601 - 6517	Edmund McOwen	Clonmullen	In reb. with Kavanaghs (D.S)
1601 - 6517	Edmund McCahir	Ballykealy	In reb. with Kavanaghs (D.S)
1601 - 6517	Gerrot McThomas	Ballykealy	In reb. with Kavanaghs (D.S)
1601 - 6517	James McBrene	Ballykealy	In reb. with Kavanaghs (D.S)
1601 - 6517	James McCahir	Ballykealy	In reb. with Kavanaghs (D.S)
1601 - 6517	Lysagh McWilliam	Kilbride	In reb. with Kavanaghs (D.S)
1601 - 6517	Morchoe McFyrr	Ballelowe	In reb. with Kavanaghs (D.S)
1601 - 6517	Mortagh McShane	Duff Ballykealy	In reb. with Kavanaghs (D.S)
1601 - 6517	Owen McAirt	Ballemullin	In reb. with Kavanaghs (D.S)
1601 - 6517	Phelim McCahir	Ballykealy	In reb. with Kavanaghs (D.S)
1601 - 6517	Rory McDonell	Killbreckan	In reb. with Kavanaghs (D.S)
1601 - 6517	Teig McShane	Co. Carlow	In reb. with Kavanaghs (D.S)
1601 - 6517	Thomas McMuiris	Ballykealy	In reb. with Kavanaghs (D.S)
1601 - 6517	Tirelagh McDonough	Kilgrene	In reb. with Kavanaghs (D.S)
1601 - 6517	Tyrlagh McBrene	Laraghteige	In reb. with Kavanaghs (D.S)
1601 - 6550	James (a harper)Donower Co. Westmeath		In rebellion with Westmeath rebels
1601 - 6555	Shane	Cork	In rebellion with Sullivan rebels
1602 - 6647	Melaghlin Duff	Wexford	Submission In rebellion with various rebels
1602 - 6664	Gerrot McDermot (horseman)Grany Co. Westmeath		In rebellion with various rebels
1602 - 6682	Cahir (yeoman)	Shangarry	In rebellion with Don Sp. Kav.
1602 - 6706	Donell	Kilcowle	(Co. Kilk?)	In rebellion with Kilk/Tipp rebels
1602 - 6765	Daniel	Kilcowle	(Co. Kilk?)	In rebellion with Kilk/Tipp rebels

Appendix 3

The Battle at Arklow Rock

The 22nd. June (1599) the Army was brought from Strongbridge[671] to the Passage (a village so named because it is on the side of the passage or ferry from the County Waterford into the County Wexford) whither the Lord Lieutenant (Essex) commanded all the boats of Waterford, Rosse and the Carrick to be gathered the next morning by break of day. But the ferry being broad and the boats not great and the carriages of our army far greater than ever heretofore in this country followed do few fighting men, (that) his Lordship coming from Waterford, the morrow after midsummer's day, found most of his horse unpassed; in regard of whereof, having lodged all his foot within half a mile from Ballyhack, he went with two companies of horse to Tintern, a house of Sir Thomas Colcloughs, there expecting the passage of the rest of the horsemen, and leaving behind the Marshal (Bingham) to hasten them with all speed, which the next morning was performed; and in the afternoon by his Lordship's directions they marched forward three or four miles over against Tintern, but more towards the heart of the country. His Lordship in the meantime being desirous to view all the coast betwixt Waterford and Wexford held his course by the seaside, and lodged that night at Ballymagir, a house belonging to Sir James Devereux, meeting the army next day at Ballybrennan, whence the day following we marched to a ford which is betwixt Enniscorthy and Ferns. His lordship employed the forenoon in viewing the state and strength of Enniscorthy, and of the troops there in the garrison, the afternoon in seeing the skirt of the Duffry, the chief fastness of Donal Spainneach, who now pretends to be chief of the Kavanaghs and McMurrough which is in Irish no less than to be king of Leinster. His lordship also went to a ground lying betwixt Enniscorthy and this fastness where the garrison not long before had skirmished with Donal Spainneach and upon the place examined the Captains of the circumstances and how they had carried themselves in that skirmish. Since our departure from Waterford till this day we saw not one rebel. Being come to the Duffry side to the very edge of the wood, some of them showed themselves, but showing themselves only without giving us so much as one alarm, though that night we lodged within a quarter of a mile of them and all the same side of the ford.[672] At Enniscorthy and this

---

[671] Strongbow's Bridge between Waterford and Passage
[672] Probably at Scarawalsh

encampment his lordship conferred with the Council of War what course from hence he should take, and whether he should carry the garrison of Enniscorthy along with him or not.

For the first it was resolved we should go to Ferns, and thence to Arklow, in regard the ways through the Duffry were all plasht,[673] and the force in a manner of all the Leinster rebels there assembled, against all which we could not have opposed above 1200 foot (the hurt men and the sick being excepted), who if they had been alone the difficulty had been far less, but they were clogged with at least thrice as many churls, horse-boys and other like unserviceable people, which of necessity were to be guarded by our troops. Besides the premises it was remembered that in all those quarters there lay no castle or fort of importance to be taken in, nor prey to be gotten, their cattle being all in Phelim McFiach's country and consequently no end could probably be found which might extraordinarily further H.M.'s service or counterpoise the incurring of so many hazards; but at Arklow it was thought fitter to leave sick men and part of our carriages, and with a light running camp to attempt somewhat upon the rebels, if we were not fought withall at our passage.

The 29th. day we marched to a place called Cooleshill[674]. In passing his lordship viewed the castle of Ferns, which he conceived to be fitter place for a garrison than Enniscorthy, were it not that the want of a navigable river for the transportation of victuals and munitions did countervail the nearness of it to the rebel's fastness. The same day, both at Ferns and at our quarters his lordship was advised that the rebels, the day following purposed to fight with us, the rather because they had two or three places where they might with advantage attempt either our Vanguard or Rearguard of foot and where the horse could not serve upon them; wherefore the next morning we marched in the strongest order we could, and to whet the rebels choler and courage, we being to pass through a country called the Kinsellaghs (which yielded maintenance to many of the rebels' hired men) his Lordship all the day long burned both in his way and on each side. The first place where his Lordship saw offer of resistance was at a village[675] on our right hand, seated on the skirt of a great wood and flanked on two sides with two groves of underwood, so as we had but one way to come to it and that of disadvantage.

At this place his Lordship being in the Vanguard and seeing the rebels put themselves betwixt us and the village and withall to drive back our footmen who went to burn it, as they had done the rest, expected their whole forces, and therefore drew all the army over a ford a little short of the village, and then having placed all our baggage and cattle behind him towards the

---

[673] Plashing was blocking up the passes with fallen trees, branches etc.

[674] Cooliseal - a townland a couple of miles south west of Gorey.

[675] This was probably Inch.

champion[676] and his horse fast by for their guard, he sent a sergeant with some light shot[677] to fire the village, commanding him to begin with the furthest houses, and at the same instant sent to possess either of the groves, having advanced our vanguard of foot towards the grove on the one side, and the rearguard towards the other, himself directing the one and giving the charge of the other to the Marshal. But soon after it appeared they were but some loose rogues sent to make a bravado for the saving of the village and that their main forces having coasted along on our left hand were laid for us before, for the village was burnt without the loss of a man, the rebels, having perceived our manner of going on, running away, having delivered only one poor volley of shot.

But four miles short of Arklow we saw their forces drawn down to a river's side[678] which for a half a mile together, ran within a musket shot of our highway, and over which there was a ford near to the sea through which our guides directed our carriages and footmen to pass; the bank of this river gave them no small advantage, for it was very boggy a good way together, but the rebels fearing the engagement of their whole force if they made good the ford, sought only at first to entertain our wings with a light skirmish, as they marched for the guard of our carriage, but soon after both sides giving fire a pace, some of our old Irish soldiers, finding the rebels to give way, unadvisedly passed over the river and made a stand with some 200 men within a harquebuze[679] shot of twice as many rebels who had also succours of both horse and foot within a small distance from them; which the Lord Lieutenant perceiving, he passed a deep ford with a hundred English horse and sent the Earl of Ormonde, who with his horse was passed at the further ford, near to the sea side, to second those, and to draw near the foot that were so disorderly engaged. Now so soon as our horse which went upon the spur[680] came with a harquebus shot of our foot, the Lord Lieutenant commanded the foot to make an orderly retreat, entertaining still the skirmish with the rebels and seeking to draw them some reasonable distance from the wood, that the horse might freely charge them. As this direction was going, the Earl of Ormonde by the mistaking of the messenger drew up his troop of horse near the other side of the wood, on the right hand, and so charged upon the spur to the very skirt of the wood, where the rebels discharged at his Lordship a volley of shot, but without any harm, only one horse of his troop hurt; on the other side Captain Esmonde, captain of 100 foot was shot through the body and through the arm,

---

[676] The country cleared of timber.

[677] Lightly armoured gunmen.

[678] This would seem to be the Clonough River

[679] A harquebus - an early type of portable gun supported on a tripod.

[680] Galloped

besides two or three soldiers more which were hurt with the bullet, the rebels loss being not inferior, for besides those who were galled, two or three of their best and forwardest men that presented themselves in the skirmish were stricken down, and so that encounter ended, and all our army was drawn over the ford towards the seaside; which way being heavy and deep, was refused by the Lord Lieutenant and another chosen, which for one mile had some small pass in it, where the rebels offered skirmish to our troops, but to little purpose, for they kept so far off that his Lordship commanded our men to spare their powder. Near the last pass, the Lord Lieutenant placed an ambush of 30 horse, commanding the army to march on, and himself staying upon a hill a musket shot off, with the rearward of horse; on which hill he made show of as many coloured coats as they had seen before, and as many horses, for with boys upon spare led horses and hackneys the number was supplied. But the rebels fearing to come upon champion ground, coasted still along on our left hand.

From this place for two miles we had a fair champion, at the end whereof was a great ascent, and yet, at the top of this ascent two high hills on either side.[681] His Lordship hastened to the top of one of these hills and discerned the vanguard, with the Earl of Ormonde and the Marshal, already advanced as far as Arklow, and the rebels' forces (800 foot and 40 horse) marching to cut off our carriages and a wing of 50 or 60 footmen. This was the fault of the guides, who carried Ormonde and the Marshal hard by the seaside, where they could not see the country nor be seen by their own wings.

The Lord Lieutenant sent to the Sergeant Major, then leading the rearguard, for 300 of his lightest foot, and all the horse, and in the meantime went with the Earl of Southampton to rescue our men who were about to be cut to pieces. The rebels stood on a bog, behind which was a shrubby wood, which joined the sand hills. The Lord Lieutenant sent all the gentlemen on horseback (Sir Edward Wingfield only excepted) with the Earl of Southampton to the plain on the right hand, while he drew down to the wings. When the rebels perceived the small number of horse and foot they came on with a louder cry and more speed than before. In this coming on, Captain Roach, an Irishman by birth, who had long served the French King, with a shot had his leg shivered, and was straightaways carried off. But immediately the Earl of Southampton with the horse gave a charge so resolute and so home, that he entered the wood as far as any bog would suffer him; Mr. Robert Vernon, Captain Constable and Mr. Coxe being all bogged and forced to quit their horses Mr. Coxe had received his death wound; Captain Constable had two wounds; and Mr. Vernon, who had killed a leader, lay under his horse till Mr. Bellington quitted his own horse to help him up. Lord Morley's son, heir to the Baron of Mountegle, Mr. George Manners, Mr. Thomas Weste, Sir Thomas Jermyn, Sir Alex Radcliffe,

---

[681] Arklow Rock and Smithy Rock about a mile south of Arklow

Sir Thomas Egerton, Captain Poole, Mr. Carew Reynolds and Mr. Heydon served bravely.

On the other side his Lordship sent down Lieutenant Bushell to lead a wing of shot at the same instant when my lord of Southampton charged; and to succour these he sent Ensign Constable. He was then attacked by the rebels, but by that time he had gotten the foot to stand firm, to keep order, to forbear noises and speeches of fear and amazement; for a poorer company there could not have been lighted on in all the army. The rebels, staying for their gross to come up,[682] gave our horsemen from the rearguard leisure to approach. Thirty of the horse were sent to the Earl of Southampton. Captain Norryes, corporal, was ordered to charge with 15 horse, who were supported by 15 others under a corporal of Sir H. Davers' company.[683] Twenty musketeers flanked the going on and coming off of the horse. The rebels were put back, and, being discouraged, they made head the other way through the bog and wood against the Earl of Southampton who repulsed them. Then came the Marshal with some more horse, Sir H. Poore with 300 foot from the vanguard and Captain Chamberlain with 200 from the rearguard. The rebels then endeavoured to secure possession of the wood and bog; but on the Sergeant Major coming up with Sir Henry Dowcra and all the ensigns of the rearguard the rebels were forced to turn their backs in disorder, "many throwing away their arms, and some so amazed that they stuck in the bog, and were overtaken and killed by our men, though being otherwise far slower and heavier than they".

His Lordship gave direction for following the chase; and then he marched away to Arklow.

---

[682] i.e. waiting for their main forces to arrive

[683] Probably meant to be Sir Henry Davell's company.

Index

—C—

—D—

D'Alton, 330
d'Artois, 135, 146
Danes, 2, 62, 63, 64, 74, 80, 143, 144, 317
Danesfort, 143, 144
Davells, 179, 194, 196, 197, 198, 199, 226, 243, 319, 330
Davis, 101, 143, 330
Davitt, 287
de Berkeley
  Sir Wm., 153
De Braose, 133
De Burgh, 133
de Cantiton, 82, 84, 330
de Cogan, 74
De Joinville, 133
de la Launde
  Sir Nicholas, 97
de Lacy, 75, 78, 79, 80, 81, 88, 97, 133
de Montmorency, 72
de Prendergast, 72
de Riddlesford, 88, 330
de Veele
  Elizabeth, 129
de Vesci
  Lord & Lady, 220
Delahunty
  Mary, 213
Delaney
  Dr. (Bishop), 298
Delvin, 181, 330
Dempsey, 252
Derenzy, 276
Dermot McMurrough, 2, 71, 83, 86, 107, 112, 128
Derrymore, 220, 221
Diarmuid Mac Mael na mBo, 68, 69, 70
Dillon, 307
Dinn Righ, 27, 28, 58, 330
Doheny, 280
Donal Reagh, 111, 153, 330
Donald
  Stewart & Linda, 222
Doneraile, 269

Donnell Reagh, 87
Doran
  Margaret, 224
Dougherty, 275
Dowdall, 237
Dowling, 78, 122, 123, 144, 147, 157, 207, 285, 330
Doyle, 87, 218, 273, 275, 276, 282, 285, 299, 300, 330
  Dr. (J.K.L.), 298
  Elizabeth, 219
  Fr., 276
  Teresa (nee Nolan), 330
Doyne, 265, 266
Draper, 255, 256, 260, 262
Drummin, 238
Drumphea, 161, 238, 303, 330
Duke of Clarence, 113, 114, 115, 124, 133, 313
Duncannon, 217, 265, 268, 300, 330
Dundalk, 97
Dungan, 293
Dunleckney, 250, 251
Dunne, 220, 221, 296

—E—

Earl of Desmond, 98, 101, 102, 103, 107, 121, 139, 142, 155, 180
Earl of Ormonde, 102, 105, 106, 108, 114, 115, 122, 124, 128, 130, 139, 141, 142, 143, 144, 149, 151, 153, 156, 157, 160, 161, 162, 168, 169, 175, 176, 178, 179, 180, 183, 188, 189, 191, 192, 200, 201, 203, 204, 234, 237, 238, 239, 241, 242, 244, 252, 254, 310, 312, 313, 316, 327, 328, 330
Echlin Henry (Bishop), 282
Edenderry, 219
Edward III, 123
Ely O'Carroll, 90, 159
England, 269
Enniscorthy, 87, 141, 159, 174, 180, 190, 192, 245, 246, 248, 249, 276, 325, 326, 330

349

Eochaidh Finn Fuathairt, 1, 3, 63
Esmonde
    Lord Thomas, 248
    Patrick, 244
    Sir Lawrence, 255
Eustace
    Edmund, 244, 269
    Francis, 255
    Hardy, 284
    James (Viscount Baltinglass), 181
    Michael, 227, 330
    Oliver, 243, 244, 262
Eustaces, 194, 265, 266, 284, 330
Everarde, 237

—F—

Farrell
    Daniel, 270
    William, 272
Faughart, 97
Feidhlimidh, 38, 39, 40, 41, 42, 43, 45,
    50, 63
Feltus, 269, 276, 277, 287, 330
Fenagh, 19, 82, 103, 217, 232, 238, 255,
    266, 268, 279, 330
Fenelon
    John, 218
    Kathleen, 225
Ferns, 61, 67, 69, 72, 73, 104, 112, 136,
    141, 158, 160, 167, 169, 176, 178,
    183, 188, 192, 196, 197, 198, 243,
    249, 299, 325, 326, 330
Finglas, 157, 158
FitzGerald, 2, 76, 80, 88, 96, 101, 103,
    104, 151, 153, 155, 156, 165, 174,
    186, 330
    John FitzThomas, 177
    Sir Thomas, 160
    Thomas (Silken Thomas), 237
Fitzgeralds, 160, 163, 165, 173, 174,
    175, 213, 216, 322, 330
FitzMaurice, 89, 92, 180
FitzPatrick, 296
FitzSimons

Mary, 224
FitzStephen, 2, 72, 73, 79, 330
Fitzwilliam, 82, 184, 186
Fleming, 80, 147, 248
Fotharta, 1, 2, 15, 17, 18, 39, 41, 47, 48,
    49, 50, 51, 59, 60, 61, 63, 64, 65, 66,
    234, 330
Fox
    Captain Arthur, 248
French
    Margaret, 230
Freynstown, 104
Froissart, 130, 308

—G—

Galway, 20, 23, 222, 229, 230, 264, 267,
    269, 270, 330
Garrenpurseen, 245
Garryhill, 134, 173, 177, 179, 181, 184,
    187, 200, 211, 212, 213, 214, 215,
    221, 226, 233, 265, 273, 320, 330
Geraldines, 88, 89, 91, 156, 163, 168,
    191, 330
Gilbertstown, 232, 257, 258, 269, 281,
    330
Gill
    Caroline, 253
Gladstone, 220
Glasnevin, 221, 287, 289, 290
Glendalough, 75, 92
Glendower, 133
Glengarry, 248
Glenmalure, 92, 94, 181
Gloucester
    Earl of, 128, 129, 137, 138, 310
Gore, 87, 136, 192, 224, 267, 269, 307,
    330
Gorey, 87, 136, 192, 224, 307, 330
Gormagan
    Henry, 244
Gowran, 61, 65, 96, 100, 106, 107, 108,
    128, 143, 153, 218, 274, 330
Grace, 1, 89, 95, 100, 104, 105, 108, 109,
    165, 167, 200, 330
Graham, 269, 276, 277

350

—L—

—M—

George, 181
Mary, 213, 298
Mortimer, 93, 98, 114, 124, 125, 126, 133, 134, 138, 139, 148, 150
Mount Leinster, 56, 79, 118, 330
Mountgarret, 176, 192, 247, 268, 293, 330
Moygane, 237
Moyle, 42, 330
Murray, 126, 277, 285, 299
Myshall, 94, 134, 145, 215, 218, 219, 220, 222, 223, 232, 234, 243, 246, 253, 255, 256, 259, 262, 266, 267, 273, 274, 275, 276, 277, 279, 280, 281, 284, 296, 300, 301, 302, 303, 330

—N—

Naas, 36, 58, 67, 96, 97, 164, 274, 330
Nangle, 103, 113
Netterville, 293
New Ross, 22, 129, 141, 147, 174, 184, 248, 278, 330
Newcastle, 94, 105, 110, 124, 153, 159, 330
Newstown, 284
Newtown, 232
Newtownbarry, 94, 195, 273, 276, 277
Nolan
Amelia, 219
Andrew, 280
Anna, 221
Anna Mary, 330
Anne Elizabeth, 222
Anthony, 230, 270
Bernard, 330
Brabazon, 230, 270
Breda, 224
Bridget, 219, 220, 225
Captain James, 248
Catherine, 220, 224
Charles, 215, 218, 219, 287
Charlotte, 221
Collette, 224
Daniel Francis (Rev.Fr.), 213

Desmond, 330
Dr., 227
Dr. Charles, 252, 304
Eamonn, 224
Eddie, 330
Edmond, 219, 222, 223
Edmund, 222
Edward, 214, 223, 225, 230, 330
Edward (Bishop), 298
Edward, Right Rev. Dr. Bishop of K.&L., 213
Elizabeth, 219, 330
Ellen, 218
Enda, 224
Eugene, 222, 223, 280
Eugennie, 223
Felix, 280
Fergus, 225
Fr. John, 278
Fr. Patrick, 330
Fr. Patrick P.P., 227
Fr.Thomas P.P., 278
Francis, 230
Gerald, 214
Gregory, 229, 267
Henry, 330
Irene, 223
James, 213, 222, 223, 227, 274
Jim, 330
Jim & Breda, 223
Jimmy, 330
Johanna, 219, 220
John, 213, 217, 218, 221, 222, 224, 230, 268, 270, 274, 330
John (Amnesty), 219
John (Rev.), 222
John (The Poet), 217
John Amnesty, 280, 287
John B., 280
John James, 305
John Philip, 230
Joseph, 222, 225
Josephine, 220
Kennedy (nee Nolan), 330
Lawrence, 216
Leasagh, 177

—O—

360